THE SECRET HISTORY OF SOLDIERS

Also by Tim Cook

No Place to Run

Clio's Warriors

At the Sharp End:
Canadians Fighting the Great War,
1914–1916, Volume One

Shock Troops:
Canadians Fighting the Great War,
1917–1918, Volume Two

The Madman and the Butcher: The
Sensational Wars of Sam Hughes
and General Arthur Currie

Warlords: Borden, Mackenzie King,
and Canada's World Wars

The Necessary War: Canadians
Fighting the Second World War,
1939–1943, Volume One

Fight to the Finish: Canadians in the Second
World War, 1944–1945, Volume Two

Vimy: The Battle and the Legend

THE SECRET HISTORY OF SOLDIERS

HOW CANADIANS SURVIVED THE GREAT WAR

TIM COOK

ALLEN LANE

ALLEN LANE
an imprint of Penguin Canada, a division of Penguin Random House Canada Limited

Canada • USA • UK • Ireland • Australia • New Zealand • India • South Africa • China

First published 2018

www.penguinrandomhouse.ca

LIBRARY AND ARCHIVES CANADA CATALOGUING IN PUBLICATION

Cook, Tim, 1971-, author
The secret history of soldiers : how Canadians survived the Great War / Tim Cook.

Issued in print and electronic formats.
ISBN 978-0-7352-3526-7 (hardcover).—ISBN 978-0-7352-3527-4 (electronic)

1. Canada. Canadian Army—Military life—History—20th century.
2. Canada—Armed Forces—Military life—History—20th century. 3. World War, 1914-1918—Personal narratives, Canadian. 4. Military morale—Canada—History—20th century. 5. World War, 1914-1918—Canada. 6. Canada—Armed Forces—History—World War, 1914-1918.
I. Title.

D547.C2C5558 2018 940.4'8371 C2018-902419-4
C2018-902420-8

Jacket and interior design by Five Seventeen
Jacket image: Front image based on William Ivor Castle, Library and Archives Canada, accession number 1964-114 NPC, item 3395810

Printed and bound in Canada

10 9 8 7 6 5 4 3 2 1

TO PAIGE, EMMA, CHLOE, AND SARAH.

WITH MUCH LOVE.

CONTENTS

INTRODUCTION

SOLDIERS' CULTURE

Major Maurice Pope, a twenty-seven-year-old prewar civil engineer and a future lieutenant-general, wrote that the Great War of 1914 to 1918 was a "huge siege" in which neither side was able to dislodge the other, adding, "It strikes me as being a test of endurance."[1] The million-man armies kept fighting far beyond any rational period of time as tens of thousands were killed, then hundreds of thousands, and, finally, millions. For soldiers at the sharp end of battle, cycling in and out of the trenches in 1915, 1917, or even throughout much of 1918, the war seemed destined to go on forever.

With the Allies and their German adversaries stalemated on the Western Front from the first months after the initial clash in August 1914, the commanders were reduced to ordering frontal attacks against the enemy's guns and defences. They had little success beyond producing mounds of corpses. There were few obvious solutions to the deadlock of the trenches, and the only way to victory seemed to be through more of everything: more shells, more men, more carnage. The German soldiers, fortified in their deep trenches, situated on the best terrain that was protected by barbed wire and machine-gun emplacements, would have to be steamrolled out of existence. New weapons—tanks, airplanes, chemical agents, and, from mid-1916, millions of high explosive shells—would kill and maim the defenders and eventually force them to give in, but not before all the armies had suffered terrible losses. This was the strategy of attrition: to kill proportionally more of the enemy than your own side lost, and eventually to force his surrender. During these costly campaigns, the infantry learned from its errors and defeats, refining tactics and training, introducing new weapons and mastering them on the battlefield to fight their way forward. But it was a bloody way to win.

And so there was a crucial factor in battle that had little to do with weapons or tactics or operations: the willingness of soldiers to keep fighting. In a long and costly war of attrition, this was essential to victory, or at least to staving off defeat. The great fear of the senior commanders was that their soldiers would collapse from the considerable strain of unending combat and the grinding effect of monotonous trench warfare. Over time, those who escaped the scythe of machine-gun fire and artillery shells would see their chances of survival shrinking, and might run away or down arms. In that imagined scenario, soldiers, units, divisions, and eventually armies would be used up, become brittle, and eventually break. The war would be lost.

The iconic images of the war are of the haggard soldiers standing at the firing line, bayonets at the ready, preparing to launch themselves into the teeth of barbed wire and machine-gun fire. The bleak No Man's Land—the dead zone between the enemy trenches and the Allies' fortifications that was filled with rusted barbed wire and shell craters—serves as an apt metaphor for the futility of combat throughout much of the war. Amid the unburied corpses and flesh-eating rats, the cries of anguish and agony resonate. We remember helpless soldiers, men caught in a no-win situation, who stumbled around like the living dead until they were put out of their misery. This is the soldier as victim. *The Secret History of Soldiers* offers another way to understand the Canadian soldier in the Great War.

"WE ARE LIKE THE RATS WHICH INFEST the trenches burrowing in the ground," Herbert Burrell wrote in his diary a few days after Christmas 1916. "Sleeping by day; grovelling in the mud at night. Mud in your bed; in your mess tin; on your food. We seldom wash. . . . One marvels at the cheerfulness of the boys who have been out here a long time."[2] Burrell, a prewar artist who enlisted at the ancient age of forty-five, would survive the war, although he remained angry and traumatized by what he had witnessed. Millions of soldiers fought along the Western Front trenches that stretched 700 kilometres from Switzerland to the North Sea. Every day thousands were killed "up the line," but hundreds of thousands more survived. How did they deal with the appalling stress? How did they cope with the slaughter of friends and comrades? "War has made me more or less callous to the suffering of others," reflected Lance-Corporal Percy Charles Read. A former bank clerk, Read had enlisted in December 1916 at age twenty and would be awarded the Distinguished Conduct Medal for bravery during the Hundred Days campaign at the end of the war.[3] Sustained combat and holding the line for extended periods indeed brutalized men, leaving some coarsened and insensitive. But most ached to hold on to their humanity.

A crucial part of the Canadian soldiers' means of coping was the creation of their own unique culture and society. Culture is the beliefs, practices, customs, and values that define groups of people, societies, and nations. Created in communities and shared to strengthen bonds and relationships, culture consists of highbrow artistic endeavours and the everyday experiences of individuals, both of which provide meaning for a group, helping them understand their collective and individual lives within a broader, constructed society.[4] Separated from civilians far behind the battlefield, the Great War soldiers' society was shaped by the abnormal environment of death and mayhem at the front, and it spawned new ways of understanding in the form of a distinctive culture of music, print, and theatre. In the landscape of killing, soldiers acted imaginatively and creatively, and their culture insulated and defined their group. They wrote and performed songs, poems, and plays, and

Canadian soldiers march off the battlefield. They leave behind the strain of battle and some of their comrades, lost to shellfire or snipers, but they know that they will soon return to the wasteland. Soldiers created their own culture to survive.

produced newspapers, all of which reflected their hard lives at the front. The development of this culture was also one of the ways that soldiers exerted agency within a consistently dehumanizing war.[5] The destructive supremacy of the war was thus met by the ongoing resiliency of those caught within it.

Most studies of war and culture focus on elites: the novelists or artists who fashioned moving visual works or stirring word pictures.[6] The British war poets Siegfried Sassoon and Wilfred Owen have been the guides to the English-language trench experience for nearly a hundred years. Painters such as Paul Nash and A.Y. Jackson, working in an official capacity, captured a profound visual record of the war on canvas. Yet the average education of the 620,000 Canadians who served during the war was of a grade-six level, and the vast majority of soldiers would never paint in the official war art program or write poignant prose or poetry. What, then, comprised the culture of the mass of men who came from every town, village, and city across Canada, and all the farmland in between, to form the Canadian Expeditionary Force?

The soldiers' culture forged in the trenches and behind the lines along the Western Front was as important to winning the war as weapons, leadership, and tactics. And it came from the soldiers themselves. It was not imposed by the generals at the top of the army hierarchy. In fact, the culture often subversively pushed back against authority. Vaudeville skits, cheeky stand-up comedy routines, and risqué songs and jokes combined with superstitions, slang, and graffiti reveal the soldiers' desire to forge their own ways of enduring. Tom Leask of the Canadian Field Ambulance wrote to a friend at home about his experiences on the battlefield, observing, "It is a very strenuous life and a hard game. The people in Canada have no idea, nor can any person have unless they have been in it. The spirit of the soldiers is wonderful. They meet everything with a smile. I sometimes think that to them Death is a joke."[7] Soldiers registered and understood the horror and trauma of the trenches and combat, but they embraced their own humanity as a way to see things through to the bitter end. The spirit of the soldiers, as Leask described, was infused by a vibrant culture that was used to guard against the tension and anxiety of having to survive unimaginable violence.

Soldiers often used dark humour as a safeguard. Sarcasm and satire helped men in uniform come to terms with the madness of the war. With its kilometres of trenches, drudgery, and death, the war on the Western Front could have sucked the laughter and humour out of those in its grip. But that was not the case. Infantryman Leslie Frost believed that the soldiers developed "a good-humoured tolerance of almost intolerable conditions."[8] This sense of humour—biting, nonchalant, at times even juvenile—underpinned the fighting men's secret culture. Cecil French, who'd been studying to be a missionary in India before his enlistment, shared with a friend his experience during one of his tours at the front, noting, "I've seen <u>nothing</u>—absolutely <u>nothing</u> yet—compared with the almost literal hell which most of the boys over here have been through, but they seem to be much the same boys as they were before. (The human frame can become used to anything, it seems). They seem happy, they laugh at danger and joke at hardship, and they have plenty to laugh and joke at, therefore, as a rule."[9] In a war where soldiers could scream or laugh, most chose to do the latter.

There was a materiality to soldiers' culture. The men gathered souvenirs from the battlefield, and sometimes these shell casings, bronze fuses, and spent bullets were forged into art. What the soldiers collected and shaped with their hands mattered, as did the objects they sent home to loved ones. These battlefield artifacts represented the war effort and were a tangible sign of service at the front. A rich vein of print culture also sustained trench warriors. As soldiers learned the art of combat and fighting through constant training and drill, it was the seemingly mundane reading material or letters from those left behind in Canada that raised and buoyed spirits. The shadow of the front-line trenches loomed over the soldiers' lives, but sport and leisure activities behind the lines and away from the shells offered diversion. Pleasure could come in the form of a good meal, a strong drink, or an encounter with a prostitute. Lance-Corporal Kenneth Foster, a prewar elevator operator who enlisted in Vernon, British Columbia, in July 1915, recounted his excitement upon escaping from the front lines to the rear areas, where he had a chance to play games, listen to the pipe bands, and see a soldiers' theatre production. "So, for that day only, all thoughts of the War were cast aside."[10]

Irreverent, salty, raunchy, and anti-authoritarian songs dominated the soldiers' society. Ralf Sheldon-Williams, a prewar farmer at Cowichan Station, British Columbia, as well as a poet and illustrator who served as a sergeant in the 10th Canadian Machine Gun Company, noted that he and his comrades welcomed the lowbrow: "Chopin, Grieg, Mendelssohn? Where are your laurels when the fighting man finds solace in 'Keep the Home Fires Burning,' 'Pack all your Troubles' and "Roses are Blooming in Picardy'? The writers of these hackneyed, stale effusions, anonymous so far as we were concerned, could move us and lift us more surely with their homely notes than all your classic masters."[11] Everyone sang in the trenches, behind the lines, in the training camps, and wherever else they went. What were officers to make of this soldiers' ditty, sung to the tune of "What a Friend We Have in Jesus"?

When this bloomin' war is over,
Oh, how happy I will be;
When I get my civvy clothes on,
No more soldiering for me.
No more pack-drill, heavy laden,
No more asking for a pass
We will tell the Sergeant-Major
To stick it up his ass.

Such songs were warbled during the conflict to give strength, to unify men, and to uplift morale, and sung after the war as a means of remembering the comradeship in times of great turmoil.

Soldiers' culture often cut against the grain of expectations back home, especially when hardened combat warriors put on theatrical plays for one another, which included popular cross-dressing performances. The characters on stage were often anti-heroes who dodged their soldiering responsibilities, engaged in crooked acts, and scoffed at authority. The home front, with its message of supporting the champions at the front no matter the cost, could never make sense of such anti-heroes, even when their sons or fathers in uniform tried to share the stories in letters. The meaning behind these deliberately unheroic actions by near-villains was further obscured by soldiers' vibrant slang and hundred-horsepower swearing. This exclusionary slang and the vulgarity deliberately distanced the soldiers from civilian society.

Soldiers' response to the prevalence of death further divided them from everyone else. Infantryman John Becker described the "black and bloated" dead, "covered with flies and maggots, a sight that would turn the stomach of one who had not grown accustomed to such sights." And yet such terrible visions often led to irreverent conduct. "It seems cruel to think of the crude joking remarks that were passed among us at the sight of these remnants of men but it was necessary to force jokes at times like these although invariably we were sick and weary and ready to quit—if there was any way of quitting." Without such cruel jokes, thought Becker, "We would have gone crazy."[12] Soldiers' psychological coping mechanisms included turning to a higher power, magical thinking, and even writing off one's life in a bid to stay sane. Soldiers who lived on the razor's edge between life and death created, invoked, and embraced superstitions, ghost stories, and supernatural beings to make sense of the bewildering and uncanny spaces of destruction.

All of these cultural acts reinforced the social group and unit cohesion, bringing men together in ways usually unknown in civilian life, and forging relationships that would be tested but rarely broken in battle. This culture was more evident and influential for the soldiers campaigning in Europe, in the front lines or the rear areas, but there were other aspects of soldiers' culture in the training camps in England, in Canada, and in the hospitals, all of which are outside the scope of this story. The soldiers' culture presented here is one that was deeply affected and infused by the spaces of violence and omnipotent death at the front, which was far less prevalent in the soldiers' culture as revealed in the camps or hospitals.[13] This soldiers' society united the men and deliberately excluded civilians. The *R.M.R. Growler*, the trench newspaper of the 14th Battalion, published for soldiers by soldiers, warned in January 1916, "It is hardly to be expected that anyone outside our own immediate circle will find any interest in what, owing to circumstances, will be necessarily crude in conception and local in character . . . our humour must be rather blunt to appeal to the men spending their days and nights in wet and muddy trenches, dodging shells, and cursing the weather, the Huns, the Quartermaster, the Transport Officer, and anything else that occurs to them. . . . Should any layman be unfortunate enough to secure a copy, we can only sympathize with him and apologise, as it was not intended that the 'Growler' should wander from the family circle."[14]

This hidden culture was one of the many trench secrets known only to the soldiers, and it is not to be found in the millions of pages of official documents produced during or after the war. Though some of the soldiers' culture was ephemeral or oral, many facets are revealed through the letters, diaries, and memoirs written by the eyewitnesses to combat as they struggled to come to grips with the fury of the war.

THIS BOOK EXPLORES THE SECRET society of Canadian soldiers in the Great War. With about one in thirteen Canadians at the time serving in uniform, and about one in three adult males, this new wartime culture was a substantial and important addition to what it meant to be a Canadian male. It has rarely been studied or presented, and yet this secret culture offers an important window into the lives of soldiers and how they coped with the strain of combat and the hard living on the Western Front.

Some 619,636 Canadians enlisted or were conscripted to form the Canadian Expeditionary Force (CEF), as counted from the official attestations of all men (and some 2,800 nurses) in all the recruiting stations and armouries during the course of the war. Additionally, close to 10,000 sailors served in the Royal Canadian Navy. As many as 50,300 other Canadians are thought to have served with British forces, although many had first "joined the colours" in Canada and then been transferred to the Imperials while overseas.[15] The CEF was the largest and most complex national organization created by the country up to that point in its history—a full fifty years after Confederation and several centuries after the first Europeans made contact with Indigenous peoples. The CEF represented the nation at war, and reflected it, too, since it drew Canadians from across the country. They came from every province, every city, and almost every community and section of the Dominion's vast rural hinterland.

Of the almost eight million people who lived in Canada in 1914, most were British subjects, as no Canadian citizenship was available until after the Second World War.[16] French Canadians made up about 30 percent of the country, but Canada remained very much a British nation within the Empire, where English was the language of politics, finance, and trade. However, Canada was more than just English and French, consisting also of Indigenous and new Canadians, the latter of whom some hundreds of thousands had arrived since the 1890s in an immigration boom.

Not all regions of Canada provided an equal number of men to the colours. The West and Ontario had the highest enlistment rates, while those in the Maritimes were lower. This followed the pattern of where British-born Canadians had settled. At the same time, men in the urban centres served in greater numbers than those from the farms, although an unknown but large number of farm hands and farmers' sons went to the cities to become soldiers. An exact indication of where enlistees came from is difficult to achieve since most of the statistics compiled after the war came from records that noted only place of enlistment, not residence.[17]

Even with these considerations accounted for, Quebec had the lowest per capita enlistment rates, as French Canadians showed little desire to serve in an English army in support of Britain.[18]

They also felt little urgency to aid France, which was remembered for abandoning Quebec in 1763. Other factors that influenced the low rate of enlistment included a higher per capita ratio of farmers than in other provinces; opposition to the war from parish priests who held an influential role in Catholic-dominated Quebec; and high-profile newspaper opposition. Not the least significant reason was a lingering resentment over language discrimination in the rest of Canada. Though most French speakers lived in Quebec, there were large numbers of Acadians, Franco-Maritimers, Franco-Ontarians, and pockets of French speakers in the West who formed the broad category of French Canadians. Still, French-speaking Canadians from all regions enlisted, although not in the same numbers as Canadians of British descent. Because of this lower rate of enlistment, and because of general anglophone hostility towards French Canada, Quebec became the primary target for an angry English Canada that bore a higher proportion of losses. As war casualties mounted, francophones were condemned as slackers who refused to share the burden.

There were other Canadians, too, who filled the ranks of the CEF. About 4,000 Indigenous Canadians served in uniform.[19] The 100,000 or so First Nations, Métis, and other Indigenous people who lived in Canada were almost completely absent from politics, and their fate, since the late nineteenth century, seemed to be assimilation, which was hastened by deliberate government policy. And yet they enlisted in proportionally high numbers, with many claiming to be responding to the King's call directly, as their ancestors had done. Indigenous people also wished to better their situation within Canadian society through military service.[20]

With the United States remaining neutral in the war until April 1917, tens of thousands of Americans enlisted in the CEF. It was thought for many years that about 36,000 American men served in the CEF, but recent studies suggest that even more Americans took the King's shilling, with perhaps as many as 57,000 enlisting during the war.[21] Thousands of other CEF enlistees gave their birthplace as Serbia, Australia, Brazil, Montenegro, Japan, and almost every other country that fought in the war. The CEF was, quite clearly, a fighting formation that drew from across the diverse dominion, even though it was largely formed of white, British, and Canadian-born men.

THE ARMY AND THE STATE tracked the Canadian citizen-soldier closely. Medical records showed that the Canadians were an average of five foot seven in height and weighed around 150 pounds at enlistment, although all soldiers put on weight while in uniform as a result of sustained exercise and steady meals.[22] The education level was about grade six for those in the rank and file, with officers having advanced further in school.[23] Almost 80 percent of the enlistees were single, and regulations stipulated that they were to be between the ages of eighteen and forty-five. About 70 percent of the CEF were twenty-one to thirty years old at enlistment, the average age being twenty-six, although those who served in the front lines tended to be younger and fitter. But age was difficult to determine, and men aching to serve lied freely. There were thousands of overage soldiers and even more who were underage, some of whom were coached and given a nudge and wink by a recruiting sergeant to walk around the block and come back in a few minutes after they'd aged a few years. Producing a birth certificate was not required for boys or men to enlist. About 20,000 underage Canadians were in uniform, most enlisting between the ages of fourteen and seventeen, and the army was loath to release them from service, even when parents wrote pleading letters.[24] Tens of thousands of additional men were turned down because of health and mental defects, revealing the poor nutritional standards and harsh conditions of early-twentieth-century Canada. In the end, about one third of all adult Canadian males between eighteen and forty-five served in the forces, fighting on land, in the air, and at sea.[25]

About 425,000 Canadians were shipped overseas, serving in Britain or Europe from 1914 to 1919, with the rest either training or engaged in military duties in Canada or other spots in the British Empire. Most of the soldiers who went overseas would eventually fight as part of Canada's primary fighting formation, the Canadian Corps, which by 1916 was four infantry divisions strong and consisted of around 100,000 soldiers. Wastage was always bringing down the number in the Corps, with reinforcements bringing it back to strength. It was the Canadian Corps that unified and galvanized the disparate men who fought for Canada and the Empire on the battlefield and who represented the nation on the world stage.

The men who formed the Corps carried names like Smith, Gagnon, Brant, and Kaminski, and they were English, French, Indigenous, and new Canadians. Even though they came from what we in the twenty-first century would see as a deeply discriminatory society, most of the overseas soldiers found that, after enlisting, they were treated as equals. A citizen-soldier became something quite different from a civilian, with service often leading to greater rights.[26] This equality within the military was most evident for Indigenous soldiers. It was illegal for Indigenous Canadians to drink in Canada; but overseas, they received the rum ration like their white comrades in arms.[27] Even more disturbing to the paternalistic Indian Agents who administered the reserves across Canada, Indigenous soldiers received the right to vote in the 1917 federal election; when the survivors returned to Canada, however, they would have to wait until 1960 to vote in another federal election. Some 222 Japanese Canadians served with distinction, and about a quarter of them were killed in battle. Jews faced a different type of prejudice in Canada, albeit no less insidious in its denial of rights and freedoms, but in the CEF, hundreds served shoulder to shoulder with their Gentile comrades.[28] Lieutenant Myron Cohen of the 42nd Battalion, a Scottish kilted unit raised in Montreal, was welcomed as a tough fighter who took on all comers. He received the Military Cross for bravery and earned the nickname "MacCohen"—denoting his acceptance within the Scottish battalion—before he was killed in combat at Passchendaele.

Within the Corps, Canadians from across the country—of different classes, races, and religions—served together. Private Frederick Robinson of the 58th Battalion, a twice-wounded veteran of the front, told his girl back home, "War is a great leveler and one rubs shoulders with probably a man who has been well educated on one side and on the other probably a most ignorant boarish [*sic*] chap who can scarcely write his name. But both these are men and we all get along like one big family."[29] Though there was one uniquely French-Canadian unit, the 22nd Battalion, most French Canadians were spread throughout multiple formations. Unless enlistees came from Ottawa, Montreal, or parts of New Brunswick, serving overseas often provided the first opportunity for a French or English Canadian to meet someone from the other "race," as the different linguistic groups were called at the time. In a country where diversity was almost never embraced, Canadians found that the other guy was not so bad, with the relationships forged in the trenches often shaking their ingrained prejudices. There were other historical rivalries, especially between the Irish, the Scottish, and the English, but these groups, too, learned to get along as they fought together against a common enemy.

The CEF was formed by soldiers drawn from all classes, but most were labourers, a distribution that reflected the makeup of Canadian society. By March 1, 1916, almost 65 percent of those who served were manual workers, and this number dipped only slightly as the war went on. Even though Canada had less rigid class divisions than Britain, it would still have been unlikely in Canada for middle-class Canadians to engage much with the labouring classes. That changed within the Canadian Corps, with the ranks filled by all types. Even the officer corps was less elite by the end of the war. By 1916, experienced rank-and-file non-commissioned officers (NCOs) were given commissions based on merit, skill, and survival, and many men without the formerly required education levels or elite background became officers. This homogenization of the junior leaders, based on battlefield expediency and combat effectiveness, was another critical marker of the Canadian Corps, and of its emerging identity as something distinct from British units. That new identity encompassed an Empire-wide respect for British culture but also for an emerging Canadian culture that was sharpened during the conflict. Corps' newspapers, cartoons, jokes, and theatrical performances all reflected this shift. Theodore G. Roberts, a writer of renown who served in Canadian uniform, gave voice to many when he declared, "Whatever a man used to be, he is now what his cap badge proclaims him."[30] It was the Canadian Corps in which the British subjects of Canada would serve and fight, and it was there that they were forged, through camaraderie, culture, and combat, into more identifiable Canadians.

Even religious differences were subsumed within the Canadian Corps. Communities in Canada were centred around the church, and small towns usually had multiple places of worship. A strong faith and connection to one's religion were a part of almost everyone's life, and the fierce battles between Protestants and Catholics were proof of how religion could breed intolerance. Few rose above it.[31] And yet, in the Canadian Corps, men from both sides of this divide would fight together. To overcome ingrained religious-driven bigotries was no small thing. The war, in this sense, was a great equalizer, and it brought Canadians together in unique ways, forcing men of different races, classes, and religions to serve together. "I am part of the works," reflected Donald Roy Macfie, born near Dunchurch, Ontario, and a prewar lumberman and farmer. "All the fellows are like brothers."[32] Within the CEF, there was an extraordinary breaking down of barriers. This was part of the nationalizing story of the Canadian Corps and the CEF.

Though the Canadian and British soldiers shared many of the same commanders, weapons, organizing ethos, and tactics, and though they were unified by a common cause, the Canadians saw themselves as different. Like the Australians and New Zealanders, the Canadians, as fellow dominion soldiers, were portrayed in propaganda as belonging to a stronger, bigger, and tougher British race than England's soldiers. According to such Canadian champions as expatriate millionaire Lord Beaverbrook, the northern climate of the Dominion forged natural-born warriors who were better fighters and tougher brawlers than the stunted, inner-city British working-class lads who had grown up with soot in their lungs and faced a life of drudgery in the factories.[33] The media magnate would orchestrate an extensive campaign consisting of journalistic accounts, photographs, film, and art to document the Canadian war effort and create a legacy.

Artillery veteran and official historian A.F. Duguid believed that "civilian soldiers when discreetly disciplined, carefully trained, vigorously led and, above all, when imbued with a resolute and unflinching determination to make their cause triumphant, could compete with and vanquish the product of a Military Autocracy."[34] Duguid's reference to discipline was a nod to the Canadians' belief that they were better brawlers than saluting soldiers, and countless jokes, stories, songs, and letters spoke to the Canadian irreverence for proper soldiering.[35] Another Canadian contemporary journalist wrote, with growing enthusiasm for the subject, that the Canadians were "men from the prairies from the wheat fields and the lumberyards of the West; men accustomed to the saddle and to sport of all kinds; men who can wield an axe more deftly than I can hold a pen; men accustomed to face death twenty times a year or more, and who have waged war with Nature or with wild beasts all their lives."[36]

This view of the Canadians as a martial race of soldier-frontiersmen also conformed to a fanciful but popular literature that emerged about Canada before the war, based on travelogues, evocative writings about the Canadian west, Mounties, "Indians," and a healthy dose of boys' adventure writing.[37] Every Canadian was supposedly a lumberjack, voyageur, or Wild West cowboy, born in an igloo or teepee and raised with a rifle in his hand. These untruths were propagated by most Canadians, too, who liked the romantic and rugged idea, and found it was far more impressive to pretend to be a windswept hunter who lived by his wits and his gun than to admit to being born in some filthy hovel in one of Canada's large cities. Canadian soldiers, generals, politicians, and publicists all played up the romance.[38] By the war's end, about 22.4 percent of the force consisted of farmers, fishermen, hunters, and lumbermen, while 36.4 percent were industrial workers.[39] But unlike the propagandist cartoons, poems, stories, and wartime histories that feature rugged, brawny frontiersmen, photographs reveal all manner of Canadians in uniform: tall and short, muscular and runty, fair and dark skinned, the dull-eyed and gap-toothed next to handsome devils flashing movie-star smiles.

It was the Canadian Corps and the maple leaf symbol that all Canadians wore that unified this diaspora of Canadians. George Timmins, who had enlisted at age forty-three with the 116th Battalion and left behind a wife and three children, said in a letter, "We can all sing 'O. Canada,' with feeling, believe me."[40] "O Canada" was sung by the Canadian soldiers long before the country adopted it as its official national anthem. In late 1916, Canadian prime minister Sir Robert Borden ordered that his overseas force would no longer be designated as an imperial one but would be remade into a new Canadian army under a Ministry of Overseas Military Forces of Canada, located in London.[41] This was a significant political change. Equally important was the rise of a Canadian to command the Corps. Though the Canadians fought with the British and under their command, by June 1917, Sir Arthur Currie, a Victoria real estate developer and prewar militia officer, became the third and last commander of the Canadian Corps.[42] He and his Corps were symbols of the country's emerging independent war effort within the British Empire.

Those who served in the Canadian Corps were not automatically transformed into diehard nationalists through their war experiences, and there were few during or after the war who gave voice to any call of abandoning the British Empire. Most soldiers embraced a series of shifting and overlapping identities. This fluidity was both a prewar and a postwar factor in Canadians' sense of self and country. The men and women of the CEF could see themselves as Canadians but also firmly retain a sense of being Scottish, English, American, Indigenous, French Canadian, Russian, or whatever identity they might claim. For others, there were influential regional or provincial links. Canadians negotiated their own distinctive frontiers, but it is also certain that by admitting these divergent Canadians into the Corps, the war played a role in shaping what it meant to be Canadian.

FOR OVER TWENTY YEARS, I have read tens of thousands of soldiers' letters, diary pages, and other written accounts in multiple archives across the country and around the world, in order to uncover the Great War soldiers' secret history. It is their words and recollections that form the basis of this book. They did not write for us—an audience one hundred years in the future—but for their families, their friends, and sometimes only for themselves. They wrote their stories to explain their foreign and formative experiences, to shed light on its grim nature, and, in many cases, to rid the war from their minds. This exorcism by pen, especially in postwar writing, can offer new insight into the war experience, which haunted the soldiers. Those who survived the trenches were never the same, but not all were scarred by the war. Some looked back on it as the most formative period of their lives. Many veterans focused their memory of the war on positive attributes like camaraderie and duty to the dead. This isn't to suggest that soldiers enjoyed the war or combat or the deprivation and dirt. But there were redeeming aspects of the war experience, such as duty to the cause and camaraderie among men within a unit, and these notions were often interwoven through and revealed within the soldiers' unique society.

Infantryman Jay Moyer wrote to a friend, Violet, in October 1916, "I was certainly glad to get out of those trenches. . . . Modern warfare is not hell, it's worse."[43] Warfare on the Western Front was indeed worse than the imagined fury of hell. Yet most soldiers found ways to endure. A forged-in-fire culture was used as a shield against the terrible strain of modern combat, and it reflected the collective and personal agency that survived in an impersonal world of death. Amid the kinetic energy of shells and sniper bullets, the soldiers unleashed their creative energy. This is a story not of resignation but of resilience.

CHAPTER 1

SURVIVAL CULTURE

Death could come at any moment along the Western Front. Herbert Irwin, who enlisted in Toronto before turning twenty and served overseas with an artillery battery, wrote to his father on the uncertainty of life in the trenches: "When the big shells come they sound like a freight train. It's funny you never seem to get used to them. The noise doesn't bother you but the more you see of their work, the more you hate them. Stray bullets seem to get more fellows than anything on the roads but a bullet's a bullet whether it's meant for you or not."[1] Soldiers recognized the role of fate in ending lives, observing with wonderment how hundreds of thousands of shells were fired to little effect other than tearing up more of the cratered landscape, or how millions of bullets scythed through the air without finding flesh. And yet there was simply too much metal to ignore the threat. Every unit lost men during every tour of the front—with the Canadian high command planning for 10 percent wastage per month per infantry unit, mostly in the absence of major combat operations, and massive carnage during the large-scale battles. With around 1,000 men in an infantry battalion at full strength, that meant 100 soldiers were expected to die, be wounded, succumb to sickness, or be lost through other means each month. By 1916, there were forty-eight Canadian infantry battalions at the front, as well as tens of thousands of gunners, engineers, machine-gunners, medical personnel, and those along the lines of communication to the rear. There was a constant turnover of units during the course of the war, and the composition of men who formed a battalion in 1915 was very different even just a year later, given the cycle of destruction and rebirth.

"Instead of fighting men alone," believed one Canadian private, "we have to fight machinery of the very latest and most deadly kinds."[2] Most of the casualties came from enemy shelling, both high explosive blasts and shrapnel. Though there were great periods of boredom, the periodic shellfire that smashed down during the day or the longer, more intense bombardments had men clawing into the dirt to escape whirling shell fragments and ear-shattering detonations. Shellfire led to about 60 percent of the total casualties suffered by Allied armies, and an even higher proportion for the Germans.[3] "We are alike; we all get a little funky in a bombardment but we will not admit it," wrote Lieutenant Ralph Lewis of the 25th Battalion, who was awarded the Military Medal for bravery. When the shells were "coming through the air you would swear that they were coming straight for you and that one had your number engraved on it."[4] Another Canadian, Gunner William Ball, writing in his diary, described the unpredictable nature of the front with particular poignancy, noting that on August 16, 1916, "three of us were sitting outside the hut tonight. I was sitting nearest the trenches, it was at dusk. A shot came down, hitting the fellow in the center sitting 2 feet away or less and talking to his mate on the other side (all being telephonists). The shot penetrated his neck and came out his mouth, after having whipped past me. I

After some battles, there were simply too many dead to bury individually, and so corpses were dragged and dropped into mass graves.

just missed it by a fraction."[5] Day after day, month after month, the unceasing casualties from shells and snipers left men feeling impotent and eager to strike back at their tormentors.

Soldiers going to war expect to encounter violence, but few imagine their own death. For the men new to the trenches of the Great War, such a fate, in fact, was almost impossible to conceive. Alan Cole, who served in the 2nd Canadian Siege Battery and arrived at the front in July 1915, later recalled, "I knew war was dangerous, people got wounded, people got killed, but I never just thought of such a thing happening to our boys."[6] Cole was shocked the first time he witnessed the killing of a comrade. And then it got easier, as relentless slaughter led to a deadening of outrage. It was difficult to fathom the industrialized violence. Artillery bombardments were withering to body, mind, and soul, as the massive explosions crumbled trenches, dismembered bodies, and liquefied internal organs. The sheer toll of casualties was staggering, and would eventually include more than 61,000 Canadian wartime dead, a number that rose to almost 67,000 a few years after the war when injured men succumbed to their wounds or other diseases.[7] About 172,000 soldiers were wounded, with about 138,000 suffering injuries while serving on the Western Front (although the method of compiling the statistics meant that these numbers included men who were wounded two or three times). The unending assault and buildup of stress led to deep physical and mental fatigue and, in thousands of men, emotional breakdown. Captain William Livingstone, twice a winner of the Military Cross for bravery and six times wounded in battle, was a dedicated warrior, but even he suffered from the accumulated exhaustion, writing in his diary, "I feel as though I should like to go thousands of miles away on some remote island and try to forget war. I am so tired. . . . Still we must keep up the morale of the troops and stick it for as many years as necessary to WIN. That's all that matters. But it will make old men of us all." Livingstone thus revealed his near collapse, even as he refused to abandon his mates or seek an escape from the "Hell . . . in the trenches."[8] Livingstone and his comrades for the most part learned to endure the relentless strain and see it through to the bitter end.

FIERCE BATTLES HAD TRANSFORMED IDYLLIC forests and farmers' fields into a wasteland of spent iron and rotting corpses that came to be called the Western Front. To escape the firepower of modern weapons, soldiers dug into the ground. The temporary ditches became semi-permanent trench systems, with multiple lines of trenches fortified with sandbag parapets, barbed wire, and hardened machine-gun nests. Within these underground cities, funk holes were scratched into the muddy walls to create a space for soldiers out of the busy but narrow pathways, while deeper dugouts, latrines, and communication trenches created vast networks. Soldiers found it extraordinary to burrow into the ground to avoid exposing heads or limbs to the fire, and to carve out what seemed to be their own graves.

But those burrowing men soon found that the cavernous and connected holes in the ground saved lives. There was varying terrain along the Western Front, but the trenches were generally dug four to five feet down and then built up another two or three feet with sandbags stacked on the ground at the top. The sandbags—jute bags stuffed with soil and mud—offered protection, and the continual act of filling them made them a ubiquitous part of the soldiers' front-line existence. Always there were the sandbags. And yet all men knew that the sandbags and their trenches were their best protection from the reaping metal from small arms and artillery that cut everything down above the ground. To become one with the earth was the only way to survive.

Soldiers tried to normalize the foreignness of the forward trenches, and nostalgia for home was evident.[9] Hunkering down in the mud, men inscribed the familiar on the abnormal, turning to symbols and names from their prewar civilian lives. Naming a space remade it into a place. It was common for soldiers to call trenches after known streets in Canada. Joseph Hayes of the 85th Battalion from the Maritimes wrote, "Our boys gave these trenches good Nova Scotia names such as Halifax, Baddeck, Borden, Sydney, Amherst."[10] And Captain H.E. Taylor noted that on the Somme in September 1916, as the Canadians advanced, "the German trenches in front of us are given Canadian names before being captured, and as they are taken, the names are absorbed into our front."[11]

Life in the trenches was dirty, smelly, and wet,
but soldiers' comradeship helped to ease the pressure.

It was not just the desire to connect with home that drove soldiers to name and rename. "All the trenches look alike," one new soldier complained of the confusing labyrinthine spaces that were cluttered with ammunition boxes, cables, detritus, and all manner of supplies required to shore up the trench walls and fight a war.[12] More experienced men found their way throughout the underground city by studying different constructions of the communication or forward trenches that revealed old and new pathways from front to rear. But all had to grow accustomed to being lost in the maze at some point. There was no getting out of a trench to study one's place in the landscape, for to do so invited a bullet through the body.

Handmade signs guided the men to their destinations. Robert James Manion, a medical officer with the 21st Battalion during the war and an MP throughout much of the interwar period, wrote, "If you wander among them [the trenches] you will see some strange names given to their quarters by the wags of the companies—such names as The Devil's Inn, Home Sweet Home, the Savoy, The Sister Susie Hotel, and other such devices."[13] Names were popular, but alpha numeric systems were also employed due to the sheer number of trenches. "Tonight we made two trips to the front trench with sand bags," inscribed George Kempling in his private diary. "The trenches are marked off in different ways. Sometimes they will be sectioned off and the sections named for cities, then farther on they'll be lettered off. Then sometimes they are numbered. On July 25th we went to the M and N trenches, last night to the O and P trenches."[14] It was also not uncommon for trenches or roads to carry cautionary names, like Whizbang Corner, Hell's Corner, or Pineapple Way, the first the name for light German artillery shells, the last a nickname for mortar bombs. Men were forever studying worn trench signs that carried the names of streets and alleys, with the soldiers' irreverent humour on display in names such as "Lovers' Lane" or placards that pointed to the firing line and read, "This way to Hell."[15]

Throughout the subterranean warren of trenches were man-made caves, some located 10 to 12 metres underground. These dugouts were areas of safety from most shellfire. By mid-1916, most of the Allied and enemy trench systems had dugouts in which soldiers sought protection from shellfire. These caves were accessed by steps and usually through an entrance that was covered by a heavy blanket impregnated with chemicals to keep out most of the poison gas fumes that were common to the battlefield by the war's mid-point. Most dugouts had crude ventilation systems and they were always stuffy and overcrowded, with walls darkened by tobacco smoke. Charles Clarke of the 2nd Battalion, who was promoted through the ranks and whose brother was killed on the Somme, warned that one had to make sure the ventilation was not blocked, as the burning of charcoal created toxic fumes, noting, "It was quite common to find some men unconscious when you called them for duty."[16] Dark and dangerous, the dugouts nonetheless offered protection from shellfire.

Soldiers turned the rough dugouts into temporary homes. Graffiti was scratched into the walls, a testament to their authors having passed through the area and an enduring memorial of sorts. The soldiers' names, units, and hometowns appeared alongside cartoons and jaunty phrases or then-risqué images of attractive mademoiselles in flimsy sleepwear.[17] Candles threw light so that men could read and write, and some dugouts contained electric torches or lamps. Most of the soldiers sprawled on the packed dirt floor, although material was sometimes scrounged to

Soldiers spent much of their time in the trenches digging, filling sandbags, and rebuilding the trench walls.

create beds of a sort. William Beattie, a prewar Presbyterian minister who served as an overseas chaplain, likened the trenches to ditches in his hometown: "Imagine trying to live for over a year in the trenches which you have seen workmen in Cobourg digging when laying sewers," he wrote in a letter home. "Men become very ingenious in their devices for making life possible."[18]

The dugout spaces were social environments for leisure activities and music. Portable instruments such as harmonicas and fiddles were popular among the trench soldiers. The men sang the latest wartime melodies, crude and lewd soldiers' ditties, but they also enjoyed sentimental dirges and folk songs from Canada. Gramophones played records and they could often be found in the officers' dugouts, although they were occasionally lent to the grateful rank and file, and such entertainments might also be scavenged from abandoned civilian homes.[19] Gunner Harold Simpson wrote to his family in Prince Edward Island, "Just below me in the recreation room the gramophone is going on a good old Canadian record which is very popular with us—'Take me Back to the Land of Promise' sung by a Canadian girl in one of the theatres in London."[20] Along the front, from either side, songs and music could be heard rising from the dugouts.[21]

INFANTRY BRIGADES—CONSISTING OF FOUR BATTALIONS of about 4,000 men when up to full strength, three of which formed the infantry component of a Canadian division—held sectors of the front, cycling through their units. Individual battalions had two companies in the forward trenches, usually about 150 men each, with the other two companies in close reserve to be rushed forward to meet any attack. Battalion headquarters, communications, and other specialists were almost always with the rear units but occasionally moved up with the riflemen. Forward companies, each consisting of four infantry platoons of about thirty-five to forty men each, were spread along a trench front, although every trench was different and there was no hard-and-fast rule. If the sandbag parapets were dissolving and dangerous to the soldiers, officers might thin out the line; if an enemy raid was expected, all riflemen were ready, with bayonets attached to their rifles.

A battalion spent around six days in the front lines, six in reserve trenches a few hundred metres behind the firing line, and another six days in the rear, where men were usually involved in carrying parties, bringing material to the isolated front lines. "A battalion at rest," remarked Private Leonard Gould of the 102nd Battalion, "is a battalion which is not actually under shell fire,"[22] but the men were still forced to carry out hard labour behind the lines. And then it was "up the line with the best of luck, chum," or so went the faux-cheery calls from those left behind to those who marched into danger. The 42nd Battalion, for example, had eleven tours in the front lines from October 29 to February 14, 1917, while the Princess Patricia's Canadian Light Infantry (PPCLI) had twelve tours during roughly the same time period.[23]

Though the trenches were plagued by daily "hates"—the salvo of shells that hurled through the air to blow up trenches or send geysers of earth and muck skyward—more often the front was a quiet place. Boredom was more common than terror, as it has always been for soldiers on campaign.[24] Infantrymen stared into the sandbags or daydreamed while searching the skies. J.L.A. Robertson of the PPCLI recounted in a letter home that he had expected "bayonet charges" and "continuous . . . cannonading & rifle fire." Instead, he observed almost disappointedly, "There are no bayonet charges. . . . And they only strafe when the other fellows do or now and then when a 'mad minute' happens along, but there is a terrible lot of mud and water and digging and fatigue and drills and waiting around."[25] Lieutenant Armine Norris, a decorated machine-gunner, offered breezy observations to his mother, writing perhaps too nonchalantly, "Don't imagine me in hourly danger of death. We are more likely to die of ennui."[26] Norris would not survive the war.

After the soldiers got over their initial fear of being killed or maimed, most learned to adapt to the monotony. Sentry duty and work fatigues filled the day, but there was always time to write a letter or read a magazine. After the frigid winter of 1916–1917 warmed up a bit in March, Gus Sivertz of the 2nd Canadian Mounted Rifles admitted that "in a quiet moment, I rolled over a trench lip—a communication trench, of course—and stretched out in the warmth."[27] Though soldiers' preoccupation at the front was to dodge their duties, only a few took to suntanning in the trenches. Sivertz would be shot in the head a month later, although he survived his wound.

Soldiers in the forward trenches spent most of their time working: digging, filling sandbags, moving around supplies, and rebuilding the trenches. The "fatigues," as such mundane manual work was called, were despised. Men swore that they had signed up to be soldiers, not labourers. However, each small victory required new trenches to be built. Even a small sector of the front required thousands of sandbags. And yet, despite the grumbling, the soldiers carried out the work. This was their home, an area of safety, and a trench in poor condition invited snipers. Lieutenant Ralph Jones of the 27th Battalion wrote to his brother in November 1915, "You may imagine how heartbreaking it is to see parapets or parados, recently built up with newly filled sandbags, cave in after a day or two of rain. Our men, though, are wonderfully cheerful considering, and go right back at the difficulty provided someone gives them some plan of the work required."[28] Jones, a prewar militiaman from Winnipeg, was killed in combat April 6, 1916, in the muddy wasteland of the futile Battle of St. Eloi. His body was lost or dismembered in the fighting so that he has no known grave, and his name is included on the Menin Gate memorial at Ypres.

The breaks in fatigues usually came when soldiers were ordered to stand sentry. Along the crooked trenches, day and night, infantrymen were at the ready. During the daylight hours, the soldiers watched through periscopes that allowed them to survey the front without exposing their heads to the waiting enemy marksmen. At night, the sentries typically stood on the wooden fire-step, a raised platform, with their upper torsos above the sandbags. They remained motionless, for to move from side to side, or to duck down, would attract attention. Even under the ghostly white flares that were shot up periodically to illuminate the front, the sentries and those men working in No Man's Land unfurling barbed wire were instructed to remain still and not flop to the ground. It was a nerve-racking business. Hundreds of men froze, statue still, holding their breath, eyes closed to what lay beyond in the battlefield.

Infantrymen shared their relatively safe space in the trenches with vile rodents that numbered in the millions. The rats lived in No Man's Land or under the wooden duckboards that soldiers laid in the trenches to keep boots out of the cold muck in the winter. Miserable unwashed men, constantly damp, recoiled in horror from the rats that were fattened on the refuse tossed over the sandbagged trench walls and on the unburied bodies of the slain soldiers between the lines. "I once took cover beside a PPCLI sergeant who had been dead about three weeks," recounted one Canadian rather laconically. "There were two rats burrowing inside him. Put me off rats for life."[29]

Even more hated than the rats were the lice that thrived in the rancid conditions. The insects burrowed into the soldiers' clothes, often in the moist armpits, seams, or the groin area. Almost everyone at the front was infested with the tiny vampires. The lice feasted on their hosts, drawing small amounts of blood, and their bites also transmitted a flu-like illness, known as PUO, "pyrexia of unknown origins." The many louse bites left skin red and raw, and irritated sufferers scratched at the site, further inflaming the area. Men with fastidious habits tried to stay on top of the infestation, but few were free for long and most accepted their fate, methodically picking the "cooties" from their clothes as they sat around and "chatted" or "crumbed" with their buddies. The men sang about them, wrote bad poetry to their tormentors, and joked about them in letters home.

A cheerful Canadian picking lice from his uniform. Several men would often sit together performing the laborious yet satisfying task, chatting as they went.

DURING THE PERIOD OF STATIC trench warfare or the large-scale set-piece battles that took weeks to plan, the Canadians, as one official report noted, "learned the lessons of War the hard way."[30] Wastage wore down the regiments and required a constant influx of recruits during the sick monotony of trench warfare, but it was in the big battles that men climbed from the trenches and where they were cut down in the largest numbers. During the four days of the intense fighting at the Battle of Second Ypres, April 22 to 25, the Canadians saw 6,000 men killed, wounded, and captured. The April 1916 Battle of St. Eloi, a resounding defeat for the Canadians, cost some 1,700 casualties. The two-week bloody affair at Mount Sorrel, from June 2 to 13, 1916, left some 8,500 Canadians as casualties (a term that includes killed, wounded, and prisoners of war). The Somme was even worse: more than 8,000 dead and 16,000 wounded in fighting from September to November 1916. Even significant victories like that at Vimy in April 1917 or at Hill 70 in August resulted in more than 20,000 casualties in sharp fighting, as well as thousands of other losses accrued in the planning and preparation phase. The horrible misadventure of the Passchendaele campaign, where the Canadians were lucky to arrive at the end of the fighting, still saw about 16,000 Canadians killed and wounded in the grim fighting to capture Passchendaele Ridge. And the greatest series of battles, the half-dozen major engagements that formed the Hundred Days campaign, from August 8 to November 11, 1918, led to more than 45,000 killed and wounded, or about 18 percent of the total Canadian battlefield casualties for the war. Even when the Canadians were winning, they were also losing shocking numbers of men in the cruel battles of the Western Front.

In this landscape of death, fear, and drudgery, officers and enlisted men understood the importance of sustaining morale, even as it was steadily eroded under the strain of waiting and wastage. "Morale" can be characterized as the general spirit of groups and individuals, and in the war this was expressed as a strong fighting spirit that supported and enhanced combat effectiveness.[31] Self-confidence, determination, staying power, a belief in the cause, trust in leaders, and a sense of fair treatment all led to high morale, which in turn allowed units and men to dig deeper to complete objectives and to refuse to let down their country, commanders, and comrades. In addition, rewards and punishments within a tightly structured hierarchy enforced the following of orders and encouraged a willingness in the men to keep fighting. In the history of recorded conflict, morale often has been the difference between victory and defeat in long campaigns.

The Great War consisted of a series of campaigns in which relentless battles were unleashed to wear down the enemy by killing his troops.[32] The long wearing-out process, known as attrition, saw armies battering one another, always keeping up the pressure. The key was to break the enemy's morale and convince his leaders and soldiers to give up. With armies consisting of millions of soldiers, and with desperate armies able to receive reinforcements faster than a follow-on assault could exploit the temporary victory, there would be no battles of annihilation in which armies were destroyed to the last man, or single titanic clashes that turned the tide. The only way to end the fighting when entire national populations were mobilized seemed to be through wearing down the enemy soldiers and civilians with constant battle until the soldiers gave up and leaders sued for peace.

Though soldiers complained mightily about their plight in between the colossal clashes and about the costly static periods of trench warfare, morale was sustained in many ways. Food was a potent motivator. Few soldiers protested against going over the top in a raid or even in a big attack, but they would scream bloody murder if they felt their ration of bread was too small or if they were stuck again with their least favourite jam. "Many men growled more angrily at the fact that plum jam came too often in the rations than the same men growled at having to go over the top and face death," thought medical officer Robert James Manion.[33] The company cooks behind the lines prepared stew for 150 men, while bakeries produced fresh bread. Alas, most of the cooks were just old soldiers who were no longer useful in the front lines and had been punted to the rear, and so weren't known for their culinary skills. Private Albert Hitchcox, who served with the 75th Battalion, told his sister Pinkie that the care packages stuffed with treats that he received from her were necessary for his survival: "I wish you could come and cook for us, as some can't cook water without burning it but such is life in a large army."[34] When food was scarce or could not be carried forward through shellfire, soldiers depended on canned bully beef. There were many types of this canned food, although most were unidentifiable meats marbled with fat and gristle. Soldiers had no love for the meat, but it was generally more acceptable than the hard biscuits that were also sent up the line. Men took to soaking and frying them, not wishing to risk breaking their teeth on the dog-biscuit-like food. In its January 1917 issue, *The Sling*, one of the many Canadian newspapers published by soldiers for soldiers, offered a fake testimonial advertisement for H. & P., the manufacturers of army biscuits: "The word 'Indispensable' does not emphasize enough the value they have been to us, using them as candlesticks, paper weights, and hammers; as well as feeling pretty safe against shrapnel and sniper's bullets, whilst carrying them in our pockets.

A private recently visited our dressing station in the early hours of the morning suffering from a choking fit. The silly fellow, thinking your biscuits were made for consumption, had managed to discover one with a flaw, and breaking a piece, had swallowed it."[35] The satirical story was easily understood by many soldiers who had tried the product and been left with aching jaws and chipped chompers. Indeed, Private Len Willans, who enlisted at age nineteen and weighed only 125 pounds, said in one letter, "One must have good teeth to live here."[36] While food was a source of much griping, a bacon sandwich or a rare tin of strawberry jam raised spirits among the hard-pressed soldiers of the line.

Cigarettes were a necessary indulgence, and most care packages sent from home contained them. With almost everyone at the front smoking, there was also an official ration of cigarettes, although these tended to be of poor quality and men yearned for "gaspers" from home. As one Canadian wrote, "Without smokes frequently

"The choicest gifts go up in smoke," reads the caption for this cartoon.

it would be awful."[37] The nicotine kept men going, and Harold Simpson professed that "a smoke is our great comfort," with cigarettes more popular than pipes. But few men campaigned without them.[38] Strong, gut-burning rum was another crucial tool for uplifting soldiers' morale. When rum jars made it to the front, the enlisted men were given a stiff tot at dawn and at night, in a ritual called "stand-to" and "stand-down." Many soldiers saw the nighttime allotment as their reward for surviving the day, and it helped them carry on. The rum was dark and thick, almost viscous, and had a very high alcohol content. It burned all the way down—and, for the untested, all the way back up again. But even with the discomfort, the drink was much loved and it gave men a chance to take the edge off their dull days. Edward Sawell, then a lieutenant in the 21st Battalion and new to the front in November 1916, worried that rum provided a "false spirit of courage," but admitted that this was often necessary in the trenches. Sawell observed that, "Aside from any mental or emotional effects, the physical effects were nothing short of marvellous. . . . Within a few minutes, the men, who had just been absolutely fed up with everything, began to take an interest in life again. A buzz of conversation usually sprang up."[39] Officers controlled the issue of rum and they often used it as part of a reward system.[40] Men who volunteered for risky jobs—a patrol, a trench raid, or a foray to bring in a dead comrade—were rewarded with a shot of rum. At the same time, the liquor was a tool that could be used to enforce discipline, with men denied it when they were being punished. Rum was part of the system of control and it was a critical component of the soldiers' culture.

Officers had a tangible impact on the lives of the rank and file. The high command of brigadiers, major-generals, and higher ranks were rarely seen or spoken to, and their support staff, the staff officers who planned operations (and all manner of logistics, training, and administration) were derided for being aloof and far from the front. They were all lumped in as the "Bloody Red Tabs," a play on the distinguishing collar marks on their uniforms. But closer to the front, the rank and file had a more intimate relationship with their own regimental officers, who led by example and shared the dangers with the men. While officers might be younger than those they commanded, they were, in the first half of the war, almost always better educated and usually came from a higher social class. As the war progressed and casualties cut a swath through the officer corps, more battle-trained sergeants and corporals were elevated from the ranks and given a commission, which improved the junior officers' general levels of command and reduced barriers with the ranks. Within the British and Canadian officer corps, there was also a strong ethos of paternalism, and officers were instructed to care for their men.[41] Officers tried to find good billets for the privates while they were out of the line, and to procure better food, a steady supply of rum, and other rewards to ease the burden. Lieutenant William Gray of the 52nd Battalion wrote that the rank and file "depend absolutely on you for their very being. You are a sort of last resort for everything in their lives, from clothes and food to seeing their effects [get] to their people after they are gone to the 'Last Parade.'"[42] This did not mean that officers befriended their men, and in fact, they generally communicated through the NCOs (sergeants and corporals). But the good ones were firm and fair, and listened for telltale signs of discontent through many channels, be it overt grumbling or masked anger as expressed in songs, newspapers, jokes, and cartoons.

The best junior officers—lieutenants and captains—led from the front, and they died in heavy numbers as they exposed themselves to danger in rallying their men over the large and lethal battlefield. Even after a unit absorbed severe casualties, the surviving soldiers could hold out long past the point of exhaustion if brave leaders inspired and rallied them to keep fighting. Canadian infantryman John Alvis described the tense period before an assault. He turned to his officers to provide moral leadership. Alvis believed that "if the officers in charge showed any jitteriness or hesitation" an operation would likely end in disaster.[43] Officers who failed the test of battle were often shipped out of the regiment into a safer job in the rear, where they could do less damage. Most, however, rose to the occasion.

A hierarchical army demands obedience, and discipline was a tool to keep men in line. Any deviation from orders resulted in fierce punishment, which included everything from docked pay to extra work to field punishment number 1, a particularly harsh act of tying a man to a structure and leaving him there for two hours a day (usually for a period of two to four weeks), where the lice tormented him and his muscles stiffened in agony. The ultimate punishment was the death penalty. Twenty-five Canadians were executed by firing squad during the war; the act was carried out by their comrades wielding rifles, and other units were marched past the bullet-riddled corpse. This involvement of other men was thought to scare them into following the rules. It might have succeeded for some, but others were furious at the treatment of one of their comrades, who were in all cases volunteer soldiers.[44]

Officers were also responsible for recommending their men for gallantry medals. Rewarding acts of bravery was a subjective process, with the officers selecting the most gallant acts in combat, and even those recommendations were sometimes turned down as they moved up the chain of command. In a significant reinforcement of the hierarchy, if an officer did not personally witness a particular act of bravery or courage, then there was little chance of it being recognized with a medal.[45] Gallantry medals for the rank and file, such as the Military Medal, were rare, while the Empire's highest award, the Victoria Cross (VC), bestowed life-long fame on a recipient. Many of the Canadian VC recipients, of which there were sixty-four during the war, received them posthumously for their acts of bravery or leadership.[46]

There were other factors that kept men fighting long beyond the span of normal endurance. At a basic level, most soldiers believed in the cause of the war and that their service was worthwhile. Future cynical generations may have scoffed at how tens of millions continued to serve as millions died or were maimed, but the soldiers of most armies assumed their countries or empires were threatened and had to be defended. Almost every nation argued that the war was a defensive one, even Germany. While soldiers may have become jaded and worn out in the trenches, most continued to see the war as a necessary struggle. However, that practical perspective was not the same thing as the flag-waving patriotism on the home front. Such public spirit faded rapidly in the trenches, where it was often replaced by vengeance or a stoic will to see the hard cause through to the end. The "dirty Huns," thought Canadians and Allied soldiers, had wreaked untold misery on the occupied Belgians and French, and had disrupted lives and societies: they deserved to be punished. The German aggression had to be met with force. And many soldiers buried comrades and friends on the battlefield with sickening regularity. "I lost my brother in the 10th Battalion," recalled one infantryman. "I lost my cousin in the C.M.Rs. I lost a lot of friends. I wanted revenge."[47] Conditions in the trenches were hard, but vengeance fired many a man to keep fighting.

Most men had a strong faith in God or another higher power to see them through the cataclysm.[48] Private Arthur Lapointe, a Roman Catholic from Matane, Quebec, assumed that his fate was beyond his control. He often committed his beliefs to his diary, including one entry on May 20, 1917, where he confessed, "I thank God for having protected me throughout my first tour of the line."[49] Assigning control to the divine eased the minds of many. Corporal Robert Miller, a twenty-two-year-old Montrealer serving in the 27th Battery, Canadian Field Artillery, wrote in his diary about the Ypres battlefield in May 1916: "Expect Germans to blow a mine tonight and if they do we will get heavily shelled here and run a good chance of being hit, but God has been good to me so far and I can trust him to bring me through."[50] The Canadian Corps was a religious army but, like the country from which it was drawn, was diverse in its beliefs. Of the roughly 620,000 who served, some 30.9 percent listed themselves as Anglicans, 22.9 percent were Catholic, 21 percent were Presbyterian, 13.6 were Methodist, and the remaining 11.6 percent were of various denominations or, rarely, atheists.[51]

Soldiers behind the lines typically attended a compulsory church parade on Sunday, given by one of the many chaplains and padres who were attached to the division and lower-level units. The sermons within the sound of the guns offered comfort to many and were tolerated by the rest. Most of the padres were charismatic figures, and those who went closer to the trenches, sharing the danger with the men, further earned the soldiers' respect.[52] The nature of the front, with unpredictable death lying like a shroud over the battlefield, pushed those in uniform to embrace a higher power for protection. Arthur Johnstone of Long River, Prince Edward Island, a student who enlisted at age

Soldiers emerge from a makeshift church somewhere in a shattered village behind the lines.

twenty-one, wrote of his comrades in the early summer of 1917, "Mother, when we see so many taken and wounded we are thankful to Him who protects and watches over us. We pray that we may be spared to return unhurt."[53] Johnstone was killed a short time after posting the letter, when shrapnel cut a femoral artery in his leg while he was manning an artillery piece.

There was no single motivator or sustainer of morale for those at the front. Soldiers were inspired and threatened, but the most significant factor for almost all men was the desire to stay the course and endure the trials of the trenches for their comrades. "This great army, drawn from all the corners of the world, and from such different classes, has a great end in common, which makes us all comrades," remarked Private Tom Johnson, a former clergyman serving with the 102nd Battalion, who, having enlisted at over forty years of age, was like a father to many of the men. "Every discomfort is common to us. We share alike a common danger."[54] The closeness of soldiers was a shield to fend off the most awful aspects of the war. Men who trained, worked, and ate together; who traded stories and sang songs together; who confided their fears and hopes to one another shared forged-in-fire relationships. Such intense feelings of camaraderie were difficult to convey to civilians. But the comradeship of the trenches did not mean that every man was a pal. There were antisocial types and bad apples. Harold Baldwin, a British-born infantryman who would lose part of his left leg during the war and who was by no means haughty, minced no words: "Most of my companions in France were savages."[55] That did not stop him from loving his comrades. In battle, they kept each other alive. In the aftermath, they comforted each other as they grieved.

BRAVERY WAS NEVER IN SHORT supply at the front. While almost every man experienced blinding fear during a relentless drumfire bombardment, the soldiers were remarkably resilient. After a brief rest from battle, 22nd Battalion officer Georges Vanier, future Governor General of Canada, wrote that he had "regained [his] former spirit of indifference."[56] Vanier's description is useful for understanding how soldiers learned to put down their heads and keep going, often through sheer willpower or indifference to danger. The sonic and physical assault during these bombardments led to the soldiers experiencing shaking and tremors, some of which lasted long after the shellfire, but for the most part these tough men continued with their tasks. A sardonic quip, the steadying hand of a chum, or a violent outburst of profanity, all combined with a hearty shot of rum, steadied the nerves in the fight to cheat death. "Courage is nearly universal, and cowardice almost as rare as the proverbial hen's teeth," observed Dr. Robert James Manion, a wartime medical officer, adding, "Most men are brave."[57] Leadership, discipline, threats, and punishment were all motivators, although in the end the Canadian trench soldiers were tough men hardened by the rigours of their service, who fought for one another and who set out to finish the dirty job that was handed to them.

While the soldiers' courage and bravery were rarely in doubt, there was a still-finite level of strain that men could endure. Lieutenant Armine Norris of the Canadian Machine Gun Corps, a generally cheerful and optimistic young soldier, wrote to his parents, "A man can face death for an hour, with a laugh; for a day, with quiet self control; but when again, again and again he comes within a hair's breadth of disaster and escapes, and when he just has to *sit* and *wait* for whatever luck brings, every fibre in his being cries for an end—any end—to the strain."[58] The rotation out of the trenches provided a respite, and longer leave to England, usually two weeks a year, helped to recharge the batteries, but over time the tension built to a crippling level.[59] Courage drained and some veterans likened it to drawing down on one's wealth in a bank account.[60] While each man was different, and rest and rewards added new "funds" to the account, over time there was little left. Ferocious battles or periods of sustained combat could break men in large numbers. So, too, could long service at the front, which exposed men to prolonged lack of sleep and constant proximity to death. Some came to believe that their only escape would be through injury or death.

Tremors and twitches contorted the faces of long-serving men made ancient before their time. "Young men in their twenties looked grey and old, at least 40 years old, while men in their thirties and forties seemed to have shrivelled into old age," recounted the 5th Battalion's Percy Kingsley, a prewar barber who went overseas in 1914.[61] Continuous service of longer than a year was rare, with those who survived that period often sent on courses or transferred to safer jobs at the rear. Some robust men lasted two or three years, but only the rarest of 1914 First Contingent soldiers made it to the armistice in November 1918 in a front-line unit with uninterrupted service.

The worst torment for the soldiers in the trenches was the unending shellfire. The physical impact of shell explosions often caused concussions, and those physical wounds were initially known as shell shock. But over time, men at the front and in the rear succumbed to the cumulative pressure of service, with seemingly stable soldiers breaking under the strain. The grisly death of a comrade or some other event could trigger extreme distress in a man already worn down from bone-deep exhaustion. He would start crying, or stare catatonically off into space, or simply lose control of his mind, gibbering madly or running through the trenches in terror. "Shell shock" was a shifting term that eventually encompassed both physical and mental wounds. The army high command understood the concussing effects of shellfire, but it was mystified by the psychological collapse of once strong soldiers. Over time, the generals far from the front feared a mass breakdown in the maelstrom of battle, an army of soldiers rendered unable to fight due to mental wounds. Authorities responded with punishment, thinking that it might stiffen the backbone of those wobbling. Officers and medical officers were instructed to be stringent in who they allowed to rest at the rear, and by the mid-point in the war, soldiers suffering breakdowns were no longer labelled with the term "shell shock." Instead, the medical officers described them as N.Y.D.N for "Not Yet Diagnosed, Nervous," and sent them to rest stations close to the front. Shell shock never became the epidemic that the army high command feared.[62] About 15,000 Canadians suffered mental breakdowns, and tens of thousands more sustained stress injuries and somehow kept going, sheltered by their mates and officers, sometimes given jobs far from the front lines or limping along until they were killed or put out of action. Countless more, too, would survive the war and return to their families and communities, forever changed by the conflict as they struggled with unseen injuries.

The medical and regimental officers were often the gatekeepers who decided which soldiers could leave the front for a temporary position in the rear, known as a "bomb proof" job. It was no easy task to sort out the men liable to drop off the edge of sanity from the exhausted majority, as all soldiers were desperately tired and pushed beyond their limits. The medical officers' job was to both care for the men and enforce discipline, and soldiers often felt the doctors were Jekyll and Hyde, one day kind, the next day heartless.[63] Anxious to escape the violence of the front lines, some soldiers tried to fabricate illnesses or trick their way past the medical officers, and this jousting was much satirized by soldiers in song, poetry, and cartoons.

With few legitimate ways to escape the trenches, many disillusioned soldiers hoped for a "Blighty"—an injury like a piece of shrapnel through the fleshy part of the leg or a bullet through the hand. A Blighty was serious enough to get a man out of the line and to England for a rest, but it did not inflict a permanent disability. It was common for soldiers to talk nonchalantly about such wounds, hoping for release from the front. "I don't know as

"The Writing on the Wall." A soldier's cartoon showing a wounded soldier with a large smile heading off to "Blighty" (England), while a sign-maker writes on a board pointing to the front: "Hell."

I'm overly eager for that honour or for a Blighty," wrote one Canadian on the Somme, "but it's popular to pretend you are."[64] Stabbing oneself in the leg or discharging a rifle into a foot was a sure way out of the line, although officers investigated and often men were charged with offences even as they lay recuperating in hospitals.[65] When they recovered, they were usually given jail time in one of the brutal military prisons, where food was scarce and physical beatings frequent. Word of the prison conditions circulated and men genuinely feared them, although the threat seems to have done little to dissuade the desperate.[66] Crafty old hands tutored those who could no longer take it on how to achieve their Blighty "ticket" through more nefarious means. The scheme of cultivating diseases like botulism in a tin of foul meat was difficult for officers to detect, while other soldiers wiped mustard-gas-infected mud in their eyes. The repercussions of such actions were painful and sometimes lethal. Catching a venereal disease while on leave was another means of escaping the front for at least a month, although it carried a different type of shame for some soldiers and was not an option for most of the married men.[67] In acts of collective humanity, the soldiers occasionally banded together to get one of their tired mates out of the line. Corporal Charles Cameron told the story of one of his older pals, Art, who was a veteran of the South African War, around fifty years old, and worn out from extended service. "We decided that he had served his country well and faithfully and his age and service merited a cushy job. Discovering that he had a bad cut on his foot, we tied a number of copper coins next to the cut, kept his boot off and marched him round the country."[68] The wound became infected as planned, and he was off to Blighty. The soldiers collectively exerted agency in how they viewed their comrades who could no longer serve, and they were often sympathetic to older men or underage soldiers (usually under eighteen) who had done their duty, even if their absence would leave the group diminished. Over the course of the war, there were only 729 recorded cases of Canadian self-inflicted wounds, although there were undoubtedly more, as many of these wounds were not tracked or were folded into other casualty categories.[69] In the most extreme cases, men committed suicide.

AN INFANTRY BATTALION AT THE front was always changing. The steady wastage from shells and snipers left a handful of men killed or maimed daily while the unit was in the line, and the big battles were far more devastating. New recruits were constantly needed to replenish the ranks. After the Somme, Private Percy Kingsley of the 5th Battalion remembered the terrible casualties and the torn-apart battalion. Around the same time, some of the old veterans who were wounded earlier in the year returned to the unit. It was good for morale to have the combat veterans back, although their return signified that even a wound would not bring a permanent exit from the firing line. In Kingsley's view, "It seemed the future led but to the grave."[70]

With no escape, how soldiers learned to cope with and endure the physical and mental trauma was crucial to staving off defeat. Writers and historians on these subjects have tended to focus on those who suffered from shell shock, a major trope of the war. Certainly, soldiers did collapse from the relentless stress of battle or from physical blows from shellfire, or were driven mad by conditions in the trenches. But perhaps we would do better to ask how or why the 350,000 or so Canadians who served at the front

A hardened Canadian soldier determined to do his duty in the trenches.

managed to "stick it"—to use the soldiers' phrase. The vast majority of soldiers found ways to deal with their terrifying ordeal and to win the internal struggle. Why didn't more soldiers break down? Why were there only a handful of Canadian soldiers' strikes (sit-down actions) in rear areas or after the war ended, and none in the front lines? How did the soldiers keep going in such conditions? While morale was sustained in many ways, it was the development of a secret, shared culture that helped the soldiers overcome the rigours of trench warfare.

CHAPTER 2

DEATH CULTURE

"If there were any grounds for superstition," wrote Lieutenant Coningsby Dawson, commenting on the Western Front, "surely the places in which I have been should be ghost-haunted."[1] Dawson, a prewar novelist and Canadian graduate of Oxford, was not alone in feeling the weight of mass death along the shattered landscape. The dirty and broken trenches, with bodies jutting from their walls, held constant reminders of the perverse sites of mass murder in which the soldiers made their temporary homes. In a site where death ruled capriciously and claimed so many, it is perhaps not surprising that many Canadians believed that the Western Front was haunted or plagued by supernatural beings and uncanny presences.

Although this was a war of machines, industrial power, and dehumanization, the magical and supernatural also found purchase in the soldiers' lives, in their belief systems, and in a new death culture.[2] The war was regarded as one of the great breaks between the past and the modern period of the twentieth century, and an ushering in of the modern period. But soldiers along the Western Front fully embraced the premodern, with its shifting and overlapping belief systems, and succumbed to the powerful influence of the mystical. Within the sites of destruction—in No Man's Land and the forward trenches—soldiers embraced "magical thinking," which seemed to offer clues to survival through recourse to obscure symbols, signs, and unscientific patterns of behaviour and belief.[3] Magical thinking and embracing the uncanny provided a sense of control in the midst of dislocation and unpredictability.[4] The Western Front was a site for spectral thinking and haunting, where the strange was made ordinary, where the safe was infused with danger, and where death was natural. Few soldiers expected to emerge alive or unscathed, and the unnatural, supernatural, and ghostly offered succour to some soldiers who accepted these "grave beliefs" to make sense of their war experience and to cope with the incessant mental and physical strain of fighting on the edge of No Man's Land.

Corporal Will Bird served with the kilted 42nd Battalion, initially raised in Montreal, for over two years at the front. He was a hardened combat veteran who admitted to killing Germans as a sniper and in battle, but also to succumbing to fear, frustration, and disillusionment. After the war, he became a much-respected journalist in Nova Scotia, was a close friend to veterans as he published stories about veterans' postwar challenges, and authored a Second World War regimental history, showing that he had earned the trust of another generation of soldiers. His memoir, *Ghosts Have Warm Hands*, is regarded by historians as one of the finest eyewitness accounts by a Canadian soldier.[5]

The title of Bird's memoir refers to an uncanny event in the aftermath of the April 1917 Battle of Vimy Ridge. After a cold night spent digging trenches and laying barbed wire, Bird stumbled to the rear through the labyrinth of trenches, uncertain as to where he would sleep. Not having had a chance to prepare a sleeping area, and having been denied a place to bunk down by a few unsympathetic types who told him to bugger off, two men from the neighbouring 73rd Battalion finally allowed him to lay with them, under a ground sheet pegged down to keep out the rain. He slipped into a coma-like slumber, and before dawn was shaken awake. Annoyed at being awoken, he tried to pull free but the "grip held." Still befuddled, he looked up with amazement at his brother Steve. Two years earlier, Steve had been reported missing in action, likely killed. What was he doing here? Why had Will's parents not written to him that Steve had escaped from a German prisoner-of-war camp? And how had Steve located him in the darkened bivvy, when even Will did not know where he was?

"Steve grinned as he released my hands, then put his warm hand over my mouth as I started to shout my happiness," recalled Will. Drawing his brother out of the sleeping quarters and beckoning him to follow, Steve moved quickly down the trench, still wearing his distinctive 1915 kit, including a soft cap instead of the steel helmet that all soldiers had worn since 1916. Steve led him through some ruins, and then suddenly rounded a corner and disappeared. Confused and distressed, Will searched for his brother, but then sobered up, realizing that he must have been sleepwalking or indulging in a hopeful hallucination. The despair over Steve's presumed death hit him anew and he collapsed into a funk hole, falling asleep but remaining perplexed about feeling the touch and texture of his brother's warm hands.

He was awoken again in the harsh light of a new day. Friends stood over him, astonished but peppering him with questions. How did he survive? Bird had no answers to their searching questions, and could not even grasp their meaning. Frustrated, they dragged him to his old bivvy, where he saw that it had been destroyed by a direct hit from a high explosive shell. The other soldiers of the 73rd Battalion had been dismembered beyond all recognition, to the point where Bird's friends had been trying to sift through the viscera to determine if they could bury a few of his body parts together.

After some prodding, Bird recounted his supernatural experience to his friends, aware that he sounded deranged. When word passed through the unit of his miraculous rescue by his dead brother, he was eventually ordered to his company command headquarters. As Bird told his story, one officer nodded supportively and, like a true believer, shook his hand, remarking, "You have had a wonderful experience." A more experienced sergeant, also present, looked at Bird as if he had lost his mind. Bird observed that neither man's reaction mattered much, for in the soldiers' world of disorder and havoc, "in a few days the matter was forgotten." It was only he who thought of it at night, before he went to sleep, marvelling again at the sound of his brother's voice, his familiar half-grin, and his warm hands.

What is the meaning of this story? Bird was convinced that something unusual had happened to him, and he even went so far as to reference the ghostly encounter in the title of his wartime memoirs. And Bird was not alone. His comrades in the trenches clung to the hope of survival by embracing death, in this sense exerting agency, even if in an unconventional manner. Life in the forward trenches saw soldiers haunting a dead land and, in turn, being haunted by it. Spectral beings, premonitions of death, and a belief in otherworldly events allowed the soldiers to cope and make sense of their disorienting war experience.

DURING THE FIFTY YEARS BEFORE the Great War, spiritualism had been embraced in Canadian, British, and American society. The attempt to understand the great beyond, to communicate with those who had passed on, and to make sense of one's own mortality drove Victorian-minded Canadians to turn to the unnatural and the supernatural. Secret societies sprang up across Canada, although speaking to the dead was generally done in the sanctity of homes and among friends. Proponents of spiritualism and spirit communication saw themselves as agents of progress who were expanding knowledge and engaging the modern.[6] The dead were thought to be ever-present in the lives of those they had left behind, and to be waiting for the living to contact them. Séances were the means of bridging the two worlds, with mediums often acting as the channel through which the living and the departed communicated. While this was a group activity, individuals could also have visions or premonitions, or might engage in automatic writing—their hands guided by unseen forces.

Perhaps the popularity of spiritualism could be explained by the fact that death was ever-present in early-twentieth-century Canada. In the crowded, fetid slums of Montreal at the turn of the century, one in four babies died before reaching the age of one, a testament to the horrible squalor and rampant disease in large urban centres.[7] Life expectancy was only fifty-two years in Britain in 1911, and likely around the same in Canada.[8] But the Great War marked an important turning point for spiritualism. The mass death in the trenches, which fell disproportionately on the young, left thousands of families grieving and seeking closure. Spiritual chronicler Hereward Carrington wrote of the loss, "The importance of psychic investigation has never been so forcefully demonstrated to us as by the present great World War. . . . Every month that passes, thousands of souls are being shot into the spiritual world—*or* obliterated altogether, according to our view of the facts. What becomes of them?"[9] Bereavement often drove these sufferers to explore beyond their known world, although it was uncommon for soldiers to engage in such actions in the trenches. Nonetheless, the soldiers were deeply affected by their spaces of hyper violence, and they would come to intimately know sudden and mass death. They fought back against it, and most found ways to cope and endure by creating and embracing a death culture.

THERE WAS A JARRING JUXTAPOSITION between the desolation of the Western Front and the green fields beyond and behind. At the front, one entered a land of carnage and corpses that was an unsettling and mysterious space.[10] It was a place that was ruled by chance. Soldiers experienced the uncertainty of life and close brushes with death: dud shells landing in trenches next to soldiers and failing to detonate; bullets passing through webbing or clothing, somehow missing flesh; shell splinters whirling into sandbags only inches from a man's face. Private Charles Olson, a prewar reporter and occasional rancher in Alberta before serving with the 3rd Battalion, wrote postwar memoirs in which he referred to himself in the third person, recalling, "The laws of chance intrigued him. He speculated upon the chance of survival in a major battle. What are your chances at Zero Hour? What are the odds when you arrive at the enemy's frontline trench? Do the odds go up or down as you advance to your second or third objective? He took pencil and pad, and with all the earnestness of a life insurance statistician, he tried to compute the odds."[11] All soldiers engaged in such mental math, a way of looking for patterns in the chaos and of attempting to cheat death. This type of magical thinking was only enhanced as friends and comrades were killed, reaffirming the need for soldiers to understand the clues to survival. Private Albert Hitchcox, who served with the 75th Battalion, confided to his sister Pinkie from the grim Passchendaele battlefield in October 1917, his thoughts tinged with dark humour: "If I don't try to stop any of Fritz's shells, everyone stands a chance of coming back safely and might be one of the lucky ones."[12] Hitchcox was wounded with a gunshot to the leg during the final months of the war but survived to go home. Destiny and doom, luck and randomness, seemed the only reliable answer to one's survival in the face of such poor odds. Private James N. Pound, a Quaker who acted as a stretcher-bearer with the 85th Battalion, wrote to his father on March 25, 1918, "Some of us soldiers are going to go through this war unharmed and somehow I feel that I am going to be one of the lucky ones." By the time his father, Asa Pound of Yarmouth Township, received the letter, his son had been killed in action.[13]

Soldiers learned to bury their friends and comrades. With lives ruled by chance and fate, it was difficult for soldiers not to become superstitious.

Two soldiers study a skull, one of the countless human remains that littered the Western Front.

On the Western Front, living soldiers became martyred corpses in the blink of an eye. The blurring of the living and the dead only added to the apocalyptic landscape. Grimy, exhausted soldiers, slathered in mud, asleep on a fire-step or in a funk hole, could easily be mistaken for the dead. It was not lost on the soldiers that they appeared to be digging extended graves—the trenches—to protect themselves from death-dealing artillery shells. And in a sick irony, the artillery bombardments often buried the living and disgorged the dead.

Human remains in varying degrees of disintegration littered the landscape. Shellfire dismembered men, while those killed in No Man's Land were often lost in the shell craters and slowly rotted away. Private John McNab of the 38th Battalion tried to capture in words the wasteland of Passchendaele in November 1917, sadly noting in his diary, "The ground is all covered with dead as far as you can see."[14] Canadian John Patrick Teahan, who managed the family's furniture store in Windsor, Ontario, before enlisting, was so disturbed by the crippling rate of loss that he believed the Western Front would soon be reduced to "one huge uncovered grave."[15] There was no avoiding the things that once were men. The stench of rotting flesh—"The smell of corruption," as one Canadian put it—wafted out of dark holes and from No Man's Land in draughts of gut-churning stink.[16] The smell of dead men worked its way into clothing and pervaded food. Some soldiers tried to describe the sickly sweet and revolting stench of the rotting dead, but for most it was beyond their literary talents. Even if the trench dwellers learned to live with the smell, particularly ripe fronts of decaying men left survivors unable to eat, with soldiers opting to go hungry rather than try to cook or consume food in such conditions. Cigarettes masked some of the olfactory assault.

The masses of the dead, buried on top of one another or spread throughout different parts of the battlefield, were like some morbid archeological dig. "These bodies lying in No Man's Land," wrote Private Donald Fraser, a Scottish-born immigrant to Canada in 1906 who had worked as a clerk in the Royal Trust Company in Vancouver before enlisting in the 31st Battalion, "made me interested in the history of this line and I made enquiries regarding the former occupants of this part."[17] Fraser uncovered the history of the battlefield by studying the layers of bodies, and even gauged when they had fought and died by the extent of their putrefaction. Some infantrymen took pride in locating the dead in other ways, with Louis Keene, a prewar artist and wartime lieutenant in a machine-gun unit, remarking, "I am an authority on smells. I can almost tell the nationality of a corpse by the smell."[18] Another

Canadian, Charles Henry Savage, recalled in a postwar memoir his fascination with the carcasses laid before him in one bloody sector:

> It was possible to read the story of attack and defence by the grouping of the dead. Here was the assault trench, broken by shell holes, each one with its circle of mangled and half-buried bodies: the German counter-barrage had been accurate. Immediately in front of the assault trench the ground was clear—it had been crossed before the enemy had had time to bring his machine guns and rifles into action. Then for fifty yards the rich harvest reaped by machine guns playing on massed men lay thick on the ground. But at one spot there were few dead: our artillery had made at least a dozen direct hits on about fifty yards of German trench. There had been no one left to resist: our men were in. But what of that circle of huddled bodies on the left? About what deadly centre had this line been drawn? A machine gun superbly handled stopped everything there. It was never reached from in front: the gunners were shot or bayoneted by our men coming in from the flanks. They died on their gun. And those men half kneeling, half lying in grotesque attitudes? The wire had not been cut in front of them: that is what is holding them up. They died on the wire.[19]

While soldiers engaged in their constant cycle through the front line, the dead remained behind. They were the permanent residents of the trenches and No Man's Land.

The dead were a part of the landscape, even becoming informal markers, much like decaying trench signs. Stealth patrols could navigate by the steadily reduced corpses of No Man's Land, with the dead acting as way-finders.[20] In long campaigns like the Somme or Passchendaele, as the Allies inched their way forward, they often incorporated the dead, in single or mass graves, into their own lines. Jim Broomhead, a twenty-year-old sniper with the 46th Battalion, spoke of his revulsion on the Somme: "I got my first glimpse of death and its stench at Poziers [*sic*]. The dead had not been removed, and they were piled three deep. What an awful sight! . . . God forbid anybody from seeing what I saw. Our barbed wire was fairly well intact, but it hung full of dead Canadians and Germans, like birds on telephone wires. The parapet had been kept built up, but you couldn't avoid the arms and legs that were sticking out of it."[21] Dead men caught on the barbed wire, like nightmarish scarecrows, were a constant reminder to soldiers of their possible destiny. But the soldiers faced their fate, even taunted it. One hauntingly bitter song, "Hanging on the Old Barbed Wire," had lyrics

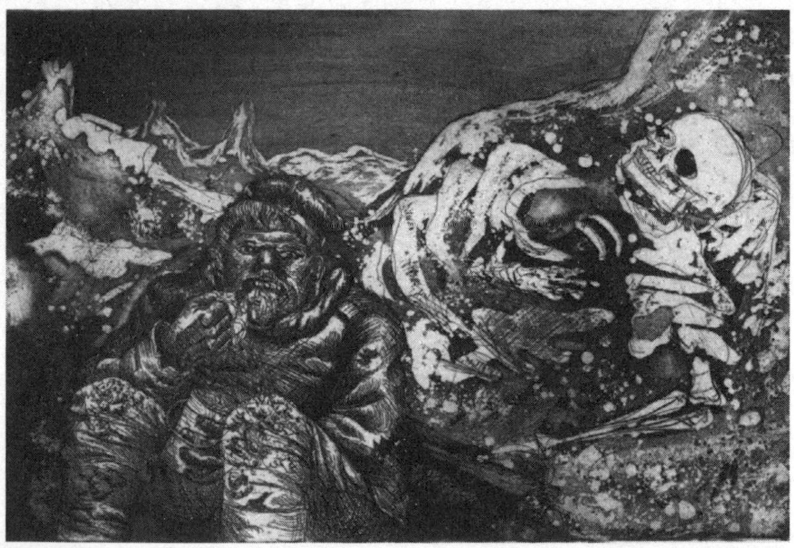

German trench soldier Otto Dix captured the ghastly nature of trench warfare in a series of celebrated prints. His Mealtime in the Trenches *depicts a soldier casually eating next to a rotting corpse.*

describing where the infantrymen would end up: "If you want the old battalion / I know where they are / I know where they are / I know where they are / They're hanging on the old barbed wire, / I saw them, I saw them / Hanging on the old barbed wire. . . ."

It is hard to imagine soldiers calling the trenches home, but they did. They had to. And within their protective space they lived cheek by jowl with corpses. Private Herbert Burrell described how the dead were "protruding through the trench walls."[22] In digging trenches, soldiers used pick axes and shovels to hack through the bones and bodies of buried men within the trench walls or underfoot. Another Canadian infantryman, Corporal John Harold Becker, wrote about digging a hole in which to curl up and shelter from the rain: "In the late afternoon I was resting in this water, soaked to the hide, when the side wall gave way and I found

A Canadian inspecting a German sniper's rifle next to a corpse.

myself lying against a corpse that had been buried there some time before. The stench was terrific but as there were always bad smells in the line, I paid no particular attention to that! I did, however, show sufficient regard for my 'na-pooed' [dead] neighbor to pack the dirt in around him and scooped myself out another funkhole a few feet to the north."[23] This is the stuff of horror movies, but rendered normal in nonchalant prose.

"It is strange how quickly we get accustomed to seeing death and hearing of the death of men we know," observed Armine Norris in a letter he wrote to his mother.[24] Some men shielded themselves from contemplating their own violent passing by trivializing the dead through seemingly deviant or uncivilized behaviour. "Along the road was an unburied hand of a soldier," recounted Lieutenant Fred Wells. "Some of our 'wags' would pretend to shake hands with it—a bit of humour along the way."[25] Body parts protruding from the walls were touched for good luck; gas masks and helmets were hung from flesh-picked bones, with ulnae and femurs emerging like white branches and tree roots. "We are all used to dead bodies or pieces of men, so much so that we are not troubled by the sight of them," scoffed one Canadian. "There was a right hand sticking out of the trench in the position of a man trying to shake hands with you, and as the men filed out they would often grip it and say, 'So long, old top, we'll be back again soon.'"[26] With the hollow-eyed and filthy soldiers looking like the living dead and living with the recently—and not so recently—killed, it is not surprising that trench soldiers developed a familiar acquaintance with the bodies of the unknown slain. Such soldiers' actions seem shocking in their callousness, but they were one way to cope with living in the land of the dead.

While the unknown dead were treated with insensitivity, one's fallen comrades were cared for, gathered, and given a grave.

This trench newspaper cartoon captures the rough soldiers' humour and slang.
SOUVENIR SAM: "This trip I'm either gonna git a decoration,
a blighty, or napoo."
HIS PAL (warmly): "All kind o' luck, boy. Hope you get 'em all."

Soldiers often risked their lives to bring in the bullet-riddled body of a man with whom they had trained, eaten, and shared stories. Others volunteered for the grisly task of burying those hit by shellfire, which usually involved collecting body parts in jute sandbags for proper burial.[27] It was considered beyond the pale to treat one's own slain mates callously. Bodies were wrapped in blankets and buried behind the lines, where possible. Informal wooden crosses were erected, sometimes with a tin metal plate attached, inscribed with a killed man's name.[28] "You ought to see the way the boys fix up the last resting places of their chums," wrote George Timmins, who had enlisted at age forty-three, was the father of three, and was impressed by the devotion of the living to their slain comrades.[29]

The paired identification discs belonging to the slain were separated, one left on the body, the other given to an officer or padre, who made note of the dead man's location for future reburial. Survivors penned letters to comrades' loved ones with the sad news of the death. While soldiers became necessarily inured to the loss of comrades, they still mourned the absence of close friends and worried about the grieving next of kin.[30] Those at home waited for information from the front with heightened anxiety after reading of the large-scale battles and campaigns and the staggering numbers of casualties in both victory and defeat. The first notifications of death usually came from an impersonal government telegram, beginning with the phrase, "Deeply regret to inform you. . . . " During the attritional campaigns, in which thousands of casualties were sustained, communities large and small were saturated by the death telegrams. Families lived in terror of the knock at the door or the telegraph boys in short pants who sped by on their bikes bringing news of death. There were agonizing cases like that of Privates John and Cyril Windle, brothers who enlisted on the same day and were killed on the Somme, with both confirmed dead on September 26, 1916. The Porter family had a similar cruel fate as brothers Frank and George died within a month of each other in April–May 1917. Their names, like that of the Windle brothers, would eventually be inscribed after the war on the Vimy monument as their bodies were never recovered.

"Ghost-haunted" was how gunner George Magee described the old Somme battlefields in late 1918, only weeks before his own death. "By that scooped-out hole yonder, where empty cartridges still strew the ground, a husky German machine-gunner

British artist Percy Smith, who served on the Western Front, produced several works in his "Dance of Death" series, in which Death is personified and haunts the battlefields where soldiers fought and died. This work is titled Death Forbids.

had lain beside his gun, repeatedly bayoneted and his head crushed in. At the bottom of those dugouts by the sunken road lay what had been men before Mills bombs bounced down the steps. Over the field to the left of the wood were the ghastly remains of Frenchmen mowed down in rows in earlier fighting for Hangard, but why dwell on the scene? In and around that demolished village the dead of three nations rest. There is something eerie still in the air, even the hardened soldier feels it."[31] Ghosts are often associated with environments of "disquiet and unmediated tragedy," and the Western Front likely saw more killing by square metre than any other place in the history of the world.[32] Prewar chemist and man of science George Nasmith seemed to feel the dead's presence on the Western Front: "I fancied that I could see the shadowy spirits of the departed ones hovering over this spot before their final departure."[33] The trench system was a porous and thin membrane, a border between life and death, particularly as soldiers stared off into No Man's Land. Private Arthur Lapointe of the 22nd Battalion, while standing sentry and watching dreamily as enemy machine-gun fire played along the front, sparking on barbed wire or whirling through the air to unimaginable destinations, wrote afterwards in his diary on May 15, 1917, that No Man's Land "seems haunted and mysterious."[34]

Like the unknown spaces on old explorers' maps, left blank or labelled with "Here there be monsters," No Man's Land was unknowable and unoccupied. Within that ghost-haunted space, some soldiers felt there were monsters, including a supposed army of deserters. Somewhere in the broken wilds that separated the two warring sides lay hundreds of such outlaws, or so the stories went. British infantryman and poet Osbert Sitwell said this of the international band of deserters:

> They would issue forth, it was said, from their secret lairs after each of the interminable check-mate battles, to rob the dying of their few possessions—treasures such as boots or iron-rations—and leave them dead. Were these bearded figures, a shambling in rags and patched uniforms . . . a myth created by suffering among the wounded, as a result of pain, privation and exposure, or did they exist? It is difficult to tell. At any rate, the story was widely believed among the troops, who maintained that the General Staff could find no way of dealing with these bandits until the war was over, and that in the end they had to be gassed.[35]

This was in fact a "monster story" for sentries and those men who patrolled the blasted No Man's Land.[36] And if ever there were a terrifying place on earth, No Man's Land fit the bill. The rumours continued to be fed by the soldiers who waited on the boundaries, staring into the darkness. Another soldier referred to the deserter army that lived "like ghouls among the mouldering dead, and who came out at nights to plunder and kill."[37] Of those who entered into this desolate land, many did not return, snuffed out in ambushes, killed by stray fire—or perhaps, as some thought, captured, murdered, and eaten by the cannibalistic deserters. But attributing the loss of comrades to an army of ghouls put a face on the unknown—even if it was a fantastic or grotesque one—and it helped men deal with the stress of uncertainty and make some sense of their senseless environment.

"Imagination ruled the nights," warned one combat veteran.[38] With the front blanketed in a darkness broken only periodically by shell- and tracer fire as well as the shimmering light of flares that cast a white glow, there was a constant feeling of unease. Kenneth Foster, who enlisted in Vernon, British Columbia, told his story of standing sentry on the fire-step, staring out over the sandbags, eyes straining to locate the enemy. "I saw all kind of funny things. Staring into so much black nothingness I would see an object, which, after a few minutes, would move cautiously towards me."[39] In this case, like so many similar soldiers' accounts, it was only Foster's tired eyes playing tricks on him. The wind rustled garbage and debris, rusty barbed wire scratched against bits of discarded kit, and the legions of rats scurried across the mountains of bully beef cans and other discarded garbage. Captain Robert Clements recounted an incident of two sentries gazing into No Man's Land. They were intermittently talking, sharing stories and swapping rumours, but they remained watchful for enemy raiders who might snatch them. After a period of quietness, the sentry on the fire-step, peering into the darkness, called softly to his mate about a shadow beyond the wire, perhaps a German patrol. Receiving no reply, he turned to find his friend's body slumped against the trench wall, headless.[40] The survivor ran screaming through the trench, raving that some monster had beheaded his friend. He was eventually caught and calmed with several shots of rum, but a search of the trench and surrounding area failed to reveal the missing head. It was an odd death, but old hands had seen worse. There was a vigorous debate: how had the Germans decapitated the unfortunate sentry without his chum knowing; or had a shell somehow taken away the unfortunate man's head while the other man dozed? In such an uncanny space, is it any surprise that rumours developed of monsters dwelling in No Man's Land?

Death Marches *is part of British artist Percy Smith's "Dance of Death" series.*

"Death was ever present, ready to pounce at any moment," believed infantryman John Lynch, an American from Baileys Mills, Ohio, who served with the PPCLI and who would be wounded at Cambrai in October 1918 and also awarded the Military Medal for bravery as a signaller.[41] Death was, in Lynch's mind, a corporeal thing, and this anthropomorphism also extended to enemy shells and bullets, all of which were described or envisioned as real things.[42] For many soldiers, death was literally a monster or animal that waited for its victims to make a mistake and expose themselves. Infantryman Harry Coombs wrote home to his brother of one lost pal: "he is among the missing, another victim of No Man's Land."[43] Most of Coombs's friends had been killed or maimed, while other comrades were lost to the empty gulf, a spectral world lodged somewhere between the living and the dead.

SOLDIERS EMBRACED DEATH IN AN attempt to ward it off. Sergeant Frank Maheux of the 21st Battalion, a prewar logger at Baskatong Ridge, Quebec, who had served in the South African War, shared this fatalistic belief: "Many times the bullets came near my head, but I always say when your time is up, any place you'll be, you go, so that don't bother me at all now."[44] More articulate with the pen, but sharing the same sentiment, was Wilfred Kerr of the 11th Battery, a future university professor, who recounted, "There was a common saying: 'If your number's on the shell, it'll get you, if it isn't, you're all right; and you can't do anything to avoid it.' More and more this attitude impressed itself on long-service soldiers at the front; and it afforded a certain amount of comfort since it relieved the soldier of the necessity of worrying whether this path or that path, this step or that step, this job or that job might lead him into serious harm's way."[45] As Kerr revealed, there was comfort in letting fate decide matters of life and death because it alleviated some of the mental pressure of confronting the idea of death claiming men at random. Summed up in the well-known phrase, "You'll get it when your number's up," this perspective found expression in the common practice of soldiers imagining themselves as dead men in order to grasp life. However, saying such things with casual bravado was perhaps not the same as being convinced of one's lot. How did married men or fathers write off their own lives? Of course, many soldiers knew there was no dodging destiny. Lance-Corporal Elgin Eby of the 75th Battalion, a prewar moulder by trade who enlisted in Woodstock, Ontario, and who was raised a Mennonite, wrote from the Somme in 1916, "I'm beginning to think when a man's time comes, he goes. Some are killed in the most unexpected ways."[46] Eby's time came at age twenty-three near Sancourt, where he was killed in action on September 30, 1918.

"The less I counted on living, the more was I likely to live," commented Gregory Clark, whose irony-infused belief afforded him the mental rigour to survive at the front. He made it home and had a rich postwar career as a much-beloved journalist.[47] Clark had accepted this fatalistic way of thinking, but he was not beyond trying to even the odds. He had a collection of magic charms and talismans that he kept with him at all times. Though all soldiers felt helpless under the fall of shells, most men tried to influence chance in their favour with some form of protection. Almost all soldiers carried lucky charms, protective amulets, and magical talismans that they felt would shield them from the unpredictable shells and bullets, allowing them to "stick it," a phrase that carried with it

The "fumsup" was a charm held and rubbed by soldiers who hoped its luck might ward off an ill fate. Many fumsups were simple in design, but this one has a wooden head and a body crafted from gold.

connotations of endurance, resiliency, and individual will to keep going in the face of stress and strain. The soldiers used their magical thinking and artifacts to push onward, with one British soldier remarking, "Nearly every man out here is wearing some sort of medallion or a rosary that has been given to him, and he would rather part with his day's rations or his last cigarette than part with this sacred talisman."[48] One such powerful charm was a "touchwood" or "fumsup," a small magical being held in the hand, with a wooden head. The name is a twist on "thumbs up" and had its origins in the thumbs-up-for-good-luck signal. This idea also found expression in the old superstition of not jinxing oneself by talking about a good deed or lucky event by saying "Touch wood" and touching something wooden.[49] Men rubbed the fumsup smooth with their silent incantations.

There were also lucky or blessed gifts, either picked up from the battlefield or sent by loved ones at home. Georges Vanier, a celebrated officer in the 22nd Battalion, wrote to his sister, Frances, that he always carried the "relic" that she gave him, and which he refused to name, perhaps in the belief that it might reduce its power to protect him.[50] It was so common for soldiers to sew magic charms, protective crosses, medals, and badges into their clothing and uniforms that doctors would instruct staff as they prepared to open up men on the operating table to be alert for hidden material on their bodies and, if possible, to save it for an injured man if he survived the procedure.[51] Corporal Francis Pegamagabow was an Ojibwa First Nation soldier who served from August 1914 to the end of the war and was awarded the Military Medal for gallantry in battle three times, becoming one of only thirty-eight Canadians to be recognized with so many medals. He carried with him a small medicine bag, admitting to its importance after the war: "the bag was tightly bound with a leather thong. Sometimes it seemed to be hard as a rock, at other times it appeared to contain nothing."[52] Anishinaabe men used talismans like this, which they called a *wadjigan*, to keep in contact with spiritual guardians, and Pegamagabow kept his talisman on his person for all four years, never looking inside the bag but certain its contents would protect him.[53] He survived the war to return to his Parry Island band, become chief, and play an important part in the struggle for Indigenous rights from the 1920s onward.

"I am sending you a piece of shrapnel that would have killed me only for my back[pack]. It buried itself in my overcoat that was in my pack, and a German bullet that buried itself in the butt of my rifle."[54] Private Herbert Durand, who enlisted in 1915 from New Liskeard, Ontario, was not alone in wanting to save relics from the front. Souvenirs that were linked to death or a near-death experience were prized by the men, especially those bullets or shell casing fragments that almost ended a man's life. British-born

George Adkins, who had come to Canada before the war and enlisted in Edmonton, wrote that "Two or three times they [the Germans] nearly landed one [a shell] in our trench. The force of the explosion threw us down and I couldn't hear nothing but ringing in my ears. I was hit on the head about four times but my steel helmet saved me. Then I had a bullet go right through a mess tin strapped on my back. I am going to keep it as a souvenir."[55] Pieces of shrapnel or bullets that were extracted from soldiers' bodies were also prized. Writing from hospital, the wounded Private Wilfred Throop told his family at home, "When I can get a box to put my pieces of shrapnel in, I will send you a piece that I found when hit and a piece that was in my hip, so you know what shrapnel looks like, and have a souvenir of the great war."[56] Surgeons with any experience at the front or back in England usually kept the metal fragments they extracted from their patients' bodies, as those who survived sought to retain them.

Early in the war, Talbot Papineau, a dashing, educated French-Canadian officer in the 22nd Battalion, barely survived an exploding shell that killed the men on either side of him. One of the slain, Sergeant-Major Fraser, was hit while Papineau was talking to him, by a shell fragment that passed through his soft cap and into his brain. In one of the more ghoulish displays of keeping death close, Papineau later recalled, "I wore his cap with a hole through it afterwards for three weeks."[57] Was it an obsession with the macabre or a display of hyper-manliness that provoked Papineau to wear the dead man's blood-stained cap? Did Papineau find comfort in having death so close to him, or was he metaphorically thumbing his nose at the Grim Reaper? Whatever the case, Papineau, too, would fall on the Western Front, cut in half by a shell during the Battle of Passchendaele, his body lost in the muck.

While the death souvenirs and talismans were varied and deeply personalized, almost all the men at the front placed faith in the protective effects of Bibles. Prayer books and religious items were carried by most soldiers, and it was not uncommon for men to repeat Psalm 91 almost mantra-like in times of stress: "I will say of the Lord, He is my refuge and my fortress. . . ." Rumours circulated about Bibles stopping a bullet and sparing a man's life. "Each day brought to light some strange incident or quirk of fate or insignificant circumstance which decided between life and death," wrote one soldier in the CEF. "The best known example, perhaps, is the pocket testament which turned aside the bullet aimed for the heart."[58] Those less inclined to ascribe such protective actions to God nonchalantly repositioned their pack of cards or metal cigarette tin over their heart. It was wise to be prudent on the Western Front and tip the odds, no matter how small, in one's own favour.

Soldiers looked for patterns in the chaos: things to avoid or repeat. They shaved in particular ways or relieved themselves according to their own personal rituals.[59] Superstitions raged: the need to avoid three on a match, the danger of being at the top of a leave list for very long, carrying money into battle (which was considered bad luck), the unfortunate consequences brought by the number 13, and a host of other notions guided soldiers in action and thought, or were to be heeded or seen as a secret warning. Enough men had been killed when on the verge of taking two weeks' leave, or been shot by a sniper after lighting a cigarette and keeping the match lit for a second and third man (giving a sniper time to draw a bead on them), to provoke soldiers to avoid certain actions. Of course, soldiers were not above having a little fun with their own superstitions. They joked to one another, "It is considered bad luck to be killed on Friday."[60] Bad luck indeed, although such beliefs could rule and ruin soldiers' lives. Charles Edmunds, a British junior officer, recounted his actions in the trenches: "You think of absurd omens and fetishes to ward off the shell you hear coming. A strong inward feeling compels you to sit in a certain position, to touch a particular object, to whistle so many bars of a tune silently between your teeth. If you complete the charm in time you are safe—until the next one. This absurdity became a dark, overpowering fatalism."[61] Such obsessive behaviour must have followed many of the survivors back to their homes after the war.

"Many are the tales told of Tommy's superstitions," observed Lieutenant Stanley Rutledge, a prewar law student and an officer with the 28th Battalion. "I would not go so far as to say that every soldier indulges in these fanciful beliefs, but it is none the less true that we have our 'lapses.' If you will remember the old witches in Macbeth, with their steaming cauldrons, recall the whining wind on the waste, swell on the mysteries of spookland, then you will know of the agencies that are urging—always urging, it would seem, our boys to swear by some charm or rule."[62] The "rules" of "spookland" were passed on, shared with new men by the veterans of the unit in countless retellings that added to and informed their potency as protective ways of thinking. Victor Swanston of the 5th Battalion noted that most of his comrades scoffed openly at such talk, but "Damn few men will take a chance, even though they don't profess to be superstitious. Of course, there is no place worse than War to give grounds like that."[63] And, of course, these "rules" could also benefit the soldiers. Things that worked or kept soldiers alive were to be embraced. Numerology was much studied, with the numbers scrutinized for meaning, including ill omens like 13 or good-luck symbols like 7, or the patterns that emerged when the desperate concentrated on finding signs that revealed the future. It was much remarked upon, for instance, that the major Canadian offensive against Passchendaele prominently featured the number 6.[64] The attack had started at 6:00 a.m. on the morning of November 6, with the 6th Artillery Brigade supporting the 6th Infantry Brigade, which advanced from a starting line in Square 6 on the Passchendaele map. Men puzzled over such things.

A MONTH BEFORE HIS LIFE was ended on the Western Front, infantryman Angus Martin, a prewar typesetter in Toronto, wrote that he and his comrades in the 52nd Battalion "have to learn to look death in the face here and pass the time of day with him."[65] In that existentially fraught environment of lethal unpredictability, some soldiers saw supernatural signs, most often in the form of premonitions. During the agonizing wait before battle, front-line infantry smoked, played cards, picked lice from their clothes, or chased rats: anything to take their mind from the struggle that loomed ahead. Most prepared a "last letter" of some kind, keeping it on their bodies or handing it to a friend who was not slated to go "over the top," in case they should not survive the upcoming battle. Yet there were others who were more certain of how and when they would die.

With the front-line soldiers—the infantry and machine-gunners—often suffering 50 percent casualty rates in battle, it is not surprising that many felt an approaching doom before a big push. But these premonitions clearly involved more than simply weighing the odds. There was frequently an accompanying uncanny feeling or a supernatural vision that shed light on the men's impending fate. Amos Mayse, born in Lincolnshire and a twice-wounded veteran of the South African War, enlisted in Manitoba, where he had been a Baptist clergyman. He confided with those at home in August 1917, "It seems strange that one should have the premonition of coming events as your dream yet it very often happens. The night I was hit, before leaving the front line trenches I had the feeling which I could not rid myself of that something was going to happen."[66] Joseph Trainor recounted sitting with his comrades in the open graveyard of the Passchendaele battlefield and overhearing two mates saying goodbye to each other: "I told them not to be silly but both seemed sure that they would not come out of it. I heard other fellows say similar things in other scraps and they didn't come back. Both of these fellows were killed soon after we got over the top."[67]

Alan Cole, a prewar school principal and the battery sergeant of the 2nd Canadian Siege Battery, wrote of one uncanny event, "Do you believe in premonitions? It was early in 1918 when a small group of us were together. Somehow or other the talk of our chances of surviving and returning home came up. The end of the war seemed further away than ever. None of us dwelt on this very much evidently except Sgt. Graham Duff. Duff was different. He was not putting on an act as he was not that type. He was utterly serious when he told us he felt he would not return. He was right. He was killed quite a distance behind the line by a fragment of a stray shell. Premonition? Coincidence?"[68]

Infantryman William Green of the 4th Battalion confided in his memoir that "A lot of men had premonitions during the war of never coming home, and a lot them, sorry to say, came true."[69] Green's statement implies, of course, that not all premonitions came to fruition. Indeed, Captain Harold McGill, the medical officer of the 31st Battalion, said as much when he described the tense days before the Battle of Vimy Ridge: "For some unknown reason I had a presentiment that I would not survive the action, a feeling that had never afflicted me before any of our previous engagements. I tell this to show how little attention should be paid to these so-called 'hunches,' for in the battle that followed I did not have even the satisfaction of experiencing a narrow escape." McGill chalked it up to an "overloaded conscience."[70] George Nasmith was another who was struck by the eerie premonition of his own death. While visiting a gun battery that was under intense fire, he felt his demise was imminent. His reaction to this sensation was to write a new will and a last letter of farewell. They were, thankfully, not used. Despite Green, McGill, and Nasmith being mistaken about the timing of their own deaths, much of the correspondence and stories describing fatal premonitions suggest they came true, partially because the accounts are related by an eyewitness and refer to a dead third party. Perhaps infantryman Charles Savage provides insight: "I had known quite a few who at various times had had such presentiments and I also knew that they were as often wrong as right; but statistics are poor consolation when you feel that way. The average infantryman was sure that he would be killed sometime, but generally he looked upon that sometime as later rather than sooner; not today or tomorrow, but in the indefinite future."[71]

Few soldiers speculated as to the origins of their premonitory visions. Such revelations may have been a part of the soldiers' sixth sense, that innate sensory protection that attuned the ears to the wail of incoming shells and caused muscle memory to react more quickly than the brain could transmit orders. Experienced soldiers knew when to dive for cover or when to run for a dugout. Corporal Charles Cameron, a six-foot-one, 190-pound tough-as-nails Highlander with the 16th Battalion, wrote of the sixth sense that he developed by around the summer of 1916, noting, "We had now served from fourteen to sixteen months in and around the front line trenches and had cultivated an animal's sense of danger."[72] But not all of the vivid premonitions can be chalked up to heightened battle senses. Infantryman Frank Iriam, a Nova Scotian who worked in Kenora, Ontario, on the railway, described an "odd experience" at the front. He was acting as an advance party to lead troops into the trenches, "when some 150 yards from the corner [near some elm groves] I seemed to sense or feel some impending evil, stopping and saying to my mate, wait a little, we will sit on that old log lying there for a few minutes and have a smoke. I felt that I was expecting something to happen. Sure enough, over came a five point nine inch shell hitting directly on the path at the corner of that elm grove. Had we kept straight on, we would have been just in time to connect with the shell. I experienced this sort of premonition on numerous occasions during my three years and seven months of front line duty."[73] This is more an allusion to an uncanny warning than to a soldier's sixth sense of caution, but perhaps the two were conflated in Iriam's view.

George Maxwell of the 49th Battalion remembered being ordered to No Man's Land as part of a work party. Tired and unhappy with his plight, he sullenly followed the engineer officer who led the group into the desolate landscape. As the men trudged forward, Maxwell, an Irish-born prewar accountant in Edmonton, became separated from the party and found, to his growing terror, that he knew neither where he was in the darkness nor even where his own lines were located. As a four-month veteran of the front, he understood that he could easily stumble into an ambush or sweeping enemy fire, but "the feeling of being abandoned in such a hostile predicament was overpowering." He began to panic and felt the urge to run in any direction when a voice in the gloom startled him, intoning, "Be seated and await deliverance."[74] Heeding the voice's command, Maxwell crouched in a crater, watching the flare lights and listening to the shells overhead. Then, in the darkness, he heard the soft whisper of his name, as one of his comrades had come back for him. Upon his return to the safety of his trenches, he asked his mate if he had spoken to him earlier; the soldier replied that he had not, that in fact he had simply come upon his silhouette in the dark. Maxwell proceeded to tell his friends about the spectral voice that had spoken directly to him but without audible sound, the voice being experienced directly in his head. His close friends were ambivalent about ascribing the voice to a supernatural manifestation, although one religious man in the section believed it was a sign from God. Each of the soldiers interpreted the voice differently, but Maxwell was sure only that it had saved his life and he was grateful, though he remained puzzled about its origin. For decades after the war, he grappled with the event's meaning.

This image, titled His Constant Companion, *suggests a soldier is being watched over by his wife or mother, likely to guide him to safety in the danger zone.*

Wartime occultist Hereward Carrington offered another account that tips more towards the supernatural. An unnamed Canadian soldier wrote home to his mother, "One night while carrying bombs, I had occasion to take cover when about twenty yards off, I saw you looking towards me as plain as life. Leaving my bombs, I crawled nearly to the place where your vision appeared, when a German shell dropped on them, and—well—I had to return for some more. But had it not been for you, I certainly would have been reported 'missing.' . . . You'll turn up again, won't you, mother, next time a shell is coming?'"[75] The pathetic nature of the story leads one to imagine it being written to comfort a worrying mother, perhaps by an unhinged son, but this "crisis apparition," as it is sometimes called in the literature,

Death Refuses, *one of British artist Percy Smith's prints in his "Dance of Death" series, depicts Death turning its back on a wounded soldier who lies amid his dead comrades.*

is similar in nature to that described in Bird's account about his fallen brother, Steve, saving his life. Can it be dismissed?

And there are other, stranger occurrences. In a letter to his mother, combat soldier Wallace Reid shared a bewildering experience he had while fighting on the Somme. In a pitched battle, with shells tearing men apart and bullets cutting down his comrades, Reid's assault force was driven out of a recently captured trench, retreating under fire back to their original lines. When they finally returned to their trenches, a German counter-bombardment crashed down, with one shell landing directly in Reid's bay. As Reid described it,

> My first thought was the certain knowledge that I was dead, also that I was glad of it. I think it was a hot stream pouring over my face and head that roused me. My head was pinned tight to the ground, a weight pressed terribly on my chest, I couldn't move my arms, nor, at first, my feet. A few seconds' working got my feet free, though . . . [then] a frantic struggle on my part to rid myself of my burden of dead men. I succeeded, rose to my feet and stood still. The sight that met my eyes in the starlight will be with me as long as I live and breathe. In front of me the shell crater, six feet or more deep and blown clear of everything in the bottom, but around the top a score or more of stark, silent figures that had been men, but a short time before—whole bodies, pieces of bodies, single bodies, piles of bodies, all stark and still. Not a sound broke the silence while I stood there—not a shot, nor a shell. For a few seconds some magic hand held up all the hellish forces that were playing over that tortured land.
>
> I waited, scarcely breathing, for something—waited, it seemed minutes that could only have been seconds. Then it

> came—invisible, intangible, but nevertheless, very real. Something came to that place of desolation, stopped a moment and passed on again, and I was the only living witness.[76]

Within a few seconds, the "spell had lifted," and the invisible presence moved on. Reid was sent to a hospital to recover, unsure about how to interpret his uncanny experience. It left him scared and anxious. He testified to his mother, "I should not be writing of these things at all, but sleeping or waking I cannot stop thinking of them." Reid felt the need to write the experience from his system, even as he did not understand the meaning of the "very real" supernatural presence.

"DEATH IS MY FAMILIAR," WROTE medical doctor and McGill University professor Captain Andrew Macphail, who served in a field ambulance unit and witnessed first-hand the carnage of combat.[77] The supernatural and the uncanny seemed natural and explicable on the Western Front. While many, perhaps all, of the stories above might be explained as products of tired, sleep-deprived minds, minds that can conjure sounds and images, soldiers were not unaware of their own exhaustion, and yet not a single Canadian soldier attributed his supernatural experiences to sleep deprivation. Those in the middle of the storm are not always the best at judging wind patterns, but Canadian combat soldiers do not seem to have even considered the possibility that their experiences were brought on by exhaustion.

"The very ground here seems to speak and night wind seemed to pluck at your sleeves and counsel you beware," wrote Canadian front-line infantryman Frank Iriam. "You could feel the pulse of the thousands of the dead with their pale hands protruding through the mud here and there and seeming to beckon you. The ragged stumps of torn trees stood like sentries looking over a scene like the aftermath of an earthquake. You could feel the presence of something not of this earth."[78] In this wasteland, many soldiers felt such an unearthly presence, and the power and frequency of the ghost stories, premonitions, and supernatural tales seem to suggest that many soldiers believed fully in these occurrences. Even more of them placed trust in the role of talismans, superstitions, and magical thinking as a source of protection against the snapping jaws of death. These reflections of trauma are part of the soldiers' constructed narrative and shared culture, one in which combatants were attempting to make meaning of their war experience.[79] Is it revealing that almost no soldier or veteran sought to debunk this type of non-rational thinking either during or after the war?

Captain Harry Coombs, a front-line infantry officer who was thrice wounded and then recognized with the Military Cross, recounted details of the artillery bombardment that nearly ended his life: "Have you ever thought you were dead? I did then. . . . I seemed to come up out of the debris and said to myself 'Am I dead?' and then I went on reasoning . . . 'I ought to be able to yell. I'll try it. Stretcher Bearers' . . . Then I stumbled toward the door. The dirt and dust was beginning to settle and I could make out the forms of all the others, not one of them moving. . . . I was still wondering whether I was alive or not."[80] The Western Front included the dead, the living, and those who were caught somewhere in between. These stories of the uncanny and the supernatural represent an impression and a repression of death. They do not appear to be the by-product of frivolous or damaged minds. They were a method, in fact, by which the soldiers ordered their minds, framed their experiences in the trenches, and found ways to cope with the unnatural strain at the front. While many soldiers had faith in magical forces or the power of rituals, they were also making real their fears in an attempt to combat, contain, or at least make sense of them. Landscapes of death bound the soldiers together in a unique society and created a space for powerful presences, fateful premonitions, and ghosts with warm hands.

CHAPTER 3

VOICING CULTURE: SLANG AND SWEARING

"Trench slang is a language all its own. No dictionary will give you the meaning of half its words," wrote a Canadian infantryman in the 7th Battalion's regimental paper, *The Listening Post*.[1] When the citizen-soldiers of the CEF enlisted, trained, went overseas, and ultimately served on the Western Front, they encountered a new, exclusive society and culture, with its own written and unwritten rules, social mores, and means to create and sustain the soldiers' identity. This closed society also had its own dialect of slang—words and phrases that further reinforced its distinctiveness.

The experience of soldiering on the Western Front required new words and phrases with which to give enhanced meaning to the abnormal, almost unreal experiences at the front. This soldiers' slang emerged and was forged in the stagnant trenches, fed by the horror and humour, the anger and joy, the comradeship and disillusionment of hundreds of thousands of citizen-soldiers. Soldiers, like any group, developed their own dialect, slang, and words to distinguish themselves, shape their identity, create meaning in new environments, and anchor themselves to place.[2] Australian soldier W.H. Downing explained why soldiers' slang was unique: "By the conditions of their service, and by the howling desolation of the battle-zones, our men were isolated during nearly the whole of the time they spent in theatres of war, from the ways, the thoughts and the speech of the world behind them."[3] The masculine society of the trenches was insulated from the civilizing effects of community, women, and family, which further led to a coarsening of the language used. This manly atmosphere encouraged—even demanded—swearing, which reinforced the difference of the trench world from the civilian realm of noncombatants, while also providing the men with a recognized protection of sorts against the strain of life in the trenches.[4] The soldiers' slang and swearing helped to forge their closed culture, weld the disparate national and linguistic groups together, and give them a voice.

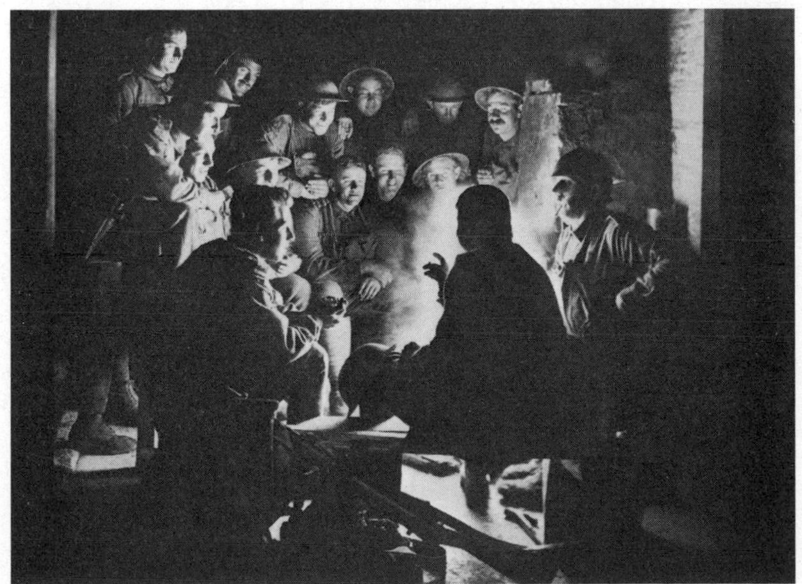

Soldiers in a dugout talking, sharing stories, and spreading rumours.

"IF I WROTE YOU ALL the slang of the army you would never understand a word. . . . It's a language in itself," believed Gunner Bertram Cox, who nonetheless was set on alerting his sister to its strange quality from the perspective of outsiders.[5] New words spawned in the trenches passed back and forth among the ranks, circling the platoon, company, and battalion, and then moving throughout the army, and finally travelling from army to army.[6] The great mingling of men behind the lines, often in the French *estaminets* (informal cafés), in walks through the countryside to visit friends in close-by units, or in joint training and leisure activities, allowed for this evolving language to pass throughout the CEF. The war drew Canadians from across the country, but service overseas, especially in the war zone, fashioned them into a coherent group. The mix of different social classes and religious groups, and the language and phrases these civilians brought to the forces, were strained through the soldiers' experience to create something new. A unique way of talking was formed, forever evolving and adapting to meet the soldiers' needs. Infantryman Leonard Gould of the 102nd Battalion observed wryly, "Nothing changes so quickly as an army vocabulary. A new word appears from no one knows where and is adopted for a season on every possible occasion."[7] As French Canadian E.L. Chicanot remarked, "The vocabulary as it existed was the same in all parts of the line, one section generously sharing with another any new words or phrase it had been fortunate enough to acquire, by passing it along from unit to unit."[8]

Will Bird, a long-service veteran and a professional writer with an ear for language, said that there were very few men who did not succumb to the pervasive slang. One such resistant man in his unit was Corporal Jimmy Hughes, whom the rank and file dubbed "The Professor." According to Bird, "He spoke with a precise manner and never used slang. The platoon thought him a granny who considered even a knowledge of French immoral."[9] Sir Andrew Macphail, a man of letters, an educator, and a physician, found much to dislike in the war, but his boorish companions in uniform were particularly trying, especially those whose "poverty of the mind discloses itself in the horrible jargon and worn out slang which they employ."[10] Macphail's solution was often to sit in gloomy silence, reading alone, unable or unwilling to lower himself to speak like his fellow comrades in arms. Even if the jargon was "fierce on ones English grammar," as Bertram Cox suggested in a letter, opting out of employing slang meant absenting oneself from an important part of the soldiers' society.[11]

Many Canadian soldiers simply parroted their British cousins—because of their own British birth, their proximity to men in the larger British Expeditionary Force (BEF), or their cultural ties to Mother England. But there were some differences between the soldiers from different parts of the Empire. Independent Newfoundlanders, whose dominion would not join Canada until 1949, took great pride in distinguishing themselves from the Canucks and other imperial troops. After the war, Newfoundlander W.C. Hawker captured some of the idioms of speech among the Empire's troops, noting, "All spoke the same language, and gave evidence of being sprung from a common stock, all had the same grand basic traditions that are known as British, yet each had its own peculiar mode of expression, its turn dialect and speech, which perhaps more than anything else, marked its individuality. This was especially noticeable when the more rugged words and forms of language were being uttered, when, in short, there was profanity without the spirit profane. Our boys possessed some beautiful and vigorous figures of speech which unfortunately cannot be placed in print, and in this dark, these were distinguishing, and, sometimes useful."[12] The language of war, as well as manly swearing, brought the different armies together, but, as Hawker wrote in a postwar article, each component of the Empire's "common stock" distinguished itself through its members' accepted slang, which in turn reinforced its distinct identity.

There were nicknames for all of the national soldiers. The Germans were known by many monikers, depending on the mood of the Allies. If the British, French, or Canadian soldier was feeling kind to the enemy across the blasted zone, aware that he was partaking in the same suffering, he might be "Fritz" or "Jerry." If anger and revenge were driving a man, the enemy would sneeringly be called a "Kraut" (abbreviated from "sauerkraut") or the "Hun," a term referring to the German barbarian tribes of old. The French soldiers were generally, and affectionately, known as "*poilus*," a French term meaning "the hairy ones." The Australians adopted both "Anzac," an acronym for Australian and New Zealand Army Corps, the fighting force first made famous at Gallipoli, and the "Diggers," first used in the nineteenth century to denote the hard work in Australian mines by gold seekers, but equally appropriate as a reference to the war's constant trench digging. The British were the "Tommies," a generic term coined in the eighteenth century that became part of the common vernacular after the Napoleonic Wars. The Americans, when they finally joined the Allied war effort in April 1917, were the "Doughboys," a term of unclear reference with origins in the Mexican–American War of 1846–1848, although Canadians sometimes, and with some derogatory tone, called the Americans the "Sammies" (after Uncle Sam). The Canadians went by several names, but there was nothing so firm or definite as the nicknames used for the British and Americans. They were sometimes referred to as Tommies or Canadian Tommies, and "Canuck" was also popular—although often a soldier would simply be labelled as "Canada." A famous song in Canada from 1915, which also made its way over to the trenches, used the phrase "Johnny Canuck," but it doesn't seem to have caught on with the other Allied armies. All of these national identifiers contributed to shaping the distinctiveness of forces at the front and helped to delineate the national armies and soldiers, perhaps no small thing when millions were crouched in ditches, slathered in mud, and hard to distinguish from afar.

English, Scottish, and Irish accents would have been heard most frequently in the ranks of the First Contingent, formed in early October 1914. About two thirds of the first 32,000 soldiers who went overseas were British-born, although many had spent years living in Canada before the war. A larger proportion of native-born Canadians filled the ranks in the years to come, bringing with them the accents from across the country, from different social classes, and from both urban and rural areas. And by 1916, as the CEF was reforming its prejudicial standards for recruiting, more Eastern European, black, and Indigenous men were allowed to enlist, thereby bringing new languages, slang, and regional dialects into the forces. The soldiers' slang helped to bring together the disparate groups that formed the CEF. One British soldier went so far as to write that once the civilian-soldier began to "use the army's language without wishing it he has ceased to be an individual soldier, he has become *soldiery*."[13] There was no single voice or accent for the Canadian soldiers, but they saw themselves increasingly as a unique force within the larger BEF, and slang and swearing gave voice to that uniqueness.

George McFarland, second in command of the 4th Canadian Mounted Rifles in the last two years of the war, recounted his experience of being on a First Army musketry course in which the Canadians mixed freely with the British troops and used their own vernacular, sometimes in an exaggerated way, to distinguish themselves. "We Canadians were a sort of curiosity, especially Ormond, who was a breezy Westerner with an amazing vocabulary of slang. At the onset he was talking a language which was like Greek to most of the chaps, and he just set himself out to use all the slang he could rake up, much to the amusement of all the rest of us."[14] Canadian infantryman Sergeant J.H. Flock, who was wounded at Vimy but survived the war, kept a little memory book in which he inscribed his favourite poems, stories, and inspirational phrases. Flock devoted one page to what he called "Canadian Sayings!" They included

> "That's the stuff to give 'em"
> "Cheers!"
> "Up the line with the best of luck"
> "Over the top with the best of luck"
> "Rum up!"
> "Hung up on the barbed-wire"
> "Wire under foot"[15]

None of these sayings were particular to the Canadians, but it is interesting that Flock believed that to be the case, as shown in his connection of the language he archived in his book to an aspect of identity construction.[16]

While some distinctively Canadian slang and profanity did exist, the English-speaking Commonwealth forces tended to speak in a similar tongue, and the common lingo, dialect, and vocabulary brought the Empire's soldiers together. "We are having kind of a windy and rainy period over here," wrote Cecil Frost to his parents in the summer of 1918. "However one learns how to get wet and merely laugh and say—'Send her down, Davy, send her down.'"[17] The phrase Frost refers to here was common to British soldiers; its origin seems to be have been in the British army, but it was obviously picked up by Canadians in the field. The Australians put their own spin on it with "Send her down, Hughie," an irreverent reference to God, brought into the army by Australian farmers who turned upwards and implored the Almighty to provide rain for their sun-burnt crops. There were other popular phrases. "'I am fed up,' was the commonest expression of all in the Tommy vernacular," thought Canadian Arthur Hunt Chute.[18] Equally prevalent was the word "jake," which, according to Canadian field artillery major William Leggat from Montreal, "appears to be the expression over here."[19] Indeed it was, and "jake," generally used to mean "fine" or "okay," was to be found in soldiers' letters home throughout the war. It is interesting that "jake" was not a commonly used term among the British soldiers, and it was therefore one of the words that easily identified a Canadian.

The most enduring of the old soldiers' terms was "Blighty," which came from the Hindustani word for "home." "You know that a 'blighty' is a wound severe enough to have a man sent to 'blighty,'—the old soldiers' name for England," recounted Samuel Honey to his people back in Canada.[20] "Blighty" was one of the most common words in Great War soldier slang, as noted by Gunner Bertram Cox, who advised, "Never say, out here, that you are going to England or London, always 'Blighty.' If a fellow gets wounded, the doctor will say, 'It's a Blighty case or if it's not too bad, a Base Case and if he has lost both arms and both legs, and both eyes shot out, one ear off and part of his nose, he might get 'a Canada.'"[21] Cox's letter employed the key identifier—"out here"—referring to service in the trenches of the Western Front, which felt very far from civilization, whether that was only a few hundred kilometres away in Britain or across the Atlantic in the Dominion.

As in all modern armies, there were technical words for items such as pieces of kit, equipment, and weapons that were common to the soldiers. This military jargon was not meant for the home front. Few civilians would have understood, for example, what a "pull-through" was for, or a "housewife."[22] Almost everything was reduced to its initials, from ranks to weapons, some of the terms being official army talk while others grew organically from within the army. *In and Out*, a Canadian trench newspaper, joked, "An Army order comprises, as a rule, about twelve words of ordinary English, interspersed with several mixed alphabets and liberally bespattered with numerals. . . . For infringing the K.R. and O. the unfortunate O.R. is paraded by an N.C.O. before the O.C., who may mercifully mete out C.B., or harshly send him to the A.P.M., who, under royal warrant and seal is empowered to inflict on him F.P., so that he may well and thoroughly understand the way of the transgressor is hard."[23] Perhaps the most interesting example of informal army slang is what the soldiers called themselves—the "poor bloody infantry" (PBI). They had other phrases, such as "gravel crunchers" and "foot sloggers," but PBI seemed to capture the experience better than anything else.

There were soldiers' phrases that demanded known responses. These phrases were spoken in a jocular manner, the most popular being "I don't think," which was used at the end of a sentence to undercut the truth of what preceded it. This type of irony would not have seemed out of place for tuned-in teenagers from the 1990s, who used the word "not" in the same manner. Combat veteran Albert Fereday offered some unintended advice on usage when he described life behind the lines: "Having concluded our tour of the town we retraced our steps to camp and called in at the Salvation Army hut and had a fine supper: 2 fried eggs, chips, bread and tea—even better than 'Blighty,' I don't think!"[24] Lieutenant Edward Sawell, a machine-gun officer who was awarded the Military Cross for bravery at Vimy, revealed the origin of one famous saying: "There were many stories of men surviving shells landing within feet of them, and coming away covered only in water muck, leading to the expression 'here's to mud in your eye!'"[25] "*C'est la guerre*" ("It's the war") was another common expression, said almost with a shrug (and usually pronounced "la gar," as in "car") as the nonchalant soldiers dealt with the strain, stress, and annoyance of discipline by blaming the war while using humour to deal with discomfort. "C'est le [*sic*] guerre," wrote Private Frederick Robinson of the 58th Battalion, in a letter to his girl at home about the need for soldiers to "endure . . . small troubles silently and like a man."[26] A variation on this expression was "*après la guerre*" ("after the war"). Often accompanied by a sad grin, the phrase came to mean something that might someday happen—like going on leave or getting the girl—but only after the war.[27] What was the use of complaining?—"there was a war on," to borrow another popular phrase.

Will Bird described some of the other catch phrases of soldiers: "On the march one heard: 'What did you do in the big war, daddy?' 'Are we downhearted? Sure we are.' Meeting another battalion: 'Thank God, we've got a Navy.' Then, 'Some say, Good old Sergeant,' but I say . . .' In the billets in bad weather: 'Send her down, Davy.' And 'Roll on, duration.' Getting ready for parade: 'Ah-ah, no [bloody] shave this morning? Ah-ah! No razor. . . .'"[28] As employed by the men, many of these phrases diminished the original meaning. For example, the question "What did you do in the big war, daddy?" was used in recruiting drives to shame men to enlist, but the soldiers wielded it ironically in their day-to-day lives, responding abruptly, "S.F.A." (sweet fuck all). "What did you do in the Great War?" remembered Tom Spears, a signaller who lived past the age of 100. "'S.F.A.,' came the reply. 'What did you do today?' 'S.F.A.'"[29] Similarly, the question "Are we downhearted?" was supposed to be answered with a rousing "No!" Bird reveals that the soldiers twisted this intention, shouting instead, "Sure we are!" Soldiers had no compunction about using facile civilian phrases or patriotic slogans to represent ironic displeasure. The much-used newspaperman tag line "The spirit of the troops is excellent" was taken up by the men, and grunted to one another as they were shelled in mud-filled trenches. Much-loved British cartoonist Bruce Bairnsfather used the expression in a cartoon signifying the importance of rum, showing that the spirit of the troops was indeed fine when supported by spirits.

There were also multiple greetings and goodbyes available to soldiers, with one of the most ritualized among the Canadian and British servicemen being

> Are we downhearted?
> No!
> Then you damn well soon will be!

The phrase in the final sentence could be "bloody well" or "fuck well" or anything else, but the sentiment was the same: if you think all is well now, wait a bit and see what the war has in store for you. Another common farewell was "Goodbyeee and fuck you!" which was taken from the popular and sentimental song of the time, "Goodbyeee," with the added vulgarity emphasizing the masculinity of soldiers' society. The "Goodbyeee" part of the expression was often drawn out with a flourish, while the "fuck you" would have been enunciated severely. And while the latter phrase would have horrified most civilians, in the soldiers' culture it was often meant as a sign of affection, friendship, and good luck. Soldiers' slang and swearing was not meant for those outside the tribe.

Soldiers' slang was also a shield, allowing combatants to trivialize death and to remake their trying conditions and environment in a language of their own choosing.[30] Objects, events, and actions were renamed in clever wordplay to provide a sense of meaningfulness, enhance familiarity, and reduce the terror.[31] The phlegmatic, stoic stance of the soldier was one of his most enduring safeguards against the strain of war. "All who reached the front looked Death in the eye every day," wrote infantryman D.E. Macintyre. "If a man were killed they said succinctly that he had 'gone west.'"[32] In fact, there was a plethora of euphemisms for being killed. A soldier was "knocked out," had "gone under" or "copped a packet," was "pushing up the daisies" or "hanging on the barbed wire," had been "buzzed," "kicked-in," or "napooed." With death so prevalent, it is not surprising that soldiers had so many words for the state of having been killed. Most soldiers expected—and many accepted—that they would get it when their "number was up," as the popular saying went, and such words and phrases allowed the soldiers to downplay the warfare's terrible unpredictability.

A postcard with a soldier aching for any rum left in the jar. The slang word "napoo," meaning "it is dead" or, in this context, "all gone," suggests the soldier's thirst will not be quenched.

Soldiers who were frightened or close to a breakdown observed that they had the "wind up," the opposite of which was the desire to "stick it." Men who were fine or doing all right were "in the pink." Those who were driven over the edge into a mental breakdown were labelled "shell shocked" by military authorities. Soldiers also used the term, but they tended to talk about their "nerves" going to pieces or being shattered. Initially, shell shock was thought to be a physical ailment caused by high explosive shells causing microscopic lesions to the brain, but it was later revealed to be a psychological breakdown from accumulated stress, lack of sleep, and relentless tension. The high command ordered that the term "shell shock" be dropped at the mid-point of the war, to be replaced by the anodyne "Not Yet Diagnosed, Nervous."[33] In later wars, the injury would be known as combat exhaustion, post-traumatic stress disorder, and stress injuries, words and phrases that have elbowed their way into common usage.

The trench talk continued for almost all elements of soldiering. A unit of men rotating into the front-line trench system was known to be going "up the line." A battle was a "show," which took some of the sting out of the potential slaughter that was soon to follow. One Canadian testified in a letter that he did not know why it was called a show, but noted perhaps ironically, "one is able to see so little of it."[34] Assaulting the enemy—the terrifying act of leaving the relative safety of the trench to advance over open ground—was referred to nonchalantly as "going over the top" or "jumping the bags." The phrase "over the top" had initially been part of the longer phrase "over the top, and best of luck," but the costs of facing enemy steel and uncut barbed wire were so ghastly that the attackers' cheerful quip "best of luck" seemed out of place, even among cynical, battle-hardened soldiers, so it was eventually dropped.

Amid the industrialization of death, soldiers reacted to the impersonal killing devices of shells and bullets by relating them to the knowable and the understandable. The rocketing shells overhead were likened to trains running or trucks driving out of control. A medical officer describing the shelling at the Battle of Second Ypres in April 1915 observed, "one after another the big German shells roared over the Canadians there with the sound of a passing train. The men spoke of them as the 'Wypers Express.'"[35] "Wypers" (often spelled "Wipers") was a play on Ypres, the name of the Belgian city that was a contested battleground where hundreds of thousands of British and Canadians fought and died. Under such heavy shelling, there were always cheeky soldiers who grunted, "his or ours?"—wondering from which side's guns the shells were coming, although not particularly caring as enemy shells or one's own "drop-shorts" were equally lethal. This deliberate practice of trivializing death helped soldiers deal psychologically with weapons over which they had no control.

A high explosive shell was slightly less terrifying when it was referred to as a "Jack Johnson," the name of the American heavyweight boxer before the war who could deliver a knockout with one punch. "Whiz-bang is the name given to a light shell of high velocity and trajectory," wrote Private Donald Fraser. "It is practically on top of you as soon as you hear the report of the gun. . . . First you hear the whiz and almost simultaneously comes the bang, then a metallic singing in the air as the pieces of shrapnel fly through the space."[36] "Woolly bears" and "Black Marias" were types of shrapnel shells; a "coal box" was a high-calibre German round, as was a "Silent Percy," which the Canadians first faced—and then added to their lexicon—on the Somme.[37] A "crump" was a 5.9-inch German shell whose name derived from the sound of its explosion and was often employed as shorthand for all manner of enemy shells. German hand grenades were known as "potato mashers" because, with their long handle and larger metal head filled with explosives, they bore a similarity to this kitchen device. The multiple types of trench mortars had names like "flying pigs," "pineapples," "toffee apples," "footballs," "rum jars," and "minnies." And referring to the enemy's "morning hate" or "strafe" was a sanitized way to describe the gut-wrenching, sphincter-clenching artillery bombardments that reduced men to red paste or drove them insane.

THE SOLDIERS' LANGUAGE COULD ALSO be playful. In this war of words, soldiers bastardized the French and Belgian languages to further shape their environment. Canadians, along with British and other dominion soldiers, delighted in shamelessly mispronouncing the names of French and Belgian towns, partly to tweak the noses of the civilians, but also because some of the words were simply hard to get the tongue around. Ypres and Albert, names of places where the Canadians fought brutal battles, were twisted into "Wipers" and "Bert."[38] Applying whimsical nicknames to these sites of mass death assuaged some of that anxiety or showed that soldiers were tough enough to deal with the worst the war could offer.

Coningsby Dawson, a professional writer turned soldier, was taken with anglicizing French words to craft a new soldiers' slang, thereby asserting a modicum of control over his environment. He was not alone in doing this, and all soldiers found ways to employ French to better express the complexities of their service. "The great word of the Tommies here is, 'No bloody bon'—a mixture of French and English," recounted Dawson, "which means that a thing is no good."[39] "Alley at the toot" was used to get men to move quickly and derived from "*Allez tout de suite*." "*Beaucoup*" was used in multiple ways, but most of them meant "plenty of" or "an abundance," and deliberately mispronounced. "San Fairy Ann," perverted from the French "*ça ne fait rien*," was a popular phrase meaning "it doesn't matter" or "it makes no difference." Similarly, "Trez Beans" was a deliberate corruption of the French "*tres bien*," and was used to denote something that was good. There were dozens of other phrases that were shaped by the local geography and by the experiences of soldiers fighting on foreign soil. However, all Canadian units had some men who could speak French passably or fluently, and there was much joy for civilians in discovering that the French Canadians could converse in their language.[40] This led to a warming of relations all along the front.

The prevalent abuse of the English language, augmented by soldiers' use of slang and bastardized French, prompts the question of whether non-English soldiers in the CEF engaged in such talk. French-speaking soldiers employed the established slang for weapons of war, especially shells and mortars.[41] Acadian infantryman Théodore Dugas, who did not survive the war, spoke of "whiz-bangs," "pine-apples," and "Jack Johnsons," although he called the heavy shells "Jock Johnson."[42] Other French-Canadian soldiers employed similar slang, although their use probably did not include mispronouncing the French language for the purposes of humour, as their English-speaking counterparts did.[43] However, Canadian infantryman E.L. Chicanot recounted that "the language of the army would have been a good deal less pungent and picturesque" without the influence of French-Canadian and French words.[44]

Simple communication remained a challenge in the CEF. English was the language of instruction throughout the force, but many of the units raised from the West, consisting of new Canadians of many nationalities, sought out men with linguistic skills to serve as NCOs or officers. In Alberta, a unit was raised under the name the Irish Guards, but the commanding officer required sixteen different interpreters to communicate with all the various disparate members.[45] Lieutenant Clifford Wells of the 8th Battalion commented in September 1916, "My platoon is composed of kilties. Some of them are Russians. They will persist in coming on parade without their khaki aprons, so that I have to call the Russian Sergeant, and administer a scolding with him as an interpreter. What peculiar workings of military officialdom caused these Russians from Western Canada to be put into a Highland battalion, it is hard to say."[46]

Soldiers use chalk to inscribe sayings and slang on their shells, messages for the Germans on the receiving end.

Soldiers who were neither English nor French often found comrades with whom they could talk in their own language. As one Ukrainian-Canadian soldier remarked, "Our boys always tried to gather together in foxholes or trenches and there hummed the Ukrainian language and song."[47] Over time, those who spoke no English learned a smattering of it from their comrades, and they also learned aspects of the soldiers' slang. For those Canadians who might not have spoken English or French—there were 4,000 Indigenous Canadians, some of whom did not speak English or French, and thousands of recent immigrants—the adoption of slang aided in easing language barriers.

Recent recruits arriving at the front had to absorb this slang to find their place in the otherwise closed society. As stretcher-bearer Frederick Noyes remarked, new men "had to learn a whole new language—a weird vernacular of war-slang, pidgin-French, barrack-room jargon and front-line wisecracks—all rolled together."[48] Most soldiers' newspapers periodically published the definitions of slang words and phrases with humorous meanings, in the hope of educating raw recruits. In the case of the *Listening Post* edition of August 10, 1917, the target of mirth was thc Americans, who were welcomed by the Canadians to the Western Front—even if they were three years late. "Study this list thoroughly," the paper advised, "and when you arrive in the trenches you will be able to greet the old soldier in his own language, whilst the shrapnel burst around and the machine-gun beats its devil's tattoo in your ears—that is, of course, if the old soldier hasn't disappeared into the deepest dug-out on the first whisper of the approaching storm. There are some things we cannot teach you by mail!"[49] Trench slang was meant to be exclusive and not easily transferred to those not sharing the dangers or drudgery of military service. But at the same time, language was one of the means by which new soldiers were incorporated into the combat unit, and through which the bonds of camaraderie were forged. Soldiers' slang was one of the secret building blocks to unit morale.

E.L.M. BURNS, A GREAT WAR veteran and a lieutenant-general in the next war, was fascinated by the swirling Canadian slang, but he struggled with the fighting man's propensity to swear. He made a brief study of it in the early 1920s and noted that constant swearing, with all its varied roughness, nuances, and severity, was highly appealing to those in uniform. While Burns had a difficult time accepting the rife profanity, he believed that it could not be ignored, noting, "It would even be false to leave the impression that swearing in the army was no more prevalent than it is in ordinary life. The truth is that the army swore excessively, and that the majority—or the loudest-mouthed, at any rate—acquired the habit of using obscene and blasphemous expletives and intensifying adjectives wholesale, so that the perception of their actual meaning soon became blunted; the most shocking of them soon signified nothing more to speaker or listener, than the 'bloody' of the English workingmen."[50] Gregory Clark, who came from a middle-class Toronto family and became a successful humour writer, said of his comrades in arms, "In some ways, the Canadian troops I am acquainted with are a brutal lot. The two commonest words heard from them are the vilest words in the language. There is something, apparently, brutalizing in the military atmosphere."[51]

Two British veterans who compiled a postwar dictionary of soldiers' slang observed, "Most men who served in the army were coarsened in thought and speech; in many the process was swift, violent, obtrusive. The agents of this corruption of the mind were these three obscene words uttered in every other sentence."[52] A decade after the war, they refused to name the three words, hoping they might be purged from popular memory and the historical record. But they were likely "fuck," "cunt," and "bugger," with "bloody" being even more common, although not in the realm of the unprintable.

"Fuck" was used in the form of a noun, verb, adjective, and adverb, and possibly in other ways as well. It was employed to give urgency to any action. One did not "come to attention," but came to "fucking attention." It was generally pronounced "fuckin'" or "fackin'," with the *g* dropped. In one rough if revealing letter, Brooke Claxton, a wartime gunner and future minister of national defence, deftly illustrates how the word was employed as an intensifier and an amplifier. Writing in the last year of the war, Claxton noted the difference, in his mind and those of many comrades, between Canadian and British troops: "We get into a hole & our feeling is 'Come on, boys, this --- thing is a hole. We've got to get into action as soon as possible so let's get it out and get to bed' & everyone jumps and & pulls & heaves and uses the brain. The Imperial says 'fuck the fucking thing. I'm going to fucking well stay in the bloody hole.'"[53] The words "bloody," "balls," "dick," "shit," and "bugger" were also used in weird and wonderfully ungrammatical ways, with "cunt" being equally popular with soldiers who even employed it as an adjective by adding "ing."

The almost constant practice of swearing further distanced soldiers from their former civilian lives. George Maxwell of the 49th Battalion remarked how men, despite a "wide diversification of backgrounds, when thrown together as soldiers, become bestial and careless, regardless of how well they might have observed the amenities as civilians." Prewar civilian life was left behind as the forging of camaraderie led to a refashioning of men. "This tendency [to swear] is insidious," wrote Maxwell. "Even the strongest willed finds the proneness difficult to resist. I think it is due largely to the absence of the mellowing influence of home-life and the concomitant feminine graces of womankind."[54] That is not to say that civilians never swore, but many soldiers warned correspondents at home that the practice became more habitual in the army, especially with no family, women, or children present to tone down the vulgarities. The isolation of the soldier within his unique clan led to a hardening effect, but it also helped to shape military societal norms.[55]

As E.L.M. Burns observed, when men have their freedom of action confined and are lorded over by others, subjected to discipline, and constantly faced with death and maiming, "the relief of

This Canadian cartoon makes oblique reference to the sergeant's colourful swearing. The caption reads: "Sergeant (who has exhausted his vocabulary): 'Would you like me to say, "please" to you?'"

strong language will often be sought."[56] Most NCOs and officers let such language go without reprimand, as they were likely to employ it too. The use of swearing was not tempered by rank, as junior officer Charles Savage observed from long experience: "A good poker face was one of the finest assets that an officer or NCO could have, and a few lusty curses delivered when things looked bad would often have a steadying effect."[57] The last commander of the Canadian Corps, Sir Arthur Currie, had a reputation for turning to profanity freely and frequently; it was not uncommon for him to fire vulgarities, machine-gun-like, for up to a minute without repetition.[58] Divisional commander Archibald Macdonell was no stranger to swearing either. "I saw him actually get wounded one day," wrote infantryman and future historian G.R. Stevens. "Somebody said, 'Be careful, sir, there's a sniper,' and he said, 'Fuck the sniper' climbed up to get a look and the sniper took him through the shoulder and he went ass over applecarts into his shellhole from which he had emerged. . . . My god, his language! You could hear him around for miles.'"[59] Except for the occasional puritanical officer, most leaders ignored the men's profanity, except, as Burns observed, "when the soldier swears in such a way as to show insolence to authority."[60] For such offences, men could be charged with insubordination or, in army parlance, "dumb insolence."

Like slang, swearing was closely linked to the Canadian soldiers' identity. Tom Johnson of the 102nd Battalion felt that swearing revealed elements of the Dominion's character: "Let me contrast the difference between the Canadian and the Englishman with one example: The Canadian swears more. His language is richer and more original in curses and obscenity. The Englishman swears too, but it is hackneyed and lacking in ideas. He swears with a sort of apology in his voice, whereas the Canadian is conscious that he is inventing phrases which are his own, so he has pride in his own language. Perhaps this is a superficial distinction, but in warfare it is one which seems essential to success. This originality tends to make him a more dangerous opponent."[61] *The Listening Post*, too, described the "signature" swearing of Canadian soldiers: "Two of our scouts who were wearing German caps, souvenirs of the recent fighting, were to their dismay, arrested by the battalion next-door; and had a deuce of a time providing an alibi. Their innocence was eventually established, and their identities proven by sheer volume of profanity. You may fake an identity disc and a pay book, but army English, Canadian army English, can only be acquired through long experience and incessant practice."[62] The profane was public and popular, and was one of the tools for shaping a Canadian identity within the larger Empire forces.

"There may be a protest in the minds of some against the swearing habit of the soldier," wrote infantryman Harold Baldwin, but "I firmly believe that if he were deprived of the power to express himself profanely when occasion seemed to warrant, his efficiency would be materially hampered. And, therefore, I have no apology to make."[63] E.L.M. Burns believed the propensity to swear came from the nervous tension and impotence felt by men confined to the trenches. "The forces beyond the power of the soldier drove men to volleys of curses in the hope of warding off the angst and perhaps 'blowing off steam.'" Some men also swore as a form of "magic spells and incantations. . . . If words of a sufficient power are pronounced in a certain unfavourable situation, something has been done to ameliorate that situation."[64] Lusty vulgarities hurled at the enemy or his shells were a verbal form of mental protection. Lieutenant-Colonel J.G. Rattray, the commander of the 10th Battalion at the June 1916 Battle of Mount

Sorrel, spoke of the talismanic effect of words, and especially profanity, when describing the harsh fighting as part of the aborted counterattack on June 3. Rattray was near the battalion's Colt machine-gunners, who laid down deadly fire all through the day, and he was thrilled by their bravery and their indomitable will, recalling, "Many of the machine gunners were using the usual expletives peculiar to the soldiers in anathematizing the Hun," firing and swearing and refusing to surrender even as the enemy closed in on them.[65] Another Canadian, Eric Harvey, spoke of soldiers swearing viciously as enemy shells rained down, remarking, "It's funny to hear the boys curse when something comes extra near. I always thought I had a very fair vocabulary even if I never utilized it, but I find that compared with some of the fellows in my section I am a babe unborn. I think if Fritz heard what he was called sometimes he'd give up the war."[66]

The soldiers' custom of swearing also underpinned issues of masculinity and virility, as men swore to enforce the uncivil atmosphere that was cultivated in the trenches.[67] There were norms and regulations to follow in emulating the manly ideals of warriors, and the practice was especially prevalent among young soldiers, who did not like to stand out as anything other than a companion in the ranks. There were around 20,000 underage soldiers—those who had enlisted under age eighteen—who served during the war, and to fit in, some overcompensated for their youth.[68] Nineteen-year-old Private John Lynch recounted that he and other young soldiers "wanted to impress the world with their toughness. We cursed louder, drank harder and behaved in a very boisterous manner, putting on a front for the veterans of the outfit, many of whom were older than our fathers."[69] Infantryman Al Symes confessed his embarrassment over the hyper-masculinity of his comrades in his diary, observing, "The eighteen and nineteen year-old lads are becoming very proficient at cursing. They work so hard at behaving like the other men. Once or twice I have been on the verge of explaining to civilians within earshot that they are only kids and will soon pass through this stage."[70] While service conferred adulthood on young men, many clearly felt the need to prove it.

While swearing met multiple needs in the army, not all soldiers partook in the litany of vulgarities. "I need hardly say that profanity was rife amongst the troops, for the most part, but I met several who were otherwise and in fact religious," wrote a seemingly shocked E.W. Russell in his postwar memoirs.[71] Gunner Thomas Walker, writing to his girl at home, noted sheepishly that the swearing, of which he claimed not to partake, "tends to make a fellow feel a little down hearted."[72] Another Canadian from the rank and file, Private William Ogilvie, a seventeen-year-old mule driver from Lakefield Ontario, testified to his own naivety when he noted, "I was amazed at the cursing, the extravagant use of the four letter words seldom heard in our quiet village. I, whose swearing propensities generally ran to such inoffensive outbursts as, 'God all fishhooks,' or 'gosh, golly,' or an occasional 'darn' or 'damn,' was now treated to round after round of obscene language."[73] Those men who did not swear—like those who refrained from using slang—were seemingly in a minority, and Victor Wheeler of the 50th Battalion, a prewar stenographer in Calgary, was surprised that "some of the signallers seemed puzzled that I did not cuss, smoke, drink, or show much interest in *les mademoiselles*. There must be something wrong, was the consensus."[74]

With officers often complicit in the swearing, or not willing to appear puritanical by enforcing censure, it often fell to the YMCA (Young Men's Christian Association) and the padres to mitigate some of the most blasphemous phrases. Padre George Wells was one concerned clergyman who agonized over the soldiers' dirty mouths, which had become, in his opinion, "steadily worse as the war raged."[75] He used his influence to drive for a "language purge." Lectures on clean living were given and pledge cards issued in the hope that soldiers would lead a better life, one without alcohol and swearing.[76] While this concern over swearing was a natural fit for the padres, they always walked a fine line with the rank and file: if they pushed too hard for men to abstain from their few meagre joys at the front, they were likely to alienate them and lose their influence. While some soldiers signed the pledge cards to stop swearing—although actually curbing their tongues was another matter—it seems that most padres tolerated the profanity, which was usually toned down in their presence anyway.

SLANG AND SWEARING WERE USED by the Great War soldiers to shield them from the unnatural strain of service at the front. These newly coined or adapted words defined groups, reinforcing the distinctiveness of the soldier from the civilian while also creating a linguistic foundation for the exclusive soldiers' culture. The custom of slang and swearing also drew together the divergent forces and nationalities that served in the BEF. The soldiers from the various dominions, colonies, and British Isles all spoke with similar slang and jargon, albeit with minor national differences, and this was one more unifying element. Yet there was a uniquely Canadian slang—or soldiers tended to think that they were speaking differently—and this further carved out the Canadian soldiers' identity.

Swearing aided in the creation of a masculine identity, too, and it is clear from the surviving correspondence and diaries that

Canadian soldiers were positively proud of their dirty mouths. However, the practice was not something normally discussed with civilians at home. It was a part of the closed soldiers' culture. Lieutenant Armine Norris generally wrote jovial letters home, but in October 1916, after the struggle of the Somme, he offered a glimpse into his usually hidden experiences, writing, "I'm afraid you're exalting me in your thought to a regular crusader and are in for some disappointment when I get back, for we'll not sprout wings but horns. This is a service where profanity is no longer an art but a habit."[77]

CHAPTER 4

THE WAR'S SOUNDTRACK

"A song to forget the horror of the trenches! A song to forget our dead! A song to forget the unforgettable! . . . Tomorrow we may be dead."[1] So wrote Charles Yale Harrison, who served in the 14th Battalion, on the appeal of singing and songs during the war. Up and down the trenches, amid the explosions of shellfire and the unmistakable ripping sound of machine-gun bullets, singing could be heard. The soldiers sang not just the songs of death and dying, but also cheerful pop songs, wistful romantic refrains, hymns, and swaggering masculine ditties about drink or women.[2] Soldiers sang on the march while exhausted and foot-sore; they sang in the rear area of the trenches as they took a break from the firing line; they sang in their dugouts in the front lines, voices rising in unison; and they even sang to their counterparts, serenading the enemy or taunting him with aggressive tunes. This was a singing war.

The voices of the soldiers were distilled and revealed through their songs. Their wide repertoire of war songs held multiple meanings for the Canadian citizen-soldiers, who were drawn from a society where song was an important form of communication and entertainment. In Canada before and during the war, piano recitals with sheet music and singing were part of the middle-class cultural experience, reinforced by an emerging entertainment industry. And the working class, which increasingly had more money and leisure time, had its own troubadours in the music halls. Canadians sang regularly and everywhere, from Toronto middle-class homes to Quebec lumber towns, and from folk songs warbled at maritime kitchen parties to the latest vaudeville tune hummed in downtown Winnipeg, while hymns were sung at church, in school, and at civic meetings.

Songs reverberated across the Dominion during the heady days of early August 1914 as an excited country found itself at war. "God Save the King," "La Marseillaise," and "The Maple Leaf Forever" echoed in the streets. Singers and songwriters went to work supporting the war effort. The established and the amateur, childhood singing sensations and military professionals: all lent their voices to the effort of urging the country onward. There were more than 500 songs published in Canada during the war, from the brazenly patriotic and heroic to the jingoistic, saccharine, and pathetic. All were readily available as inexpensive sheet music.[3] "We'll Never Let the Old Flag Fall" became the most popular Canadian song of the war, sung at patriotic rallies, fundraising events, and recruitment drives.[4] But it was not just patriotic songs that were on everyone's lips. The First Contingent soldiers who left Canada in early October 1914 were issued a songbook published by the YMCA, *Songs for Soldiers*.[5] It contained mostly hymns or uplifting songs, but these were often already known to church-going soldiers. Other units published their own regimental song books, like the one for the Dawson, Yukon, formation Boyle's Machine Gun Corps.[6] Titled *New War Songs*, it contained all manner of humorous ditties, including "Marching on to Berlin," "I'm Der Kaiser," and "It's a Long Way to Dear Old Dawson,"

Thousands of songs were written in support of the war effort. This one, "K-K-K-Katy," had the tagline, "The Sensational Stammering Song Success Sung by the Soldiers and Sailors."

Toronto songwriter Morris Manley, who wrote many hits during the war, offered "Hello Canada" for soldiers and civilians. Song sheet music often had colourful and dramatic covers to attract the eye. Here, the soldiers in the cover image are drawn from across the country, but they seem to be wearing sauce-pans on their heads instead of helmets.

This song, "We'll Love You More When You Come Back Than When You Went Away," was published in Toronto for the "Brave Defenders of the British Empire."

which was sung to the tune of the popular song "It's a Long Way to Tipperary." The songs were a part of life aboard the transport ships and in the training camps in southern England.

At the front, singing was a way for the soldiers to forge a vibrant and communal society.[7] Further to the rear, behind the lines, pianos were set up for collective singing. The band section of some units—often brass and pipe formations—were also available to strike up a song for morale or to provide a steady beat on the march. Private William Davidson of the 72nd Battery, Canadian Field Artillery, a farmer from Brockville, described his impression of the bands to his fiancée, Grace, in May 1917: "One hears some fine band music out here. Heard the Princess Pats Pippers [*sic*] band last night, my but it was great."[8] Waring Cosbie, who served with the 10th Field Ambulance and survived the war to become a surgeon and professor at the University of Toronto, described the importance of music and its normalizing effect. "You would laugh to see how strangely War and Peace are mixed out here," he wrote in a letter home.[9] And of course Highland battalions had their bagpipers, who led the soldiers everywhere they went, even over the top into the face of the enemy guns. These formal musical groups, when combined with the ad hoc instruments of soldiers—mostly harmonicas, flutes, and violins—made for a convivial atmosphere all along the front. Inventive soldiers could make music on almost anything, from rusty saws to blocks of wood. Infantryman Will Bird described one "Old Bill" who "made a type of music with tissue paper on a comb."[10]

When live music could not be secured, gramophones played the latest hits. Even in the firing line, an officers' mess or a dugout might have a gramophone, with Decca creating a dedicated trench model.[11] These contraptions were not always appreciated by some

Organized bands, especially pipers, could inspire men to keep going in the worst of conditions on the Western Front.

of the older men. Colonel J.J. Creelman, the crusty commander of the 2nd Brigade, Canadian Field Artillery, described one in his diary, a new "Columbia gramophone" that had been purchased by the junior officers, lamenting that the "infernal thing is at present ripping out *Humeresque*."[12] A younger officer, Lieutenant Andrew Miller, was more in tune with the popular culture, writing to his "dearest Ruth" about a small party that he and fellow officers had in a dugout: "After dinner we had various selections on their gramophone . . . to help to lend cheer to the occasion. . . . With your letter coming and the music[,] even if it was only a gramophone[,] and our concerted efforts accompanying it in songs we knew and the company of fine fellows I think it was the happiest evening I have ever had in France. . . . So you see it is not all shells and war and frightful things over here.[13] The gramophone and the sheet music connected soldiers to civilian culture, but they also provided the base—a jumping-off point—for the men to parody the songs and make their own cultural artifacts.

THE WAR'S SOUNDTRACK

MUSIC WAS SO IMPORTANT THAT soldiers quoted lyrics to communicate with friends and family at home, making it one of the few shared cultural references between front and home. Amos Williams noted to his loved ones that although life in the army was not casy, "wc can only do as thc song so wiscly & philosophically put it: 'What's the use of worrying! It never was worth while, Pack all your troubles in your old kit bag; And smilc—smile—smile.'" He added, a little more seriously, "It's pretty hard however to smile sometimes."[14] Williams was using the lyrics from the ubiquitous "Pack Up Your Troubles" to communicate his feelings across the literal and figurative ocean that separated soldiers and civilians. Alfred Andrews, a prewar lawyer, spoke of a frustrating night in the trenches when his officers got lost and his formation wandered blindly in the underground world of darkness and dead-end alleys. Andrews laughed it off, noting, "Everyone was tired and mad! Ah it was a lovely war all right!"[15] The latter phrase came from the popular song "Oh! It's a Lovely War," which had singers sarcastically professing to love the war:

> Oh! Oh! Oh! It's a lovely war . . .
> What do we want with eggs and ham
> When we have plum and apple jam?
> Form fours! Right turn!
> How shall we spend the money we earn?
> Oh! Oh! Oh! It's a lovely war.

"Pack Up Your Troubles" and "Oh! It's a Lovely War" were two of the most popular songs of the war, and they both conveyed the idea of soldiers grinning and bearing the strain through humour and satire.

A significant feature of the soldiers' songs was that they recycled prewar and wartime civilian popular culture. Songs with religious themes were popular because the hymns, as noted by First Contingent soldier Richard Graeme, "had a stirring tempo" but also lent themselves to "parody."[16] The songsters and lyricists of the unit added new phrases and choruses to existing songs. Adapting popular songs had a twofold advantage: the informal composers did not have to come up with new melodies and those who listened to the new songs instantly recognized them. The quick-witted among the units were encouraged to improvise lyrics and phrases on the fly. While a few musical professionals or gifted amateurs filled the ranks of any given unit, this was an egalitarian war of voice, and no special equipment or skills were required to sing.

There were multiple versions of soldiers' songs. As many of them had no single author and changed with the currency of many mouths, this made it difficult to find the definitive versions of songs, since they were, for the most part, never committed to paper.[17] The songs born of parody were cynical, bawdy, and at times infused with antiwar or anti-military attitudes and rhetoric, but they were not mutinous. The soldiers were blowing off steam, and officers for the most part did not object to even the raunchiest songs. One contemporary soldier suggested that songs came "from the ranks, especially from the private soldiers," and almost all originated within the exceptional environment of the Western Front.[18] Different songs fit different moods: monotonous marches required uplifting tunes, which assisted in putting the soldiers into rhythmic step; working on a labour party digging trenches might evoke angrier songs; and sitting in a dugout at night with one's comrades was the right setting for a sentimental ballad.

The most important and popular of these songs, believed combat veteran Will Bird, were the "satires on the war." These were thinly veiled attacks against the boredom and banality of military life, as well as against the patriotic ideals that underpinned much of the talk on the home front. The song "I Don't Want to Die" was an example of how the soldiers stripped away the high-flown words of honour and duty, creating a very different, almost antiwar message:

I want to go home, I want to go home.
I don't want to go in the trenches no more,
Where whiz-bangs and shrapnel they whistle and roar.
Take me over the sea, where the Alleyman can't get at me.
Oh my, I don't want to die, I want to go home.
I want to go home, I want to go home.
I don't want to visit la Belle France no more,
For oh the Jack Johnsons they make such a roar.
Take me over the sea, where the snipers they can't get at me.
Oh my, I don't want to die, I want to go home.

"I Don't Want to Join the Army" was another variation on the anti-heroic theme, with the singers howling irreverent lines:

I don't want to join the army,
I don't want to go to war.
I'd rather hang around Piccadilly underground.
Living off the earnings of a lady whore.
I don't want a bayonet in my belly,
I don't want my bollocks shot away.
I'd rather stay in England, in merry, merry England,
And fuck this bleeding life away.

In the soldiers' songs, the patriotic discourse of the home front, with its exalted speech-making of one more push, was buried under a chorus of deliberately shocking satire, anti-conformity, relentless vulgarity, and merry-making. This was the grousing of everyday soldiers put to song. The cynicism expressed in the songs did not mean that the soldiers were willing to give up or embrace defeat. In fact, to sing about the army discipline, which in its extreme form was much hated, or about escaping the trenches, was a way of coping with the strain at the front and finding strength to go on. Chester Routley of the 18th Battalion was so taken with one untitled and impertinent song that he wrote it down from memory in his postwar memoirs:

They say we're going over the ocean
They say we're going over the sea,
They say that we're going to Blighty,
But it all sounds like bull-shit to me.
Bull-shit, bull-shit, it all sounds
Like bull-shit to me, to me,
Bull-shit, bull shit, it sounds
Just like bull-shit to me.[19]

These satirical send-ups also allowed for the trivialization of mud, lice, and sudden death.[20] In the strange world of the trenches, where lives were ruled by fate or military discipline, one simply had to grin and bear it. This sentiment was expressed in many ways, but the soldiers' song "Never Mind" (also known as "If the Sergeant Steals Your Rum") captured it well:

If the sergeant drinks your rum, never mind
And your face may lose its smile, never mind

He's entitled to a tot but not the bleeding lot
If the sergeant drinks your rum, never mind
When old Jerry shells your trench, never mind
And your face may lose its smile, never mind
Though the sandbags bust and fly you have only once to die,
If old Jerry shells the trench, never mind
If you get stuck on the wire, never mind
And your face may lose its smile, never mind
Though you're stuck there all the day, they count you dead and
stop your pay
If you get stuck on the wire, never mind

Some troops added their own fun to the lyrics by mimicking officers or NCOs, either in speech or tone, to personalize the song for their comrades.[21]

A Canadian violinist entertaining two chums. The soldier on the right has his gas mask in a pouch on his chest, at the ready.

Though soldiers liked to take their superiors down a notch, reminding those in power that the rank and file were on to their tricks, they reserved a special vitriol for those at home who would not fight. The anonymous satirical attack on conscientious objectors, "I Don't Want to Be a Soldier," was sung with vigour:

I don't want to be a soldier, I won't be compelled to fight:
I much prefer to stay in England than to battle for the right:
Others may be patriotic and answer King and Country's call,
But my conscience won't allow me—no, my conscience won't
Allow me—or I'd sacrifice my all.
Chorus
I don't want to be a soldier,
I have nought worth fighting for;
If I had, my conscience tells me
It's not right to go to war
I don't want to be a soldier, I feel quite happy singing psalms,
Tho' I've often heard the bugle sounding the call to arms:
I would rather be a shirker and sleep upon a feather bed,
Than to doss within a dug-out—a dirty, muddy dug-out—
And plaster Ticker's jam upon my bread.[22]

"It won't be good to be a chap who stayed at home, when the boys return," wrote one Canadian stretcher-bearer in a letter about those young men who did not serve. "This thing is just a bit too serious. We know what it is here."[23] Motivated by anger at the unfair burden shouldered by those at the front, many soldiers dreamed and sang lustily about postwar revenge against the slackers at home and their own abusive superiors. The moving "When This Lousy War Is Over," which was sung to the tune of "What a Friend We Have in Jesus," fantasized about postwar payback.

> When this lousy war is over no more soldiering for me,
> When I get my civvy clothes on, oh how happy I shall be.
> No more church parades on Sunday, no more begging for a pass.
> You can tell the sergeant-major to stick his passes up his arse.
> When this lousy war is over no more soldiering for me,
> When I get my civvy clothes on, oh how happy I shall be.
> No more NCOs to curse me, no more rotten army stew.
> You can tell the old cook-sergeant, to stick his stew right up his flue.
> When this lousy war is over no more soldiering for me,
> When I get my civvy clothes on, oh how happy I shall be.
> No more sergeants bawling, "Pick it up" and "Put it down"
> If I meet the ugly bastard I'll kick his arse all over town.

Such feelings of anger and discontent could be aired safely in the songs, in a way that they could not be presented in private letters home, which were censored, or in direct talk with superiors, which could result in confrontations and punishment.

There were also multiple songs devoted to the popular subjects of booze and sex. "Here's to the Good Old Beer" and "Drink It Down" were celebrations of alcohol, and even abstainers were known to join in to the chorus to be a part of the social activity.[24] The songs of drink quenched a thirst of the spirit and facilitated male bonding.[25] The rough culture of the soldiers was revealed more boldly, and bawdily, through sexual songs such as "My Nelly, Skibboo," "I'm Charlotte, the Harlot," "Oh, Florea's [or Florrie's] New Drawers," and "Three German Officers." The most famous dirty song of them all, "Mademoiselle from Armentières," with its ever-changing and increasingly vulgar lines, is known to have at least 700 recorded versions. And this doesn't include most of the unprintable ones, with the lyrics degenerating into incest and bestiality.[26] "Certainly some of the verses we sang were pretty ripe," said Ernest Black in his memoirs, with little more than a literary shrug.[27]

The more blasphemous the song, the more it was sung with gusto, with some of the raunchiest songs being belted out on the march. Soldiers were not known as foot-sloggers for nothing, and it was not uncommon for them to march in their heavy hobnailed boots for kilometres behind the lines, carrying gear weighing more than sixty pounds. Lieutenant Thomas Dinesen, a Danish national who enlisted in the CEF and would later receive the Victoria Cross for fierce fighting at the Battle of Amiens, recounted the joy men took in shouting irreverent lyrics while on the march:

> Again and again we go back to the good old *Pack Up Your Troubles*; or else we roar so that the whole countryside may hear: *The Gang's All Here!* But the best of the lot is the everlasting and ever-varying song of *Mademoiselle from Armentières*:
>
> Oh, madam, have you any good wine?
> Parley voo,
> Oh, madam, have you any good wine?
> Parley voo,
> Oh, madam, have you any good wine,
> Fit for a soldier from the line?
> Hinky dinky, parley voo.
>
> It continued, "Oh, madam, have you a daughter fine? Yes, I have a daughter fine. Then . . ." Our imagination pictures the

continuation of the song in lusty and vivid colouring, although in any case we have now turned our back on all such pleasures for some time to come.[28]

Singing relieved some of the boredom and burden of the march and "Mademoiselle from Armentières" was popular because of its jaunty tune and full-on obscenity, but its multiple verses allowed different voices to take up the song and add their own absurd or mocking lines. Canadian soldier Ralf Sheldon-Williams described an occasion when he and others were singing on the march and some lyrics of the song left commanders' "necks a shocked old rose," but he added, "Still, boys will be boys and soldiers soldiers."[29] He remarked that not only were the soldiers part of a hyper-masculine society, but that soldiers in general were a breed apart from other men. Perhaps the song Sheldon-Williams was referring to is "Do Your Balls Hang Low?":

Do your balls hang low
Do they dangle to and fro
Can you tie them in a knot
Can you tie them in a bow?
Can you sling them on your shoulder
Like a lousy fucking soldier
Do your balls hang low?[30]

Marching several kilometres a day remained brutally hard while in full kit and wearing hobnailed boots, but singing often bawdy songs kept up morale and passed the time.

Captain William "Wild Bill" Livingstone, a former electrical engineer from Big Bras d'Or, Nova Scotia, was wounded six times and awarded the Military Cross twice by the end of the war. He remembered the power of song from an incident in the summer of 1918: "I never saw the Bn [battalion] in better condition, and I think if some of the pacifists cranks could have heard those men sing on the march, it would have made them hide their heads in shame. Men, many of whom have gone through three years of this game. Men determined to 'carry on' to a victorious issue, and after three years of war, singing! Like they used to in the old days in Canada. Singing as they march back to the same old Hellish scenes that we have all grown so sick of. Truly as much of the old stick-to-it, undaunted, spirit as our race has ever shown."[31] Singing on the march restored the fighting ethos of the warriors. The 44th Battalion, as they marched away from the costly fighting at Amiens, on the morning of August 25, 1918, and headed toward another big battle, was attacked by heavy Gotha bombers. The men dived for cover in terror as anti-aircraft fire raked the air and the bomb blast sent reverberations through the earth. The men were shaken up, but the men of A Company cheekily began to warble "I Want to Go Home," spurring Lieutenant E.S. Russenholt to remark, "confidence is completely restored."[32] Soldiers were of course susceptible to fear and even wrote about their feelings in their diaries or in letters home, but there was a masculine bravado that was especially revealed in their songs that was important for sloughing off the worst of the war.

In the soldiers' world of bluster and swagger, sentimental songs, somewhat surprisingly, were just as important as the vulgar ones. "Roses of Picardy," "Keep the Home Fires Burning," "Hold Your Hand Out, You Naughty Boy," and "Dear Old Pal of Mine" were all sung with feeling. These songs, with their maudlin and at times tearful lyrics, seem at odds with what combat soldiers might be expected to enjoy. There was nothing ironic or subversive about the sentimental songs, but they touched the men to the core. Few sang or heard them unmoved.

Victor Wheeler of the 50th Battalion told the story of his shattered unit marching to their rear billets after moving off the devastating Somme battlefield in December 1916: "Corporal Arthur Howard Cross entertained us singing both old favourites and contemporary War songs. . . . Finally he sang *The Roses of Picardy* as a farewell to the Somme in Picardy. We implored him, 'Sing it again, Cross. Please sing it once more.' Seeming to realize how much that song meant to us, Cross sang many encores—until every hardened soldier, recumbent around the sides of the low mud-whitewashed walls of the high pitched roof, was in tears.[33] Such poignant songs were a form of nostalgia, reminding men of a better time, away from the killing.

An addition to the popular sentimental songs were the hymns that had been a part of the men's civilian lives in a society where the church played an important role. Church padres encouraged the singing of such songs, as did the YMCA. Singing religious songs brought tremendous relief for some men, but this did not always mean that soldiers were particularly moved by the experience. Major R.S. Cockburn, a British soldier at the front, remarked "there is nothing the men enjoy more than singing hymns; but they do not sing them (as some would have you and me believe) because they are religiously inclined . . . they sing hymns because they wish to hear their own voices, and because most of them happen to know the words."[34] Hymns were often sung in unexpected places like the trenches or in contexts that seemed oddly suited to the sentiments expressed. Canadian Harold Simpson wrote, "Many a time I have seen the bunch of men playing poker and at the same time singing *Nearer My God To Thee*, *I Am Thine O Lord* or *Abide With Me*."[35] Whatever the hymns' meaning was to the soldiers—spiritual or otherwise—singing them evidently brought solace to hard men in a hard place, while forging a new sense of community.

No single song or even genre represented the Canadian soldier overseas. And even the signature song of the war, "It's a Long Way to Tipperary," went through cycles of popularity. "Tipperary" was on everyone's lips at the start of the war, even though it had been a hit the year before in 1913. Its bouncy lyrics captured the optimistic spirit of 1914:

It's a long way to Tipperary,
It's a long way to go.
It's a long way to Tipperary
To the sweetest girl I know!
Goodbye Piccadilly,
Farewell Leicester Square!
It's a long long way to Tipperary,
But my heart's right there.

The song had both little and everything to do with the war. While it was written before the conflict, "Tipperary" was about leaving behind a loved one and then finding a way home. It resonated with many men and women who battled the loneliness of separation brought on by the war effort. However, by the second year of the war, the soldiers overseas sang it less often because it was so popular on the home front. The song had moved out of their own secret stash of material to enjoy wider circulation and acceptance, and that left soldiers searching for new tunes that they might own exclusively. Attempts by new men to sing it were shouted down by their hard-bitten compatriots, although this treatment was also likely part of the sometimes harsh acclimation process experienced by reinforcements to the established trench community.[36] However, it was acceptable for the soldiers to parody the song by inserting racy or vulgar lines, such as "That's the wrong way to tickle Mary, it's the wrong way you know."[37] The lyrics would get increasingly "ticklish" as the song went on, underscoring the propensity of soldiers to take ownership of such popular songs by parodying them.

In a letter to his family, Lieutenant J.S. Williams observed that a particular parody was "much circulated over here," adding, "It absolutely reflects the impression and feelings of the men, and officers as well, in my opinion." The song was an adaption of the popular weeper "Someone to Sing Me to Sleep." The soldiers' version, "Far, Far from Ypres," was also published in an early

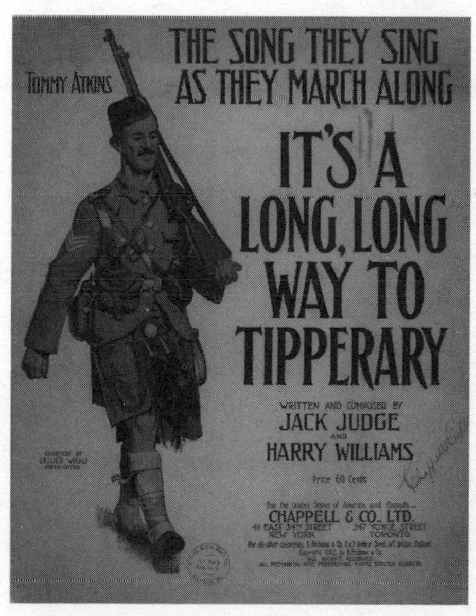

"It's a Long Way to Tipperary" was the most popular song in the early part of the war, but soldiers grew tired of it, refusing to sing it or changing the lyrics to make it their own.

issue of the Canadian trench newspaper *The Listening Post*, thereby codifying it for the thousands who read it:[38]

Sing me to sleep where bullets fall;
Let me forget the war and all.
Damp is my dugout, cold are my feet,
Nothing but bully and biscuits to eat.
Sing me to sleep where bombs explode
And shrapnel shells are a-la-mode.
Over the sandbags helmets you find,
Corpses in front of you, corpses behind.
Far, far from Ypres I long to be,
Where German snipers cannot pot me.
Think of me crouching where the worms creep,
Waiting for someone to sing me to sleep. . . .
Far from the star-shells I long to be,
Lights of old London I'd rather see;
Think of me crouching where the worms creep,
Waiting for someone to sing me to sleep.[39]

The song expressed the trench dwellers' deep longing to escape the clinging mud, dead-eyed snipers, and unburied corpses, and was pitiful in the way it implored the soldiers' loved ones to remember them in their misery, or at least to offer something as simple as a lullaby to ease their discomfort.

Death and its trivialization remained a dominant theme in the soldiers' songs. "The Bells of Hell" was one of the most cutting songs of the war, and creepy in its faux cheerfulness, as it wished doom on one's luckless mates while one stayed safe. Several versions had the refrain

The bells of Hell go ting-a-ling-a-ling,
For you, but not for me. . . .

The Canadian trench newspaper *The Brazier* told its readers in November 1916 that "Parodies on popular songs are always in demand. Here's a new one on an old song. The air is, *She only answered ting-a-ling-a-ling*." The newspaper's editors changed "for you" to "for Fritz" (one of the slang words used to describe the Germans), which takes a little of the wanton meanness out of the song:

The bells of Hell go ting-a-ling-a-ling,
For Fritz, but not for me;
For me the angels sing-a-ling-a-ling,
They're waiting there for me.
Oh, Death, where is thy sting-a-ling-a-ling.
Oh, grave, thy victoree?
The bells of Hell go ting-a-ling-a-ling
For Fritz, but not for me.[40]

To sing about death in this cavalier manner was perhaps to offer up a psychological shield to the murderous conditions at the front, where, by the war's end, the vast majority of infantrymen who served in the trenches would be killed or wounded.

Taunting other units with songs was part of the soldiers' culture that embraced comrades and shunned outsiders. Though the CEF and the Canadian Corps were bound together in many ways, there was an intense rivalry between divisions, brigades, and smaller units. This sense of competition was stoked by officers who sought to instill pride and unity of purpose in their men. Most battalions had a song or two that praised the formation and its victories while claiming toughness and disdain for the enemy.[41] Most of these were sung for instant laughter, but the 3rd Battalion had a popular song to the tune of "Put on Your Old Grey Bonnet," whose lyrics "reflected invidiously on the personal habits and appearances" of the 2nd Battalion, according to one bitter soldier from that latter unit.[42] Whenever the song was sung, the 2nd Battalion would shout it down with profanities, which of course only caused the men of the 3rd Battalion to bellow the offending song even louder.

THERE WERE OTHER CANADIAN-COMPOSED SONGS that were unique to the men from the northern dominion and that were sung with pride. Canadians serving in British units, like Private Wilfrid Fletcher, who had enlisted from Lethbridge, Alberta, and who was fighting in late 1914, sometimes sang to distinguish themselves from their British comrades. Fletcher wrote home that he and twelve other Canadian mates in the regiment were known as the "Canadians. It is quite a distinction. . . . We have sung 'The Maple Leaf Forever,' 'Casey Jones,' 'Red Wing,' and 'The Old Star Trail,' until the whole garrison knows of the thirteen lucky Canadians."[43] Fletcher's luck ran out early and he was killed on October 29, 1914, during the Battle of First Ypres. Canadians sang the old songs of the Dominion as a badge of courage, but they also made up new ones. *Tommy's Tunes*, a collection of songs published by a Royal Flying Corps officer, F.T. Nettleingham, was prefaced with the belief that "a nation's songs and other musical efforts reveal the actual character and culture of a nation in a way that is unapproached by any other art."[44] Armine Norris, a machine-gunner who would be killed in the final months of the war, told his mother about the latest popular song in his unit—one of the few, he noted slyly, that was "fit for publication."

We are the boys from the mountains and the plains,
We are Canucks, you see.
We come from the East and we come from the West
To fight for the Land of the Free.
And now that we're here like the rest of Britain's sons
We don't care a ----- for the Kaiser and his Huns.
C-A-N-A-D-I-A-N-S
We are—we are—we are Canadians.

This untitled song was composed by one of Norris's mates, who was later killed, leading Norris to observe to his mother, "You'll understand why we don't sing it often now."[45] Though the Canadians fought in an English-speaking army as part of the British Expeditionary Force, there were visible minorities in the ranks who also expressed themselves in song. French Canadians sang the popular English tunes as well as French songs like "La Madelon" and folk songs from Quebec. Stanislas Tougas, who enlisted on October 29, 1914, a few days after his eighteenth birthday, and who served with the 22nd Battalion until he was killed on August 28, 1917, wrote in French and noted that he and his comrades sang both French and English songs, including "Minuit," "Chrétiens," "O Canada," and "Vive la Canadienne."[46] Georges Vanier, also of the French-speaking 22nd Battalion, described his unit marching through France singing "'La Marseillaise' and 'O Canada'. . . . The women along the route were enthusiastic, cheering us up and encouraging us."[47] Later, he said that he and his men "sang Canadian songs," while another of the Van Doos, Private Arthur Lapointe, recounted the comfort in turning to "the old songs of French Canada."[48]

What songs other minorities in the CEF—from Indigenous men to Ukrainians, from Jews to black Canadians—sang were likely the same as those sung by their white, Anglo-Saxon comrades, along with whatever songs they brought with them from their own communities. Canadian infantryman Andrew Napier observed in September 1915 that in the camps, his battalion—which was "very cosmopolitan, [and filled with] Canucks, British, French, + some Indians"—sat around "playing cards + singing all the latest choruses."[49] Katsuji Nakashima, a Japanese Canadian serving in the Canadian Corps, wrote of the night before the assault on Vimy Ridge, recalling, "Everyone had the strained look of men waiting to go into battle. At nine in the evening we joined the *hakujin* in singing songs, the words of which we did not understand."[50] Language barriers could be brought down by songs because they could be sung without full command of their language of composition. The songs of the war were thus a means by which some of the differences between the soldiers—of language, ethnicity, region, and class—could be more easily overcome, and they assisted in forging new bonds within the soldiers' tribe.

SINGING WAS A WAY FOR soldiers to exert agency. Either individually or in groups, to sing was a choice made by the men and was rarely a requirement imposed on them from above.[51] The stalemated nature of the war, with its long periods of boredom, lent itself to soldiers searching for new survival strategies and means to mark their service as separate from civilians far from the front. There were songs of leisure, but also songs of coping and opposition. A dirty or subversive song could be sung teeth-bared, and few officers would step in to moderate their men.

Singing was integral to the identity of both imperial and dominion soldiers. The laughing, cheering, smiling Tommy was idealized throughout the British Empire, and this was how soldiers saw themselves in contrast to the grim, robot-like Germans. Humour in all its forms, but especially as it was expressed in song, would carry the soldiers through their hard days.[52] After the Canadians captured the ruined village of Courcelette on the Somme in September 1916, Lieutenant F.G. Newton wrote, "The British Army sings no hymns of hate, but the rollicking ragtime songs of the music halls are, as it were, barometric measures of their morale."[53]

Amid the horrors of the battlefield, even in sloughs of despair like Passchendaele, with its sea of unburied corpses and gas-infected mud, the soldiers sang their songs. "In circumstances worthy of Hell," remembered Major F.T. Coghlan of the 43rd Howitzer Battery, the sound of rough male voices could be heard singing in chorus the old songs of "A Long, Long Trail," "Pull for the Shore Sailor," and "A Bicycle Built for Two."[54] Singing calmed nerves and soothed jagged fears. Mike Mountain Horse, an Indigenous soldier from the Blood First Nation Reserve who enlisted in May 1916 and would be awarded the DCM for bravery, revealed that during one intense artillery bombardment he sang a traditional war chant that allowed him to release "his pent-up feelings."[55] "A common song (even now and then a dirty song)," believed Lieutenant Henry Simpson, "can make one glad and sad beyond words, because one has heard men singing it times without number."[56]

Officers and men, usually separated by their rank, could sing together. In mid-1916, the Canadian trench newspaper *The*

Forty-Niner described a recent "sing-song," the third in a series, which had been a great success: "All the officers of the staff were present and shedding their 'august majesty,' which is so necessary on active service."[57] While singing was often carried out by the rank and file, at times it offered an accommodating language to draw the unit together. Soldiers were bound through blood and belonging, but songs welded them even tighter within the closed society.

The soldiers' songs formed some of their fondest memories of the war. A single bar or refrain could spark deep feelings among veterans in the postwar years. The songs were badges of identity. It was a strange and shocking war that few predicted and fewer still knew how to end; at times it provoked disillusionment or a howl of anguish, and at other times a grin or a belly laugh. As a Canadian trench warrior remarked in a letter home, "I often think of the nights we spent singing together."[58]

CHAPTER 5

TRENCH STORIES

Lieutenant Stanley Rutledge was both exasperated and amused by the constant rumours that circulated through the trenches. Even as shells and bullets claimed lives, there was a never-ending chatter among soldiers. Rutledge described how in a single dugout "one can hear more rumours, more complaints, more jests than in any other part of the line." He noted further that as men huddled together to escape the cold, they talked freely, trading wildly in speculation and hope: "One chap has heard that the Kaiser says the war will be over before Christmas (this, by the way, is our annual rumour). 'Honest, boys, I was talking to "Jim" (one of the drivers), and he said he had it straight from "Bob" (who is batman for a staff officer)—ad infinitum. . . . An afternoon quilting party at Mrs. Smith's could not compare."[1] Rutledge was struck by all the gossip and idle talk and he felt the phenomenon was important enough to recount to his parents before his death at the end of 1916.

Rumours tend to emerge in times of crisis or ignorance, and the unending tension on the Western Front, mixed with the soldiers' forced inactivity, constant fear of death, and lack of knowledge of the strategic direction of the war, made the trenches a breeding ground for tall tales.[2] These stories played an important role in the lives of Canadian soldiers, who listened to, speculated on, and spread gossipy tales day after day. Such stories were another way of coping with the strain of combat and the uncertainty of daily operations. Though they were often harmless, absurd, and unnoticed by civilians who were not members of this unique society, these malleable narratives provide insight into the experience of soldiers and their secret culture. Rumours were a multilayered form of social interaction, and even if most soldiers understood their inherent inaccuracy, they listened intently, passed them on, and waited for the next tale that might aid in making sense of their trench experience or at least help them manage the unknowable.

WHILE THOSE AT THE FRONT bore the heaviest load and experienced the war in its fullest brutality, all soldiers were caught in the slipstream of ever-changing events and often had only the slightest idea of what was happening beyond their limited sector. "The closer we got to the war the less we knew of it," lamented Lieutenant James Pedley of the 4th Battalion. He and his troops felt "cut off from the world."[3] Lieutenant-Colonel C.B. Topp of the 42nd Battalion, thrice wounded and awarded three different medals, shared his thoughts on the soldiers' narrow vision: "At best the infantryman's knowledge of the war in general was necessarily circumscribed and naturally his attention was very largely centred upon the particular task to be carried out along the limited section of the front occupied by his own Battalion, Brigade, or Division."[4] The front-line soldiers knew almost instinctively when to duck, how to keep rats from eating their food, or what route to take through No Man's Land on a patrol, but they knew little about the overall direction of the war or even the factors affecting its possible outcome.

Within this vacuum of knowledge, rumours flourished. "Nowadays a whisper passes like a prairie fire along the line, and although we find some are untrue, still never an action occurs that has not been preceded by the 'unseen courier,'" observed the Canadian trench newspaper *The Iodine Chronicle*, published by the 1st Canadian Field Ambulance.[5] These "wild and unsubstantiated stories and prophecies," as two contemporary commentators referred to them, often originated at the latrines, one of the few places where the soldiers had rare precious minutes to themselves.[6] Here, men talked and gossiped, passing along whatever local wisdom they had gleaned, before returning back to chums to impart the latest "intelligence."

Dugouts were another place where rumours circulated freely. Away from the prying eyes of officers, the rank and file, often with rum-loosened tongues, spouted their theories and expanded upon all aspects of the war, usually while playing cards, reading, or writing letters. George Timmins, who enlisted as an "old man" at forty-three, wrote to his wife that the soldiers' boredom led to much idle chatter. But sometimes the conversations were very animated and involved large groups of debaters. Timmins noted that his chums in the 116th Battalion often sat around and held mock peace conferences, where "we draw up terms & settle the war offhand, to our own satisfaction." The terms, he said slyly, required Germany to pay a "huge indemnity," rebuild Belgium, hand over occupied territory, and reimburse "Canada's sons for their trouble."[7] Dugouts were a safe area in which to complain. As Will Bird testified, "All grousing was reserved for the higher-ups, the 'brass-hats' and the 'big bugs' responsible for everything.

December 1, 1917. THE LISTENING POST. *Special Christmas Number.*

HOW RUMOURS GROW.

IN an army which is dependent on the London papers a day or two old for exact knowledge of what is happening on its own particular front, it is inevitable that rumours of all sorts should travel from unit to unit, and grow increasingly grotesque until they break down from sheer overweight of untruth.

Rumours are generally born in the brain of some person whose occupation leaves him sufficient time to concoct and spread a tissue of half-truths, sufficiently highly coloured to appeal to troops whose one and everlasting hope is change.

A few samples of the ordinary types of rumour are :—

"The Division is going back to Canada for a three months' rest."

"The war will be over by (movable date)."

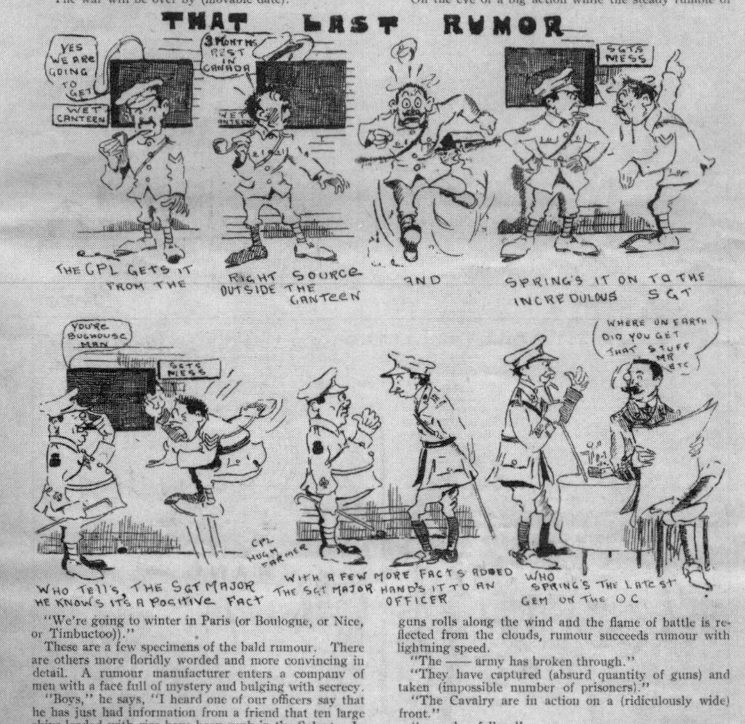

"We're going to winter in Paris (or Boulogne, or Nice, or Timbuctoo))."

These are a few specimens of the bald rumour. There are others more floridly worded and more convincing in detail. A rumour manufacturer enters a company of men with a face full of mystery and bulging with secrecy.

"Boys," he says, "I heard one of our officers say that he has just had information from a friend that ten large ships loaded with rice have been sunk in the Solent. In about five days' time there won't be a grain of rice to be had for love or money. Now, you mark my words. THERE'LL BE NO RICE!" (Loud cheers from the troops.)

Some will remember the rumour which passed along the line two years ago: "There is to be no cheering in the front line when peace is declared." There was the master touch about that. It sounded official and authoritative. It conjured up visions of Christmas at home, but that was two years ago, and here we are!

Batmen are, perhaps, the busiest spreaders of rumour. Their association with the brains of the army gives them a sort of reflected authority, and their unique opportunities of finding out what is passing through the official mind give them the widest scope. When a batman says "Straight goods from the Mess," he is sure of a respectful hearing.

Strangely enough chaplains' batmen are generally the worst offenders, and their product is marked by its wildness and originality.

It is a notable fact that although one may be convinced of the utter falsity of a rumour, that does not usually prevent one from passing it along.

On the eve of a big action while the steady rumble of guns rolls along the wind and the flame of battle is reflected from the clouds, rumour succeeds rumour with lightning speed.

"The —— army has broken through."

"They have captured (absurd quantity of guns) and taken (impossible number of prisoners)."

"The Cavalry are in action on a (ridiculously wide) front."

"—— has fallen."

"The Huns are evacuating ——."

"The Russians, Italians, or French have broken through at ——."

So it goes, and although most of these reports are grossly exaggerated, there is often a kernel of truth in them which keeps hope at high tension, until the papers bring expectation back to within reasonable limits.

31

The cartoon "How Rumours Grow" was published in The Listening Post *and illustrated the origin of rumours, starting with a soldier who overhears officers talking in a wet canteen, and then following the spread of the rumour through the unit.*

The men were unselfish among themselves, instinctively helping each other, knowing each other, each with a balance and discipline of his own. We endured much."[8] Cantankerous talk allowed soldiers to let off steam, and all manner of conversations raged in the holes in the ground. These were places where the secret history of survival was revealed by old hands to new men. Those fresh at the front were wise to listen. In fact, with battalions and units suffering horrendous casualties and often losing half the force in the big battles, the informal talks were crucial for passing along tips, lore, and legends of the Western Front, as well as for reinforcing the regimental stories that inspired and bound men together.

Sergeant Thomas Clark Lapp, a wartime gunner, revealed in a letter to his family in Belleville, Ontario, that "The things that affect us personally—rations, mail from home, leave, working parties' patrols, vermin, mud. etc.—are talked of most, but the range of subjects include politics, religion, literature, poetry, and sometimes war. No debating society ever had more earnest speakers than I have heard in my experience of some five months in France."[9] Unscripted and uncontrollable, the rumours filtered from the dugouts and travelled up and down the line, shared by many mouths, appeasing or creating worries, addressing the unknown. Sometimes the stories were little more than escapism; at other times, they underlined a complex means of discourse as they revealed hopes, anxieties, and fears. But the rumours were always a part of the soldiers' secret culture. *The Listening Post* addressed the widespread promulgation of rumours, noting, "In an army which is dependent on the London papers a day or two old for exact knowledge of what is happening on its own particular front, it is inevitable that rumours of all sorts should travel from unit to unit, and grow increasingly grotesque until they break down from the sheer overweight of untruth. Rumours are generally born in the brain of some person whose occupation leaves him sufficient time to concoct and spread a tissue of half-truths, sufficiently highly coloured to appeal to troops whose one and everlasting hope is change."[10]

The rumours bulged with a sense of secrecy, yet not all of them were false. It was hard to keep anything from the soldiers for long. Informal back channels of information leaked from officers, often through signallers or batmen (the officers' servants), with the stories soon spreading from man to man, and then jumping units to move laterally and vertically along the trench systems. One of the most common reason for the circulation of rumours was the men's stark need to hear who had lived or died after big offensives, with soldiers hunting for news on friends or family members. Hopes rose and fell with each story of miraculous escape or certain death. Not all of them were accurate. There were even cases of men hearing from others of their own passing. Some took it with a soldier's perfected shrug, but Lieutenant Georges Vanier of the 22nd Battalion was less forgiving of one such rumour of his own death that reached him, complaining, "I cannot understand who spreads these rumours that do no one any good and that very often do a great deal of harm."[11]

But rumours were not always inaccurate fantasies. A front-line unit knew it would be relieved at some time—but when? was the question on everyone's lips. The war would end too at some point, but when? In the trenches or rear areas, opinions were not held back. With time on their hands, anyone with an answer was at least worth listening to, and perhaps what they had to say was even worth repeating. "It is a notable fact," thought one soldier, "that although one may be convinced of the utter falsity of a rumour, that does not usually prevent one from passing it along."[12]

Few forthcoming operations were a surprise to the soldiers, even though the high command and officers often tried to keep them secret for fear of loose talk that might inform the enemy if a soldier was captured or overheard by a spy behind the lines. When the 2nd Battalion was part of a diversionary force moved north to the Ypres front before the Battle of Amiens in August 1918 to deceive the Germans as to the location of the main attack, it started tongues wagging among the Canadians: "It was all very mystifying," wrote Captain William W. Murray. "The rumour-factory worked overtime. Corporal Jones had heard Sergeant Smith say that Captain Green was told by Major Brown of the colonel's conversation with General Griesbach, in which the General declared emphatically that the Second [Battalion] were going to the Marne. All nonsense. The Canadians were going down to fight with the Americans. And so on. The Battalion just revelled in these mysteries."[13] Aware of the soldiers' propensity to gossip, the high command took the unprecedented step prior to Amiens of having a note pasted into every man's pay book: "KEEP YOUR MOUTH SHUT." It was clearly for naught.

Idle gossip and salacious rumours: these were all part of the soldiers' day as they engaged in monotonous fatigues, cleaning kit, or clearing their bodies of lice. Men snorted at the stupidity of the war effort and then whispered conspiratorially that they had heard about some new plan, a new weapon, or forthcoming relief. Most experienced men knew to accept any rumour with a pound of salt, although that did not lessen the social enjoyment of listening to and partaking in raucous debates on the individual merits of each circulating tale of grouse and gossip. This camaraderie of the trench in fact encouraged such interaction and reinforced the strength of the social group.

A number of enduring rumours that circulated in the trenches might be classified under the broad rubric of wish-fulfillment. The most popular and common stories tended to revolve around the end of the war. Bill Hutchinson penned a letter on New Year's Eve 1916, remarking, "There seems to be all kinds of peace rumours floating around, hope some of them are true, though I can't see it yet."[14] He was right, of course, that the fulfillment of this wish was still very far off, but he nonetheless allowed some leeway for the hopeful possibility. Private Leo LeBoutillier of the 24th Battalion wrote to his "Mums" on April 27, 1916, "We hear great rumours of the war ending May 27th or during the summer. Let's hope it is true."[15] Perhaps for LeBoutillier, the inclusion of a specific date gave credence to the rumour; but he did not live to see the end of the war, dying of wounds sustained during the Vimy offensive in April 1917.

Whispers of the Kaiser's death, usually via assassination or insurrection, circulated periodically, repeated no doubt because this was one of the few genuine ways that the war might end.[16] In *The Listening Post* column "We Have Heard People Say," the paper poked fun at the loose talk: "That the war will end soon. . . . That the mud WILL dry up. That all the old boys are going back to Canada for 6 months rest (I don't think). That the Bosches have no ammunition (guess again)."[17] Clearly, there were so many gossipy stories that had been passed around so many times that veterans laughed them off, showing both their bravado and their experience, a way for old hands to distinguish themselves from the new men. There is more than a little irony in the fact that the armistice of November 11, 1918, was learned of by most front-line soldiers through the rumour mill before it went into effect. Hardened after months of intense combat and false rumours, few expected the news to be true.[18]

ONE OF THE MOST ENDURING rumours of the war focused on the leaning golden Virgin and Child atop the ruined Basilica at Albert. "The Legend is that when the statue falls the war will be over," wrote Major W.H. Hewgill of the 31st Battalion. "If I was sure of this the Virgin would certainly come down tonight."[19] Seen by nearly every Canadian as the troops marched into the devastated Somme battlefield in the late summer of 1916, one can imagine the men's silent prayer that some shell would knock down the statue before they had to go over the top. "The rumour amongst the troops was that when the statue fell, the war would end; consequently we did not think it was right for the French Engineers to strengthen it with cables, as they had done," complained gunner Arthur Catchpole.[20] But despite being bolted down, the Virgin finally fell in April 1918, when British gunners knocked down the statue to stop the German gunners from using it to range their artillery fire. The war did not, of course, end, but the image of the fallen Virgin Mary, holding Jesus in her arms and seemingly offering Him in the name of the sufferers below, was ripe with pathos.

A virulent form of rumours were those about German atrocities committed during the first days of the war. Stories of the cruel German occupation circulated throughout Europe, and then the world. The brutal invasion of Belgium had involved a draconian campaign of suppressing a seemingly large-scale armed uprising among the population. German soldiers experienced their own fearful bogeymen in the form of the *francs-tireurs*, or "free-shooters." The insurgent attacks by Belgian freedom fighters, or terrorists in the eyes of Germans, led to hysterical reactions and harsh reprisals. Though these free-shooters represented only a small percentage of the population, delusions, myths, and rumours circulated through the Imperial German Army, intimating that their

A view of the golden Virgin and Child atop the Basilica in Albert on the Somme battlefield. A widely circulating rumour carried the message that when the statue fell the war would end.

comrades were being picked off one by one through frequent ambushes, poisonings, and other grim endings. Fernand van Langenhove, a young German sociologist serving in the army, was even given freedom to study some of the hyper-reactions of his countrymen in Belgium.[21] He argued that many of the rumours contributed to a "myth-cycle" that spread contagiously through the ranks to shape a collective belief. Tales of murder and assassination were repeated endlessly, but there were often only a few variants. The anxiety produced by the threat of the free-shooters, more than their actual military effectiveness, led to German reprisal atrocities, with some 5,000 civilians executed. These cruelties were documented by the British and spread widely to demonize the enemy; after the war, the atrocity stories were downplayed and seen as just another form of wartime propaganda. It was not until many decades later that, through careful scholarship, the wartime rumours were proven true and the Germans revealed to have executed thousands of innocents.

One of the most enduring rumours of the war, based upon a seemingly fervid mass hallucination, centred on the small British regular army during their desperate retreat from Mons in the opening month of the war. Pressed by overwhelming German forces and retreating day after gruelling day, the desperate army fervently hoped that it might be saved. In this fraught situation, a legend sprang up about angels intervening between the retreating British and the Germans, although there were many versions told and retold.[22] Armoured knights, ghostly bowmen, or shimmering angels, depending on the rumour, swooped down from the heavens and blocked the German armies from pursuing and overrunning the British troops. In other versions, ethereal bowmen fired on the Germans, forcing them back, a story no doubt influenced by the British army's retreat past the medieval battlefield of Agincourt. In fact, the British were able to outrun the Germans, but the story instantly became a legend among the British forces, fuelled by the fighting men's desire to see the war as a crusade, and it was soon codified for mass consumption in a best-selling book by journalist Arthur Machen. The story of otherworldly bowmen saving the British Tommies was accepted by many as truth, and even after the author publicly outed himself, admitting his story had no grounding in fact, countless anxious British people, grappling with private fears for their loved ones or nation, refused to believe him.[23] Stanley Rutledge observed that the supernatural tale circulated among the Canadians, too, even though no Canadian units were at Mons: "It was told in semi-poetic language. And

Arthur Machen's short story "The Bowmen" presented the idea of ethereal bowmen who intervened to save the retreating British army from Mons. The story, based on widespread rumours, was republished the next year in The Bowmen and Other Legends of the War *(1915), the cover of which is featured here.*

then we all hoped it had really happened. Glad to believe, you know, in such a manifestation of righteous judgment." Even when it was revealed that the story was a fabrication, Rutledge noted there were "many who will not disbelieve the vision."[24]

In this war that Britain and Canada framed as a fight for justice and civilization, the British Empire forces were seen as literally on the side of the angels and the evil Hun as raping, burning, and murdering his way across Europe. In such an environment, a particularly sick rumour circulated among troops and civilians that gained significant currency. It was said in hushed tones that the British naval blockade had choked Germany of fats necessary for the war effort, and that, accordingly, the enemy high command had responded by transporting their own soldiers' corpses back to an unknown factory to render them into nitroglycerine or tallow for candles.[25] Demonstrating the influence of the story, Canadian infantryman Herbert Clemens wrote home in jest that his recently enlisted brother would have a chance "of getting a whack at those beastly body boiling Sausage Eaters."[26] Lieutenant James Pedley of the 4th Battalion also took note of the "corpse-factory yarn," commenting after the war, "We half-believed these things at the time, for we were in a mood to believe anything that indicated that our enemy was in hard straits. But I don't think we cared much whether he buried his dead or boiled them."[27] Many of the men may have scoffed at such extreme characterizations of the enemy, as well as at the story of the corpse factory. But the effectiveness of the Royal Navy blockade, coupled with the perceived brutality of the German *Kultur* that had unleashed submarine warfare, aerial bombardment, and poison gas, stimulated soldiers' belief in the possible validity of rumours that illustrated the Hun's barbarity, even towards their own people. The truth about the corpse factory legend was not revealed until nearly a decade after the war, when John Charteris, who had been the BEF's senior intelligence officer, let it slip that the British had planted the rumour and encouraged its spread.[28]

There were also battlefield atrocity stories, the most influential among the Canadian forces being the supposed crucifixion of a Canadian soldier during the Battle of Second Ypres in April 1915. The rumour morphed into a powerful myth, whose intensity increased with each retelling. Many Canadians claimed to have seen the crucified soldier, yet they all had different versions. The story was reported back in Canada, and by the time Frank Maheux of the 21st Battalion arrived on the Western Front in September 1915, he told his wife in broken English that "they found the poor 6 Canadians killed in a barn they were nailed with a baynette in each hand and it was marked in English 'that show you Canadiens to stop in Canada."[29] Maheux interpreted the story as a cruel warning to the Canadians, a criticism of their decision to fight by Britain's side, but others made their own meaning out of the powerful rumour. So prevalent were the stories that the Canadian high command investigated the matter, eventually concluding that it was untrue as helpful soldiers stepped forward to offer testimony that was conflicting, unreliable, and at times obviously untrue given unit locations during the battle.[30] Brigadier R.G.E. Leckie testified, "I heard rumours that such an incident took place during the second battle of Ypres," but after a thorough investigation, he could get no "reliable information" from supposed eyewitnesses. Combat veteran Hamilton Gault was less charitable, remarking, "I am inclined to think that much of this was due to irresponsible gossip."[31]

The image of an executed Canadian was tenacious, however, and the story was passed on to new recruits through constant chatter. The crucified Canadian who died in prosecuting this war for civilization was a powerful religious image that resonated with the

Rumours circulated of German soldiers who crucified a Canadian during the Battle of Second Ypres. The stories spread widely and were also captured in print. This is an American recruitment poster from the Philippines that illustrates the Germans' barbarity with the crucified Canadian.

largely Christian army, and an important symbol that would have been easily communicated to new soldiers. Private Leonard Gould testified that his whole battalion was shown a barn door as part of their training, which was "identical [to the] one on which the Canadian sergeant was found crucified."[32] The same thing happened to the 102nd Battalion, men drawn from British Columbia, who arrived in France in August 1916.[33] And George Ormsby, a recent arrival to the 15th Battalion in the aftermath of it being nearly wiped out at Second Ypres, revealed to his wife that a survivor of that battle told him, "the boys found [a Canadian soldier] crucified to a door with bayonets through his hands and feet." This rumour served to indoctrinate Ormsby into the unit, reinforcing in his own mind why he was fighting. "I trust you will be proud that I have had the courage to get out and fight against such a domineering race," he declared to his wife. "Should Germany win this war then may God help Canada—in fact the whole world."[34]

The story of the crucified Canadian was widely believed in the Canadian Corps, and often employed as a justification to show no mercy to the Hun. British infantryman and poet Robert Graves accused the Canadians of having "the worst reputation for acts of violence against prisoners." But he also noted that the "Canadians' motive was said to be revenge for a Canadian found crucified with bayonets though his hands and feet in a German trench. . . . How far this reputation for atrocities was deserved, and how far it could be ascribed to the overseas habit of bragging and leg-pulling, we could not decide. At all events, most overseas men, and some British troops, made atrocities against prisoners a boast, not a confession."[35]

This violent behaviour was payback for the enemy's acts of barbarity: the supposed crucifixion of one of the Canadians' own was preceded by the German pillage of Belgian towns and execution of civilians, and followed by the sinking of the civilian steamship *Lusitania* in May 1915 and the execution of nurse Edith Cavell at the end of that same year. In retaliation for real and fabricated German atrocities, William Gosford of the 5th Battalion had been instructed by his officers that the next time his unit was in the line, they were to take no prisoners: "shoot the bastards or bayonet them."[36] Barlow Whiteside, a graduate of McGill University and, at the time of the crucifixion rumour, working in a field hospital, shared his rage with his sister, to whom he wrote of the supposed act carried out "in cold blood, a form of death to which the most debauched murderer would think too hideous."[37] In the end, there is no evidence to suggest that the crucifixion occurred, but enough Canadians believed it had happened for many of them to think twice about offering mercy to the Germans.[38] The only way to address such barbarity, Whiteside insisted to his sister, was to "exterminate the enemy."[39]

RUMOURS WERE A COPING MECHANISM to make sense of the uncontrollable swirl of chaos at the front. But there was meaning in many of these rumours and they often reflected the soldiers' fears and concerns. "We hear the Germans now have a gas that clogs rifle and machine guns, so that they cannot be fired," wrote Major Agar Adamson of the PPCLI in April 1916. He added, sensibly, "This may be a fairy tale."[40] It was, but there was a continuous anxiety in the trenches, fed and passed along by rumours, that the enemy would unleash some new terror weapon.

Poison gas was a most terrifying weapon, largely because it seemed so alien. Soldiers could well understand bullets or shrapnel, but poison gas—which corrupted the lungs, the eyes, and with later variants, the genitals—was even more fearsome. This was not "fair" war, in which soldiers fought soldiers; instead, science was weaponized and unleashed to kill anonymously.[41] Rumours spread about new gasses that made the soldiers' eyes and fingers fall off upon exposure, while other tales circulated about chemical agents that shot out "electric waves destroying everything" in their path.[42] Perhaps Canadian infantrymen could be excused for imagining other super weapons when their own rumour mill had been accurate in unmasking the pending arrival, in the early fall of 1916, of great metal beasts that looked like caterpillars and had the odd name of "tanks."[43]

Some rumours were a tangible representation of transgressive behaviour. In a war where written words were censored, where soldiers could be punished for looking at an officer the wrong way or jailed for damaging their own bodies through self-inflicted wounds, there was space for subversiveness in oral communication.[44] Discipline and control were an essential part of the army and were integral to functioning military units. But rumours could not be controlled; nor could they be curtailed. They were a form of resistance. Yet instead of wielding them to bring about sedition or mutiny, the rank and file used them as a means to push back against the oppression of their own voices and actions by creating their own narratives, fantastic as these may sometimes have been.[45] The army high command seems to have tolerated rumours in the way they allowed grousing. "Officers are very leery if there is no grumbling going on because they think there is something afoot," wrote Canadian infantryman John MacKenzie, expressing a sentiment held by both the rank and file and officers. "As long as there's grumbling, and complaining," Mackenzie observed, "it's a good symptom."[46] Rumours created a space for communication between the leaders and the led, much like other forms of soldiers' culture, with attuned officers able to gauge the morale of the men through the circulating stories, especially those that diminished the high command or were laced with fury.

For much of the war, rumours had circulated about how First Contingent men—soldiers who had been overseas the longest and whose numbers were steadily thinning—deserved an extended leave to Canada. In rumour after rumour, leave was "promised" to the men, and each time it proved to be an illusion. A growing sense of anger germinated as a result of these seemingly broken promises. *The Iodine Chronicle*, a soldiers' newspaper, noted, "There is a restlessness among the boys, and here and there one sees small groups of soldiers gathered, and in deep discussion. No, you are wrong, it isn't revolution, but the rumour has gone forth that the remainder of the old first are going to have leave to Canada, and they are telling what General -------'s batsman and Colonel ------'s groom said that they were told by the boss."[47] In early 1918, Sir Arthur Currie, the Canadian Corps commander, acted on the rumours, granting leave to several hundred of the longest-serving men in desperate need of a break.[48]

Following the armistice on November 11, 1918, two Canadian divisions were selected to be a part of the Army of Occupation in Germany. Anxious to go home, the troops were quarrelsome and receptive to rumours. There was no easy solution to the demobilization problems, and Currie and his generals tried to keep the soldiers busy with sports and educational classes.[49] Still, the soldiers grumbled, and especially about Currie. According to the rumours circulating among the quarrelsome troops, the commander had sacrificed his men in the bloody Hundred Days campaign, volunteering them for every battle, and all in the name of elevating his reputation among the British. The casualties in the Hundred Days—which rose to more than 45,000—were proof, it seemed, of Currie's wasteful and indifferent nature.[50] Bored and angry soldiers could look around and see how few of their mates were still with them and how many had been buried in shallow graves. Victor Odlum, the respected commander of the 11th Infantry Brigade, observed worriedly to a politician in early 1919 that the rumours were rife throughout the camps: "Sir Arthur, in order to acquire honour for himself, had sacrificed men needlessly, and some of them were very bitter on this score. . . . In short, they charged him with having no regard for the lives of his men."[51] These accusations were not just the result of a nefarious group of conspirators seeking advantage or revenge. Some of Currie's own soldiers believed, added to, and spread the stories that undermined their general.[52]

Rumours had power in the Canadian Corps. The subversive gossip and idle chatter snowballed, in this case, to a systematic assault on Currie's reputation. Though the rumours were inaccurate, they reflected a deeper anger among Canadian soldiers over the perceived spearhead role of the Corps in the final months of the war. The battles during this period had forged an elite reputation for the Canadians, but at the cost of tens of thousands of casualties. During the war, there were few organized attempts by the army to suppress the many rumours about Currie's callousness. And after the war, when they rose to a level of damaging ferocity against the corps commander, it was too late, and the rumours about Currie entered into the lasting memory of the war.

THE SOLDIERS' APPETITE FOR RUMOURS and knowledge was insatiable. From the scandalous to the scurrilous, from the monstrous to the mundane, speculative and sophomoric rumours circulated through the trench system, passed from man to man and from unit to unit. While many rumours seemed beneath contempt for experienced men—especially the persistent talk of leave being imminent or the end of the war being only a final push away—other wish-fulfillment rumours had remarkable tenacity. Most rumours had more bark than bite, although some certainly had sharp teeth, as witnessed by the rumours that inspired the execution of prisoners as retribution for the supposedly crucified Canadian, or the nasty gossip that damaged Sir Arthur Currie's reputation.

A reflection of the soldiers' closed culture, rumours often sprang from casual conversations, shared gossip, and unbridled wish-fulfillment. Soldiers were forced to turn to one another to understand the unfolding events of the war that not only shaped their lives but could very well extinguish them, too. Rumours reflected the need of soldiers to make sense of their strange world in times of crisis and unending tension, and they were a crucial part of their society.

CHAPTER 6

"SOMEWHERE IN FRANCE"

Lieutenant Clifford Wells was an atypical soldier as he held a master's degree and had completed a year of study towards a doctorate of philosophy. Wells served as a lieutenant in several infantry units and read voraciously in the trenches, often requesting books, magazines, and novels from his family in Canada. He was different from the majority of his comrades in arms in the breadth and depth of his reading, but, like most of the men at the front, he used writing as a cathartic release and as a way to order his thoughts. As he noted in one letter, "You ask about my diary. I will send it home at the end of the year, if you will send me one for 1917. My diary is just a brief record of where I am, and what I am doing. My letters are the fullest record of my experiences. Many things I cannot write about, but will describe when I get home."[1] Killed on April 28, 1917, in the aftermath of the Vimy battle, Wells never came home. While there were more than 61,000 Canadians who did not make it back to tell their stories, the living and the dead left traces of their war experiences in the form of letters, diaries, poetry, and prose.

In an age before instant communication, letters were the only means for soldiers to communicate over long distances. Most Canadian soldiers, unlike their British counterparts, did not have a chance to see their loved ones when they went on periodic leave to Britain. And so, clever phrases and stirring imagery were an important means of sharing stories and making sense of the war, as soldiers, families, and friends traded letters across the Atlantic. While more than half of the CEF had not reached a grade-six level of education, and thousands of the men were illiterate, soldiers of all education levels usually put enormous care into their letters. Poetry was also an important outlet for many men, allowing for evocative word-pictures to convey emotions and experience, and poems were often quoted in letters. And yet not all experiences were shared with those who waited at home. In a world where lives were ended abruptly and violently, some soldiers felt compelled to keep their thoughts private, but expressing themselves in diaries also allowed these soldiers to leave a record of their war service. Others were more dedicated or ambitious and wrote about their war lives in long-form stories, usually after being wounded at the front and being discharged to Canada. Their memoirs were sometimes published for a broader audience during the war, while others remained buried in desk drawers for decades. Though the sword remained mightier than the pen, and the shell trumped all, words mattered to the soldiers. The written word played a key role in their lives as it normalized their experiences, allowed them to stay in touch with friends and family, eased some of the boredom, and documented the momentous events through which they lived. This print record reveals much about the soldiers' secret society and culture.

ONE OF THE HIGH COMMAND'S more unenforceable orders decreed that no soldier was to keep a diary for fear of providing the enemy with usable intelligence. The directive was widely

Soldiers wrote tens of millions of letters during the war, while countless others kept diaries.

ignored, and countless soldiers, from Sir Douglas Haig, the commander in chief of the British forces, to the lowest rankers, recorded their experiences at the front. Their diary entries ranged from the mundane to the sensational, and along with letters and sketches, these personal accounts documented the war and revealed the inner lives of the soldiers.

Most soldiers used small journals that could be easily stored in a pack or in one of the soldier's service dress uniform's many pockets. Writing under the faint glow of candlelight at night or during a daytime quiet period, soldiers committed their personal thoughts to the small pages. These entries ranged from a few words a day to long, descriptive missives that spilled out over several days, with additional spidery script running up and down page margins.

Each diary reflected the individual character of its author and his daily experiences. Class and education didn't determine the type of entry, with some officers and generals scribbling only a few daily notes while the rank and file could sometimes produce long, descriptive passages. Lieutenant Harry McCleave of the 13th Battalion noted in his little book, "This diary is merely a brief account for the purpose of aiding to remember places and dates afterwards. No attempt is made to give details, impressions etc."[2] McCleave kept the diary for about six months until he was shot in the arm and suffered a compound fracture of the leg on October 8, 1916, while fighting on the Somme. The twenty-four-year-old who had turned down a Rhodes Scholarship to enlist died two days later from complications.

Private Donald Fraser of the 31st Battalion decided to keep a journal after watching a friend recording the events of the war in a small book. "I saw him jot down particulars in a notebook and promptly thought that I would do likewise, notwithstanding that it was contrary to regulations." The friend later lost interest, with Fraser speculating, "probably like most he thought it of more importance to devote his whole time to the art of keeping alive than looking for copy."[3] Private Fraser found solace in the writing regime and he kept a detailed account until his severe wounding at Passchendaele in November 1917. Many soldiers turned to writing as a means of disconnecting from the daily tribulations of the war, even if for only a few minutes. The intimate experience of writing in a diary brought some calm to those who kept them. A young James Robert Johnston, who was only eighteen when he enlisted from Notre Dame, New Brunswick, and who served with the infantry, machine-gunners, and transport, observed, "My diary was, largely, a means of escape from the war."[4]

A diary was a written record of all aspects of the soldiers' distinct society, from the quality of food to the trials of combat. High-level strategy was rarely mentioned in them, except for the latest rumour about when the war might end. The weather was of more than passing interest to men who were, for the most part, homeless and living with the elements. Writing about the weather also hearkened back to a prewar life when people talked about such things in everyday chat as opposed to spending every moment fearing for their lives.

William McLellan, who enlisted from the University of Alberta in 1916 and was serving at the front with the mounted rifles by the next year, wrote home about his diary, noting, "I've kept my diary up to date. Its getting to be a pretty interesting epistal [*sic*] now. . . . If you still have those other diarys of Mine, keep them, will you, so that I can fill mine in when I get back."[5] McLellan started his diary as a way to pass the time, but over several months it grew to be a full and rich story of his wartime experience. He survived the Western Front and returned home with his war record and his record of war. McLellan, like many diarists, kept at his work because of the expectation that he would one day be able to use it to reflect back on his time overseas. In that sense, the diary was a labour of hope: soldiers kept it with the aim of surviving to read and reread it someday. Carman H. Thornton of the 2nd Battalion, from Woodstock, Ontario, shed light on his own motivation, asserting, "I am beginning this diary for two reasons. First that I may derive some pleasure reading it when my soldier days are over or if anything ever happens to me and it is lucky enough to reach home, the folks might like to read it."[6] To keep their diaries safe, most soldiers sent their prized writings home when they were completed at the end of each year, the books stained with mud, grime, and water. Almost all diarists provided a forwarding address in their diary so that it could be sent to their next of kin if they were killed. It was not meant to be buried with them.

Some soldiers used their diary as a last letter, leaving a record in case they should go under. In April 1917, Private Jack McClung of the PPCLI was nineteen years old and about to go into his first battle at Vimy Ridge. Son of the activist and author Nellie McClung, he had enlisted against his mother's wishes and he now faced the grave uncertainty of combat. McClung confided his thoughts about the moment to his diary, writing in pencil in one of the tunnels carved into the chalk beneath the ridge: "Easter Sunday night & we go over the top tomorrow morn at 5:30. I guess a fellow has more sensations & feelings in this short night than in his whole life. . . . Each of us is trying to hide the real state of his mind. I know how much I am thinking about Mother, Dad and all the kids."[7] McClung's inner turmoil reflected that of tens of thousands of Canadians who agonized in the final hours before attacking fortress Vimy. McClung survived the war, although with a serious wound. Thousands of others were not so lucky. Private Donald Gordon marched with the 8th Battalion and had lied about his age when he enlisted against his parents' wishes. In April 1915 a sniper's bullet took his life. He was only eighteen. Among his personal possessions was a Bible bearing the inscription "Goodbye, Mother, Forgive me."[8]

"I AM WRITING THIS FROM a forward line where daily the price of blood is paid," noted Sergeant Thomas Clark Lapp from Brighton, Ontario, who had left behind his job at a printer.[9] He survived a gunshot wound to the abdomen shortly after writing this letter to his wife, and was returned to her three years after leaving the

Letters, postcards, and care packages from home kept up the soldiers' morale at the front.

country. By the summer of 1917, the British Expeditionary Force was sending eight million letters home per week, and Canadians posted around eighty-five million letters during the course of the war.[10] With the letters criss-crossing the Atlantic, replies following inquiries and then sparking new questions, letters were a lifeline to keep those overseas connected to those at home.[11] It could take two to three weeks for a letter to travel from a soldier's hand to his home, and just as long for the return message to make its way back.

Letters from afar were absolutely essential for sustaining morale. "You can't understand how much mail does mean to us over here," wrote Claude Williams to his father. Having finished his second year as a medical student at the University of Toronto before enlisting, Williams was gassed and awarded the Military Cross at the front, but survived the war.[12] Soldiers needed to know that they were remembered by those at home. And in turn, wives, children, and elderly parents were constantly on the minds of those overseas. Lieutenant George Ormsby wrote to his wife and two children, "I am dreadfully homesick and I am longing to be home with you and the children again. . . . Every time I go to sleep I dream that the war is over and that I am back again home. For comfort I read your letters and look at your pictures and I can tell you they are a great comfort to me."[13] Ormsby's war ended on the Somme with a terrible wound, but he returned home to his family and went on to build a life as a fruit farmer in the Okanagan Valley.

Even as citizen-soldiers were remade into trench warriors, almost all retained a deep connection to their communities and to prewar interests that continued into their service—pursuits that included everything from sports to politics to culture. In their letters, farmers wanted to know how their crops or livestock were faring. And all soldiers had an interest in hearing about which young men from their street, town, or village had enlisted, and which of them were shirking their duties.

In addition to wondering about home, there was a more powerful sentiment on display. Nostalgia was a driving emotion for every soldier as men looked for anything that reminded them of the lives they left behind. Dominion chewing gum, tobacco, and newspapers were all snatched up when the YMCA or Salvation Army received shipments for sale behind the lines. The link to their past lives offered a mooring of sorts. Soldiers dreamed of returning home. Private Evelyn Elgood, a prewar telegraph operator who served as a signaller in early 1917, remembered how he had put in eighteen months of service by early 1917, "and had very few illusions or ambitions left—except that I might someday get back to the Salmon River Valley in British Columbia, and farm. A far off Dream."[14] He made it home, returning with a new wife whom he had married while on leave from the front.

Though letters provided emotional sustenance, it was not easy at the front to summon the will to settle oneself down and write. There were constant trench duties, from standing sentry to engaging in back-breaking manual labour. Officers had less hard labour but were responsible for the men and thus carried all of the weight of command. Everyone was sleep-deprived and worn down, and often a lassitude settled over men who focused all their energy on survival. Dr. Charles Willoughby from Cookstown, Ontario, who served in the Royal Army Medical Corps in Mesopotomia and then on the Western Front, believed that "The army spirit unconsciously gets hold of you and you rest content to do as little as possible and all the times you are forgetting the little bit you ever did know."[15] Under such conditions, it was difficult for the men to fully concentrate on writing.

For other soldiers, there was a desire to explain what was happening to them, but they flailed at the task. William Muir, writing from a hospital to his mother after being wounded at Passchendaele, struggled to describe the trauma: "I can't write it down but hope to get back and will tell you then Mother, it is awful, awful, awful—ain't a name for it."[16] Capturing the bewildering, kaleidoscope-like experience of combat, with its howling terror and wild confusion, was especially difficult. Metaphors of trains or trucks out of control were used to describe the shellfire, while the sound of bullets whizzing through the air was compared to animal noises. Self-censorship hid other aspects of the truth, as soldiers failed to capture on the page what they saw, felt, and did. Others did not want to burden those at home with unnecessary worry. Almost always the sensory experience—the reek of the trenches, from the mounds of garbage, from unwashed men, and from rotting corpses—was absent from the letters. Often men chose not to document these grim experiences or perhaps grew used to such unpleasantries, with the masculine ideal of toughing out the hard bits a common trait among almost all the trench warriors.[17] "I cannot begin to describe the awfulness of war and wouldn't if I could," wrote Lieutenant Andrew Wilson to his wife in November 1917. He would survive the trials of war for a year before being wounded in the final months of the Hundred Days campaign, which allowed him to return to his wife and two children in Rosetown, Saskatchewan.[18]

And yet, many wrote to relieve the strain. "You needn't marvel at my being able to write seven pages or so about my first trip over the bags," remarked Armine Norris of Toronto to his mother. "I was bursting to tell someone about it. . . ."[19] Clearly, the transferring of pent-up emotions to the page could be a cleansing release. But after surviving a brush with death by artillery shelling, infantryman John Sudbury, who enlisted from Montreal at age twenty-one, told his loved ones, "I wrote an eight-page letter to you yesterday and on reading it prior to posting I decided to destroy it on account of its gloom."[20] Not all secrets from the front were communicated to those at home.

LETTER WRITING PRESENTED A CHALLENGE: a soldier had to gather his thoughts, find a dry spot, and secure paper. But to make matters worse, there was the added constraint of formal censorship. The problem for the rank and file was that almost all of their letters were read by their own officers, who were to ensure that they were not passing along information to their correspondents that might assist the enemy or undermine morale at home.[21] Conventional history says that the soldiers could not write anything for fear of stiff punishment; in reality, the censorship was sporadic at best. Officers disliked the time-consuming and invasive task of scrutinizing their men's correspondence, and reading fifty or more letters a day, with soldiers' chicken-scratch writing straining the eyes, led to much skimming or even wholesale abdication of the annoying chore. Some officers—usually those new to the front—followed the letter of the law, striking out certain passages with black markers or even cutting out offending sentences via delicate razor work, but most grew lax in their task. Others simply objected to the intrusive task. "I feel like a burglar reading all these young fellows letter's to their sweethearts and wives," wrote Lieutenant D.E. Macintyre of the 28th Battalion, a decorated and aggressive trench raider who worked for the Grand Trunk Pacific Railway before the war. "Some of them write really beautiful letters and I think they all write to someone at home."[22] The soldiers whose letters were being examined were even less pleased by the idea of the officers peeking into their intimate thoughts and confessions. In all cases, words were chosen carefully.

There were rare green envelopes—usually issued once or twice a month—that allowed soldiers to write more freely as they were excluded from censorship from one's officers, although the letters were occasionally opened further to the rear.[23] As in all things in the army, some soldiers were made an example of to discourage the great mass. Men who were caught leaking sensitive information were punished with docked pay or field punishment, and the consequences could be even worse if the battalion's commanding officer wanted to send a message. One form of punishment was to deny the entire battalion or unit the use of green envelopes, and to reveal the culprit to the disgruntled men. Precisely what type of information was allowed in the green letters was often unclear,

CHRISTMAS, 1917: SOMEWHERE IN FRANCE.

"Somewhere in France," states this cartoon in a Canadian trench newspaper.

although soldiers knew not to mention their unit name or location. The phrase "somewhere in France" became an inside joke, both during the war and afterwards, and seemed to capture the sense that soldiers were lost in the maelstrom of battle.

The limits to what the Canadians overseas were allowed to reveal to those at home were mirrored by the soldiers' correspondents, who often shielded the men from the hard truths of the war's effect on their lives. Families struggled with a father or son away; wives and children were desperately lonely, sad, and worried; but most of the soldiers' families buried the reality of such trials and offered supportive and positive messages in their letters overseas. Soldiers were also voluntarily guarded in what they wrote, choosing to reveal different things to different correspondents. In a letter that Garnet Dobbs posted to his sister, he asked her to keep some of the dangers he described from his wife, noting, "My one and only reason for not telling her is to keep her from worrying and I know she does worry over even what little she knows from the tone of her letters. . . . I can't explain the situation [at the front] by writing like I could if I was talking to you."[24] Soldiers frequently shared with siblings their distress about being infested with lice, but would refrain from telling their mothers. There is also evidence from surviving letters to suggest that sons wrote differently to fathers, and certainly to brothers in uniform. Such letters were more revealing and often more masculine in tone and description than those to female recipients. Canadians in uniform were not shy about warning an enthusiastic sibling not to enlist. In the aftermath of the Somme battles in December 1916, Toronto-born Jay Batiste, through an intermediary, urged his younger brother, Bruce, to stay home. "Tell him he is too young to last long out here and that one from our family is plenty and not to dare enlist even as a bugler. I would tell about this in stronger lingo only am afraid of the censor."[25] The elder Batiste was killed at Vimy Ridge in April 1917.

ONE OF *The Listening Post*'s poignant cartoons, from the April 1918 issue, depicted a soldier in a series of near-death encounters, with shells and mortar bombs dropping around him, mines beneath him, and bullets slashing the air above. A final panel showed the soldier struggling to find the words to describe his experiences in a letter, with a caption underneath: "Those hairbreadth escapes we were to relate in that next letter home invariably end up in the bald language of the f.s.p. [field service postcard]—'I am quite well, etc.'"[26] Here, the phrase "I am quite well" serves as an ironic comment on the difficulty soldiers had in finding the words to describe their unique experiences, but it is also a direct nod to the field service postcard, known as a "whiz bang" after the German high explosive shells that seemingly arrived out of nowhere. The f.s.p., as it was sometimes known, was a simple prewritten card on which soldiers struck out words to deliver a message. These cards were a quick way to reassure families and friends that a soldier was still in the land of the living. As one Canadian gunner noted in a longer letter, "I have sent several 'Whizz-Bangs' so you will know I have been OK."[27] The cards were a stopgap measure in between letters and they were commonly sent after a battle by exhausted soldiers. Samuel Honey was a prewar teacher born in Conn, Ontario, who went by "Lew" and served as an enlisted man and then a lieutenant with the 78th Battalion. He would be awarded the Military Medal, DCM, and Victoria Cross before his death in battle at age twenty-four on September 30, 1918. Two years before his end, he wrote to

Those hairbreadth escapes we were to relate in that next letter home invariably end up in the bald language of the f.p.c.— I am quite well, etc.

his family on November 5, 1916, "I won't have this [his letter] ready for the censor until late tonight and it won't get to the postman until tomorrow. The F.S. card ('whiz bang' some of the boys call it because it's short, sharp and much to the point) doesn't have to go through such formality."[28]

Soldiers completed the f.s.p. by striking off preprinted lines that did not apply, and no extra notes could be added or the card would be destroyed. The first line consisted of "I am quite well," the second line was "I have been admitted into hospital," and the third line read "I am being sent down to the base." Generally, if all was as usual, the soldier was left with the option "I am quite well." The whiz-bang was well suited for the illiterate, but the standardization of response left much unstated. There was no entry for "I am terrified of what lies in store" or "I have survived the battle, but I may never be the same." Soldiers nonetheless accepted these restrained communication tools, but seized them, too, as a target ripe for satire. The whiz-bang phrase "I am quite well" was repeated slyly among the soldiers, with suitable rhetoric, relish, and irony. A man up to his waist in mud, soaking wet, and being helped out of a sinkhole, upon being asked by his saviour, "You all right, mate?" might give the weary response, "I am quite well." In irreverent gallows humour, D.E. Macintyre was informed by folks at home that the local paper in Moose Jaw had reported him killed in battle. In his diary, he wondered if he should send out a field service postcard saying, "I was killed in action but am quite well."[29]

Soldiers at the front were also enthusiastic collectors and senders of pictorial postcards. The soldier-as-tourist had much to choose from when he left the line, with an enormous market operating in the cities and towns to feed the soldiers' desire for material to send home. Even closer to the front, among the ruins of

A field service postcard, in which the soldiers struck off the passages that did not apply to them.

NOTHING is to be written on this side except the date and signature of the sender. Sentences not required may be erased. If anything else is added the post card will be destroyed.

I am quite well.

I have been admitted into hospital
{ *sick* } *and am going on well.*
{ *wounded* } *and hope to be discharged soon.*

I am being sent down to the base.

I have received your { *letter dated* ___ / *telegram* „ ___ / *parcel* „ ___ }

Letter follows at first opportunity.

I have received no letter from you
{ *lately.* / *for a long time.* }

Signature only.

Date

[Postage must be prepaid on any letter or post card addressed to the sender of this card.]

(92088). Wt. W3497-293 2,250m. 3/16 J. J. K. & Co., Ltd.

A comedic field service postcard published in The Dead Horse Corner Gazette.

One of the drollest things of the war, says the *Windsor Magazine*, is a field-service post-card—" amended form "—which a wag produced " to save platoon commanders and censors much labour and searching of heart." It is arranged like this—to be crossed out at will, of course :—

My { own / owner / ownest } { dear / dearest / darling / duck } { babs / girlie / sweetheart / wife / sister / mother } } in-law

I am { fairish / pretty well / in the pink ! }

I am / We are } up to { my / our } { ankles / calves / knees / waists / necks / eyes } in { slush / puddle / water / snow / garbage / dust }

Have { not / just } received your { card / letter / parcel / box / packing-case }

Belgian and French towns, postcard hawkers manned makeshift carts from which they sold their wares.[30] The postcard was a popular form of communication before the war, and it was estimated that in France some 125 million of the quick mailers were printed in 1910 alone, and that in Germany during the war some 9 million were printed each month.[31]

There were thousands of different types of cards. Images of war-shattered French cathedrals and towns showed the destruction wrought by the Hun. Other postcards were sentimental in tone and depicted wistful soldiers pining for a girlfriend or a mother. The wartime culture was reflected in many postcards, even if their full meaning and humour is in some cases obscured a hundred years later. What is to be made, for example, of the infantilization of soldiers, as was done in a popular series of cards depicting little boys and girls dressed as soldiers and nurses and engaged in drill or sassy talk? Humorous postcards were the most popular types of cards, judging by how many have survived to this day. They portrayed sausage-eating Germans, fat and ugly in their oversized helmets, as bumbling fools or degenerate barbarians. In Belgium, Canadians were drawn to reproductions of Mannequin Piss, the

A postcard from British soldier-artist Fergus Mackain's series, "Sketches of Tommy's Life." It reads: "Sometimes you get so far in the rear, marching in, you are good as lost when you come to a spot where different trenches branch off."

Another of Mackain's "Sketches of Tommy's Life." It reads: "One of the bright spots in our life," as privates wait for a sergeant to issue rum.

boy of legend from centuries before who put out a bomb by urinating on it. His image was repurposed in this war as he sent a shower of urine on fleeing Germans. "Sketches of Tommy's Life," by British soldier-artist Fergus Mackain, depicted soldiers engaged in all manner of mundane and dangerous tasks at the front. This large series contained postcards featuring the importance of rum, letters, and leave, as well as those illustrating the simple everyday existence of soldiers. Pictures of French pin-up girls in lingerie were also prized, although they were perhaps more likely to be squirrelled away among a soldier's possessions than mailed.

Selecting the right card for a child or girlfriend was a brow-furrowing experience. An unknown Canadian who struggled with English wrote to his lady friend, Flo Reid of Galt, Ontario, on the back of a card depicting a newly married couple. In child-like language, he wrote, "This is us wen war is over and I can cum back to

A French postcard for soldiers to send to their sweethearts in Canada.

An English postcard of a British Tommy yearning for his girl at home. A stanza of a love song, "I Just Want You," is included on the card.

you."[32] The spelling might have been off, but the sentiment shone through. Other soldiers shyly sent postcards bearing images of loving couples or of a woman waiting for her man who had enlisted and gone overseas. Much was left unsaid in this suggestive card, although soldiers hoped the message was received. In this sense, postcards are a fitting metaphor for the soldiers' experience of the war, and an excellent representation of the soldiers' secret culture. The cards contained messages of love, hope, concern, and bravado—but they were also hard for civilians at home to decipher. A hundred words were not enough to shed much light on the trench experience, even when recipients tried to read between the lines.

THE TOMMIES in the trenches
And the men behind the guns,
In the lulls between the fighting
Find their inclination runs
To writing bits of poetry
Just to pass away the time.
So if you will kindly pardon
Us, we'll fill this page with rhyme.

Such was the cheerful sing-songy banter about poetry in the March 1916 edition of *The Brazier*, newspaper for the 3rd Canadian Infantry Brigade.[33] Poetry was an important form of expression in the late nineteenth and early twentieth centuries. It was estimated that 50,000 war poems were written around the world each day in August 1914, and more than 2,000 poets had their works published in Britain during the war.[34] The best-known English-language Great War poets, British officers Siegfried Sassoon and Wilfred Owen and Canadians John McCrae and Canon Frederick Scott, had Empire-wide fame, as they provided important insight into the war experience through their evocative language.

The rank and file emulated the famous officer-poets by penning their own poetry. Simple and sometimes clumsy rhyming informed much of their work, but the subject matter was inspired by and indeed born in the trenches. Most often this type of soldiers' doggerel focused on the small pleasures in the men's lives, the annoyances of senseless discipline, or the value of friendship, and it occasionally took a savage swipe at those in the rear. This verse offers a balance to some of the "high diction" poetry that has become iconic for representing the war, and the soldiers' poetry and trench doggerel offers another way to explore the closed soldiers' society.

Whether a unit was in the front lines or the rear areas, it was common for a few of its poets to stand and deliver. Many critics joked that one of the many casualties of the war was the finely crafted poem, as, for the most part, emotion overshadowed talent, but the soldiers' verse was part of the mass culture embraced by these warriors. Poetry was a means of connecting with other soldiers and with loved ones at home. The most gifted poets, as well as some with few gifts, were encouraged to publish in the trench newspapers as an outlet for their literary expression. Robert Hale, a British-born tradesman who had enlisted from Montreal, penned a touching poem to his girl, Alice, in a February 22, 1915, letter:

> Remember me is all I ask
> But if remembrance proves a task
> Forget me.[35]

This three-line poem captures much unstated worry, heartache, and love. Hale was wounded three times at the front and returned home to Alice. They married in 1920.

One of the more successful early war soldier poets was Frank Brown, a sergeant and sniper in the PPCLI. He put pen to paper upon his arrival in England and during his brief stint on the Western Front before he was killed in February 1915. His poems—characterized as "born in war"—were published as *Contingent*

Ditties and Other Soldier Songs of the Great War. Much of Brown's poetry was influenced by the songs of the day, which were a powerful influence on cultural expression. The preface to the small book characterized the verses as "sincere, strong, and musical," noting approvingly, "they are the sort of poems which appeal to the lettered and the unlettered alike. . . . Here are his poems, good honest stuff, brave in thought and patriotic in ideal, as befit a soldier of the Empire."[36] His patriotic verse "The Call" was typical fare:

> The Flag's in danger! needs there such a cry
> To rouse the loyal blood of England's sons?
> Must Englishmen be urged to take up arms
> And set their strength against marauding
> Huns?
> We need no other strength but Might of Right;
> The courage of a cause both just and dear
> No conscript rolls need we to swell the ranks.
> The British soldier is a volunteer.[37]

The Dead Horse Corner Gazette complemented Brown's poetry, noting that the "volume sounds the true note of Imperialism" and that it was "couched in the language the men of the Dominion best understand."[38] These were not cynical antiwar poems, although Brown was killed early in the war and perhaps his experiences would have been presented differently in his work had he survived. But it is rare to find the theme of disillusionment in soldiers' wartime poetry. In fact, the views of disillusioned war poets were always in the minority, even if these poets' work was embraced more strongly in the late 1920s and then again after the 1960s.

Private Victor Swanston, a First Contingent man from View Haven, Saskatchewan, was an enthusiastic writer of doggerel. On July 30, 1915, he wrote, unconcerned about French diacritics, the poem "Apres La Guerre":

When to the prairie you get back,
With not a drink in your old shack,
You'll miss your rum and "Cognac" —
Apres la Guerre.
All the "fag" tobacco you buy,
And cigarettes, won't satisfy,
Unless they're rolled in "Riz la Croix" —
Apres la Guerre.
When some friend strays in for tea,
You'll say, "Old Chap, du pain finnis."
But call around again "Compres"?
Apres la Guerre.
Your Staff of Life while you're out there
Will be a simple Bill o' Fare
Of fried sage hens, and "Pommes de terre."
Apres la Guerre.
There's one thing, though, you'll miss each day,
When breaking "bones" or stacking hay,
And that's the old Estaminets—
Apres la Guerre.[39]

Swanston's poem—an homage to the wartime pleasure of cigarettes, rum, *estaminets* (local eateries), and comradeship—is a prediction voiced to his mates that even as they wished to see the end of the war, those who survived would look back from their future hard lives on farms and lumber camps and realize that there were indeed redeeming aspects of service overseas. This poem was an important celebration of comradeship and future nostalgia, and a declaration that would prove prescient for many veterans in the years to come.

Infantryman John Sudbury offered a typical soldiers' poem, an ode to "Our Pal—the Sandbag."

The sandbag is a wondrous thing
To us in France today
He's used for every kind of job
In every kind of way.

A suit of clothes he makes complete
When your uniform is wet
And if he's stuffed with dirt or sand
Makes a dandy parapet.

We use him every night, you know
To bring the rations up
And afterwards as tablecloth
On which to have our "sup".

If torn to shreds and greased a bit
With candle fat, He's fine
On which to boil a cup of tea,
A stove for any time . . .

There's one I've always near me
Used as a refuse bin

I hope 'twill come in handy
To put the Kaizer in.[40]

Sudbury noted that the poem was compiled in the trenches while he was on sentry duty a mere thirty metres from the German lines. The poem, topical and funny, made its way around the battalion, and Sudbury acquired the nickname "Poet." One might smile at the absurdity of a poem being written to a sandbag, but this multipurpose object was one of the most common things in the soldiers' lives, and its presence often meant the difference between life and death.

The soldiers' poetry reflected their distinctive society and culture in the trenches. It was poetry of the unnatural made natural: of men forced to stand in mud and rub whale oil on their feet to keep their toes from rotting off. This was a war in which rats scurried over trench dwellers' bodies and faces, the same rats that ate the rotting flesh of men lying in the open only dozens of metres away. Much of the poetry written in this bizarre, terrifying environment was juvenile and simple, but it reflected the subjects that mattered to the rank and file.

"The Pardon Came Too Late" chronicles the execution of a soldier by firing squad. The unfortunate man is sentenced to death and shot by his comrades, with the pardon from the high command arriving only after bullets end his life. The pathos-filled twist at the end is that the executed soldier deserted to bring comfort to his lonely mother.[41] The poem is undistinguished except that it openly addressed the issue of executions: in the course of the war, twenty-five Canadians were shot by firing squad for the offence of desertion.[42] *The Iodine Chronicle* printed that the author, Private John Fannon, a driver on a horse team, dropped out of school at a young age and travelled North America with a circus. "He cannot read or write," observed the paper, "although he has a wonderful memory, for he can sing songs by the hour, some of which he makes up himself."[43] The poem was evidently written down by another soldier as Fannon recited it aloud.

Charles Olson, a prewar reporter and rancher in Alberta who served with the 3rd Battalion, penned hundreds of poems and informal "sing-songs," as he called them. In his memoirs—in which he called himself Private Kenjack Pamjoy, a pseudonym based on the names of his four children—Olson observed, "The almost instantaneous fame of Colonel Mc[C]rae's 'In Flanders Fields' brought to every man at the front an irresistible urge to burst into song." As a consequence, "Men who had ample desire but little aptitude to write verse" turned to Olson to supply the goods. Writing came easy to him and he sold his poems and songs for a few francs. His "sing-songs" were poems or songs that he composed for men who desired to partake in the informal soldiers' get-togethers behind the lines. As Olson explained, "This interesting war-time institution enabled officers to mingle with their men and thus helped to sustain the morale of both. There was an urgent need for talent. Piano players were invaluable, while musical talent of any description was eagerly sought. Men who could sing won instant popularity, and as popularity creates competition, there was always a demand for something different. Everyone looked for good parodies on popular songs. . . ." Limericks were especially popular and sometimes the word play was accompanied by music. At parties, one man would start with a song, and he would be followed by others, with each succeeding comrade having his turn to sing. "Those who could not sing often volunteered to recite some dramatic poem while the pianist played a subdued accompaniment." The best-known poems of Rudyard Kipling and Yukon poet Robert Service were recited frequently, but Olson was called upon to create new ones, and perhaps unsurprisingly, "While melodrama with plenty of pathos was in demand, the general preference was a judicious mixture of humour and drama in keeping with life at the front."[44]

The vibrant and ever-shifting oral culture of stories and poems in the trenches was occasionally captured in letters, diaries, and journals. Sergeant John Flock enlisted with his father, Robert, from Weyburn, Saskatchewan, in January 1916 and was wounded at Vimy.[45] He kept a memory book in which he inscribed his favourite poems and stories from the front, as well as inspirational thoughts, mixing gallows humour with pathos and sentimentality. He recorded Kipling's "Recessional" next to some doggerel called "Click of the Chips on the Table," a poem about gambling. Some of the material is his own, including a poem, "The Men of the Rank and File":

> Who are going to win this world wide scrap?
> And change the face of Europe's map
> For dignity don't care a rap?
> The men of the Rank and File.
> Who love their little bit of fun,
> And fight the harder when tis done?
> Who grin when some clerk calls out "Shun?"
> The men of the Rank and File.
> Who left their happy homes to fight,
> While cold-feet, slackers sat back tight?
> Who'd face the devil for the right?
> The men of the Rank and File.

Flock's attempt at poetry is infused with anger as he condemns the slackers at home and exalts the soldiers' service in defence of their homeland. This was exactly the type of writing that resonated with soldiers.

Poetry entertained, and it was a part of the soldiers' mental shield. Robert James Manion, a medical officer with the 21st Battalion and a future leader of the Conservative Party back in Canada, described his faith in poetry, noting, "My favourite pastime while wandering through the trenches was to quote to myself all the poetry which I had ever learned, finding that with one line of a poem once known one could gradually by repeating it bring back the whole poem almost perfectly from my subconscious memory." Manion, who was well educated and read voraciously at the front, observed that the trenches could be "the most unpoetical of experiences," but that he still found solace in words.[46] The poets of the CEF were not historians, but more than a few sought to mark their place in the war. Soldiers knew all too well how a shell or bullet might cut short their lives. Their poetry was testimony from the front, bearing witness to service and forming a legacy of Canada's war experience. While few versifiers achieved fame beyond the bounds of their unit, the substance of the soldiers' poetry remains an important window into their lives and culture, and another means by which to understand the secret history of the soldiers.

"I DON'T LAY CLAIM TO being much of a writer, and up till now, I never felt the call to write anything." So wrote Alexander McClintock, a CEF combat veteran. McClintock was a twenty-two-year-old American from Lexington, Kentucky, who crossed the border to enlist in Montreal in November 1915 with the 87th Battalion. In his 1917 published memoirs, *Best o' Luck*, McClintock recounted much about the soldiers' experience, including some of the brutal aspects of close-quarters combat and the terror of long-range shelling. His war ended on the Somme with twenty-two wounds to his lower body. He recuperated for many months, was in tremendous pain, and was haunted by his war experience, but McClintock wished to get his record of service straight and to tell his story. "I believed that my experience was worth relating," he explained, "and I thought the matter published in the newspapers by the professional writers sort of missed the essentials and lacked the spirit of the 'ditches' in a good many ways despite its excellent literary style."[47] McClintock also had ghosts to exorcise. His writing might have alleviated some of the trauma he suffered, but he committed suicide on June 28, 1918, exactly one year after he was discharged from the CEF.

A number of memoirs were published during the war to take advantage of the hunger of those on the home front to understand the soldiers' experience. British soldier Ian Hay's 1915 memoir *The First Hundred Thousand* was a massive hit throughout the Empire and sparked many more soldiers' accounts. Hay was a prewar novelist and a decorated soldier, and his wry account of the war revealed a jaunty, see-it-through attitude. Other writers mimicked his prose, while some wrote to correct the ultra-patriotic nonsense of the journalists who sought to prop up morale rather than to reveal the harsh realities at the front. This first generation of writing from the coalface of battle presented some of the hard truths of the trenches, although no soldier openly questioned the war in the midst of the titanic death struggle, with untold numbers of comrades killed and many more still fighting in the line.[48] In Canada, over 200 wartime and postwar memoirs were published, and many more were written for family and friends only.[49]

Another popular genre of postwar writing was soldiers' published letters. Families sometimes reprinted their loved ones' letters in local papers, while some soldiers had their collected letters published in book form. Lieutenant Armine Norris, a machine-gun officer, posted a letter to his father in which he described almost being killed on the Somme and the sight of the shocking rows of dead who were caught by machine-gun fire. Yet he also observed, "I'd like to go over the top again, Dad, even knowing the hell that follows, for it's the crowning experience of a lifetime. It's madness, of course, but it's glorious."[50] Norris was killed during the war, but his experience was captured in his collected, published letters, where he depicted the war in all its lunacy and glory.[51]

SOLDIERS ADMITTED TO NOT KNOWING much about the strategic direction of the war, but they knew of things that we can never know. All were troubled by the tragedy at the front, by the events they witnessed, and by what they did to survive. Putting these experiences down on paper in personal diaries or letters relieved some who suffered with their thoughts. Communicating with those left behind in Canada sustained morale and restored the fighting spirit, and almost all soldiers relied on missives from their families and friends. "You cannot imagine how, over in this land, a letter from home cheers and encourages," remarked Private Frank Cousins, a former teacher. "Without it one feels lost, and, as it were, stranded in a sea of desolation."[52] Cousins survived the war, studied to become a lawyer, and worked as a legal partner with future prime minister John Diefenbaker, another war veteran, before dying in his sleep in June 1927.

The surviving Great War diaries, poetry, letters, and memoirs reveal soldier-witnesses grappling with the war and with how to wrestle it onto the page. There was a rich print culture from soldiers who spent large parts of the war dodging both shells and the sergeant-major. Writing in the war zone was no easy task for even the most articulate of soldiers, but their hard-won accounts provide insight into suffering and survival. In September 1917, Private John Davidson, a prewar farmer, wrote to his fiancée, Grace Wells, in Glengarry County, Ontario, "Grace, there is heaps I would like to tell of my travels the last few days but cannot here. Will try to tell you in the years to come."[53] The gunner in the 72nd Battery made it home. Tens of thousands never did, and many more who returned never found the words to talk about their war, but their print culture survived in many cases to reveal the inner life of soldiers and provide a word-picture of their secret society.

CHAPTER 7

TRENCH NEWSPAPERS

Under the heading "The Ancient Order of Lead Swingers," Private C.B. Eversick put out a call in the pages of *The Listening Post* for "all experts at swinging the lead"—an old nautical term for a sailor who tried to avoid hard labour by faking his work. The goal was for these soldiers to band together to share ideas in order to trick the medical officers into letting them escape from the front. The author, going under the moniker "Eversick," invited soldiers to join him and other club members, including Lord Windhupp, Sir Verey Badheart, and the Duke of Wellinrear. "All windy soldiers are welcome," the ad read, in the club of cheaters, fakers, and scared soldiers. The group's hope was to pool their talents to help one another to "outwit telepathic pill-throwers" (the medical officers); to "concentrate expert ingenuity for the purpose of discovering diseases and ailments hitherto unknown to medical science"; and to discover the place and units where "sympathetic army doctors (just out) and the cushiest Field Ambulances (newly organized) were situated."[1] This anti-heroic "call to arms" brought these artful dodgers from the shadows into the open, even if the article was clearly written with tongue firmly in cheek. And yet *The Listening Post* was the most popular and widely circulated Canadian soldiers' trench newspaper. How could this treasonous club even be mentioned—let alone admired—in a paper that was read by regimental officers and even generals? This type of content was far different—dangerously so, some might complain—from the heroic material presented in the civilian press that encouraged everyone to dig deep for the war effort. What, then, was the role of trench newspapers like *The Listening Post*?

Canadians before and during the war were a newspaper-reading people. In 1911, there were 143 daily newspapers in Canada and the average family read two and a half papers a day.[2] Soldiers carried this intense interest in print news into the service. From early in the war, British papers were sold along the Western Front, with *The Daily Express* having the highest circulation, followed by *The Daily Mail* and *The Daily Mirror*, while pictorial papers fed the public's appetite for a glimpse into the war.[3] French and Belgian refugees often purchased papers from dealers behind the lines and then peddled their wares to troops in the rearward areas, with cheeky children calling out their papers for sale within the range of shellfire. Worried soldiers were known to hand out gas masks to the young newspaper boys, and more than a few kids were safely squirrelled away in dugouts during bombardments, the sympathetic soldiers holding tight to the crying kids.

The Canadian and British newspapers tended to be aggressively patriotic in their tone, supporting the war effort and sustaining morale on the home front. There was no money to be made in doom-and-gloom predictions, and almost all the British newspaper barons were co-opted into the war effort, with most mainstream papers in English Canada taking a similarly supportive stand. There were few grey areas for the popular press to debate: every last sacrifice was needed against the barbarous Hun,

Children delivering fruit and newspapers to front-line Canadian soldiers.

and formal censorship ensured that truth was not the first consideration. The papers' jaunty prose was also underpinned by a message of hope: that the enemy was near collapse and that the heroic boys of the Empire would soon deliver victory.[4]

Front-line soldiers on both sides were often frustrated by newspaper accounts of the war. The infantry mired in the mud of Flanders or digging for their lives on the Somme knew from first-hand experience that the enemy was not on his last legs and that "one more push" would not lead to the enemy's surrender. The French soldiers had a revealing term for the patriotic propaganda in their papers: *bourrage de crâne*, or "skull stuffing."[5] It became common for those in uniform to warn family and friends back home that nothing could be trusted that had been printed in civilian society. "Don't believe all you read," Lawrence Rogers cautioned his wife in December 1915. "We don't."[6] Another Canadian soldier was more wistful about the relentlessly optimistic journalistic stories, remarking, "These newspaper accounts are sometimes very funny."[7] A third, Private Harold Peat, was scathing: "We boys read those editorials and letters, and wondered how sane men could waste time in writing such stuff, how sane men could set it in type and print it, and more than all we wondered how sane men could read it."[8]

Yet there was a paradox at play. The soldiers remained intimately connected to their loved ones at home and desperate for any information about the larger war effort. Many soldiers explained in their letters that they had no idea what was happening at the front, beyond their limited view in the trenches, and even then the rampant rumours made most information unreliable. Wilbert Gilroy, a prewar dentist in Winnipeg who served with the Canadian Dental Corps, optimistically told his mother in March 1916, "We have held our end up fairly well and the papers say we have regained some of our lost trenches," but he went on to note, ironically, "Although we are very close to the stirring scenes, and hear the noise, and see the results, yet we have to rely on the newspaper for actual information."[9] Officer Stanley Rutledge echoed Gilroy, lamenting, "We know little about how the war is going."[10]

THE INDEFATIGABLE LORD BEAVERBROOK, who had established an official photography, art, and film program to document the Canadian war experience in 1916, turned his hand the next year to issuing a daily newspaper, the *Canadian Daily Record* (*CDR*). Offering a summary of domestic and international news, and illustrated with official photos, the *CDR* circulated 17,500 copies daily (with an increase to 35,000 during the December 1917 federal election).[11] Sir Richard Turner, one of Canada's most senior generals, wrote in March 1917 that he felt the *CDR* was "a very interesting little paper and I am sure that the news it contains will be most welcome to the Canadian troops," but the newspaper was largely viewed as an official organ of the army.[12] The soldiers wanted something that was their own.

Soldiers responded to the unreliable home-front press or semi-official publications that spouted the "army line" by producing their own newspapers. These soldiers' papers were published in most of the armies involved in the war. They thrived, for example, in the British, German, and Australian forces, and there were an estimated 400 such journals in the French army alone.[13] The most popular BEF paper was the widely circulated *Wipers Times*.[14] With the Canadian units boasting an abundance of civilian-soldiers who had been newspaper editors, journalists, writers, and cartoonists before enlisting, some entrepreneurs began their own papers with their unit officers' blessings.

The trench newspapers consisted of journals, broadsides, and news-sheets printed by the soldiers for the soldiers.[15] Though many of the newspapers were crafted in or near the trenches, the term "trench newspapers" also encompasses those periodicals that were produced behind the lines at bases in France or in England. In fact, some newspapers had started up even before a single Canadian unit had entered the firing line, with the first papers originating in the training camps in Canada and continuing on the troop ships that carried the CEF across the Atlantic. The 14th Battalion's Private C.D.B. Whitby, a *Montreal Gazette* journalist, created *The Fourteenth Battalion Bugler* aboard a troopship in October 1914. It contained gossip, verse, shipboard sporting events, and a tearful account of the demise of "Vic," a cheerful pup that had been adopted as semi-official mascot.[16] The paper was a crude single-page production, but it was popular among the troops. No. 1 Field Company, Canadian Engineers, published a newspaper on board S.S. *Zeeland*, with the editor, Sergeant J.A. Taylor, calling it the *Sham News*, a play on both the type of material printed and Sam Hughes, the minister of militia who was a character of immense ego and overbearing personality, and the butt of many soldiers' jokes.[17] The 16th Battalion, a Highland regiment of amalgamated militia units from Victoria, also published an unnamed publication in October 1914. The unit's historian suggested that it captured and conveyed "items of Battalion gossip, told of the ten to one odds bet in New York against the safe arrival of the convoy in England, published Canon Scott's first war poem, and informed the interested of the aching tooth to be had in exchange for a headache, and the Crown and Anchor set for sale at the guard room."[18] Two of the items were obscure jokes, while Crown and Anchor was an illegal gambling game that was confiscated by officers when found, and Canon Frederick Scott was to become one of the most beloved poets in the Canadian Corps. Though the Canadians did not have a troopship literature as lively as that of the Australians—largely because the Australian voyage was a month in duration and the Canadian trip only about ten days—there was still a desire by Canucks to mark their unique experience of the voyage overseas.

In December 1915, the *Dead Horse Corner Gazette*—surely the most dramatic Canadian newspaper title in history—told its readers there was a "trench newspaper fever."[19] By this, the editors meant that every unit in France was cobbling together writers and editors to produce its own battalion paper. The first Canadian newspaper on the Western Front was the 7th Battalion's *The Listening Post*, with its inaugural issue published in August 1915.

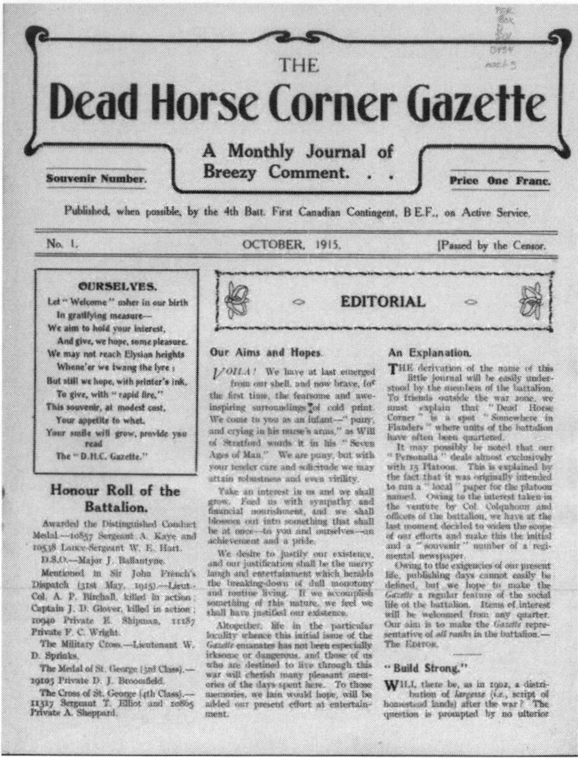

THE

Dead Horse Corner Gazette

A Monthly Journal of Breezy Comment. . .

Souvenir Number. Price One Franc.

Published, when possible, by the 4th Batt. First Canadian Contingent, B.E.F., on Active Service.

No. 1. OCTOBER, 1915. [Passed by the Censor.

OURSELVES.

Let "Welcome" usher in our birth
In gratifying measure—
We aim to hold your interest,
And give, we hope, some pleasure.
We may not reach Elysian heights
Whene'er we twang the lyre;
But still we hope, with printer's ink,
To give, with "rapid fire,"
This souvenir, at modest cost,
Your appetite to whet.
Your smile will grow, provide you read
The "D.H.C. Gazette."

Honour Roll of the Battalion.

Awarded the Distinguished Conduct Medal.—10857 Sergeant A. Kaye and 10538 Lance-Sergeant W. E. Hart.

D.S.O.—Major J. Ballantyne.

Mentioned in Sir John French's Dispatch (31st May, 1915).—Lieut.-Col. A. P. Birchall, killed in action; Captain J. D. Glover, killed in action; 10940 Private E. Shipman, 11187 Private F. C. Wright.

The Military Cross.—Lieutenant W. D. Sprinks.

The Medal of St. George (3rd Class).—19103 Private D. J. Broomfield.

The Cross of St. George (4th Class).—11317 Sergeant T. Elliot and 10865 Private A. Sheppard.

EDITORIAL

Our Aims and Hopes.

VOILA! We have at last emerged from our shell, and now brave, for the first time, the fearsome and awe-inspiring surroundings of cold print. We come to you as an infant—"puny, and crying in his nurse's arms," as Will of Stratford words it in his "Seven Ages of Man." We are puny, but with your tender care and solicitude we may attain robustness and even virility.

Take an interest in us and we shall grow. Feed us with sympathy and financial nourishment, and we shall blossom out into something that shall be at once—to you and ourselves—an achievement and a pride.

We desire to justify our existence, and our justification shall be the merry laugh and entertainment which heralds the breaking-down of dull monotony and routine living. If we accomplish something of this nature, we feel we shall have justified our existence.

Altogether, life in the particular locality whence this initial issue of the *Gazette* emanates has not been especially irksome or dangerous, and those of us who are destined to live through this war will cherish many pleasant memories of the days spent here. To those memories, we fain would hope, will be added our present effort at entertainment.

An Explanation.

THE derivation of the name of this little journal will be easily understood by the members of the battalion. To friends outside the war zone, we must explain that "Dead Horse Corner" is a spot "Somewhere in Flanders" where units of the battalion have often been quartered.

It may possibly be noted that our "Personalia" deals almost exclusively with 15 Platoon. This is explained by the fact that it was originally intended to run a "local" paper for the platoon named. Owing to the interest taken in the venture by Col. Colquhoun and officers of the battalion, we have at the last moment decided to widen the scope of our efforts and make this the initial and a "souvenir" number of a regimental newspaper.

Owing to the exigencies of our present life, publishing days cannot easily be defined, but we hope to make the *Gazette* a regular feature of the social life of the battalion. Items of interest will be welcomed from any quarter. Our aim is to make the *Gazette* representative of *all ranks* in the battalion.—THE EDITOR.

"Build Strong."

WILL there be, as in 1902, a distribution of *largesse* (*i.e.*, script of homestead lands) after the war? The question is prompted by no ulterior

The editor was the battalion's medical officer, Captain George Herbert Gibson, a doctor, professor of medicine, and the author of an instant history, *Maple Leaves in Flanders Fields*, an account of the 7th Battalion that he wrote under the name Herbert Rae.[20] His commanding officer complimented him later in the war, remarking, "It was Capt. Gibson's genius which stamped on the paper the character which has since endured. He made it a journal of broad interest instead of restricting it to purely local news."[21] After *The Listening Post* brought acclaim to the 7th Battalion, other commanding officers took notice.

In France and Flanders, the papers were published episodically, with an issue usually appearing every four to six weeks, and there were no daily offerings. A higher level of authenticity was accorded to those papers produced closer to the front. *The Listening Post* claimed in November 1915 that it was a "special paper for particular people" that was "written in the firing line—(as a matter of fact some of our material has been lost through the caprice of a German shell)."[22] Occasionally the editors of the emerging trench newspapers took shots at one another, deriding a competing paper for being published behind the lines, sheltered from the coalface of battle.

In the first issue of *The Listening Post*, the editor expressed that the paper was designed to "break trench monotony."[23] *The*

THE LISTENING POST

BRITISH COLUMBIA — CANADA

PRINTED BY KIND PERMISSION OF LT. COL. V. W. ODLUM. D.S.O., OFFICER COMMANDING 7th CANADIAN INFANTRY BATTALION.
EDITOR. CAPT. W. F. ORR. — CENSORED BY CHIEF CENSOR, 1st CAN. DIV. — NEWS EDITOR. L/CPL. H. MAYLOR.

No 18 BRITISH EX. FORCE, FRANCE, MAY 18, 1916. Price 1d

Experiences of a Manchester Recuiting Canvasser.

Contributed by a friend of the "L. P."

It seems a far cry back to the dull grey days of November last when the clament call of Lord Derby for more recruits was ringing through Great Britian. Manchester, that busy Metropolis of the North, had already done her duty nobly. Lord Kitchener had said so, and personally visited the City to show he meant it. Still more men were needed. The National Register taken in August which gave full particulars of every resident in the British Isles over sixteen years of age, revealed the fact that there was still a considerable surplus who had not been moved by the call. The Derby scheme of attestation by which a man could enlist and be placed in a class to be called up according to his age and responsibilities, needed canvassers to explain. The present writer volunteered for the duty and was appointed to visit a district of the City contiguous to the docks of the Manchester Ship Canal. My appearance on the scene left no doubt that whatever part of the Country had not done it's duty, this particular district had risen nobly to a great occasion. In long rows of tenements it was only necessary to call at houses here and there, for already the majority of their former elegible occupants had gone. And of those left. Who were they? What were they? Well, for the most part, married men with large families and small wages, "waiting for the single men to go first", together with the halt the lame and the blind. Mr. Asquith's pledge, since redeemed, to book in the single men, at that time seemed but half convincing to the man with a brood of children clattering at his heels, "Let him do it and we'll follow" was the opinion pretty freely expressed.

(To be Continued)

Sensational Robbery.

LITERARY WORLD RECEIVES A SEVERE JOLT.

Early this morning it was discovered that yeggmen had broken into the strong room of the Editorial Offices and carried away the great Poetical Masterpiece "Gawd, how my eyes grew dim", composed by the world famous poet, Pioneer N. McLean.

Great as was the shock to the artistic world when the famous "Mona Lisa" painting disappeared, it was a mere 'seven days gossip' compared with the disaster caused by the loss of this poem. Letters and telegrams of condolence are pouring into the temporary office hourly. Noteworthy amongst these are letters from Rudyard Kipling, Ally Sloper, Ella Wheeler Wilcox, Bud Fisher, Sam Gothard, Bob Edwards, Robert Sievier and Horatio Bottomley. The whole of the Secret Service machinery has been set in motion and early results are breathlessly awaited.

Serious charge against Pte. Richards.

CAUGHT WITH THE GOODS

SUSPECTED OF TRADING WITH THE ENEMY.

As a result of being brought up before Capt. Lees, on a charge of violating the "Defence of the Realm Act".

Pte. Richards has been interned pending further developments. The news caused a deal of consternation among his comrades who had never suspected him of having anything German (barring a razor) about him. Had he not, in a moment of utter recklessness decided to wash himself, he would, in all probability be still at large. Whilst this painful operation was in progress, thousands of German 'Marks' were noticed about his body.

Everyone he has been in contact with are being closely watched, and early developements are anxiously expected.

So eager did his comrades wish to share the spoils, that a rush was made for his blanket and towel.

After a careful examination of the suspect, the M. O. has ordered him to be isolated.

A word from the Transport.

Dick Turpin may have been a dare-devil, but his historic ride to York was a Sunday School picnic compared with my nightly jaunt. Yes, although I say it myself, there is more excitement in one mile between our transport and the trenches, than would fill all the penny hair-raisers that I ever got spanked for reading. Dick may have loved Black Bess, but it was merely flirtation compared with what I think of my two Gee Gees, and the Hun that does hit one had better look out

If he only so much as gives one of them a "Blighty", it will be, "Good night Adolph". I shall quit this job and go in the Infantry and start a battle all by myself. It will be the beginning of the end for all the Herr Hermans.

Loaded up with Maconachies, bully beef, biscuits, and other delicacies which men leave home for, we start in the direction of the flare-lights. This is a signal for all the German snipers to load up their magazines and machine gunners to fill a new cartridge belt.

The wagons rattle over the cobbles, in and out of shell holes and make enough noise to scare Berlin—ZING-SPLUSH, ZING—PHUT—why don't they shoot at somebody else? I never hit a German in my life. I've too much respect for my hat. At last we get there, unload, about turn, out of range, breathe easier, arrive home, unhitch, in my dug-out, have a smoke, good night.

Yorky.

Front page of The Listening Post, *the most popular of the Canadian trench newspapers produced on the Western Front.*

Dead Horse Corner Gazette published its first issue in October 1915, and the editor similarly hoped the paper would alleviate the "dull monotony and routine living" of the trenches by capturing some of the soldiers' experiences in print. The name itself "will be easily understood by the members of the battalion. To friends outside the war zone, we must explain that 'Dead Horse Corner' is a spot 'Somewhere in Flanders' where units of the battalion have often been quartered." The editor, Private R.W. Trowsdale, declared, "Our aim is to make the Gazette representative of *all ranks* in the battalion."[24]

The *Silent 60th*, which started publishing in early 1916, flippantly remarked, "The magazine is not intended as a serious contribution to current literature, but rather to cause a little amusement among the boys during their leisure hours in rest."[25] And yet the papers were also a forum for the soldiers' observations. They provided a space for discussion, humour, and irreverent observation. Polished prose was mixed with maudlin verse; fierce patriotism existed side by side with stories of soldiers acting unsoldierly and dodging their duties. The newspapers themselves were a means by which soldiers could express their outrage and wit, their concerns and complaints. While the editors of *Vic's Patrol*, the trench newspaper for the 24th Battalion, suggested that the "simple grousing" in their paper did "not constitute disloyalty," prose or poetry that growled at conditions and discipline were a warning of sorts for officers that trouble was brewing in the ranks.[26] This type of oppositional journalism was an important way the soldiers could kick back against authority.

As soldiers languished in their trenches, dugouts, and gun pits, humour was one of their primary mechanisms for coping with and combatting the drudgery of war. Even the worst suffering and privations were scoffed at with masculine ribbing, mirth, and satire. "The gift of humor is as priceless as the gift of physical courage," believed Canadian T.W. Johnson.[27] In the mad war of the trenches, with soldiers surrounded by death and horror, the silly and the superficial were an important shield. Much of this humour was part of a rich oral culture of men trading jokes, swearing non-stop, and hurling insults in rapid-fire succession, and little of it was written down except in the private letters and public trench newspapers. Drawing upon the soldiers' culture, the papers were rife with the inside jokes and references that connected with their soldierly readership. Lieutenant-Colonel P.G. Bell wrote revealingly for the inaugural issue of *In and Out*, a journal published for a Canadian field ambulance late in the war, "The number of trench journals produced by the War has been so large as possibly to induce in the minds of the public a wonder as to what good purpose may be served by them. In the first place, they serve as chronicles, recording a great deal of the lighter side of a Unit's daily life, and, in the second place, as an outlet for the soldier's literary skill and yearnings."[28] An easily added third role of the papers was to provide a forum for soldiers to embrace the absurdity of war, as expressed through satire, irony, and head-shaking mirth. Thomas Clark Lapp was convinced that "this unfailing sense of humor accounts in a large degree for the splendid morale of the Canadians."[29] Perhaps—to borrow from the great satirist group of the late twentieth century, Monty Python—the soldiers learned to look on the bright side of strife.

THE FIRST ISSUES OF CANADIAN papers were usually little more than pencil sketches on notepaper, reproduced through sheets of carbon. Later, as the newspaper craze took hold, the publications became more sophisticated, longer, and professionally produced. They were replicated with spirit duplicators (a copying device that used wax and pressure), and some units even had access to small printing presses.[30] The rush to produce Canadian papers starting in late 1915 coincided with a period of trench warfare in between the big battles of Second Ypres in April 1915 and St. Eloi in April 1916, a time when second and third divisions arrived on the Western Front and the Canadian Corps was formed. With some 40,000 Canadians at the front by September and then 60,000 a few months later, they were a captive group and one open to reading about their own war.

Though the editors of the newspapers were typically those with a higher education, the selection of articles, cartoons, and poetry had to reflect the mentality of the rank and file or the paper would slip into irrelevance. Censorship unavoidably affected what could be presented in the papers, but the content could not be reduced to patriotic pablum. For the editors, there was no dodging their audience, as they might be digging a trench with their readers—the rank and file privates—the next day or sharing a tour of sentry duty. And soldiers were not shy in telling the editors what they liked and did not like about the papers.

The regimental newspaper *The Twentieth Gazette* was first published while the 20th Battalion was in Canada, training in Toronto. Editions were printed in England in the training camps and then on the Western Front when the unit arrived in September 1915. The two founding editors were Harry Wreford Clarke, a prewar commercial artist, and Sergeant William W. Murray, a future journalist and regimental historian. Both were tough, frontline men, the first and second scout sergeants, whose exceedingly dangerous positions involved prowling though No Man's Land nearly every night while at the front. Neither of them were prewar journalists, although according to one officer, "They developed quite a news instinct, and made the publication popular by being bold enough to take a sly dig at the Commanding Officer, to feign respect for majors, to treat captains with cynicism, to be distressingly sarcastic about subalterns, to be openly insulting about sergeants, to be abusive about corporals, but wise enough to be extremely polite about privates."[31] Like most of the trench newspapers, *The Twentieth Gazette* was aimed at the rankers who made up the vast majority of the battalion.

The trench newspapers were not created by the high command in order to shape opinion. They came from the ground up and responded to the concerns of the men; at the same time, editors who received complaints from their readers could give as good as they got. Major George Boyce, the editor for *The Iodine Chronicle*, grumbled in a cynical piece called "Editor's Diary," "Am informed today that there is by far too much poetry in the 'I.C.' Later another eager soldier informs me that there is too much prose in the same journal." On the next day, his published journal entry reads, "Bitterly criticized for not giving enough knocks in our papers; say I ought to be more personal. Later am held up by another disgruntled reader who says we are much too personal, and all such items should be discontinued at once."[32] Boyce's feedback, likely exaggerated to make his point, revealed the constant bellyaching and carping on the part of his readership. And while Boyce was a major, many other editors were NCOs and even privates. *The Forty-Niner* was edited by the 49th Battalion's Private Fred Johnson, and the assistant manager, sub-editor, advertising manager, circulation manager, and financial secretary were all NCOs or privates.[33] Only the manager was an officer,

Lieutenant F.S. Winser, a prewar militia officer and civil engineer. All received commentary, regardless of rank. There does not appear to have been any undue influence exerted on these lower-ranking newspapermen by officers demanding that they tone down the criticism. All of this was quite remarkable in an organization—whether the battalion or the army—whose functioning depended on the preservation of hierarchy. Attesting to the importance of this type of informal communication, one British paper observed that *The Listening Post*, whose co-editors were a captain and a lance corporal, "speaks volumes for the democracy of the corps, and the excellent relations between the commissioned and non-commissioned ranks."[34] That the papers were allowed to criticize the war effort and the high command, and even poke fun at the absurdity within the battalion, was also a hidden factor in how the leaders and the led, officers and the rank and file, functioned in the forces.

"MANY LITERARY COMPOSITIONS IN VERSE and prose, some of exceptional quality, have been received, and in thanking these valued contributors, we must confess that the success of our paper has been largely brought about by their efforts."[35] Despite this praise for their contributors, the editors of *The Iodine Chronicle* hoped for more content, as did all papers. Editors beat the bush by walking through the trenches, chatting with men, encouraging them to offer a joke, song, or piece of doggerel to their paper. "If you hear a good story, write it up and send it to the editor," pleaded Corporal John Ward, editor of *The Forty-Niner*. "If you cannot write it, tell it to someone who can, for it is only fair if you get a good laugh that you should pass it on."[36]

Many rankers and officers did not feel they had the literary chops to write for a newspaper, while others could not be bothered to spend their limited free time in such endeavours. *The Listening Post*, in May 1916, responded with a sharp and long editorial when the editor heard that there had been grousing by the soldiers about its content. "Did YOU say that the last number of this paper had too much 'would be' poetry in it? Well listen; the men who wrote that poetry probably put in their spare time at rest billets composing those little poems, whilst YOU were perhaps playing 'Black Jack', or maybe playing a 'Mouth organ.' . . . Now, what have YOU done towards filling up our eight pages? . . . We admit to publishing stuff that would get a civilian editor cast into an asylum, or prison, but, 'there's a reason.' This is YOUR paper; it is only through your interest that it can exist. If we engaged the services of some professional arm chair war correspondent to write and edit the paper, we should soon get stony, and the paper—'Na poo.'"[37] Referencing the word "napoo," soldiers' slang for "killed" or "dead," the editor was warning that the paper would expire without their contributions. Some of the papers withered away during the war, but more than a dozen had a long and rich publication run.

The newspapers were always in a state of flux and were never published according to a preset schedule. The movement of a unit to a new front could disrupt publication, along with shortages of paper or ink. More damaging was the death or injury of critical members of a paper's staff or frequent contributors. By early 1917, *The Listening Post* had lost several of its editors to injuries in battle, although they were replaced by other willing men.[38] Between the first and second edition of *The Forty-Niner*, the original editor was run over by a car in London. Corporal John Ward took over as editor and he was later replaced by Private Fred Johnson.[39] *The Dead Horse Corner Gazette*, founded and edited by Private R.W. Trowsdale of the 4th Battalion, who had been a prewar journalist by trade and was older than most of his comrades, ended one edition with a final dispatch from Blighty.[40] Writing from a hospital to his comrades, he and the paper were out of action for a while after he was wounded in the thigh and hand during the Somme, although another editor took over and the paper was publishing again within a few months.

The high command also had an impact on the papers' content and message, though stringent censorship does not appear to have occurred under their watch. While civilian-soldiers, journalists, newspaper men, and cartoonists had flocked to the ranks, they were also in the high command. Major General David Watson, the commanding officer of the 4th Division, had been general manager of the *Quebec Morning Chronicle*, while Brigadiers Victor Odlum and E.W.B. Morrison edited papers before the war, and so did the mercurial minister of militia and defence, Sam Hughes, in his early career, in an effort to boost his political voice. They were sympathetic to the trials of publishing in the war zone, and both Watson and Odlum recognized the value of the papers in raising the profile of their formations. In the French army, General Joseph Joffre ordered in March 1916 that officers should resist interfering with trench newspapers. He acknowledged that these were important tools for the French soldiers to "amuse" and "divert" themselves from the ordeal of service at the front, and that independent papers boosted "confidence, cheerfulness, and courage."[41] The general advised that the officers should ensure that there was not outright harm to the army's overall message or discipline, but that the interventions should be minimal. The

British and Canadian high command also viewed the papers with mild benevolence. They understood the soldiers' strain and knew that disrupting the publication of the papers would be viewed poorly by the rank and file. But despite such tolerant attitudes, there was some interference. In October 1916, the Canadian Corps passed order 1857, whereby trench journals were to be examined by official censors at corps headquarters before publication.[42] While the censorship appeared to be of the same sort exerted over letters—consisting of removing the name of units and battles—there was some unwanted meddling and evidence of delays to publication. "Fate is unkind, and the work of editing even so small a journal as ours is not all honey," complained editor John Ward of *The Forty-Niner*, even before the censorship order. "The Censor will not allow certain articles, one is not allowed to mention casualties in any shape or form, and we must bow our heads in silent grief to those of our boys called Home, and names must be left unmentioned."[43] Ward's open assault on the censors was regarding their denial of the 49th Battalion's wish to commemorate their fallen comrades, something that rankled one of the censors, who felt that listing the slain soldiers might aid the enemy. A later editor of *The Forty-Niner*, Lieutenant R.G. Dorway, blamed the delay of one issue on the fact that "service conditions and censorship regulations placed many stumbling-blocks in the way." But he went on to say that "through it all the magazine has been kept going with the object in view of having a written record of the more intimate doings and happenings in the Battalion that are not permitted in the terse wording of the Battalion Diary."[44] While surviving records do not reveal what editors were forced to withhold or pull, the *Dead Horse Corner Gazette* opined that "it's a safe bet to prophesy that if a soldiers' journal were run after the war, it would contain more on the *real dope*!"[45] There was surely some censorship, but what remained still managed to be daring at times, even impertinent.

The Listening Post, published by the 7th Battalion, was the best-selling newspaper on the Western Front—in any army—and its circulation eventually rose to 20,000.[46] The battalion commander and brigadier were proud of the paper, and its success spurred other commanders to establish papers to encourage morale and showcase their own units. There was a natural tendency in the Corps towards rivalry, which manifested itself on the battlefield in the desire of officers to pull off bigger raids than other battalions, and behind the lines, in sporting matches. This spirit of competition was also reflected in the trench newspapers. Papers went up and down the line, carried with the rations and mail, distributed throughout the battalion, then the brigade, and throughout the CEF. A good newspaper brought credit to its regiment or battery, and in the competitive CEF, this was appreciated by commanders. As almost all of the CEF units were raised during the course of the war, commanding officers understood the value of forging the tight bonds that linked men to their regiment, battery, or brigade, and papers were a good way to do that.

IN THE SUMMER OF 1916, *The Listening Post* proudly published a compliment from one old veteran: "You know the 'L.P' just smells of the TRENCHES."[47] That was the goal for most of the soldiers' papers. Despite the desire of many men to escape the front, there was an equally strong need to bring to light the experience of the trenches: from rats to mud to shelling. Sometimes the complaints were simply intended to draw attention to the hardship and drudgery of service; at other times the soldiers scoffed at the privations and death, showing a manly disdain for whatever the war threw at them. Either way, they wanted to talk or read about these issues. The weather conditions were particularly trying for soldiers, and food was a source of incessant grievance and therefore fodder to feed dark humour. Bully beef, hard tack, and gluey jam could inspire doggerel, cartoons, or angry lamentations. Rum, cigarettes, the enemy, the slackers on the home front, and much more were discussed, spoofed, and joked about in the papers. There was a fierce debate between soldiers and temperance advocates at home over the army issue of rum: the soldiers saw it as an absolute necessity for propping up morale while abstainers on the home front worried it would lead to moral degradation. The latter attitude rankled the soldiers, and the trench newspapers were filled with angry rejoinders. For example, *The Listening Post* said of the fretful abstainers, "Till they come and share the crapping/At the side of fighting men/They should stop their yapping/Never to commence again."[48]

Criticism and grousing formed the life blood of the Canadian newspapers. The *R.M.R. Growler* of the 14th Battalion claimed that "as the name will suggest, our columns are open to every grouch in the Battalion, and a growl on any subject, whether the grievance be either real or fancied, will be joyfully received and have immediate insertion."[49] However, this grumbling did not equate with hopelessness or despair. In fact, the reality was the opposite. Railing at the trials of the trenches was a sign of the infantry clinging to life. To wail about one's own artillery dropping shells short of their target was not to demand that they stop firing, as mass death would result without the protective artillery screen, but it was a flag to note that short shells killed men, and, even if little could be done about it, the dirty secret was out in the open. Ordered into harm's way, soldiers felt they had a right to kick back a little bit. "It would be strange if they took this right away from us: sheep still bleat loudly at the door of the abattoir," wrote one scathing French soldier in his trench newspaper, *Le Bochofage*.[50]

The papers were a safe space to codify some of the soldiers' gripes directed towards the war effort or their officers. Most newspapers had a section where soldiers could demand information or put queries to be read by all. These notes were framed along humorous lines, but there was some bite to them, and the officers were wise to realize that this cantankerousness had a purpose. *The Listening Post* offered one variation on this, with a list of soldiers' queries:

> Why the M.O. doesn't issue a dose of pain-killer, just by way of variety?
> When are our reinforcements coming?
> Why the sencor dosent issue more green envulopes?[51] [*sic* throughout]

The first query, a swipe at the medical officer, the MO, refers to the hated number 9 pills that were given for almost all ailments. These were laxatives and men despised them, especially when every soldier dealt with constant aches, pains, colds, and ill health resulting from their trying existence.[52] Private Archie Selwood, who went to France with the 72nd Battalion at age thirty-five, remarked on the stringent medical examinations: "Unless there was blood, we got little sympathy."[53] The MOs were also sometimes unhappy about their role, and one Canadian in the job described his "chief duties" as consisting of convincing "a sick man that he is not sick."[54] The second query, about reinforcements speaks for itself, although it also refers to the truth that battalions were always short of riflemen, a situation that created a strain on the survivors who had to work harder, stand sentry more often, and expose themselves to danger more frequently. The final, deliberately misspelled query is about green envelopes that were not to be censored by regimental officers. Together, these comments, and many more like them throughout the papers, were a way for the soldiers to vent their frustrations within a safe context.

The newspapers were willing to spoof almost anything, including the soldiers' attitudes and culture. Gallantry medals were sniffed at and accused of being handed out with the rations to the underserving.[55] For those tough souls who claimed to have few allegiances to King and country, *The Listening Post* needled, "Nobody seems to have the nerve to admit that he enlisted for patriotic reasons; but the party who said he joined up to get a clasp-knife and a razor must have been pretty keen."[56] Even the soldiers' slang was diminished, with *The Iodine Chronicle* pointing out the most "hackneyed sayings" to come out the soldiers' mouths—for example, "Any more for any more?" "Say, I hear there's a war on," and "toot sweet."[57]

But the deepest anger and vitriol was reserved for others. *The Silent 60th* was a cheerful magazine, but in the June 1916 "Things we would like to know" section, there was a loaded question: "What is Colonel Gascoigne's private opinion of the Ross rifle?"[58] This was a hot-button issue for the soldiers, as the Canadian-made Ross rifle had failed on the battlefield in 1915 and its jamming in battle had contributed directly to the death of their comrades.[59] The Canadians were nonetheless slow to adopt the British-made Lee Enfield because of the evangelical fervour of the dominating Minister of Militia Sam Hughes, who believed the Ross was the best rifle in the world. The 60th Battalion, within the 3rd Division, was still using the Ross in June 1916, by which time other Canadian units had switched over to the Lee Enfield, and the men were putting their colonel's feet to the fire. In a similar vein, *The Dead Horse Corner Gazette* had a caustic section known as "Things Unlikely to Happen," which, in the October 1915 issue, included

> "A full issue of rum for the privates."
> "Fair prices at the estaminets."
> "The cooks voluntarily giving up their jobs."
> "An immediate return to civil life."
> "The M.O. to lose his stock-in-trade of No. 9's."[60]

All of these were common complaints by the rank and file and an indication of the things that mattered to them. The 27th Battalion's *Trench Echo* 1915 Christmas edition took a shot at a staff officer who, while inspecting a section of the front under heavy fire, asked a subaltern, "Have all your men shaved this morning?"[61] While the story sounds apocryphal, weirder questions and inappropriate requests were given voice during the war. The rank and file always liked to hear about the inanities of those in the rear who did not understand the real war at the front, especially stories about the staff officers being seemingly out of touch with the issues that mattered to the fighting men. Following the popular theme of thrashing the uppers, *The Listening Post* continued to swipe at authority figures in one mock advertisement, "Be an Officer." It was a mail-in correspondence course soldiers could take to become commissioned. The advertisement claimed, "Why remain in the ranks? No more working parties, no more pack drill. Frequent passes to Blighty." It also observed that officer wannabes should consider "a

Three Canadians give toothy and toothless grins while reading a paper in the trenches.

small extra fee for our special courses for paymasters, quarter masters, chaplains, censors, transport officers and other bomb-proof jobs."[62] The rank and file viewed these rearward officer positions with skepticism because they were far from harm and hard work.

One of the harshest attacks on an officer came from the irreverent *Dead Horse Corner Gazette*, in which one inquiring soldier (likely speaking for all the rankers) wanted to know "whether the officer of a certain Canadian battalion who ordered one of his men to pick up scraps of paper from the top of a communication trench in broad daylight attended the man's funeral?"[63] The paper allowed for this type of grievance to be heard by the officers in a neutral setting, and it showed the rank and file that they were not alone in their justifiable anger. Such statements also reinforced the authenticity of newspapers, underscoring that they were written for the rank and file and not the officers.

In such instances of pushback against authority, the trench newspapers created a space for disobedience and dissent within the accepted parameters of the hierarchical army. The printed criticisms could range from breezy and gentle prodding to sharp blasts from furious men. While in France, the 5th Canadian Field Ambulance had its own paper, edited by Pete Wise and carrying the title *The La Clytte Bladder and Empire* and later *L'Echo de Godewaersvelde* (after a village in which the unit frequently billeted).[64] Another name under consideration had been the "Latrine Gazette," which perhaps speaks to the regard in which the editor held his paper. The "Weekly Eye-Opener," as it was sub-titled, was based on the "proposition that all men were born equal," wrote cynical stretcher-bearer Frederick Noyes, "excepting non-coms and officers, who were the works of the devil." Noyes added, "To every issue the men looked forward with delightful anticipation; the officers and noncoms, with mistrust and dread, for the editor's pen was often dipped in acid."[65] The paper was short-lived, switching from a daily rag to a bi-weekly, and then becoming episodically printed throughout 1916 and 1917, but many men in the ambulance joined in to assist the editor and provide copy. Through their combined efforts, observed Noyes, "their many sly digs at officers, non-coms, cooks, mail men and quartermaster stores hangers-on did much to curb abuses and make life a little more worthwhile for the lowly buck privates."[66] It was difficult to know if the airing of grievances helped to relieve the abuses and nonsense directed at the rank and file by some of the more egregious officers during the daily ritual of work, training, and hard labour in the trenches, but the privates seemed to think that it did.

Though the papers were rife with dark humour and biting satire, there were also patriotic verses and heroic accounts of the

Allies defeating the evil Hun. Soldiers believed in the cause—the need to stand by Britain, to defeat German tyranny, and to liberate the oppressed—and not all patriotism was knocked from them in the wasteland of the trenches. Private Walter Hill offered a good old-fashioned patriotic song, "We are coming Mother England," in the summer 1916 issue of *The Listening Post*. The song noted that the Canadians were crossing the Atlantic to defend Britain against the Hun. The war, in Hill's mind—and in this he echoed many millions in the firing line and on the home front—was a fight for civilization against an enemy *Kultur* that was diabolical, as revealed by the Germans' use of "deadly gas."[67]

The papers and their contributors were overtly proud of the Canadian soldiers and their peculiar ways. *The Brazier* printed a short story that played up the irreverence of the Canadians: General E.A.H. Alderson, the first corps commander from late 1914 to May 1916, is visiting the front, "seeing things for himself." He comes across a transport section and encounters a "very well-groomed and well-kept team." Alderson, a former cavalry officer, compliments the men on keeping their horses trim and healthy. "To his great surprise and secret amusement, the driver replies: 'Thanks, Cap; a little encouragement once in a while don't do a fellow any harm.'"[68] Whether true or apocryphal, the story and the cheeky response speaks to the casual charm of the Canadians while also painting the "secretly amused" general in a fine light as he easily accepts the non-soldierly ways and moves on without reprimand or comment. The Canadians liked to portray themselves as different from British soldiers, and many of the jokes and stories in the newspapers highlight the Canadians' seemingly contradictory characteristics of mischievous irreverence for authority. This image is all the more interesting given that about half of the CEF was British-born, but even these Canadians were perceived by both themselves and others as different from the citizens of the island kingdom.

LIEUTENANT-GENERAL SIR ARTHUR CURRIE WROTE to congratulate *The Listening Post* on its second anniversary in the summer of 1917, remarking, "For over two years *The Listening Post*, full of piquant satire and wholesome humour, has regularly appeared, and has done much to drive away dull care. Its influence for good has been truly great."[69] The Great War newspapers, products of the trenches and the men who fought in them, serve as an important window into the soldiers' culture. In a war of unyielding discipline and unbreakable hierarchy, the Canadian papers were

Two chums reading in the trenches.

strikingly anti-authoritarian. *The Iodine Chronicle*, the second-longest running Canadian newspaper, noted towards the end of the war that in its pages "officers and privates find scope for criticism which is often daringly outspoken."[70] The shots against authority were in fact often subtle, but they were bold within the context of the authoritarian hierarchy of the army. However, there was nothing subtle about the one paper that suggested that a strategist (i.e., a general) is "a person who doesn't care how many lives he risks as long as he doesn't risk his own."[71] Sometimes the Canadian trench papers bared their teeth against the authorities.

How and why the officers allowed the newspapers to survive provides a glimpse into the hidden history of the war. The papers were seen by both officers and rankers as a way for the lower ranks to negotiate officers' authority rather than as a negation of it. *The Brazier* codified the stories circulating in the ranks after the bloody Somme and before Vimy in February 1917, complaining, "Rumour has it that we are going to have a rest. When is it likely to begin? After three weeks of strenuous training and the infinite variety of squad drill we are reduced to the verge of nervous prostration and anxious enquiries may be heard as to when we shall be returning to the Line."[72] This stark admission of the soldiers needing a rest was a clear message to the officers. There were others like it in the papers that became a safe forum for the expression of unpopular ideas within the army hierarchy.

A lot of effort was required to keep publishing these papers. Their appeal had to extend beyond a few keeners; they resonated with much of the rank and file or they would fold. "It is a pleasure to know that even though one does not kill Germans," observed one editor in a moment of self-appraisal, "he has been the means of bringing a little pleasure in this none too gay life."[73] The papers in fact went above and beyond this humble sentiment. They were important for helping the soldiers vent their frustration and keep up their spirits, and for leaving a printed legacy. All soldiers realized they were living through momentous events. Men aimed to bear witness. As well, given the soldiers' fleeting existence, with lives snuffed out after just weeks at the front, it was important that the soldiers' war—the war as seen and experienced by those who fought it at the front—be codified. Finally, and perhaps most importantly, these papers bound together unit members who both read and chuckled at the shared familiarities and added to them with irreverence. All of this seemed at odds with proper soldiering, at least at first glance, but the papers were a by-product of the spaces of death on the Western Front. As William W. Murray said of the trench newspapers, one of which he edited, they were "one of the oddities of a war that was altogether odd."[74]

CHAPTER 8

DRAWN AND QUARTERED

"It is often said that a picture is worth a thousand words," declared John Diefenbaker, one of the two Canadian prime ministers who were Great War veterans. "A cartoon, well done, is worth a thousand pictures."[1] Another veteran of the trenches, Adolf Hitler, who would leave a malignant legacy in world history, wrote of cartoons, "At one stroke . . . people will understand a pictorial representation of something which it would take them a long and laborious effort of reading to understand."[2] Had Hitler's forces successfully invaded Britain in 1940, he would have executed a large number of politicians and intellectuals. The list included cartoonists, whose pens could destabilize the establishment, skewer the powerful, and ennoble those in the ditches.[3]

Canadian soldier cartoonists carried out their work behind the lines and in the trenches. Some of their drawings were published in the trench newspapers, while others were never viewed beyond the soldiers' private notebooks.[4] The trench cartoons drew upon the combat experience, depicting fatigue, life in the trenches, work parties, interactions with the enemy, difficult officers, and ungrateful civilians.[5] The cartoons often contained exaggerated figures or farcical elements that appealed to the soldiers, as well as visual in-jokes that were not easily deciphered by those not in uniform. Soldiers' cartoons, like the soldiers' culture that they both documented and were a part of, were secretive and not meant for outsiders.

BRITISH OFFICER BRUCE BAIRNSFATHER WAS the most popular cartoonist of the war, admired by British, Canadian, and most other Allied soldiers, including the French. Bairnsfather had been a prewar cartoonist with *The Bystander*, a British paper with a large working-class readership, and he had found a prewar niche with his cartoons that lampooned upper-class life. When war was declared, Bairnsfather was quick to enlist and his service with the infantry at the front immersed him in the unique soldiers' culture, which he captured in his drawings. The "poor bloody infantry" groused and grumbled about the food and mud as well as the danger and mind-numbing discipline, and it all became fodder for Bairnsfather's cartoons. But his caricatures went beyond the physical discomforts to address the stress and strain at the front: the fear of standing sentry, the agony of suffering under shellfire from which there was no place to run, and the dislocation from civilized society. Despite serving as a lieutenant in the line, and later as a captain when he became the army's only official cartoonist, he always treated the rank and file with respect. Bairnsfather's beloved characters Old Bill and his cockney sidekicks Alf and Bert epitomized the experience of "Everyman" at the front. The dishevelled, pipe-smoking, walrus-moustached Old Bill and his companions were not cowards, but they certainly were not heroes in the traditional sense.

While serving at the front, Bairnsfather drew cartoons for the men, handing them out on single sheets of paper. He also etched and drew larger murals on the walls of abandoned buildings and

Captain Bruce Bairnsfather, the most popular cartoonist of the war.

trench dugouts. His popularity grew and his first collection of cartoons was published in early 1916. *Fragments from France* would eventually sell an astonishing 250,000 copies.[6] Bairnsfather found inspiration in the rank and file, especially the anti-heroic ones that populated every unit, remarking, "I love those old work-evading, tricky, self-contained slackers—old soldiers."[7] His Old Bill spent his time grumbling and seeking cover from shells. He was unabashedly unheroic. Patriotic citizens on the home front were aghast at such a characterization of their hero-soldiers, whom they supported in the fight against the Hun. Indeed, there were those who initially viewed Bairnsfather's cartoons as unpatriotic, almost treasonous. That perception only changed when the soldiers themselves offered a chorus of approval of the cartoonist's depictions.[8] The civilian critics retreated, yet they remained unsure as to why soldiers would embrace these unheroic images.

"These cartoons by Bairnsfather are very good and true to life," wrote Canadian infantryman Basil Morris, a prewar civil engineer who did not survive the war.[9] Bairnsfather's most famous cartoon, "The Better 'Ole," revealed in grim humour that during a bombardment there was nowhere to run or feel safe, as two desperate soldiers searched for a "better" hole in the ground in which to find protection. The cartoon was so popular that soldiers repeated the phrase ad nauseum to each other, and even made a pilgrimage to see Bairnsfather's original mural drawing. Lieutenant Raymond Massey, who served with the artillery and would later become a famous actor, remembered being dragged by two friends, shortly after he arrived on the Western Front in early 1916, to a little *estaminet* in Ploegsteert, or Plug Street as the soldiers called it, to see "the original of a famous cartoon." The three Canadians entered the ruined building, and "on one wall, half blown down, was the Bruce Bairnsfather drawing of Old Bill and Alf looking over the edge of a crater. The caption was still intact: 'If you knows of a better 'ole, go to it!' The artist's signature was clearly visible."[10] Soldiers travelled from afar to visit the hidden work of art.

"Well, if you knows of a better 'ole, go to it."

Captain Henry Clyne, a prewar accountant in Vancouver who would be awarded the Military Cross for bravery, remarked, "Our first long winter campaign against a welter of mud and caved-in trenches now began. The life was hard and dreary but often cheered by Bruce Bairnsfather's famous and cogent cartoons featuring 'Alf' and 'Old Bill,' that did so much to portray our kind of existence for those at home."[11] The soldiers thought that the cartoons authentically captured the real war at the front, revealing many of their unspoken worries and the evident hardships of campaigning on the Western Front. Bairnsfather's Old Bill and the other characters in his cartoon chronicles were instantly recognized by any British or Canadian Tommy, who saw themselves in the cantankerous warrior. He endured as they endured; he growled as they growled. The cartoons' irreverent, grim, and humorous view of war struck the soldiers: this was no pandering, no condescension, no "eye-wash." Even the generals understood Bairnsfather's value as a source of support for the soldiers, with one of them, Sir Ian Hamilton, suggesting that he was "the man who made the Empire laugh in its darkest hour."[12] Bairnsfather's cartoons crossed national boundaries because his illustrations were less about a particular nation's stories than about what united the common soldiers—namely, dealing with the strain and finding a way to keep in the fight.

Canadian infantryman G.R. Stevens described the popularity of Bairnsfather and his messages, remarking, "His gallery of characters—Old Bill, Alf, Bert, his fed-up privates and his sardonic sergeants—became celebrities in their own right and their cross-talk became a common coin of conversational exchanges wherever English was spoken. 'Where did that one go?' 'If you knows of a better 'ole go to it!' 'What time do you feed the sea lions, Alf?', 'There goes our blinkin' parapet again!' 'Who made that 'ole?

Mice.' 'They've evidently seen me,' and a hundred other catchphrases portrayed a world war as Britons wanted to see it—stimulating, dangerous but on the whole a rather amusing business."[13] The characters' phlegmatic sentiments, as captured and presented by Bairnsfather, were also the means by which the armies of civilian-soldiers coped with the strain of the war, pushed back against authority and hierarchy, and interpreted their wartime experiences. They represented the infantry's ability to endure the awfulness of war with a wry smile and a shrug of the shoulders. In other drawings, the soldiers were frightened and bewildered by the shocking experiences at the front, and soldiers could point to these situations to help express their own terror or discomfort. Lieutenant Ralph Jones of the 27th Battalion felt that Bairnsfather's cartoons "are so true to life that we almost cry laughing at them. The artist has been, or is, out here + knows whereof he sketches. There is one, for instance, of a patrol, hair on end + absolutely scared stiff by imaginary huge Bosch heads in a cloud just above him."[14] Here, Jones

"Where did that one go to?"

was trying to explain his own fear of moving through No Man's Land, with the enemy ready to pounce at every step, and he used the cartoon to help talk about his anxiety. Jones might have delved deeper into the hair-raising disquiet of nighttime patrols in other letters or when he made it home, but he was killed two months later at the Battle of St. Eloi in April 1916.

Forced to confront a world of destruction, soldiers often had trouble describing their fear and exhaustion in letters, either because of formal military censorship or because of a simple inability to put words to paper. In the face of such obstacles, Bairnsfather's cartoons offered a common language, one of understood symbols that allowed soldiers to speak to one another and sometimes even to those at home. Lieutenant Maurice Pope could write to his parents in early 1916, "I am well physically, but very tired mentally. This work is quite a strain on one and these nights I am living Bairnsfather's cartoon—'This ----- war will be the death of us yet."[15] Soldiers adopted the classic Bairnsfather phrases, using them as recognized cultural references to help them communicate. Hugh Kay of the 43rd Battery noted that during an artillery bombardment, if one listened to the men taking shelter in their dugouts, "you might hear faint snatches of 'Where did that one go to 'Erbert,'" a reference to the cheeky Bairnsfather cartoon in which stunned soldiers are wondering where the shells are falling.[16] Percy Willmot of the 25th Battalion wrote to his people in Cape Breton in an attempt to convey the experience of the trenches, using a cartoon as a shared point of reference: "You remember the Bairnsfather picture of the 'Night before going into the trenches,' with the officers exhibiting a most woebegone cast of countenance."[17] The cartoonist's catchphrases or images became one means by which soldiers could voice their experiences.

FORMER TEACHER SAMUEL HONEY SHARED with his parents how much he admired Bairnsfather's cartoons for capturing "incidents and situations at the front in a humorous light, but yet with a great deal of grim reality underlying the humour. The exact extent of this reality, I never realized until I actually took part in similar incidents and situations."[18] Honey confessed that he wished he had a talent for drawing like Bairnsfather in order to better share his experiences, but he did not. However, other Canadians did, and their drawings and jokes were consumed throughout the CEF.

With the Canadian forces recruiting across the country and from all professions, there were many cartoonists in their ranks. Some were inspired by Bairnsfather and made no apologies for "sampling" his work. *Oh, Canada*, a wartime publication, included several cartoons that played on Bairnsfather's success, with titles like "A Figment from Flanders (with apologies to Captain B –nsf-----r.)," which depicts two scared Canadians working in the darkness of No Man's Land, either repairing or cutting through barbed wire, and bears the caption, "Say, George, when we get back to our farm in Ontario I'll bet the old snake fence will be good enough for me!" "Same here! I don't never want to see anymore of this blame stuff again (*And so say we, all of us!*)."[19] Here and in other mimicking cartoons, the Canadians were building on the accepted war-weary message established by Bairnsfather and other soldiers' cultural creations like songs and poetry. While not overtly anti-heroic, the depiction of men admitting fear and fatigue was far different from the hyper-patriotic speeches on the home front or the caricatured portrayal of superheroes on war posters. Canadian cartoonists presented all manner of subjects, with the anti-hero figuring prominently, although at least one cartoonist in *The Brazier*, the trench newspaper for the 3rd

SHORTY: "Here, pull that blinkin' flap down, or we'll both catch our death o' cold."

Two Canadian soldiers in a dugout, nonchalantly worrying about the cold as shells detonate around them. The caption reads, "Shorty: Here, pull that blinkin' flap down, or we'll both catch our death o' cold." Of course, the cartoonist makes it clear there are many other ways that the soldiers will catch their death.

Canadian Infantry Brigade, queried politely whether Alf and Old Bill and other characters of their ilk truly represented the Canadian soldiers. There was no answer to that question in subsequent issues of the paper; however, the same issue included the image of a dopey-looking Canadian soldier who could pass for Alf's twin, dreaming of happy times and tasty food away from the trenches.[20]

Cartoons were popular among editors of the trench newspapers as they created visual appeal in newspapers that were, by and large, made up of short essays, jokes, and poetry. *The Listening Post* boasted one of the most talented cartoonists in the CEF.[21] Private Hugh Farmer, a prewar baker who enlisted in his early thirties and earned multiple charges of drunkenness and misconduct during the war, was described by another envious trench newspaper editor as being "good enough to put him in the Capt. Bairnsfather class."[22] His drawings of Canadians usually presented them as stronger, fitter, and better-looking than Bairnsfather's sad-sack figures, but Farmer also embraced anti-heroism. One of his cartoons in December 1917 depicted a soldier trying to get out of the firing line by applying for a transfer to the motor transport unit. The officer asks, "What do you know about motors?" The private replies, "Only that they don't go into the trenches, sir."[23] This was gentle humour, no doubt, and with a simple punchline, but it was also a blatant acknowledgment of a haggard soldier looking to escape the front. And for good measure, the image insulted the transport soldiers in the service corps, positions that were usually derided by the infantry as "bomb-proof."

Some Canadian cartoonists were even more daring. *The Iodine Chronicle* made light of a bar fight in "Activities on the

December 1, 1917. THE LISTENING POST. *Special Christmas Number.*

THE ANCIENT ORDER OF LEAD SWINGERS.

Inaugural Meeting to be held far from No Man's Land.

ALL experts at swinging the lead are hereby notified that it is intended to form a new branch of the above association with special powers for dealing with refractory M.O.'s. All interested are requested to attend the meeting, which will be held two days prior to the next attack on the Western Front. The provisional committee, comprising the names of many eminent leaders of the cause, such as Lord Windhupp, Sir Verey Badhart, and the Duke of Wellinrear, have secured for this occasion a well-fortified dug-out in Absentee Square, facing Deserter Lane (map ref. 4½—4½, No. 9 Iodine). The M.F.P. will not be on duty, so prospective members need not carry their entrenching tool handles. All windy soldiers are welcome.

cushiest Field Ambulances (newly organised) in the Corps area.

NOTE.—Further suggestions will be open to discussion.

An appeal, largely signed by prisoners of war and conscientious objecters, has been addressed to commanding officers, requesting them to facilitate the attendance at this meeting of all ranks, and we are assured that defaulters and those in clink will be excused from DUTY on this occasion.

N.B.—Subscriptions, for the propagation of the praiseworthy objects of the above association, will be thankfully received by the Secretary of the above new branch.

PTE. EVERSICK, C.B. (toujours).

Temporary Branch Office: Swingit Ave., Billetville.

OFFICER (to applicant for transfer to M.T.): "What do you know about motors?"
PRIVATE: "Only that they don't go into the trenches, sir."

An anti-heroic cartoon from Private Hugh Farmer, who published regularly in The Listening Post.

Western front (Un-official)," which portrayed a wild brawl in an *estaminet*.[24] Alcohol-fuelled battles were not uncommon behind the lines between the Canadians and other national forces, or even among chippy Canadian units, but this drawing contains broken wine bottles used as weapons, as well as knives and pistols. With temperance groups at home already worried about soldiers' seemingly unfettered access to alcohol, either in wet canteens or via the daily rum ration, a cartoon depicting beer-soaked berserkers would have been no laughing matter.[25] But it was directed towards the soldiers, who well understood the pleasure of having a blow-out party before returning to the front, and who would perhaps have relished the angering effects that hyper-portrayals of drinking would have had on the temperance groups at home.

The hardships of the trenches remained the primary topic for most cartoonists—and writers of poems and prose, for that matter. Infantryman Richard Day, in a cartoon published in *The Listening*

"Hope springs eternal in the human breast." The jar contains rum, or so the soldier hopes.

Post, illustrated the harsh reality of the front—with its heavy emphasis on manual labour—in contrast to the idealized war that many men felt they were signing up for in Canada. The accompanying snide caption, "Come for a rest at the front," likely elicited a smile or chuckle.[26] Other trench newspaper cartoons focused on unpleasant aspects of the soldiers' everyday lives, such as the shortage of water for bathing, the eternal search for lice by "reading the shirt," and the fact that hard tack biscuits were most useful for lining the floor of a dugout.[27] *The Canadian Sapper* featured a drawing of some sad-sack Tommies in trenches filled with water, wondering if they might secure some torpedo nets to protect against U-boat attacks, a theme also presented in several Bairnsfather cartoons.[28]

THE IMPORTANCE OF LEAVE WAS emphasized by all soldiers in their letters, and it is not surprising that the cartoonists had their own opinions on this topic. *The Listening Post*'s cartoon of December 1, 1917, was particularly good at mashing up the subjects of leave and shell shock, with a dazed soldier returning to the Western Front from a period of leave. He's clearly had a good time on "vacation" in Paris or London, but it has also taken off his edge and left him vulnerable to the unending strain of the front, and he shakes with palsy and is drooling. "What's wrong, chum, shell-shock?" asks a mate, giving him coffee to soothe his nerves. "No, back off leave," the returnee responds.[29]

The front was indeed hellish, but home was also viewed with some ambiguity. The home front was both desired and despised, and both views were expressed in trench paper cartoons. "Just Dreams!," a cartoon in *The Twentieth Gazette*, depicted a soldier

COOK: "*What's wrong, chum, shell-shock?*"
BILL: "*No, back off leave.*"

fantasizing about civilian life: having fought in battle and received leave as a reward, he then enjoys his time as he walks down a city road with a girl on his arm.[30] That was the place where soldiers wanted to be, and there was much nostalgia for loved ones and the community left behind.[31] But not all cartoons presented a positive image of the soldiers' relationship to civilians. Soldiers hated those who they believed were shirking their duty—men back home who were making money or living soft lives while the soldiers risked all overseas. *The Listening Post*'s November 1915 issue took a typical shot at the slackers back home, drawing one of them as effeminate, clearly from the upper class with his fancy walking stick, and strolling nonchalantly past a "Your King and

Country Need You" sign with an upturned nose.[32] The soldiers believed that those at home could never understand their torment—neither the physical nor the mental strain—but, in a contradiction that the soldiers easily squared, they relied heavily on the home front's moral support, in the form of encouragement, love, and material comforts. For soldiers, there were both good and bad civilians—those who supported them, and the rest.

Life after the war, or *après la guerre*, as the soldiers wistfully referred to it, was a subject of much speculation. Cartoonist P.G. McGibbon published in *The Silent 60th*, the regimental paper for the 60th Battalion until the unit was broken up in the aftermath of the Vimy battle. One of his cleverest cartoons, "When This Gory War Is Over," showed a soldier after the war, unable to cope with his reintegration into society. The veteran sleeps with sandbags on his feet; he rents a dugout for his family; his wife and children must present themselves to him, backs ramrod straight, for daily parade; and the "pop, pop" of the motor bike sends him fleeing in terror, as the sound reminds him of incoming shells.[33] There was no glory in the aftermath of the gory war that, for many soldiers—should they survive to be veterans—would go on forever.

Like the songs, skits, newspaper accounts, and almost everything else produced by the soldiers, there was a healthy dose of anti-authoritarianism in the cartoons. It was easy and fun to taunt the officers, and *The Splint Record* took a jab at the officers with the cartoon "Things that Never Happen," which showed an officer refusing leave.[34] With officers receiving about four times as much leave time as enlisted men, the inequality was a source of friction between the leaders and those they led. For good measure, the officer in this cartoon is depicted with a large bottom and a flamboyant wave, as he girlishly turns his legs inward in an act of "cheerio!"

"When This Gory War Is Over"

Adding some blood to the cartoon, the Canadian officer granting the leave is depicted as a fat upper-cruster with a monocle. Another cartoon from *The Forty-Niner* showed unhappy infantrymen billeting with pigs on a farm while the officers enjoyed better quarters. It was a reminder to the commissioned class that the rank and file would not accept these indignities without some pushback.[35]

"Things that never happen. An officer refusing his leave."

SOLDIERS ADMIRED THEIR TOUGH COMRADES and brave leaders. They relied on one another for survival, and all soldiers appreciated those men whose courage on the battlefield was expressed through knocking out deadly machine guns or carrying a wounded mate out of a fiery killing zone. There were NCOs who inspired all with their professionalism and skill, and long-service men at the front were respected for their knowledge and sheer survival skills. The best officers shared the danger with their men, leading from the front and often dying in front of those they led.

While everyone in the unit knew of fearless men by word of mouth, gallantry medals were another way to single out the uncommonly courageous. The British War Office established new medals during the course of the war, including the Military Medal (MM), the Military Cross (MC), the Distinguished Service Order (DSO), and the Distinguished Conduct Medal (DCM), with the

MM and DCM given out to NCOs and other ranks, and the MC and DSO reserved for officers. Even though these medals were awarded with more frequency as the war went on, and some deserving soldiers went unrecognized while others reaped the benefits of friendships, patronage, or being at the right place at the right time, the medals were nonetheless scarce. A study of one unit, the 14th Battalion, suggests that only four in a hundred men received a gallantry decoration, while seventy-one out of a hundred could be expected to be wounded or killed.[36] The Empire's highest award for gallantry, the Victoria Cross (VC), which could be issued to officers or the rank and file, came with immeasurable glory and transformed a soldier into a legend. But of the sixty-four VCs awarded to Canadian soldiers or airmen during the war, twenty-eight were awarded posthumously.[37]

And yet the soldiers also accepted the anti-heroes depicted in cartoons, poetry, and other cultural products, with scoffing at bravery, proper soldiering, and even medals becoming established practice. A joke in the June 1916 *The Listening Post* offers some insight:

> Bill: "Say, here that Jock Robinson got the D.C.M."
> Fred: "What for?"
> Bill: "I dunno."
> Fred: "Blimy, why ain't I got one too, I hid in the same dug-out."[38]

The joke here speaks to the sometimes liberal dishing out of medals, although, again, soldiers were often deeply impressed by men with medals. The contradictions sat easily in the soldiers' society.

The most perplexing cultural figures were the "old soldiers," who were popular in songs, poetry, and cartoons. These were the

One of the anti-heroic cartoons by Private Hugh Farmer, who published in The Listening Post. *It reads:*
"Lieut: Now Pte Coldfeet, if you were in the trenches, and the Germans were coming to attack what steps would you take?"
Pte Coldfeet (Promptly): Long quick ones Sir."

men who had served at the front for several years and who no longer had a warlike demeanour. They had seen most of their buddies killed or wounded, and they knew that the true purpose of life as a trench warrior was to avoid work and to survive. The dodging of responsibility frequently involved deceiving NCOs, officers, and medical officers—cannily tricking those in power, usually with fake illnesses or injuries. Volunteering for anything, these old hands advised the new men, was a good way to get oneself killed. These malingerers and anti-heroic types offered those in uniform a way to view the war with a grim smile and an apathetic shrug, another subtle means for civilian-soldiers to exert agency. In a cartoon in *The Listening Post*, Hugh Farmer captured such anti-heroism and codified one of the popular quips among soldiers. In the drawing, a nattily dressed officer speaks to a Canadian infantryman, appropriately named "Pte. Coldfeet." The lieutenant asks, "Now Pte. Coldfeet, if you were in the trenches, and the Germans were coming to attack [,] what steps would you take [?]" Coldfeet replies promptly, "Long quick one's [*sic*] sir."[39] To those who were not a part of the soldiers' culture, cartoons depicting anti-heroic actions, gallows humour, and biting satire could be shocking, even misconstrued as evidence of soldiers' wish to abandon the war effort. Had the army been reduced to cowards? Had rot set in to the once proud fighting forces? The truth was that while some soldiers were always close to succumbing to the stress of combat, most understood their role in the war and the need to win, and they were not anxious to abandon their mates in the lurch. But representations of anti-hero helped the soldiers deal with the strain engendered by the boredom, banality, and brutality of trench warfare. "It is the soldier's privilege to grouse," wrote Armine Norris, an enlisted man who later received a commission. "These are the same kind of men who, with eyes wide open, entered hell to die for people and a country that had never done anything very special for them."[40]

A cartoon from *The Forty-Niner* summed up the appeal of the "old soldier." In the drawing, one such soldier stands at attention before his commanding officer at a court-martial, where he is being punished for returning late from leave, and looks the worse for wear after two weeks of drinking in England. On being asked why he was late, the private replies respectfully, "Sir, I was hurrying to catch my train and I met the Salvation Army Band playing 'God Save the King.' I had to stand at attention as became a Forty-Niner, and it caused me to lose my train by about a minute." The commanding officer, who knows he is hearing a tall tale, nonetheless replies, "Dismissed," thereby letting the "old soldier" off the hook.[41]

Using his wits, the old hand talks his way out of a tight situation, and his commanding officer grants him that escape without either man losing face. Visual stories like these offered powerful and popular messages to the Canadian soldiers, who wanted to know that they had a chance of escaping some of the worst examples of disciplinary punishment through their street smarts and slippery actions.

NOT ALL CARTOONISTS SOUGHT TO publish in the newspapers. Men sketched and doodled in notebooks and journals, capturing many aspects of the war, and good cartoons were passed around with approval and hearty laughs, then pinned to the wall of dugouts or near latrines. Like those who offered memorable jokes or limericks, skilled cartoonists soon distinguished themselves among their peers with their deft drawings and cruel caricatures. Cartoons could be ripped from the journals and sold or given to mates.

Talented artists tried to capture the war experience visually. Louis Keene, a prewar artist and newspaper cartoonist, published his wartime memoirs, *"Crumps": The Plain Story of a Canadian Who Went*, and liberally sprinkled drawings and sketches throughout it. His book starts with a brilliant evocation of soldiers' culture, as a sad-sack Old Bill character reclines in the mud and sings

> The CRUMPS'; they whistle
> An' roar!
> I don't wanta go to the trenches
> no more,
> I wanna go, acrost the sea,
> Where the Allemands cant
> git me.

Ho! Hi! I don't wanna die!
I wanta go home
I wanta go HOME!

Keene served as a lieutenant in a suicide squad, as the soldiers sometimes called a machine-gun section, before being wounded in 1917 and sent home to Canada. Somewhat surprisingly, he healed and re-enlisted as part of the 4,000-strong Canadian contribution to the Siberian Expeditionary Force late in 1918, which spent a miserable half year in Russia assisting, where they could, the Whites against the revolutionary Red forces. Keene sketched and painted to fight the boredom, and he left a strong legacy of art.

Herbert Heckford Burrell was an overage soldier who served on the Western Front with the 1st Canadian Mounted Rifles, usually in the role of stretcher-bearer. Burrell, an accomplished prewar artist who had worked for *Punch* magazine, sketched throughout his service, creating a multi-volume diary filled with seething visual commentary on the soldiers' hardships. One wicked depiction was a pen-and-ink drawing of a rat, with the caption, "one of our trench friends."[42] Another prewar artist, Private Harold Harvey, who had exhibited at the Royal Academy, enlisted in the First Contingent and went overseas to the trenches. Harvey drew cartoons of much of what he saw, which were later published as *A Soldier's Sketches Under Fire*, but, as he noted, "There were many happenings—repulsions of sudden attacks, temporary retirements, charges, and all things of that sort that would have made capital subjects, but of which my notebook holds no 'pictured presentment,' because I was taking part in them."[43]

Some of the soldiers' cartoons even made it home during the war. *Maclean's* magazine offered Canadians a cartoonist's view of the Western Front when it published the work of Gunner G.D. McRitchie and Driver H.W. Cooper in several issues. In the November 1916 issue, McRitchie offered a cartoon titled "When They Come Over," which depicted a soldier jumping for cover, any cover, in this case behind a flower, as a shell soared over him.[44] In another cartoon, a sergeant holding a broken jar of rum, the essential tool for bolstering morale, is quaking before a none-too-pleased colonel; it is titled "That Awful Moment," and the caption reads, "When you have to explain how you broke the rum jar on the way to the guns." Driver Cooper created a series of cartoons and drawings to accompany a story, and he prefaced the piece by noting, "There is nothing picturesque about war and there is nothing picturesque about these sketches: they show rubbish heaps and broken walls and soldiers in uniforms . . . but they give momentary glimpses of things as they are over here." He took the time to capture the "most important thing in a soldier's life," and promised, "it is not going to be a story of a charge, or the gaining of decorations or of a big advance. The most important thinking in a soldier's life is when he goes on leave! He thinks of it for weeks in advance and he lives on the memory of it for months after he has come back."[45] At least one overseas soldier nodded in approval at the cartoons that had made their way back to the trenches, writing, "I have read a couple of articles from McLeans [*sic*] and they sure are good. If you read the trench letters of Driver Cooper you get a pretty fair idea of what it is like out here and the sketches are good too. His pen pictures of how our feelings run are correct."[46]

However sharp the satirists' wit, there were still boundaries. The cartoonists' prodding of authority never questioned the right of rule. Nonetheless, such jabs reminded those at the top that consent needed to be earned. This coded warning was presented in relatively non-threatening pictorial language, but there was truth in the violence and mayhem depicted. Exaggeration and hyperbole were tools of the cartoonists' trade, and while not all of the cartoons were fair or nice, especially in their portrayal of

TOMMY, AFTER MEETING MR. TICKLER,
"Na then, show me where Mr. Maconochie lives."

Soldiers' culture could be difficult to decipher for those outside the closed society. This cartoon depicts a Canadian Tommy beating up "Mr. Tickler." He goes on to say, "Na then, show me where Mr. Maconochie lives." The joke only makes sense if the viewer knows that Tickler and Maconochie were types of canned meat, which the soldiers grew tired of in the trenches. This soldier is seeking out the manufacturers of the food to deliver some payback.

civilians, these works from the trenches revealed aspects of the soldiers' secret culture. Bairnsfather's Old Bill and his other cartoon comrades railed against the system, sometimes beating it, often simply enduring it. But they were not beaten by it. Bairnsfather's success in capturing that idea in his cartoons led to his tremendous success. Even as the cartoonists and their audience embraced the anti-heroic, there was something quite heroic about the soldiers' stoicism in facing the worst that the war could throw at them.

CHAPTER 9

MATERIAL CULTURE

"I never saw such men as the Canadians are for souvenirs—helmets, buttons, belts or anything at all. Men take the greatest risks for the sake of some souvenir off a dead Fritz. A saying of the German prisoners is 'the English fight for honour, the Australians for glory, and the Canadians for souvenirs.'" So wrote Canadian Great War infantryman Lieutenant R.S. Hicks over the winter of 1916, describing the Canadians' reputation for scavenging and collecting war material.[1] The statement was an exaggeration, although much repeated by soldiers and even printed in a Canadian trench newspaper.[2] Canadians may have excelled at collecting keepsakes, but other Allied soldiers and the Germans also gathered all they could from the battlefield. This collection of material culture from the battlefield and enemy soldiers was another aspect of the soldiers' closed society.

In a war of unprecedented death and destruction, where soldiers' lives were expended in sickening numbers for minimal gain, why was there a desire on the part of the fighting men to collect objects and material from the battlefield? Souvenirs are defined as remembrance objects, even mnemonics of events, and yet soldiers actively pursued these representations of death, suffering, and loss. The instinct was so strong among Canadian soldiers that they embraced a new name to encapsulate the act: "souveneering." The term, which encompassed the gathering of souvenirs on the battlefield and the fleecing of valuables from prisoners of war, was used by British soldiers who engaged in the same collection of goods, and the Canadians adopted the word.[3] Battlefield trinkets, German Iron Crosses, and even shrapnel extracted from flesh were prized trophies, but soldiers had even stronger connections to these material objects, which reveals something important about the soldiers' culture. Souvenirs held multiple meanings, and these harvested battlefield relics were proof of service on the Western Front and a sign of victory over the enemy. Bullets, shrapnel, badges, and pins also made a unique gift for loved ones at home, with these items providing a link to the soldier at the front. One of the soldiers' most evocative uses of souvenirs was in turning them into art. By twisting steel casings and soldering bullets and shrapnel, soldiers took the remnants of death-dealing weapons and transformed them into sculptural works that held deep meaning for those at the front.

SOLDIERS HAVE ALWAYS SOUGHT THE spoils of war. For much of human history, armed men who risked life and limb augmented their meagre pay (if they received any) with loot and trophies. In premodern times, prisoners were ransomed for money or sold into slavery. Treasures and goods were pillaged from the conquered. But much had changed by the time of the Great War. Massive armies of civilian-soldiers were now the norm, and these soldiers were paid consistently (at least in the British Empire armies), though few of them expected to grow rich from their service. In

Canada, as throughout the British Empire, the conflict was portrayed as a just war against German aggression. With France and Belgium overrun and occupied, the Canadians, who arrived on the battlefield in early 1915, saw themselves as a force of liberation. Strict rules and discipline ensured that the armies, for the most part, did not "live off the land" like the forces of old, stealing from civilians whatever they needed to survive and damning those same wretches to privation and starvation. The static nature of the front, which dictated that soldiers spent weeks, months, and sometimes years on the same battlefield, created strong connections to places like Ypres, the Somme, and Vimy Ridge. These foreign battlefields became very familiar, and the trenches were the soldiers' temporary homes.

In this blasted landscape of barbed wire, sandbags, muck, and unburied corpses, there were few obvious sites of interest. But over time, the shattered tree that defied the shells, the red poppies that struggled up through the mud, and even the dead hanging on the old barbed wire became identifiable markers in the warscape. The ground was poisoned with metal and gas, churned by shells and high explosives, cratered and ripped open, but it held treasures.[4] Amid the craters, the shells' brass nose caps often survived intact, along with tons of splintered shell-canister shards. These weirdly shaped objects became souvenirs for most soldiers at the front, with almost all men carrying a few around in their packs until they could figure out how to get them home. As Private Donald Fraser recounted in his diary, "Many of the fellows are busy gathering souvenirs, mainly nosecaps. SP 10 [a trench system] is the happy hunting ground."[5] Experienced soldiers learned to dig about a third of a metre below the centre of a shell crater, with one soldier remarking that the surviving brass caps were "beautifully made, and [had] about a dozen fine adjustments for timing."[6] Soldiers banded together with like-minded chums and went exploring for their buried treasures. The thrill of the hunt bonded men, and separation could be painful. Infantryman John McNab wrote about the loss of his friend, lamenting, "He was out sniping, and took too many chances and got sniped himself. I could not believe it at first. . . . I sure miss him here, for when we were here before he slept with me, and we used to go out souvenir hunting together, but now he is gone."[7]

The best prizes were often to be found in No Man's Land. One Canadian trench newspaper joked, "Real estate in No Man's Land is placed there for the express purpose of allowing one to dig for souvenirs, and on no account is one allowed to use it for any other purpose."[8] Though trench newspapers often made light of the soldiers' trials and privations, the blasted area between the trenches was a lethal space, swept almost continuously by small-arms fire. Captain William E.L. Coleman, having been awarded the Military Cross with Bar (in effect receiving the award twice), remarked incredulously to his diary on October 23, 1915, that it was a misty morning and hard for enemy snipers to see targets, so "many Canadians dangerously went into No Man's Land on a 'souvenir hunt.'"[9] "Hopping the bags," as the soldiers called the reckless act of leaving the safety of the trench, Canadians would then set about crawling in broken ground, moving from crater to crater, seeking their souvenirs. Victor Swanston of the 5th Battalion talked about collecting in No Man's Land under the cover of darkness: "Percy and I slipped out through our wire into No Man's Land tonight and 'Believe Me' the place was just 'lousy' with shell noses. We gathered about a sand bag full of them and crawled back into our trench."[10] Swanston and his mate were exposing themselves to enemy fire and their own trigger-happy sentries to collect the brass shell caps that would later be sold or traded behind the lines. The risks associated with "souveneering" did not dissuade many soldiers. No doubt most of the men already believed they lived in a perilous world and that fate would claim them when it was ready. H.M. Urquhart, who served as a major in the 16th Battalion before being wounded, observed that the Canadian Tommy "was prepared to jeopardize, indeed, lose, his life, in such trivial pursuits as souvenir hunting."[11]

While the massive popularity of collecting souvenirs in No Man's Land made it more than a trivial pursuit, there were more hazards to be feared than those posed by the enemy. Amid the hundreds of tons of twisted metal were countless "dud" shells, ordnance that had not exploded but that remained unstable and liable to detonate at any moment. Soldiers prized the nose-caps and the fuses that remained intact. Infantryman Kenneth Foster described an occasion when he and three mates went out in search of souvenirs. One of the soldiers, Matthews, "would pick up 'duds' and attempt to remove the nose-cap, foolish boy, considering that he knew nothing about them and there were four reasons why he should leave them alone. I was one of them." After Foster and the others convinced Matthews to stop messing with live ordnance, he stopped, but the collecting habit was too ingrained, and Matthews was killed a short time later after he collected and then tossed away a German grenade that detonated.[12] This was not an isolated incident. Harold Simpson, a gunner in the 2nd Canadian Siege Battery, recounted one funny story of how his battery mates searched for souvenirs on the Somme, especially the fuses of dud shells: he came across one of the gunners straddling an eight-inch dud "with a hammer and cold chisel, trying to

Bruce Bairnsfather captures two dopey soldiers engaged in chiselling off a fuse from an unexploded shell. The humour here comes from a dangerous task being engaged in so lightly by the soldiers.

The Dud Shell — Or the Fuse-Top Collector

loosen the fuse, and yelling at our mascot dog as he approached him, 'Get out of the way, you darn fool! Do you want to get your head blown off?'"[13]

The soldiers' quest for souvenirs was driven partly by their need to augment their pay. New recruits to the front were good customers, being especially willing to purchase German souvenirs, weapons, and kit. Will Bird, who served from 1915 to 1918, recounted how in one of his first tours back from the trenches he bought from an engineer a German Luger and a sawtooth bayonet for a mere ten francs (about two Canadian dollars).[14] The relics were proof of his having made it to the sharp end of battle, even if he had not personally captured the items in question. Captain Frank Morison of the 16th Battalion had seen fierce fighting throughout 1915, with most of his company being wiped out in two major battles, but he wanted an Iron Cross—an enemy gallantry medal—to show for his service. And he was not above

A photograph of Canadians emulating Bairnsfather's cartoon characters.

paying for one, remarking, "One of my lads obtained an Iron Cross last Thursday. I tried to buy it from him but he desired to send it home. German souvenirs in the shape of rifles, bayonet, helmets and the like are so numerous that they sicken you. If I can locate a cross however I shall certainly keep it."[15]

Trophies could also be used to trade with other units to acquire prized cap badges, collar tags, or other patches or markers on uniforms. Many soldiers created souvenir belts, which acquired the odd name of "hate belts."[16] By sewing several belts together, soldiers had a ready-made surface on which to affix badges and pins that they acquired through trade, purchase, theft, or "souveneering." Infantryman C.J. Bell of the 29th Battalion took a stable belt made of beige cloth with leather and metal buttons and eventually attached fifteen British cap badges to it.[17] John Lynch of the PPCLI remembered one occasion when his unit encountered exotic French

Canadian soldiers holding and wearing the spoils of war, including German pickelhaube *helmets.*

Algerian troops behind the lines. As wine flowed, the men mixed freely, and "They fairly mobbed us and insisted upon trading their badges, buttons and knickknacks for our badges and buttons as tokens as esteem and to be kept as cherished souvenirs."[18]

While some of the souvenirs were presumably sold, others were kept as memory items. Private Harold Peat, whose service at the front was limited to a few months in 1915 before he was wounded, brought back home a leather belt decorated with the cap and regimental badges from his dead comrades to remember them.[19] The determined act of collecting and assembling such mementos were a tangible representation of the soldiers' hope that they would survive the war.[20]

Survivors' trophies were inscribed with victory and loss. Arthur Lapointe of the 22nd Battalion described his cut-up unit after the

August 1917 Battle of Hill 70, noting, "We set off and pass through a number of villages, whose inhabitants are roused by the shouts of our men as they display trophies taken in battle. I myself have on the spike German helmet I found on the day of the attack."[21] Writing in his diary on April 10, during the battle of Vimy Ridge, infantryman Théodore Dugas was no less revealing about how souvenirs served as signs of victory, remarking, "C'est une grande victoire pour les Canadiens. Pourtout où j'ai passé c'etait un massacre de Boches. J'ai enleveé plusieurs trophées, entre autre un casque allemand, un helmet et un revolver."[22] Battlefield booty represented success and survival, and through collecting souvenirs, soldiers materialized the defeat of their enemies. After the titanic battle of the Somme in late 1916, in which 24,000 Canadians were killed or maimed, along with an estimated one million Allied and German soldiers, *The Listening Post* observed, "Everyone collected souvenirs. There were gas masks for ma-in-law, buttons for the baby, parcels from dear, old Wurtemberg for immediate consumption, suitable gifts of all sorts. They bulged out of every privates' pockets. . . . Everywhere there were tokens of Fritz."[23] These mementos could be picked up from the dead, from overrun dugouts, or from defenders who discarded them on the battlefield while fleeing from the front. But the most common method of acquiring souvenirs was by stealing them from German prisoners of war.

Soldiers were instructed by the high command to collect any sort of documents or orders they found in overrun dugouts or in the possession of enemy officers to aid the Allies in knowing their opponents. Most Canadians used the opportunity to pat down and relieve all prisoners of their valuables.[24] After Vimy, infantryman G.R. Stevens joked that "there was a brisk trade in souvenirs, with pickelhaubes [spiked helmets] and Luger pistols galore; an

Canadian soldiers gathering up prisoners' wallets, documents, and whatever else the captured men might have, as they move from the trenches to the rearward cages.

astonishing number of the prisoners wore wrist watches that they would not need in the future."[25] George Kempling wrote in his diary about the large number of prisoners on the Somme: "Our lads would walk alongside them hollering 'souvenir' in their ears and grab their hats or cut the buttons from their coats. As a rule, the Germans were like frightened sheep and were very passive under this ordeal."[26]

The prisoners were passive because they feared for their lives. It was not uncommon to execute prisoners on the battlefield, especially in the midst of the chaos of combat, with adrenaline pumping, fear prevalent, and revenge on the mind of men who had just seen their best friends torn apart by shell and shot, or remembered the rumour of the crucified Canadian at Ypres.[27] As Lieutenant

C.B.F. Jones observed after combat, the terrified Germans who had thrown down their arms "began to pull out watches and souvenirs" and hand them to Canadians as a sign of non-resistance and passivity.[28] Most German prisoners weighed the odds and came to the conclusion that a watch or a Luger was not worth protesting over, especially when one's life was in danger during the march from the battlefield to prisoner cages at the rear.

The act of stealing from prisoners had the unintended advantage of creating a period of post-battle cooling down. Stripping prisoners of their personal effects—watches, rings, money, and even personal letters and photographs—was common practice among the soldiers in all armies. This fraught interaction was part of a complex interplay of power. There were informal signs and symbols to surviving on the battlefield, with prisoners crying, "'Mercy!' 'Mercy!'" to every Canadian they met," according to Lieutenant James Pedley, "and the victors in turn yelling 'Souvenir!'"[29] Prisoners hoped that their hurried, fumbling offer of souvenirs would buy them some good will from those who would decide their fate. Moreover, taking the time to sort through a prisoner's photographs of his loved ones at home was a crucial step in humanizing the enemy, and it reminded soldiers of their shared humanity with those they had captured. Divesting the prisoner of his valuables, a process sometimes accompanied by other acts of humiliation—such as threats and both verbal and physical abuse—was an act of disempowering a defeated foe, but it also allowed for a soldier to cool off from the frenzy of battle and to see the enemy as a man like himself. The "souveneering" impulse saved German lives.

The gathering of souvenirs extended to robbing the dead. Soldiers in search of prizes often rifled freely through corpses, picking through blood-soaked uniforms, hands brushing away the flies and trying to avoid the maggots. Private George Hatch described the scene after a bloody engagement: "Germans by the thousands lying dead. Every one of us were hunting for souvenirs."[30] John MacKenzie, who enlisted at sixteen and was fighting at the front by eighteen, also took part in gathering souvenirs, although at times he felt his comrades could go too far. One of his company mates came back boasting of his newly acquired golden wedding ring taken from a slain German. MacKenzie was sickened by the macabre act, noting, "I wasn't very pleased about it."[31] N.A.D. Armstrong reacted even more violently when he saw Allied soldiers rummaging through the dead, both German and Canadian, during the August 1918 Battle of Amiens. "Battle, terror and sudden death no doubt numbs the brain and feelings of a certain type of a man who then will commit any sacrilegious act possible. The penalty for looting a dead comrade should be death on the spot. This would act as a deterrent if public in orders."[32] Armstrong believed many of the pillagers at Amiens were not the front-line soldiers but the rear-area service corps men, who, in his mind, did not have the same code of honour in treating the fallen enemy or even their own comrades. While that may have been the case in this instance, the front-line infantry were, in general, just as likely to search enemy dead for possessions. For most men, though, there was a line not to be crossed when it came to relieving Canadian dead of their goods, an act that went against the soldiers' code because those items were sent back to the grieving next of kin.

While the newly killed were open to all comers, grave-robbing seemed beyond the realm of the acceptable. Canadian infantryman Herbert Heckford Burrell recounted in his diary in May 1917, "Passed a ghoul on the way back, disinterring dead soldiers (not from cemetery or clearly marked grave though) with a spade, hunting for souvenirs. He had unearthed a German soldier and secured the helmet with a small cross attached, and said he could obtain a 100 frcs. for it. I was too disgusted to talk to him and passed. I regret I did not have him arrested, did not notice if he was a Canadian or Imperial. . . ."[33] Burrell was a long-service veteran at this point and was clearly dismayed at the grave-robbing. Most of this activity was confined to the search for prized objects rather than the collection of body parts, the latter of which was sometimes seen in the racialized Pacific campaign between the Americans and the Japanese during the Second World War. Though there were disturbing accounts on the Western Front of soldiers digging out gold teeth for their value, there appears to be no mention of "dark trophies," a term referring to collected human remains such as skulls or earlobes.[34] Private Ernie Thomas, a stretcher-bearer at Vimy, recounted with disgust how one of his comrades spent his days and nights digging for the dead who lay in the trenches from previous battles: "I seen him digging through old skulls trying to find gold teeth. French skulls, German skulls."[35] This deviant behaviour was too much for most soldiers to accept, although it was no doubt stimulated in part by the rough, masculine coping mechanism of soldiers who lived with death every day. "While in Canada I was a little shaky when I saw any dead body," wrote Private George Hatch. "Here it is like walking over rye straw."[36]

Claude Williams, a former medical student, shared with his mother his fascination with corpses and his particular take on the art of "souveneering":

> You can hardly move anywhere without stepping into a pile of bones or some other sign of our dearly beloved departed, very few of them English though, all German and French, we can

> always tell by the clothing and equipment they have on. You know how seemingly morbid I am about "stiffs" etc., well, I used to go searching about everywhere for good specimens of bone for my collection, I now have nearly a whole skeleton rigged under my bed, the worst of it is he is a composite of a French and Hun. I don't know whether that will agree or not, I will have to put a little English in to temper it down. It is funny how hardened and accustomed you do become to these things though, the sight is so familiar that you never think twice about it, but I must stop, I must write something that the rest will appreciate.[37]

Although Williams seemed to know he had crossed a line in writing about his bone collection, the practice was clearly not taboo in his own unit, where his reconstruction of a skeleton must have been carried out with at least implicit approval. Most soldiers were not interested in such things, encountering enough corpses, skeletons, and bones while serving in the trenches.

WEAPONS ARE THE TRANSFORMATION OF material into agents of destruction and killing. Steel becomes shrapnel; saltpeter and sulfur become gunpowder or propellant; chlorine chemicals become poison gas. Yet so too can these weapons become objects of art. Casings and cartridges, bullets and shell nose caps, were transformed by the trench soldiers from objects of death into objects of art. This material culture—known as trench art—ranged from candlestick holders to cigarette cases, from walking sticks to letter openers, and from little toys to jewellery. Created in the trenches and behind the front lines, this art was popular with the soldiers and collected by many of them.

The military authorities overseas created an official art program in 1916 that would eventually produce more than a thousand works of art, with over a hundred British and Canadian artists sent to paint along the front. Most of them used watercolours in the field, painting every day, before returning to studios in England where they used oils on large canvases.[38] These works were displayed during and after the war, and they remain a powerful visual legacy. Trench art was very different, however, as it was ignored by the established military forces, but its creation was also deemed illegal because it used recyclable military material that was declared off limits. Brass was expensive, and vast foraging units scoured the battlefield picking it up, along with discarded helmets, water bottles, rifles, and almost everything else. The military authorities claimed ownership over all shells and shell casings, with the idea of collecting them and reusing the metal to forge new weapons. But declaring that the art was illegal did little to dissuade artists, although most of the wartime pieces were not signed by their soldier artists for fear of retribution, or only initials were engraved, with some of the slyer soldiers using their wives' or towns' names as identifiers.[39] Trench art by its very nature, then, was unsanctioned. No artist ever seemed to be prosecuted, but the official artist program also made no effort to amass examples of this battle art. It was left to the soldiers to create and collect it.

"A couple of weeks ago I sent home a small box with a few souvenirs I had made up and among them was a paper-knife which I asked Nell to forward to you," wrote Garnet Dobbs to his friends Lottie and Walt. "This was one of my first attempts and is not just as 'nifty' as I would have liked it to be but I was very much handicapped at that time for tools and did the best possible with the tools at my command. . . . I might state that the handle

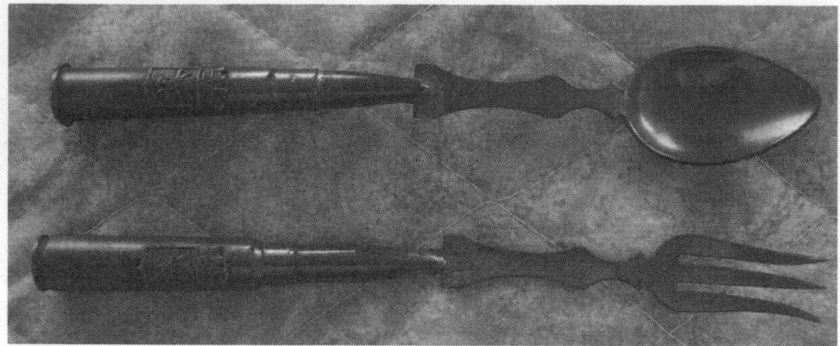

Trench art spoon and knife formed from bullets.

Trench art shell casings engraved with "Ypres" and "Yser."

of that knife is a Boche bullet. The engraving looks as though it was a souvenir of a drunk but wait till you see some of the later work."[40] Sergeant Dobbs, from Belleville, Ontario, was proud of his trench art, even as he struggled to craft something for those at home. Without workshops or proper tools, soldiers were hampered in their work. And yet there was an authenticity to this rough and jagged art forged in the combat zone.

Soldiers often gathered brass casings and turned their creative attention to the exterior, on which they engraved designs and names using a metal pick, while other tools allowed for the bending of the metal. While military crests and names and dates of battles could be scratched in with pride, there were also many works with complex pastoral motifs, including flowers, leaves, or other flora. Some soldiers lacked the necessary skills to carry out this intricate work, and so entrepreneurs behind the lines set up shop to deal with the trade coming in from this quarter. Engineers could pursue a solid black-market wage in this pursuit, as did civilian metalsmiths. Chinese labourers behind the lines, who eventually numbered around 140,000, sometimes augmented their meagre pay by inscribing Chinese characters into the shell casings or other forms of art for a commission, adding an exotic flavour to the object.

Pens and letter openers were crafted from spent bullets and scrap metal, and photo frames made with bullets and shrapnel were popular and often sent home, occasionally enclosing a picture snapped of the man in uniform or his mates in London. There were also flower vases and water jugs, but much of the trench art centred on smoking. The soldiers were heavy smokers, and

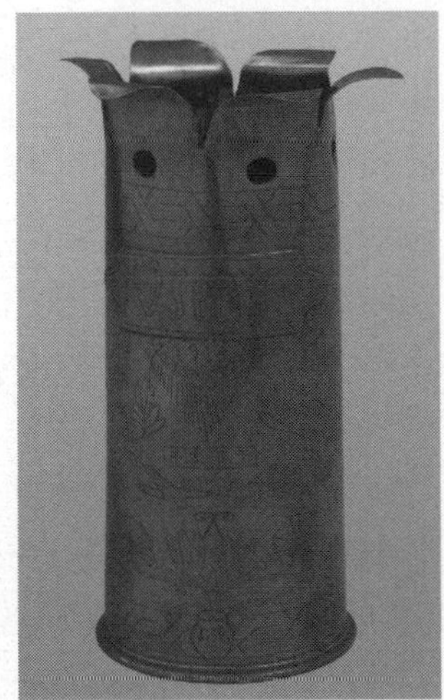

Trench art engraved with "Vimy" and Chinese characters.

lighters, pipes, ashtrays, matchboxes, and tobacco holders had a functional purpose as well as that of a memory object. They ranged from simple and plain to intricate and gaudy. In the post-war years, the conflict of the trenches was remembered daily, sometimes, hourly, with each use of the tobacco trench art.

While metal objects remained the most recognizable form of trench art, there were other works made from chalk, wood, and textiles. With a chunk of chalk, a knife, and some patience, soldiers could carve their own trench art. Percy Kingsley, a First Contingent man who was wounded at Festubert in May 1915 but returned to the front carrying shrapnel in his arm, described the creative use of clay on the Vimy front: "Some of our boys made some sculptures with this clay which was wet enough to work like putty."[41] Not all of the art fashioned by the soldiers was meant to be sent home. Thousands of men took the opportunity to etch their names and hometowns into the soft chalk of the tunnels and caves below ground that protected them from shellfire. The more adventurous tried their hand at carving women, animals, or regimental crests.

Gunner Philippe Gagné of the 13th Battery wrote to his wife in September 1917, ". . . I have been on the battlefield for two years and let me assure you that I have seen so many atrocities, but if we are healthy, that's all that matters. I hope that you have received the package I sent you. It contains souvenirs made of small shrapnel from the battlefield. I can't put a finishing touch on them because I don't have any tools here. Give me the birth dates of the children and if I can, I will send them more mementos from the battlefield."[42] Despite the lack of tools at the front, artist-soldiers would not be deterred. Private Arthur Lee of the 3rd Canadian Engineers turned his skills towards crafting a match box and a bracelet. The bracelet was made from French bullets that he

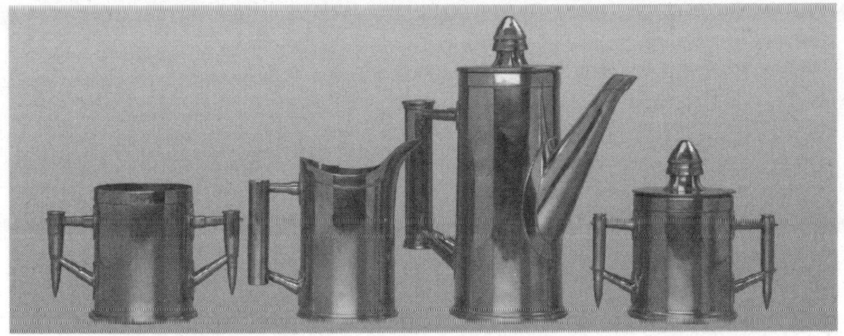

Elaborate trench art tea set created from shell casings, bullets, and shell fuses. This was forged by Corporal Frank Cameron of Barrie, Ontario, who served as a signaller in the 2nd Canadian Division. He worked on the set for four years, sending each piece home as he finished it.

carefully laid on a track where a light rail train flattened them, while the matchbox was made on the Lens front from a German shell case and held brimstone matches that had a tendency to explode in one's pocket as a result of friction.[43] Working long hours, Lee used a small hammer and file, along with a needle, to engrave the pieces.

The trench art reflected the taste and needs of the soldiers. Unlike the official war art, the art born of the trenches came from the masses of fighting men themselves. This art, created through the transformation of weapons of death into artful artifacts, was one more example of how soldiers were able to exert their own agency in the trenches.

WITH ALL THE TROUBLE SOLDIERS went through to gather their trophies and trinkets, and the time they might spend creating art from them, they found that they could not easily send them back to Canada. Leo LeBoutillier of the 24th Battalion wrote home about his souvenirs after the June 1916 Battle of Mount Sorrel, remarking, "I have had a lot of souvenirs more caps of shells and hunks of shrapnel but I have thrown everything away, too heavy to carry. . . . I only wish I could have kept all the souvenirs I picked up, but it's impossible to carry them."[44] Gunner Roy Grosgrey sent a similar baleful letter to his loved ones, noting, "We could get lots of souvenirs but can carry hardly anything."[45] Lieutenant Clifford Wells explained to one relative in Canada who was seeking a souvenir, "Certain articles only can be taken as souvenirs. German rifles and revolvers are taboo, although they are sometimes smuggled across to Blighty. I carried a little German novel that I picked up in a captured trench for some time, but finally threw it away. That is the fate of most souvenirs."[46]

Some soldiers despaired at dumping their loot and often buried their souvenirs in the hope of coming back some day to collect their booty. Most never returned, knocked out by a shell

This postcard shows a soldier with war souvenirs hanging off his kit bag and rifle. The title, "The Optimist," suggests that despite the improbable number of these souvenirs, the soldier is hoping to sell them or get them home.

or bullet, or simply unable to travel back to that sector of the front before they were demobilized. Captain Herbert McBride of the 21st Battalion wrote, "We had found that, although we might gather and accumulate the most wonderful collection of these trophies, whenever we made a move, it was necessary to ditch the whole lot. Personally, I buried several cartloads of junk in various parts of West Flanders, in the hope that I might sometime, get back to dig it up."[47] How many others dreamed in the postwar years of returning to France to find their treasure trove?

"This war will undoubtedly go down to posterity as a 'War of Souvenirs,'" remarked one trench soldier dryly.[48] It has not, even though the soldiers placed great value on these artifacts. Souvenirs and trench art were a means for the men in the trenches to personalize the vast impersonal mechanism of the industrial war, and they offered a way for soldiers to exert their own agency. Caught in a system in which they were always subject to orders from above, the soldiers embraced the hunt for souvenirs, as well as the found treasures, as theirs alone. Even when the army tried to issue warnings about the collection of live ordnance, reminding the men that it was illegal and that brass casings and fuses should be recycled, soldiers refused to follow the rules.[49] These men were not easily cowed. But while most soldiers were obsessed with souvenirs, many developed a reasonable perspective after some time at the front. Gunner William Curtis asserted wisely, "Getting souvenirs does not occupy my mind. It's myself I want to bring home as a souvenir."[50] All soldiers would have agreed, although many preferred to head home with packs full of memory objects gathered from the fields of slaughter.

CHAPTER 10

SOLDIERS' CULTURE BEHIND THE FIRING LINE

The infantrymen in the front lines dreamed of being released from the death and destruction. In February 1917, Corporal Harry Hillyer wrote, "We have been fighting now over 6 months and I should like to go out and have a rest, we all need it . . . 2 weeks would make a lot of difference if it is only for the change of food and a good sleep and the opportunity of buying some food if it is only fish and chips and eggs."[1] Hillyer, who had enlisted as a boy sailor in the Royal Marines in 1900 before emigrating to Canada in 1905, was killed with a bullet to the head a little over a week after writing this letter.

In a four-battalion brigade, there were usually two battalions of 650 to 750 men each in the front lines, and two in reserve. Of the two at the front, one or two companies were up in the line, each composed of 150 to 200 men, with the other two or three situated in depth to absorb any attack. In this sense, a front-line trench on an established front might actually be several lines of trenches extended back several hundred metres. A soldier's length of service in the forward trenches was usually four to six days.

This period of extreme danger was a strain for all the officers and men, who had to be hyper vigilant for enemy raids, carry out patrols, stand sentry, and always be prepared to scurry for cover from shells, mortar bombs, and bullets. There was little time for rest, and the hard labour of expanding trenches, digging latrines, and filling sandbags was physically demanding. After their tour in the forward trenches, the company moved to a rear area for a period of rest and recuperation, usually about six days, and the units in reserve shuffled forward. And after a spell, the whole battalion was cycled to the rear and replaced by a sister unit. Though the return to the rear area was not all giggles and treats, with many soldiers ordered back to the front on work fatigues—more digging or laying barbed wire—the men were generally able to rest and engage in leisure activities while there.

The mud-splattered infantrymen, their eyes red with fatigue, shoulders hunched in exhaustion, and legs on the verge of collapse, marched out of the trenches to one of the small towns behind the lines. Depending on the ravages of war, there might be only a few structures left standing in a town, but usually there were barns and buildings. Major B.F. Gossage of the 4th Brigade, Canadian Field Artillery, described the village of St. Omers in his diary on September 19, 1915, declaring, "We are all terribly surprised at the people living in ruins + also right in the danger zone + places where shells drop every day."[2] Hundreds of thousands of French and Belgian civilians were forced to survive under German occupation or were driven from their homes, but thousands more lived in the war zone.

Soldiers were sometimes billeted with families for a fee that the army paid. James Balfour wrote home in August 1915 after a tour at the front about finding relief in sleeping on the floor of a

Canadian soldiers resting in a purpose-built structure to hold many men behind the lines.

French house, noting, "We took off boots & putties the first time for 5 days."[3] Barns were a more common spot to keep the large numbers of men. Private George Hancox of the PPCLI, who enlisted at age nineteen and gave his prewar occupation as the "operator of a motion picture machine," described one drafty stay in a series of bombed-out farm buildings, complaining, "We had only our blankets or greatcoats for bedding and on the whole our standard of living was lower than the poorest slum dwellers."[4] Barn fires were distressingly common, as exhausted smokers drifted off to sleep mid-cigarette.[5]

Officers usually gave their men the first full day of leave to stitch the holes in their clothing, relax with cigarettes, and eat a hearty meal. Hot baths were arranged for the lice-infested homeless men, and these were often set up in converted breweries. "I don't suppose that prior to this experience in the war zone I ever properly understood or appreciated the meaning of a bath," wrote Lieutenant William Gray, a prewar journalist in Port Arthur, Ontario. "It is something you look forward to, and back at, and is as important as a Sunday School picnic to a boy of ten."[6] Sometimes the lice survived the steam cleaning of their clothes, but they were much reduced in number and men could usually find some relief for a while. After the first day, officers soon tightened up the discipline, guided by the old adage that a soldier without duties was a soldier likely to get into trouble. Lieutenant J.S. Williams's take on keeping the soldiers busy while on leave was that it kept "the men from brooding and that does not give time for depressing conversation between them."[7]

The training and lectures began anew. But this was at a more relaxed pace than that of front-line duties, and a talk about how to clean one's gas mask or the latest codes in signalling was almost a rest compared to the frenzy of dodging shells in the forward trenches. However, the training behind the lines was more intense, especially as of late 1916, when the officers began keeping the men engaged in subjects such as fire and movement tactics, how to follow a creeping barrage, and, by the last year of the war, advancing in fighting formation with tanks.[8] Some soldiers noted dryly that "rest" like this was enough to make a man yearn to return to the front. Perhaps that was the point.

With the private's $1.10 a day equating to about five francs, the Canadians were flush for a short period after receiving their earnings. Pay was a source of conflict between Canadian and

British troops, as the Canucks were paid almost five times as much as the British Tommies. "They call us the millionaire army," gloated Harold Simpson, a young Prince Edward Islander who had never been so flush.[9] Paymasters doled out spending money, usually fifty to seventy-five francs at a time to each man, aware that most soldiers were sending half their pay back to families or next of kin, and that giving them any more money would only lead to trouble. But even with such limitations on their funds, some men promptly went to try their luck with the unit's card sharks and dice masters, who were frowned upon by the authorities but flourished nonetheless. Crown and Anchor—a dice game heavily favouring the man who owned the board—seemed the most popular way to lose money, but there were many games. It only took being cleaned out a few times for a new man to become wary of claims by the old hands with sticky fingers that they need only play to double their pay.

"THE BOYS ROAM THE VILLAGE to see what they can purchase," observed Private Donald Fraser in his diary. "Almost every house in Belgium will supply you with eggs, coffee and bread. . . . The boys are so glad of a change that some of them consume as many as twenty eggs in a day."[10] Private Arthur Lapointe, a French Canadian from Matane, Quebec, serving with the 22nd Battalion, wrote in his diary in the summer of 1917 about buying milk, eggs, and butter, and even the occasional bottle of wine in the local villages, noting that all of it "helps us to forget past weariness and suffering."[11]

The most popular and happy places for soldiers were the local *estaminets*. Civilians opened up their houses to feed those returning from the trenches, running taverns from their living rooms and refitting larger structures to look like restaurants of sorts. Weak beer and *vin blanc*, along with plates of eggs and fried potatoes, were consumed, and all offerings, according to one Canadian, were "a veritable Godsend for the soldiers."[12] These eateries were also sanctuaries of camaraderie, bonhomie, and raucous song.

A burly Canadian soldier enjoying a drink in an estaminet. *There is no accompanying caption for this wartime cartoon and none would have been required for soldiers who well understood the importance of a drink behind the lines.*

Gunner J.C.K. Mackay of the 20th Battery described his visits to a series of *estaminets* in the summer of 1916, observing, "The mademoiselles were pretty and did a roaring trade in Malaga wine."[13] *Estaminets* could be located easily, as alcohol-fuelled songs rose into the night sky. "Our spirits are high," wrote one Canadian of his time at the rear. After a night of unruly fun in the establishments, one could almost claim, as did Lieutenant Stanley Rutledge, "It is not such a bad war."[14]

While out of the firing line, the Canadians had many interactions with French and Belgian citizens. The civilians sold goods to those in uniform and were grateful for the men's sacrifice on their behalf, but they still considered them an occupying army.[15] In parts of Belgium, the residents were positively hostile to the Allied forces, as they saw the soldiers as an alien force that ate their food and tore up their villages. In France, however, the reception was generally positive. Canadians spoke fondly of helping women with household chores, sharing treats with malnourished children, and aiding the elderly left alone on farms. But there was also friction, with soldiers sometimes regarding civilians as ungrateful and the civilians viewing the warriors from afar as boorish brutes and looters. One point of contention was the sale and purchase of goods. As many of the French had been forced to flee their land or villages, they sold fruit or cigarettes at high prices in order to survive. The soldiers, on a brief break from their long war of hardship, felt cheated. A frustrated Clarence McCann, a New Brunswick driver in an artillery brigade, wrote that the French around his sector in March 1916 were graspers and exploiters, stating bluntly, "I don't believe there is a meaner race of people on the earth."[16] Soldiers were not always innocent babes in this relationship, however, as many of them annoyed the French or

Belgians by tramping through gardens, stealing chickens, and pilfering firewood.

Soldiers looked for pleasure where they could find it. "When living in the trenches and amongst the ruined houses there, we take no interest in women and love beyond the usual jokes and funny stories," wrote Thomas Dinesen, who was to receive the Victoria Cross for uncommon valour on the battlefield. But behind the lines, "with so much spare time on your hands," noted Dinesen, many soldiers went in search of women.[17] Away from the stress of battle, young men made old before their time became young again. J.H. Hunt of the 52nd Battalion, who lived in Port Arthur, Ontario, before the war, described the prevalent attitude: "Eat, sleep, drink and be merry, for tomorrow, you may die."[18] It is no surprise that many of the Canadians sought female companionship behind the lines. In turn, the French and Belgian women

Two Canadian soldiers chat with French women after working in the fields.

became practised at resisting the amorous advances of the men who tramped through their villages.

With their attempts at romance frequently unsuccessful, it was not uncommon for Canadians to turn to prostitutes. There were tens of thousands of women selling their bodies behind the lines, most of them refugees from the fighting.[19] Regimental and medical officers were instructed to lecture their men on the dangers of sex with prostitutes, while the YMCA offered moralistic pamphlets that warned of permanent shame.[20] One YMCA booklet, *If Every Man Were Straight*, claimed there would be "no suicides by women, no illegitimate children," and fewer babies born blind or dead, if men abstained from sex that spread venereal disease (VD).[21] (By "straight" the booklet referred to men walking the straight line and avoiding temptation. The word was not a reference to homosexuality, which was a punishable offence that could lead to jail time for the rank and file and cashiering for an officer.) However, hellfire and damnation speeches by the lieutenant colonel, medical officers, chaplains, and even special civilian experts failed to curtail the growing VD epidemic.

Though few of the Allied soldiers were innocents, the Canadians in particular had a reputation for promiscuousness and the pursuit of prostitutes, likely because of their high rates of pay and because men could not return home while on leave as married British soldiers did. The First Contingent in 1914 had been plagued by venereal disease, with the level at one point reaching a shocking 28.7 percent of the force.[22] Harsher punishments followed, as the impact of venereal disease on the fighting forces was significant: more than thirty days of treatment on average for syphilis meant a significant loss of men from the lines. Pay stoppages were put into effect as punishment for those who contracted a disease, and more than a few married men were forced to write painfully inventive letters home to explain why their salary had dried up.[23] Realizing the futility of moral lectures, the high command eventually ordered that official, regulated brothels be set up and prophylactics issued.[24]

Authorities far from the front blamed the VD epidemic on the "harpy" prostitutes supposedly preying on the helpless soldiers, but there was a little more understanding among most officers closer to the sound of the shells, who better knew their men.[25] Private Victor Swanston wrote in his diary on March 8, 1918: "Fritz has been shelling and bombing the devil out of the towns 'round here for the last ten days. He got a bunch of French girls today. This was a whorehouse, the girls were inspected (medical) once a week. The soldiers were marched over to the whorehouse and lined up to await their turn with the girls." Afterwards, continued Swanston, the men's genitals were inspected for disease. Swanston commented on one comrade who was diagnosed with a venereal disease. The man claimed in his defence that "he had contracted the disease by 'pissing up against a wagon wheel.'" A bemused officer replied, "All I can say is, it's a hell of a place to take a woman."[26]

"RIGHT UP THE LINE WHERE it was not fit for man or beast to be, you would find a hole in the side of a bend, big enough for one or two men, and they would be handing out free tea, cookies and a few cigarettes to anyone going by," wrote James Robert Johnston, an eighteen-year-old driver of mules, describing the YMCA. "This was one of the great morale builders."[27] In many of the villages, as well as closer to the front, the YMCA and Salvation Army established canteens to sell goods to the Canadians. The goods were usually sent from across the Atlantic, and so Dominion gum, chocolates, magazines, and tobacco were all available at modest prices, and sometimes for free. The YMCA and "Sally Anne" looked to aid the soldiers physically and spiritually, but also to keep them from other distractions like drinking, gambling, and sex.

The canteens behind the lines were more established and sophisticated by the summer of 1916. The large wooden huts that became the norm could house many men and they had tables for soldiers to write letters and space to listen to music played on a few battered pianos. The canteens were dry—meaning that they sold no alcohol—and prices were generally low, the staff caring, and the area open to all. For some men, it was simply nice to get out of the rain and into something that resembled a comforting

YMCA staff provided coffee, tea, and snacks to tired soldiers along the Western Front.

house. Private John Watson of the 4th Battalion, who was wounded on the Somme and again at Vimy, sent a letter to his father before the latter battle, noting, "I am writing in the YMCA building. The boys are playing the organ, dancing and singing. Mostly every song is about mother at home, and wife and baby. It would make your heart melt if you only heard them."[28] Across the Western Front for all the British, dominion, and colonial forces, there were some 10,000 YMCA Red Triangle Huts that offered much-sought-after goods and shelter from the cold while also sponsoring talks on religious, spiritual, and moral issues.[29] Towards the end of the war, the huts contained lending services for both books and sports equipment.[30] Canadian Corps commander Sir Arthur Currie enthused over the aid from the Salvation Army, asserting directly to the organization, "One of the most important factors in winning a fight is the morale of the troops, and it is in helping to raise and maintain the morale at a high level, that you have done so much. . . . The men forget the sights of war and seem to get a fresh start through your programmes, your concerts, your sports and your canteens."[31]

The Salvation Army and the YMCA offered soldiers candy, magazines, and books from home that stirred up fierce memories. This nostalgia was a powerful motivator for men and it also acted as a shield in the face of much hardship. Letters were an overt fulfillment of this need to stay connected to home, but the need was filled in many ways, especially by the receipt of photographs. "I want you to send me some snapshots of yourself and baby and myself and anybody else you can spare," Corporal Harry Hillyer told his wife in a letter. "All these fellows have their pockets full of snaps and I should like some myself."[32] André Bieler, who was one of four brothers who served overseas in the war, wrote to his parents of taking time every day to look at the pictures that were sent along in the letters from home, noting, "that makes me feel good."[33] Bieler survived the war to return home and become a well-known painter; two of his brothers joined him, while one remained forever buried on the Western Front.

Some soldiers were also interested in capturing their war experience with their own cameras, even though photography at the front was outlawed as of March 1915 by order of the British high command.[34] Senior generals feared that military intelligence in the form of photographs would be passed to the enemy, and periodically throughout the war there were orders pressuring officers to enforce the rules and regulations.[35] Beginning in the summer of 1916, Canadian official photographs were commissioned to document the war, but some of the irrepressible Canadian soldiers sneaked portable cameras into the trenches almost from the start.[36] Private Victor Swanston, who liked to document the war by composing bad poetry, keeping a diary, and sketching cartoons, was not the type to be cowed. He wrote in his diary on February 19, 1916, that his friend Doug Burrage came by the trenches to see him and to hand over his camera. "He was scared to pack it around any longer, it being strictly against Army Orders," Swanston related. "I'll try to get some snaps as soon as it is fine."[37] However, it was difficult for soldiers to practise photography since the developing solution and fragile glass negatives were not easy to carry in and out of the trenches, although many overcame this by using portable Kodak cameras that operated with film. George Ormsby was born in Ballycastle, Ireland, and in 1895 immigrated to Canada, where he farmed and operated a general store in Lumby, British Columbia. Writing to his wife, Maggie, in early August 1915, Ormsby asked her to send him a camera, as he was hoping to shoot some "valuable pictures," both in the trenches and behind the lines. Trench rumours suggested that "some papers in England offer and pay as high as 200 (pounds) for good snap shots," and, Ormsby enthused, "I have seen scenes which beat anything."[38] The fee of 200 pounds was an enormous sum, and the "scenes" he had witnessed had occurred at the bloodbath at Festubert in May of that year, where he had been a machine-gunner. Ormsby asked his wife to send the film and developing solution clandestinely in empty preserves jars, noting, "you know we are not allowed to have cameras but I think I can manage it so that nobody will find out." He had one final request: he needed instructions on how to use the camera as the contraption was a mystery to him.[39]

H.R. Alley of the 3rd Battalion recounted that much of the war was "just utter bloody boredom," and that reading relieved some of the ennui.[40] While trench soldiers spent much of their time at the front simply trying to survive, there were moments to quiet the mind. "Our reading gamut is usually a queer mixture, but we all read," wrote one Canadian to his folks in Cobourg, Ontario.[41] Reading restored many men, reminded them of their individuality, allowed them to escape the Western Front through their imagination, and lightened some of the brutality of service. And while reading was usually solitary in nature, soldiers often read aloud to groups of men in the dugouts, because of the shortage of material, the challenges faced by illiterate comrades, and the communal nature of the act that was similar to gossiping and storytelling.[42] This reading culture bound the soldiers together, both in the dugouts of the front lines and in the rear areas where there was more time for such things.

The soldiers consumed all manner of books and novels, with no particular preference for war-related material. Reading was

Cartoon of a hard-bitten soldier deep in concentration as he reads a romantic novel. The caption reads, "Diversion," although the soldier's rapt gaze suggests he is perhaps enjoying the book as more than a simple distraction.

important enough for most men to write home about it in their letters. Books by Rudyard Kipling, Arthur Conan Doyle, Gilbert Parker, Jack London, H.G. Wells, Jules Verne, and Nat Gould, who was known for his horse-racing novels, all circulated among the men. Spy novels and adventure stories were the most popular, but nothing was wasted. Armine Norris witnessed one mate absorbed by a cheap novel, holding the pages up to the light to decipher them, as the book had a bullet hole through it.[43] Lieutenant Clifford Wells offered a wish list in one letter home and noted, "all reading matter is carefully preserved and passed around."[44] Most soldiers wanted light reading, although some men liked to be challenged beyond the lowbrow. Captain Robert Clements described one fellow officer in his 25th Battalion, a banker who was pleased to receive, and who studied in detail, the Bank of Montreal annual report for 1915.[45]

Civilians were remade into soldiers when they enlisted, but almost all of those in the war retained links to their past lives, communities, and professions. Donald Macpherson, who was studying education at the University of Toronto when he enlisted, was likely not typical when he revealed, "Shakespeare has continued to be my chief companion, both on and off duty."[46] Macpherson, who would be wounded and awarded the Military Medal at Passchendaele, was not alone, and trench editions of Shakespeare could be purchased in London and carried into the trenches. The tiny print was not good for the eyes, but the contents were perhaps a tonic for the soul.

Reading provided a common frame of reference for the soldiers, and it was a way to stay connected to friends and family at home. More than a few learned men believed that books saved them from the deadening ennui at the front. Books saved lives in other ways, too. Gunner Harold Innis, who would later become one of Canada's most influential intellectuals, was nearly killed by a German shell splinter while serving to the east of Vimy in the summer of 1917. As the shell exploded, a shard of steel ripped into his right thigh, causing a painful if non-lethal wound. Another piece whirled through the air and into his back, which might have ended his life.[47] However, the second splinter found no flesh as it was absorbed by one of his many books.

"THE TOWNS AND VILLAGES HERE are deadly dull in the evenings," wrote Private Ernest Taylor in December 1915. "If people were enterprising enough to start a good picture show they would make piles [of money]. A Canadian soldier did have a miniature one going here for a few nights. . . . The screen was not much larger than a good-sized pocket handkerchief, but the pictures were quite clear, and the room was packed with soldiers."[48] Taylor was killed five months later, and he therefore missed the rise of much of the entertainment that would soon spread behind the lines to entertain Canadian soldiers, raise morale, and pierce the dullness of the war.

Cinema had mass appeal. Before the war, twenty million tickets a week were sold in England as crowds were drawn to the flickering, silent images on the screen.[49] After repeated demands from the front, Ottawa supplied a cinema to each of the four Canadian divisions in the spring of 1916, and experienced projectionists were culled from the ranks.[50] *The Brazier* reported in its February 1916 issue that the 3rd Infantry Brigade now possessed a "moving picture machine" that projected films in barns where the troops were billeted. When the unstable celluloid occasionally burst into flames from overheating, soldiers ran for the exits and continued with a "jolly sing-song as part of the evening's entertainment."[51]

A steady rotation of films arrived at the front: mysteries, melodrama, "pathetics" (emotional films), official war films (documentaries), and, the most popular of all, comedies. Lieutenant Lawrence Rogers, a medical officer who would be killed at Passchendaele, wrote in March 1916, "We were marched down to another picture show this week and personally I think it a very good institution as it keeps the men in good spirits and breaks the monotony of things."[52] By the second half of the war, the films were projected in purpose-built cinemas that had a shabby elegance, with seats and curtains usually cobbled together from abandoned and wrecked French or Belgian villages in the war zone. The films were silent, but they were often accompanied by a piano or even a marching band that also engaged in bursts of song, to the roaring approval of the men.

The pictures allowed soldiers to gather in a safe area within the war zone, restoring spirits and reinforcing morale. Corporal Robert Miller, a twenty-two-year-old from Montreal, inscribed in his diary the conditions of the Ypres battle front in April 1916, before adding, "Went out to a movie show last night which was pretty good. It was funny to think that nearly all the men there would be in the trenches in a day or so."[53] Stanley Rutledge, whose life would end after he transferred from the infantry to the flying services and went down in a plane crash, described one film night in a soldiers' theatre, observing, "It is situated about a mile from our rest billets. . . . It was quite a relief after an experience dodging whiz-bangs and shrapnel shells. The boys laughed boisterously, and the antics of the actors, which would be boresome to the civil theatre-goer, were loudly applauded."[54] As Rutledge revealed, the men in the war zone, desperate for jokes and humour, were not choosy about their films.

Soldiers attending the films were a rowdy bunch. They laughed loudly, stood and shouted cheeky comments, and a few clowns even rushed forward from their seats to greet the shaky images on screen. This was an opportunity to let off steam and momentarily set aside the strain of the trenches. It was a chance for the men to enjoy freedom from the stentorian demands of officers and NCOs, who generally let this nonsense go in the cinemas. *The Listening Post* scoffed gently at the soldiers' "interactions" with the actors: "It was a moving picture show in a YMCA hut, a thriller of the most heart-rending sort. The hold-up man had just pulled his gun on the unarmed hero, when from the audience came shrieks of 'Kamerad! Kamerad; Married man me!'"[55] The harsh joke invoked the familiar world of the battlefield, where captured German soldiers pleaded for their lives, invoking their married status in hopes of staving off execution.

There were many wartime celebrities, such as Harry Lauder and Bruce Bairnsfather, but highest on the pedestal was the shabby "Little Tramp." Played by Charlie Chaplin, his characters were wildly popular before the war, during it, and afterwards. There was much to like about the dishevelled Chaplin, who challenged authority while stumbling over his own feet, and he was a hero to the rank and file.[56] Like Bairnsfather's Old Bill, the Tramp was the little guy who was soldiering through life with quiet dignity, and, in his few war films, simply trying to survive the bloody war. "In the evening we all went around to the moving picture show and saw our old friend Charlie Chaplin," wrote William Antliff, a prewar commerce student at McGill before serving in a field ambulance on the Western Front.[57] The satisfaction for viewers of a Chaplin film was not in witnessing the achievement of money or fame, although the Tramp did sometimes succeed in getting the girl; more important was the reclamation of dignity and self-respect, and sometimes the delivery of a come-uppance to the wealthy and sophisticated. Chaplin's penguin waddle was hilarious from the perspective of the soldiers, who had been drilled to walk with precision and in unison. The Tramp lived by his wits and outsmarted his betters. Soldiers liked to think they did the same with their officers.

The theatre troupes at the front, whose performances rivalled films in popularity, almost always included a Chaplin-like character, who was easily identified by his threadbare clothes, absurd moustache, tell-tale visual ticks, and antics. He might have been referred to by a different name, but everyone knew that this was Charlie. One of the jokey songs that the soldiers parodied was the popular "It's a Long Way to Tipperary," with a new version that made fun of facial hair:

> It took a long time to get it hairy,
> 'Twas a long time to grow;
> It took a long time to get it hairy,
> For the tooth-brush hairs to show.
> Good-bye, Charlie Chaplin,
> Farewell, tufts of hair;
> It took a long time to get it hairy,
> But now my lip's quite bare.[58]

The song was even more of a hit since soldiers occasionally referred to their own moustaches as "Chaplins," with a nod to Charlie's distinctive hair on the upper lip. There was also the popular wartime tune "The Moon Shines Bright on Charlie Chaplin," which imagined Charlie in uniform in a foreign theatre of war. The humour worked its way into the soldiers' publications, and included this joke in *The Iodine Chronicle* under the title "Charlie Chaplin Again":

> Sentry: "Who goes there?"
> Army Chaplain (visiting trenches): "Chaplain."
> Sentry: "Good night, Charlie."
>
> (Note: The above joke has been suggested as suitable for the "I.C." by about 123 and some odd readers. Our thanks to them.)[59]

Always in tune with the soldiers' point of view, Bairnsfather penned a highly praised cartoon that showed a silhouetted image of Charlie Chaplin on the Western Front under a moon-lit sky.

Chaplin's appeal cut across nationalities. In a January 1916 letter, Canadian Ernest Taylor described the atmosphere at one screening: "The room was packed with soldiers representing dozens of different regiments, English, Scotch, and Canadians, and to hear them laugh at the antics of Charlie Chaplin you wouldn't think they worried much about meeting the Germans or going in the trenches."[60] Even the French—who had 1,200 mobile cinemas behind the lines—liked Charlie, whom they called "Charlot."[61] One YMCA worker believed, "All of the picture shows are good . . . but Charlie Chaplin is the soldiers' favourite," adding, "When word comes down the line, Yankees, Poilus, and Tommies link arms and hit the trail for The White Screen."[62]

Chaplin's most famous war film, *Shoulder Arms* (1918), was released a few weeks after the armistice, and most soldiers saw it while undergoing the dreary demobilization process. The film situates Private Charlie in the trenches, unluckily wearing 13 as an identification number, dreaming of his life in America. Having replaced his trademark bowler hat with a helmet (which the soldiers sometimes called a "battle bowler"), Chaplin struggles with the terrible conditions in the trenches, using a gramophone speaker as a snorkel to breathe above the water rising round him, and laying out a single mousetrap to deter the multitude of rats. Nonetheless, Chaplin bumbles his way to victory and even captures the Kaiser through a series of unlikely events. Lieutenant Bill Hutchinson of Dorchester, New Brunswick, who served with the 36th Battery, Canadian Field Artillery, wrote as he waited to be demobilized in the camps at Kinmel Park, Rhyl, "We went to the

Charlie Chaplin as an infantryman in the film Shoulder Arms *(1918). Chaplin, the great anti-hero, was a favourite of the Allied soldiers.*

pictures and saw Charlie Chaplin in "Shoulder Arms." Had a great laugh, as I hadn't seen him for months."[63] Hutchinson described Chaplin as if he were an old friend. For many Canadians, he was a comforting figure of anti-authority, humour, and hope who allowed them to shrug their shoulders and be the unlikely heroes that they were.

SOLDIERS CARRIED THEIR LOVE OF games with them overseas.[64] In fact, on the home front, many of the amateur and professional sporting leagues temporarily closed down as hockey, baseball, and lacrosse players joined the colours, serving both in the ranks and as officers. There was an accepted belief in the forces that sports bred manliness, competition, and teamwork, all of which were essential for raising and maintaining morale. In *The Dead Horse Corner Gazette*, former Olympian Captain Edward Archibald urged his comrades to participate in sports, declaring, "The man who is in the best shape will stand the hardships better, for never had men greater hardships to go through, and never did men go through these hardships with a better spirit than our boys."[65]

Toughness and speed were exalted on the sporting battlefield. So, too, were men who showed grit by overcoming injuries. To solidify inter-rank relations, officers sometimes played with the other ranks, an interaction that wasn't necessary but was considered good form. Officers could affirm in this way that they did not shy away from manly sport or from mixing it up on the field. It was not uncommon in these intense matches for a few elbows and kicks to be delivered in scrums as payback to superiors for past punishments. William Antliff of No. 9 Field Ambulance observed that new officers were initially stiff and formal and bent on enforcing discipline, and so would maintain a distance between themselves and their men, but over time they learned the subtle art of leadership. Antliff noted, "In these days, there is a remarkable spirit of camaraderie and the boys certainly appreciate it. The officers from the 2nd in command down often come out and play ball with the fellows and no one minds the kidding which goes on."[66] And when officers chose not to play, they could at least be a part of the cheering crowd. "In sports of all kinds," commented one trench newspaper, "officers descended from their giddy altitudes of discipline and became almost chummy. They held the tape for you in the different heats, fielded the cricket ball or loaned you their shorts and sweaters, and you rubbed 'flashes' with them in the crowd without having to salute and look as though you realized the enormity of your offence."[67] This levelling sporting culture was crucial in easing some of the inherent tension between leaders and the led.

The games were also part of the recovery process from trench terrors. After the April 1916 Battle of St. Eloi—a quagmire of mud, rain, shellfire, and unburied corpses—men at the front collapsed under the strain. Lieutenant D.E. Macintyre of the 28th Battalion wrote in his diary a few days after being rotated from the front, "A number of officers and men have had to be evacuated on account of shell shock. Several men went temporarily insane. However, most of the men are quite fit again and football and baseball games with bands playing are a great help."[68] Similarly, at the Battle of Mont Sorrel in June 1916 the Canadians took a tremendous pounding from enemy artillery, and the 16th Battalion's war diary recorded that when the shaken survivors stumbled out of the line, their officers set up soccer matches against nearby British teams, adding, "Sports of this kind appear to have a great brightening effect on the men, especially if they have been subjected to any artillery fire."[69] The officer writing up the 31st Battalion's war diary in June 1917 described a sports day, noting, "Most of the events resolved themselves into inter-company rivalry and the men had full play for the exercise of that 'esprit de Corps' as applied to a company which is so productive of the best result in military life."[70]

Baseball was one of the abiding passions of Canadians, and those at the front were no exception. There were amateur and semi-professional teams, and games against the Americans—whom the snickering Canadians called the "Sammies"—could incite wild, nationalistic pride or end in the head-hanging shame of defeat.[71] Closer to the front, behind the lines but within range of shellfire, platoons and companies competed against one another in games of

Canadians playing baseball in front of a sizeable crowd. Big games like this, especially against American teams, brought out intense nationalistic passions.

"pick-up-and-play," although there were also all-star teams composed of professional or semi-professional players. These elites were kitted out with matching uniforms and new equipment, usually supplied via home front donations to the Salvation Army or YMCA. This sporting culture was a crucial aspect of the soldiers' society, binding together those at the front and providing another method of coping with the strain of service in the war zone.

The inter-unit games were very popular, with much money changing hands in wagering. Fans catcalled and jeered the other team's players, and the Canadian approach to heckling the other side's players, fans, and perhaps even mothers, was surprising to the British, who were not used to such offensive remarks. Chaplain B.J. Murdoch observed how the British Tommies and their officers were taken aback when watching Canadians play, especially as "one side would yell at the other, trying to rattle the pitcher." Murdoch noted with much amusement, "To them, it seemed rather abusive."[72] One

Canadian lieutenant-colonel described the feisty atmosphere: "the supporters of different teams . . . shouted such witticisms and jeering remarks at the players—irrespective of rank—as bewildered the British officers. . . . It was bad enough to hear a private tell a non-commissioned officer who was pitching that he had 'a glass eye,' but it seemed to them as if discipline had completely broken down when a crowd of all ranks kept yelling in chorus at the batting of a Brigadier-General, 'He swings like a gate, the blighter—he-swings-like-a-gate.'"[73] Such reports illustrate the Canadians' nationalistic pride in their sport-driven, easygoing relationships that differentiated them from the "stuck-up" British. Or at least they liked to think they were different, and this was another way for the Canadians to define themselves within the larger Empire-wide war effort.

By the summer of 1917, the Canadian divisions regularly set up sports fields and tennis courts behind the front lines, especially around Vimy Ridge, the Somme, and the Ypres salient, where the Canadians spent months in static warfare.[74] Soccer and baseball were the most popular sports, but there were also multiple boxing leagues, with soldiers competing at different weight classes. Officers and mounted units enjoyed horseback games, in which strength and skill were tested in tug-of-wars and rowdy rounds of climbing atop a horse and attempting to send one's opponent crashing to the ground through a mixture of wrestling and roughhousing. Track and field competitions were easy to organize, and some units took to lacrosse with a passion. All of these activities culminated in two major Canadian Corps multi-sport events on Dominion Day (July 1) in 1917 and 1918. On the latter occasion, about 50,000 Canadian soldiers took part in a jamboree of competition and patriotism, with the Canadian prime minister, Sir Robert Borden, in attendance.[75]

There were no wartime sporting dynasties established, as all winning teams faced the grim prospect of having their star players killed or maimed in the real battles they were facing. The 25th Battalion fielded a winning baseball team in the first two years of the war, but, according to Captain Robert Clements, it "had been smashed on the Somme in 1916 and never really did get going again."[76] Sergeant Chester E. Routley revealed one bad day when a "shell had dropped right about the centre of the hut and left seven dead besides several wounded. Charley (Chuck) Bothwick, the centre forward in our football team, was in there and amongst other wounds he lost his left foot from that shell. Just before that, we had won the Corps championship in football, although [after the loss of Bothwick] we never got that far up again with our football team."[77] Losing a star to machine-gun or artillery fire would be unthinkable on the sporting fields of Halifax, Toronto, or Vancouver, but the Canadian soldiers understood that death and maiming were a daily part of life at the front, with its vulnerability to chance and fate.

MAJOR D.J. CORRIGAL OF THE 20th Battalion wrote about the good times behind the lines and the many cultural activities available to the soldiers, observing that his comrades' "chief items of interest were the daily football games between the company teams." As the soldiers competed on the pitch, local bands played all manner of songs, with which the athletes and spectators sang along heartily. "Some of us would walk, even as far as Ypres, others would sit around writing letters; others again played cards, and many visited the estaminets." There was no shortage of leisure activities behind the lines, but as Corrigal and so many others lamented, "The periods out of the line were always too brief."[78]

CHAPTER 11

SHOCK TROUPES

The soldiers' "concert parties," observed Private Victor Wheeler of the 50th Battalion, "contributed to lightening our spirits, relaxing our nerves and lessening our apprehensions."[1] And yet mounting plays, putting on skits, and partaking in variety shows seemed a far cry from soldiering to some of the more hard-bitten generals. As the war dragged on, however, even the high command understood that the civilian-soldiers required entertainment to combat boredom, provide an outlet for cultural expression, and restore morale.[2] The soldiers initially turned to one another for the provision of entertainment shows, but there were semi-professional troupes as of late 1916 on the Somme. By 1917, all four Canadian divisions had full-time entertainers, which often included musical bands and cross-dressing actors, and in the final year of the war, there were more than thirty theatre groups. Stage performances, much like songs, newspapers, cartoons, jokes, and poetry, reinforced the soldiers' sense of community while also creating a safe environment in which they could comfortably air grievances.

Starting with the arrival of the first Canadians in England in 1914, thousands of young men in uniform sought amusement as a distraction from their military duties in the squalid training camps. Some turned to alcohol, with predictably bad results.[3] Officers and moralizing groups like the YMCA feared for the well-being of the soldiers, who were almost always regarded as naive new-worlders in the cruel old country, easy prey for the perils of drink and prostitutes. The authorities sought to engage the soldiers in other activities. Private Jack Stickney, who enlisted in Edmonton and served with the 4th Battalion until his death in December 1915, wrote of the senior officers' plan for the Canadians on Salisbury Plain in late 1914, remarking, "The War Office is paying the expenses of London Concert Parties to come down here three times a week to give us entertainments and they are top-notch too."[4] The entertainers—singers, actors, and sketch comedians—were greeted with visible pleasure by the Canadians, as thousands stood in open-air theatres or smaller venues to hoot and holler in support.

After the Second Contingent arrived in England in early 1915, the cost of entertaining tens of thousands of Canadians rose significantly, with the Canadian YMCA paying a hefty $9,000 a month.[5] Those cash outlays grew as more Canadian soldiers arrived, and there was the added logistical challenge of getting civilian troupes to France. One regularly featured performer was the Scottish entertainer Sir Harry Lauder, who made many trips to the Western Front, playing for the soldiers when they were out of the line. He was much loved, especially by Scottish Canadians, and after Lauder's son was killed in battle in December 1916, he travelled the front and rear areas constantly, sometimes in a car with a small portable piano, calling himself "The Reverend Harry Lauder MP Show."[6] His most famous song, "Keep Right on to the End of the Road," was written after his son's death, and it is sung to this day, most notably at games of the Birmingham City Football Club.

Even with the abundance of touring shows, there were simply too many Allied troops along the front for everyone to have a chance to see a performance, and the Canadian officers and men realized they would have to make their own entertainment. In the dugouts of the front lines, and when rotated out of danger, soldiers banded together to put on shows for one another. After the slaughter of Second Ypres in April 1915, Captain Richard Ponton of the 2nd Battalion described how his decimated unit had been gutted in the fighting and then given a rest behind the lines. There, at a concert, "The Colonel made a splendid speech and the talent was all right, but oh, how we missed some of the good fellows that we had four weeks ago at Winifred, who made our concert, then by the bonfire, such a grand success; we can never forget."[7] Ponton, who was sent home to Belleville, Ontario, early in 1916 as medically unfit, also observed that some of his chums stepped up to fill the ranks of unit entertainers as others fell in battle.

Musicians, comics, magicians, and poets entertained their chums in the trenches and behind the lines. Often the performers spent their free time composing poetry and songs, which were first tried out in the trenches among close mates, usually in a dugout by candlelight. Success there might lead to a larger audience behind the lines. A battalion at full strength was around 1,000 men, who could be a daunting audience, especially given the masculine tradition of ribbing, heckling, and cheeky talkback. Nonetheless, scouting officer D.E. Macintyre observed of the shows, "They do a lot of good."[8]

Soldiers' theatre productions flourished in the summer of 1915. They had their origins in the music hall performances of songs, skits, and jokes that were popular in Canadian cities at the time.[9] In Toronto alone, the city's four vaudeville theatres, with total weekly sales of 150,000 tickets, outpaced the three highbrow theatres in sales by at least four-to-one.[10] This music hall culture, brimming with crude caricatures, irreverent songs, and slapstick skits, was transported to the front, although revamped to meet the tastes and expectations of the army. After a hard day of training or work fatigues, the soldiers had an opportunity to unwind and take in a show. "It was here that the one big family spirit prevailed," wrote Jack McLaren, a soldier-entertainer who always leapt to amuse his mates. "The audience and actors became one and thus banished all their worries for at least a little while . . . men who died the following dawn with the song still on their lips."[11]

Frederick Noyes, a stretcher-bearer in the 5th Canadian Field Ambulance, recalled a concert party from this same time: "Bob Ferris was the star comedian and this American-born Lancashire lad from the Canadian army did much to brighten the war with his droll monologues and his songs, 'I'm Not So Young As I Used To Be,' 'Try a Little Piece of My Wife's Cake,' 'That was Me Last Night in Poper-in-je,' and 'I was Standing on the Corner of the Street.'"[12] Songs and skits were performed on makeshift stages that were sometimes as crude as a few ammunition boxes stacked together. Stephen Beames of the Canadian Field Artillery, who returned to his battery after suffering a head wound at Second Ypres, described the entertainers in late 1915, enthusing, "There was a lot of talent around there that winter. . . . We had a number of professional musicians and entertainers among us, including a Metropolitan Opera basso with a wonderful voice."[13] In these intimate settings, the men came together and threw off the war, if only for a few hours. One review in *The Dead Horse Corner Gazette* gushed, "The shows were excellent and this was accentuated by the fact that the entertainers were all amateurs."[14]

Lieutenant Gitz Rice was a Canadian singing star, with his hits "Dear Old Pal of Mine" and "Keep Your Head Down Fritzie Boy" sung at the front and throughout the Empire.

By the summer of 1915, a number of touring soldier-entertainers emerged. The most famous Canadian was Gitz Rice, who was born in New Glasgow, Nova Scotia, and studied at the McGill Conservatory before enlisting at age twenty-three with the Canadian Field Artillery. Rice performed up and down the line, singing popular songs and winning over his comrades with a jocular, soldier-friendly showmanship. His song "Dear Old Pal of Mine," in which a nostalgic soldier laments to his girl, "Oh, how I want you, dear old pal," was a monster hit.[15] Lieutenant Rice's songs were recorded and sold throughout the Empire, sung and recorded by others in both English and French, and used in wartime plays. Rice's fame extended to the United States, and his music was featured in *Getting Together*, a touring Broadway musical used to recruit Americans. Rarely had a Canadian made such an impression, and Canadian soldiers were proud to claim Gitz Rice as one of their own.

THE SUMMER OF 1916 SAW the establishment of more formalized theatre and entertainment groups within the Canadian Corps. The longest-serving Canadian infantry unit, the Princess Patricia's Canadian Light Infantry (PPCLI), had arrived on the Western Front in late 1914 and had fought steadily since then. After suffering heavy casualties, the battalion had received reinforcements, including several companies composed almost exclusively of university students. In informal gatherings, the clever students turned soldiers acquired a reputation for mounting smart, witty, and lively entertainment shows, and in June 1916 the PPCLI Comedy Company was formed.

The PPCLI Comedy Company's first show was to be performed after the Battle of Mount Sorrel. The unit had lost more than 400 men there, and the regiment that arrived at Steenvoorde to see the command performance was shattered.[16] Jack McLaren, an original member of the Comedy Company who had recently graduated from the University of Edinburgh, reacted with dread as his weary comrades filtered into the hot, poorly ventilated hall. The first couple of songs were met with dead eyes and withering silence. But the jokes, songs, and skits soon won over the battle-hardened footsloggers, and by the end of the performance the Patricias were laughing and cheering. It was a remarkable indication of how entertainment could provide succor to the soldiers suffering from deep exhaustion and mental wounds.

The popularity of the PPCLI Comedy Company, according to Jack McLaren, "spread from shell hole to shell hole."[17] Soon the troupe's reputation was established in the 3rd Division and units were clamouring to see the shows. Lieutenant Clifford Wells of the 8th Battalion in the 1st Canadian Division wrote about seeing a nighttime performance with about 400 comrades, remarking,

"The men enjoy it immensely. The singing and acting were really excellent. One song in particular you would have enjoyed. It was sung by a man wearing his full equipment—rifle, bayonet, entrenching tool, haversack, pack, waterbottle, rubber boots slung over his shoulder, gas helmet, steel helmet, etc. He came on the stage looking as tired, bored, unhappy, and disgusted as anyone could, and sang a song the burden of which, was, 'I have a motto—Always merry and bright.'"[18] The actor, of course played the last line with a dismal countenance, a sinking Eeyore-voice, and sad-sack eyes. The audience loved it and there was round after round of cheering and encores.

"There is an abundance of talent in this company and the concerts were greatly appreciated," reported *The Brazier* trench newspaper in a review of a PPCLI Comedy Company evening of entertainment. During the company's first couple of months, the songs were generally chaste and many were so popular that the audience called out for encores. The players on stage obliged. Perhaps the most popular tune was "The Bad, Bad Boy," a duet sung by Jack McLaren and Fred Fenwick. The latter's impersonation of the "good, good girl" was, according to *The Brazier*, an extremely clever piece of work in which Fenwick, dressed in drag, strutted and curtsied across the stage. Another member of the troupe, W.J. Cunningham, played Charlie Chaplin and "made friends with his audience from the start. His make-up is excellent and the gestures and antics of the original 'Charlie' seem to come natural to him." The paper concluded, in a comment intended more for the senior officers than the rank and file, "Their efforts are worthy of every encouragement."[19]

The 3rd Division's commander, Major-General Louis Lipsett, a British general and one who had a good sense of his men's morale,

One of the many Charlie Chaplin impersonators in the Canadian forces. Theatre troupes usually featured one such performer to appeal to the soldiers' demands to see their friend Charlie.

soon visited the PPCLI Comedy Company, and as one entertainer recounted, although the general noted that the members of the troupe had "volunteered to come over and fight . . . he felt that we would be doing our country a greater service by staying out of the line as permanent entertainers."[20] The entertainers no longer travelled along the dangerous front lines, remaining in the rear areas to greet trench warriors with songs and skits as they trudged back from the firing line. The "soldiers of the song" continued their important service as the Canadians moved to the Somme battles in September 1916, where all four Canadian divisions would eventually fight, with the battles raging until November and the casualties rising to 24,000. Time in the rear was needed for the men to recuperate from the bloodbath at the front, with rest and sports restoring some of their vitality. The role of the theatre groups gathered in importance as weary men grew desperate for relief from the crushing weight of the savage battles.

Though the initial PPCLI Comedy Company shows were rather tame and filled with "clean humour," they soon changed, as the brutal nature of the fighting on the Somme dictated more biting satire. The performers understood their audience and they crafted their content to appeal and provoke. Incorporating the latest rumours, grievances, and revelations into the show, they always kept their material up to date. They could be sharp-edged and anti-authoritarian, and in one popular skit, the acting provost marshal (military police officer), a near-sighted lout who is always arresting the wrong soldiers, goes on leave, arriving at his house to find his wife on another man's knee, being unfaithful to him. He shoots her and her lover dead, only to discover he is in the wrong home.[21] The humour was dark indeed, often poking fun at authority and revealing the men's fear of female infidelity. Allan Murray of the Dumbells, another popular theatre group, noted that the PPCLI Comedy Company "were superb, no one ever came near them with their satire, they would tear anything and everything to pieces in the most joyful manner."[22]

Like the soldiers' newspapers, cartoons, and songs, the PPCLI Comedy Company —and the theatre troupes that followed and emulated them—took liberal swipes at the officers. This sense of humour pandered to the enlisted men, as officers and NCOs were mimicked, their affectations, speech, and mannerisms exaggerated for comic effect. Even the long-time commanding officer of the PPCLI, Lieutenant-Colonel Agar Adamson, was a victim. Adamson was well liked by the men, but he never lost his appeal for professional soldiering, and he sported a much-derided monocle. Howard Ferguson, a runner in the Patricias, called him a man of "peculiarities and eccentricities."[23] But Adamson, who was a strict disciplinarian, could poke fun at himself. "Our new

Comedy Show was most excellent," wrote Adamson to his wife. "One of the players dressed up to represent me. He was so clever. I recognized myself at once. He rather gave me a roasting. . . . His efforts at mimicking me highly amused both men and officers and I really had a rather bad time, although in a most friendly way."[24] Ralph Hodder-Williams, an officer in the PPCLI, observed, "Skits, choruses, plays—many of them daringly personal—were hugely appreciated."[25]

The YMCA was also involved in providing formal entertainment for the soldiers. Millions of dollars in funds were raised by Canadians back home to pay for YMCA cinemas, concert parties, loan libraries, and the famous Beaver Hut in London, a drop-in centre for soldiers on leave. There were six YMCA officers per division who organized the entertainment facilities, and the most famous of these was Captain Merton Wesley Plunkett, a grocer from Orillia, Ontario, who had achieved local fame by singing in a quartet with his brothers before going overseas with the 35th Battalion. After transferring to the YMCA, Captain Plunkett continued performing, putting on variety shows in training camps in England. There, he recruited one of his brothers in uniform, Al Plunkett, who had been wounded at Mount Sorrel. The Plunketts returned to the Western Front during the dark days of the Somme battle in late 1916, setting up shop in a YMCA canteen in Albert, a few kilometres behind the front lines. In addition to serving coffee and treats, Mert and Al Plunkett performed for the battle-weary soldiers. "We would do some old minstrel songs and jokes, of which the boys were very fond," recalled Al after the war.[26] One of the Plunketts' contemporaries enthused, "Never were songs and hymns and passing jokes employed to more noble purpose than in lifting these men out of their depression and helping

Mert Plunkett of the YMCA became famous for entertaining troops on the Western Front and for establishing the Dumbells, a popular soldiers' theatre troupe.

them to win one of the greatest victories of the war—the victory of the human spirit over the awful conditions of carnage and death."[27]

The Plunkett brothers' YMCA hut behind the Somme battlefields had a stage made of old packing cases and a couple of gaslights and candles to illuminate the area. "It was in this atmosphere that every evening at five o'clock . . . crowded by Canada's best—a thousand seated, and hundreds standing to join in the impromptu songs played by the Captain as the requests were called out from the audience," remembered Al Plunkett.[28] The brothers sang in harmony and periodically Mert invited soldiers up on stage to sing a tune, tell a joke, or play the piano. The Plunketts' fame spread and Mert eventually established a troupe called the Y Emmas in early 1917, which was later renamed the Dumbells.

Captain Mert Plunkett was, in his brother's words, a "social-worker-at-war."[29] The high command recognized the morale-boosting value of the Plunketts' shows, and soon each of the divisions established full-time entertainment groups. Auditions were held for the few prized positions, with those selected escaping the trenches and being given an opportunity to entertain their comrades. It is not melodramatic to say that the auditions sometimes made the difference between life and death. Each troupe showcased about a dozen different performers: comedians, singers, dancers, pianists, female impersonators, and a handful of stage crew. Almost all were well-established prewar performers, although some new faces made the cut.

As the Canadians spent several months preparing for their assault on the seven-kilometre-long slab of mud and shell craters known as Vimy Ridge in April 1917, the Dumbells and other groups toured the rear area of the Canadian Corps, setting up a stage or taking one over from another troupe. Far from the fall of shells and under a big tent, regimental bands often accompanied the performers, and weary soldiers, sometimes only a day off the front lines, would trudge into the venue seeking some relief. Jack McLaren of the PPCLI Comedy Company recounted that they did some of their "best work" in between the large-scale battles, and it was not uncommon to see wounded men in the crowd and those with "a touch of shell shock." For McLaren, "the finest compliment came from the CO of a dressing station over the road who came across one day and said: 'You boys are doing more for the troops than I can. Keep it up.'"[30]

Machine-gun sergeant Ralf Sheldon-Williams remarked, "To us there was more of the 'pep' we needed in one 'rag-time' or sickly sentimental lyric than in ninety-and-nine fugues and symphonies. The concert parties, permanent and itinerant, knew this and catered wisely to our needs. Their bill of fare was strictly topical, and cheap old 'gags' and hoary 'patter songs,' so be it they had a bearing on our lives, were never wearisome."[31] The stage performances were popular and lowbrow, and were decidedly part of a closed soldiers' culture. The content may have varied with each theatre troupe, but the songs, skits, and plays were focused on the soldiers' experiences. There was much for the entertainers to poke fun at or complain about, from discipline to food, from lack of leave to the ever-present threat of death.

Soldiers' theatrical fare also mimicked the popular shows and songs in London. Men returning from leave shared the newest songs, especially from the contemporary long-running West End musicals *Zig-Zag*, *The Maid of the Mountain*, and *The Bing Boys Are Here*. *The Bing Boys* offered the soldiers "Another Little Drink" and "If You Were the Only Girl in the World," two wildly popular songs that made their way into soldiers' concert productions. The sentimental and sappy "If You Were the Only Girl in the World" had the lines

> If you were the only girl in the world,
> And I was the only boy,
> Nothing else would matter in the world, we'd say,
> We could go only loving in the same old way.
> In a Garden of Eden just made for two,
> With nothing to mar our joy,
> There would be such wonderful things to do,
> I would say such wonderful things to you,
> If you were the only girl in the world,
> And I was the only boy.

Soldiers liked the song but that did not stop the entertainers from parodying the lyrics, with one wag offering "If You Were the Only Boche in the Trench":

If you were the only Boche in the trench,
And I had the only bomb
Nothing would matter in the world that day.
I would blow you up into eternity.
Chamber of Horrors, just made for two,
With nothing to spoil our fun—
There would be such a heap of things to do,
I should get your rifle and bayonet too,
If you were the only Boche in the trench
And I had the only gun![32]

The Bing Boys was so popular that soldiers adopted the name informally for the Canadian troops, adapting it slightly in tribute to their beloved corps commander, Sir Julian Byng. The Canadian Byng Boys would wear the name proudly throughout the war, although it became less frequently used after Sir Arthur Currie took over the Corps in 1917. *Chu Chin Chow* was another popular show that was performed an astonishing 2,238 times in London.[33] It had a lavish set, and featured songs and dances, slave girls, and mystery. The adaptions that were performed at the front interwove soldiers into outlandish situations taken from the original storyline.

The music hall tradition demanded audience participation. The same jokes and songs and skits were performed again and again, and audiences joined in, singing, shouting out lines, and becoming part of the play. Civilian songs and jokes were updated for performances at the front, and the old familiars became new groaners. Some of the content was deliberately set to appeal to Canadians. Jokes about the Ross rifle or other failed Canadian kit would not have resonated far outside of the Canadian Corps, but they were much appreciated by the Canucks. The talented Jack McLaren riffed on one of Sir Harry Lauder's famous songs, "Roaming in the Gloaming." In McLaren's version, it became

> Roaming in the gloaming, Ross Rifle by my side
> Roaming in the gloaming, could nae fire it if I tried,
> It's worst than a' the rest, the Lee-Enfield I like best,
> I sure must lose it roaming in the gloaming.[34]

Such songs reflected aspects of the soldiers' separate society (even though by the time McLaren performed the bit, the rifle controversy had largely been settled, with the Ross having been discarded in the summer of 1916 in favour of the more robust, British-made Lee-Enfield). "We have hidden our seriousness," recounted McLaren, "in laughter and song."[35]

Containing in-jokes and slights directed at officers; a grin-and-bear-it attitude towards the monotonous food, mud, and fatigues; or perhaps a sly mimicry of the sergeant-major who skimmed off the rum—these shows were created exclusively for the soldiers. The PPCLI Comedy Company even wrote one skit, *Old Nick*, in which they likened the British and Dominion officers, NCOs, and generals to Kaiser Wilhelm and Satan. The troupe played the gag with a straight face as the army's senior staff were sentenced to hell. Satan greeted these "evil" figures one by one: first the sanitary sergeant (the NCO who forced men to dig latrines or clean up human waste), then the sergeant-major, the paymaster, the general, and finally the Kaiser. With each appearance of a hectoring NCO or officer on the stage, the excitement built among the audience, stimulated by catcalls and shouted demands for comeuppance. When the final villain, the Kaiser, received Satan's crown, handed over by the King of Darkness himself, the crowd roared with approval. The image of the Kaiser as demon was not uncommon, but more than a few officers must have raised an eyebrow at the positioning of one of their own generals only one level of evil below the Kaiser.[36]

Of a similar thematic bent was "I'm on the Staff Now," a popular and rollicking ditty sung from the perspective of a staff officer who has no work to do while the rank and file toil in the trenches. Easy cheers or jeers were secured by entertainers whenever they directed their theatrical assault on staff officers. In a running gag, and unbeknownst to the rank and file who were singing along with the entertainers, the troupe planted one of their own actors in the audience, dressed as a staff officer. At the conclusion of the song, the red-faced officer jumped to his feet, shaking with rage, screaming bloody revenge, and stormed out in a huff.[37] After a few shocked seconds of silence, the onstage entertainers cracked a joke that brought down the house, referring to the staff officer being late to plan another murderous operation.

How could such ribbing happen in an army built on blind discipline and fierce punishment? It was tolerated because the officers understood the value of letting men blow off steam, poke fun at the absurdity of the war, and get some of their own back. The stage was a safe zone for this type of performance, and it allowed for an open negotiation of power. Moreover, once the officers sanctioned such performances, they became more difficult to censor. Nor did the officers seem to want to take such restrictive actions. They knew that creating a space where the men could have a laugh at their own or superiors' expense would engender a tighter bond between the leaders and led—men who shared the common danger of the front. Moreover, many of the fighting officers had little love for the staff officers far to the rear, and so why not allow the men to take the piss out of them?

But the stage shows were not just about skewering the high command. Every performance had highs and lows, comedy and satire mixed with maudlin songs and sentimental skits. A wistful song about a girl left behind could bring the crowd to tears. And just when a sentimental song had turned the crowd misty-eyed, the pace could change wildly with a raucous, bawdy tune about drinking or searching for sex with a farmer's daughter. "Oh! It's a Lovely War!" for example, was a devastating, satirical, and cheerful song, and one of the most popular on stage or on the march, and whose lyrics always changed with each group or performance:

Up to your waist in water,
Up to your eyes in slush,
Using the kind of language
That makes the sergeants blush;
Who wouldn't join the army,
That's what we all enquire,
Don't we pity the poor civilians
Sitting beside the fire?
Chorus:
Oh! Oh! Oh! It's a lovely war,
Who wouldn't be a soldier, eh?
Oh, it's a shame to take the pay.

The song was irreverent, catchy, and infinitely hummable, and it easily became an iconic song of the war.

Stand-up comedy routines were also a part of every show. The humour was direct and almost always related to the soldiering

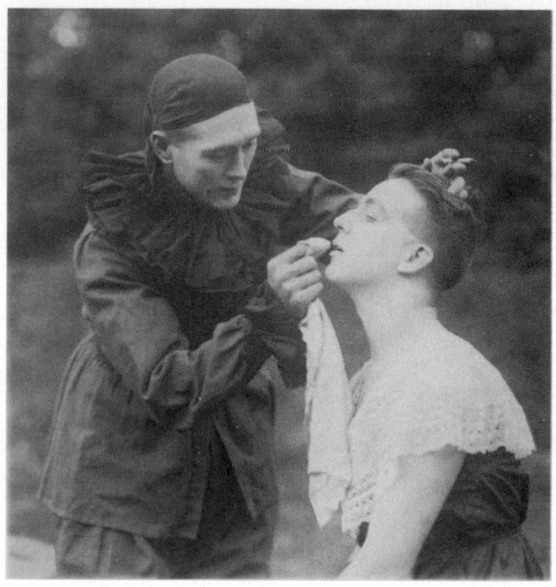

Soldier performers getting ready for a show.

experience. Leo LeBoutillier of the 24th Battalion, who fell at the Battle of Vimy Ridge, wrote before his death, "We had a concert given by some of the boys of the first division, it was very good, a minstrel show and they had some excellent jokes about the trenches and everybody in general, one I remember, they asked the whole class where Flanders was, each described as nice as he could being in Belgium, etc. but it did not satisfy the fellow who asked the question, so he told them where Flanders was 'one half was under water and the other half is in sandbags' and he isn't far out."[38] These types of jokes were universal, appealing to soldiers of all nationalities, and Canadians often visited British and Scottish theatre shows if they were in the same sector. A front-line medical doctor described a concert that he attended in 1917, in which he was quick to note that the comedy was "All done by men who have been over the Top, or at least front line work," and that it therefore carried a sense of authenticity. "The plot is laid in 1967, and its really awful clever. War still progressing, and the men's grandsons were rolling up. Leave only granted once in twenty-one years."[39] The never-ending war—where the scant leave was reduced now to once every two decades—was a popular trope in theatre, cartoons, and songs, reflecting the sombre reality of a war that was consuming this generation. And yet the soldiers found humour in it, or at least it was true enough to their experiences that they could chuckle at their own collective plight.

"THERE IS A CONCERT PARTY belonging to one of the Scotch Divisions at this place, I went to see them the other night and they were simply immense," wrote Canadian infantryman James Evans, who was a prewar merchant in Miniota, Manitoba, and who served until his death on September 1, 1918 near Arras. "They put on a Musical Comedy, all the ladies' parts are taken by men & hang me it's hard to tell the difference if we didn't know."[40] Female impersonators had been a staple of British music halls for many years, and the military had a tradition of garrison soldiers putting on plays for one another in which the women's roles were played by men.[41] On the Western Front, these "ladies" were immensely popular, and their success with the Canadian soldiers was due to the complex interplay in the men's lives of a celebration of the anti-heroic, a rejection of traditional military values, and a longing for female companionship.

Corporal Jim Pickard of the 76th Battalion recounted his experience of trying to join the famous Dumbells theatre group. He did not make the cut, but he provided a description of their show: "The first time I saw them was after the Battle of Vimy Ridge, when we were out on rest—and what a reception they got.

The men went wild when they heard those old songs. Some of the artistes were outstanding. Red Newman used to sing, 'Oh, it's a lovely War,' and it brought the house down. . . . Everyone was singing these songs, you know, and we picked them up on the mouth organ. Whenever we were out on rest and we heard that the Dumbells were in the locality, we'd walk miles to hear them, and every performance it seemed they got better. Of course, when Marjorie came on there was pandemonium. . . . She was a wonderful impersonator, or rather, he was."[42] The female impersonators were a central component of each show. Outfitted initially in what articles of clothing could be scrounged behind the lines, and sometimes wearing mops as wigs, later in the war the entertainers were dressed in fine dresses, stockings, high heels, and an assortment of boas and colourful fans.[43] The Maple Leaves Concert Party of the 4th Division had "Gladys," played by Edmund Bullis, who was famous for his rendition of "Come and Cuddle Me." Allan Murray played "Marie" with the Dumbells, and Fred Fenwick morphed into a bevy of beauties with the PPCLI Comedy Company. But Ross Hamilton of the Dumbells was the most famous drag queen, with his character "Marjorie." Hamilton was a prewar performer from Nova Scotia and he played Marjorie to be every soldier's girl back home. His signature song, "Hello My Dearie," brought down the house every time:

> Hello, my dearie I'm lonesome for you.
> I want you near me, Oh! Honest I do
> Come over, I'm all alone
> That's why I called you by phone.
> Loving like this is, some people admire.
> But cuddles and kisses you can't send by wire.

After the war, Hamilton toured the country as Marjorie, and he remained a standout on the music hall circuit for many years.[44]

Most of the soldiers' eyewitness accounts clearly indicate that they knew that the "beautiful" performers on stage were men. Claude Craig, a railway operator before the war who served with the 28th Battalion, wrote of a July 1918 performance, "Went to the Dumbell show in the evening at the Y and enjoyed it very much as it was very fine. They had one of the best 'WOMEN' that I have ever seen and who can sing just the same and a good deal higher than some women."[45] Major D.J. Corrigall of the 20th Battalion remarked that it was good to "see a genuine English girl" when he returned to Blighty, "as our own 'Marjories,' though excellent, were imitations slightly muscular."[46] Indeed, contemporary photographs reveal most of the impersonators to be very masculine. Craig, Corrigall, and most of their companions enjoyed the cross-dressing aspect of the show, perhaps needing to believe in the authenticity of the feminine form in their presence.

The drag performers sang sentimental melodies, sometimes with a suggestive wink, which allowed soldiers to embrace the idealized image of girls left behind. While there was a blurring of identities unfolding on stage, there is no evidence of real sexual confusion.[47] In a popular Canadian cross-dressing show, Ross Hamilton as Marjorie would saunter into a "mess" on stage, where every officer would stand at attention as she was seated. Then in a loud, hoarse, unmistakably male voice, "he'd call for a drink—and the illusion soon vanished."[48] This act and others like it drew more on the traditions of farce, misunderstanding, double entendre, and pun than on latent homosexual desire. Even if soldiers were ogling the drag queens on stage, they were actually "indulging in delightful fantasies that brought them substantial

One of the many popular cross-dressing artists in the Canadian theatre troupes behind the lines.

memories of the girls they had left behind," believed British infantryman Eric Hiscock.[49]

The actors in drag also performed a transgressive role in allowing the rank and file to strike back against certain types of officers. There were many stories of officers being smitten with the "women" on stage. Canadian Alwyn Bramley-Moore observed of the cross-dressers in a company concert, "The girls were excellent; one of the officers fell in love with one of them, and had to be told it wasn't a real one. He is still busy making excuses, they say."[50] Corporal Jim Pickard described the female impersonators, and especially Marjorie of the Dumbells, as being so convincing that "a lot of those young British officers wanted to make a date with Marjorie. She was so good that they couldn't be convinced she was a female impersonator."[51] Even a senior representative of the YMCA repeated the story that the cross-dressers were so winsome that "young officers could scarcely prevent themselves from falling in love."[52] But while this may have been true of some exceedingly naive officers, it seems more likely that such stories were a form of anti-authoritarian rumour, spread by the rank and file. It is most telling that those who "fell in love" were almost always the inexperienced officers. The rank and file repeated the story, creating narratives to needle a few of their more dainty officers who were unschooled in the ways of the world.

Cross-dressers always caused a sensation. They were reported on extensively in the papers and remarked upon in letters and diaries. In many cases, the "women" were the stars of the already popular theatre shows. The trench warriors' embrace of the cross-dressing anti-hero, like the adulation they expressed for the equally anti-heroic Old Bill, Charlie Chaplin, and malingering "old soldiers," was a form of pushback against traditional soldiering, and perhaps even against the supposed masculine ideal of soldiers. It may have been particularly appealing to civilian-soldiers who had exchanged everyday clothes for a military uniform. The cross-dressers' popularity was likely also a reflection of the deep loneliness of the overseas soldiers. Dr. Norman Guiou, a medical officer and one of the pioneers of blood transfusion, believed, "Each man might privately prefer the concert party 'girl' that most reminded him of his girl back home."[53]

SIGNALLER SANDY BAIN WROTE ABOUT his visits to three YMCA venues behind the lines, one of which showed films while the other two hosted theatre productions. The battalions were able to cycle through the area, with their soldiers attending films or live performances. "These concert parties are very good, and contain some splendid talent. The Second Division Concert Party, known

The Woodpeckers, one of the Canadian theatre troupes, entertained the soldiers. In this image, each character is identified with a sign around his neck: flag seller, allotment worker, munitions worker, profiteer, and Tommy Atkins (who represents the common soldier).

as the 'C'Toos' are especially good, and the boys crowd into the tents, glad to get a chance to hear some of the songs and jokes, and have their minds distracted from the stiff work that has been going on up the line."[54] In August 1917, Canadian infantryman Samuel Honey, a former schoolteacher who was destined to win the Victoria Cross but lose his life in combat, wrote to his parents about a play put on by the C.T. Perrots, called "Live Rounds," noting, "They pulled off some very clever comedy."[55] Canon Frederick Scott, who supported the soldiers' spiritual well-being and morale, observed of the performances that "a stranger could not have told from the roars of laughter that shook the audience from time to time that we were about to face the fiercest ordeal of the war."[56] Indeed, sustaining humour in the death zone was not easy. And while much of the material presented on stage was frivolous, light, and populist, it played a crucial role in soothing the battle-fatigued soldiers. One Canadian official document claimed that "in no other of the armies on the Western Front did the program of recreation assume such large proportions, and in none was it so potent a factor in maintaining morale."[57] The army high command had come to recognize the value of theatre for the shock troops in its role of sustaining and bolstering a fighting spirit. In the long, attritional war, soldiers needed to continually train and hone new tactics. But they also needed to recover from their ordeals and replenish their dwindling reserves of courage.

Though the soldier-entertainers were fortunate in escaping the strain of the trenches, they often performed multiple shows a day under difficult conditions. It was even more wrenching for them to know that the audience of mates and countrymen were enjoying but a brief respite from the front. Accomplished pianist Jack Ayre recalled the poignancy of these shows, confessing, "I get a lump in my throat when I think that some of the brave lads we entertained at 5 o'clock were dead at 7:30 in No Man's Land."[58]

CHAPTER 12

ENTRENCHED CULTURE

"One wonders how human beings live in such a Hell of fire and flame," wrote Private Frederick Robinson of the 58th Battalion, a Chicago-born, twice-wounded veteran of the Canadian Corps. Robinson penned the letter in June 1918, after fifteen months of service but before the full storm of the Hundred Days campaign, in which more than 45,000 Canadians were killed or wounded in the series of battles to defeat the Germans.[1] Robinson survived, and so, too, did Driver Clarence McCann of the 23rd Battery, Canadian Field Artillery, who in an April 22, 1916, letter asserted, "My future life is ever before me. I am always thinking of what I will do."[2] McCann spent much of the war dreaming of escaping the trenches. He made it back to his home province of New Brunswick, although with chronic pain from gas poisoning. His condition slowed him down, but he found ways to cope and he would eventually father seventeen children. Harold Simpson, a gunner from Prince Edward Island, contemplated what awaited him after the fighting stopped, noting anxiously, "A fellow has been through a battle and his soul is sick with the horror of it all, for no matter how hardened one may be the sight of shattered broken men is a cruel one. . . . The memory follows him, haunts him. Even in his dreams he sees again those cruel, gaping wounds, hears those heart-rending cries of pain and his whole being revolts. It is unbearable. He must forget for a time."[3] Soldiers like Robinson, McCann, and Simpson were conflicted over the war. Many wished to leave it behind and find a new life, free from the filth and violence of the trenches. But few were able to forget the war. And a surprising number of soldiers would find solace in the memories of their service, with the war, a deep scar, running across their lived history.

Soldiers carried with them the burden of the war years but also the joy of comradeship. For those who had previously never left a farm or travelled far from their birthplace, the war had brought great adventure. The historic sights of London or Paris were never to be forgotten. Canadians from all parts of the wide-ranging dominion had met one another, served together, and relied on each other for survival. And as part of their service, the soldiers had created a new and vibrant society. Would the secrets of survival resonate beyond the deadly trenches, where much of the culture had been spawned, and would this culture still matter to the soldiers as they returned to their civilian lives? Many soldiers were unsure. "Nobody can understand what we go through unless they have been here," wrote Major B.F. Gossage in his diary during the war.[4] Infantrymen Will Bird was even more pessimistic about fitting back into postwar Canada, so intensely was he affected by his overseas experiences. "We were prisoners, prisoners who could never escape," he declared. "I had been trying to imagine how I would express my feelings when I got home, and now I knew I never could, none of us could. . . . We were in a world apart, prisoners, in chains that would never loosen till death freed us."[5] Many soldiers had written off their lives on the

Western Front. Now that they had outlived the war, they wondered if they had been saved or resurrected. Certainly they were no longer the same men who had left years earlier. Despite the millions of letters and postcards from the front that had provided a glimpse of the war to those at home, almost all "returned men," as the veterans were initially called, knew it would be difficult to share their stories and experiences with outsider civilians.

Throughout 1919, hundreds of thousands of Canadians returned to a changed country. Canada had stood side by side with Britain and had earned the right to take part in the peace conference in Paris that would lead to a new world order. The home front, too, had been galvanized as never before. Canadian food and shell production had been enormously important for the nation's allies during the course of the war, with hundreds of millions of bushels of wheat sent overseas, and in 1917 alone, one quarter of all shells fired in the British army manufactured in

A Canadian soldier returning home to a grateful country, with the woman symbolically representing Canada. The caption reads, "Your motherland will never forget." The soldier has two German souvenir helmets hanging off his backpack.

Canada. To prosecute the war to the fullest, the government had intervened forcefully in the lives of Canadians, introducing an income tax, putting the hard sell on war bonds, and even conscripting young men for service. But the tensions of the lengthy war, the search for recruits and then the forcing of men to serve against their will through conscription legislation, the turning of the majority of Canadians against those of German or Ukrainian descent, and the continuous loss of soldiers had all led to division and fragmentation.[6] The country would never be the same.

The massive wartime debt forced the postwar federal government to create new powers and taxes. Tens of thousands of injured soldiers required prolonged medical treatment, some for the rest of their lives, and new hospitals and facilities were established across the country to care for them. Records show that Canadian soldiers suffered some 172,000 physical wounds, although that figure includes multiple wounds to the same combatant. Tens of thousands more would suffer psychological trauma ranging from nightmares and dark thoughts to crippling anxiety and mental collapse. While the term "post-traumatic stress disorder" would not come into being for more than half a century, it was acknowledged at the time that the war had irrevocably imprinted itself on those who had served.

Canada's loss of more than 61,000 service personnel—eventually rising to over 66,000 in the immediate postwar years—had gutted communities. Almost every town and village lost their young to the war, with larger cities reeling from the absence of thousands of men who would never return. Grieving and spent, Canadians turned their attention to ennobling their sacrifice. The British Victory Medal, issued to all Canadian and Empire soldiers, was inscribed with "The Great War for Civilisation 1914–1919." The war was regarded as a just crusade to liberate democratic nations and defend them against military oppression. A hundred years later, this perception has shifted, with the nobility of the cause becoming less accepted. Even though issues like fighting to liberate the oppressed and respond to aggression still resonate, the need to provide a rationale has perhaps been obscured by the war's nine million dead and its conflicted legacy. Whatever the case, in 1919 there was no desire to denigrate the war effort—too much blood had been shed, too much despair poisoned the land. To frame the losses overseas as futile would have further damaged the fragile country that had been pushed to the brink in the struggle for victory.

There were symbols to mark the war and help heal the country. Armistice Day was observed as of 1919, with commemorative rituals and the observance of two minutes of solemn silence, and it continues to this day as Remembrance Day.[7] The red poppy was issued starting in 1921, as both a fundraiser for veterans and a wearable sign of remembrance. John McCrae's "In Flanders Fields" was read and recited at Remembrance Day ceremonies, and continues to be so, although its meaning has changed over time, from a wartime martial poem that encouraged Canadians to keep fighting to a postwar call to honour the dead and their sacrifice.[8] The poem's appeal, when combined with the other symbols of remembrance for the dead, demanded grave reflection throughout the English-speaking world. In almost all cases, the wartime death culture and the dark humour that accompanied it did not survive the transition back to Canada.

THOUGH SOLDIERS ONCE HAD SCOFFED at death or feared an anthropomorphized monster that could strike without warning, those beliefs were largely left behind in the wasteland of destruction. The unknown dead had been treated with callous disregard and gallows humour, but in the war's aftermath the dead were sanctified. Most nations created agencies to care for the fallen, and the British Empire's dead were interred in thousands of Imperial War Graves Commission cemeteries around the world.[9] With the bodies left overseas, the missing and killed had their names inscribed on thousands of monuments across Canada.

There had been a rising belief in spiritualism since the late nineteenth century, with its advocates framing it as a misunderstood form of science. During the war years, many grieving parents and widows turned to séances and mediums to channel the spirits of the departed. The organized churches were aghast that wide segments of the mourning public had turned to such paganism for answers.[10] With violent deaths and missing bodies—more than 18,000 Canadian soldiers had no graves—those left behind embraced the spiritual realm in pursuit of comfort and closure. Seeing an opportunity, photographers produced "spirit photographs" that seemed to capture ghostly apparitions. These photographs were derided as simply underdeveloped images, but true believers regarded the hovering forms of the fallen as proof of a presence that extended beyond death.

When the séances did not provide clear answers for the anguished, the next of kin invested strong meaning in the material culture of their deceased loved ones. The memory items of the dead grew in importance after the armistice. Their letters were written testimonies of motivations and mentalities, of aspirations and service, and, as such, they acted as the literary legacy of a fallen soldier.[11] They were treasured by survivors as proof of a duty discharged. These private archives included postcards,

More than 61,000 Canadians were killed during the war, with the number reaching more than 66,000 within a few years as veterans succumbed to wounds, illness, and disease. Most of the fallen were buried overseas in the Commonwealth War Graves Commission cemeteries.

"whiz-bangs," and additional letters of condolence from other soldiers that were sent to soothe a family's pain after a comrade's death. Some of these condolence missives were marred by platitudes, but most were moving evocations from anguished pals or sympathetic padres attempting to find comforting words for parents hollowed out by grief. Many families curated scrapbooks that documented a soldier's service and death, and some even published letters in commemorative biographies.[12] Surviving photographs of sons, fathers, uncles, and brothers—often only a handful because of the rarity of photographs from the front—were also enshrined in homes. Canada's lost citizen-soldiers, wearing their military uniforms, offering carefree smiles or stern gazes, jauntily holding cigarettes or posing with a friend, would forever look outward from a dead past. In other families, the deaths were too painful to acknowledge, and their son or father's absence was rarely commented upon.

Most of the war's soldiers—the survivors and those buried in the overseas cemeteries alike—had sent home their prized war trophies. In early 1917, Waring Cosbie wrote to his family in Toronto that he was shipping souvenirs and trench art, ". . . a German helmet, a silk blouse . . ., and a Tobacco jar, made from two howitzer casings, which by the way might be made into a very unique clock for the smoking room."[13] Cosbie wanted to be reminded of the war every single second of the day, and he lived a long and rich life as a surgeon and professor of medicine at the University of Toronto. Georges Vanier expressed to his mother mid-war his future plans for his souvenirs, which he had smuggled from the front and given to a priest in Paris to mail home: "When mounted, they [shell fuses] make splendid paper-weights. I wish you would keep them for me in their natural state and when I return, we will decide what to do with them."[14] During the war, these trophies became objects of hope—in that the soldier aimed to survive the war to be reunited with their relics.

Souvenirs, talismans, and trench art acted as a hinge between the present and the past, between animate and inanimate worlds, and they reflected the changing relationship among veterans, their families, and combat objects. The next of kin used the artifacts as a mnemonic link to the fallen, a symbol representing an absent father, son, or brother.[15] Certainly the trench art that made it home was not kept solely for artistic reasons, since it was, in most cases, mundane and workmanlike. The arsenal of war was transformed into memorial objects and this material culture mediated

An example of one of the many trench art vases brought back by soldiers as souvenirs and memory objects.

grief and provided some comfort for the next of kin. But the engraved 18-pounder casing that held flowers or the tray built from an artillery fuse in which to drop spent ashes had a different and visceral meaning to those who had served overseas and survived the war. The memories of the war, those of both comic camaraderie and nightmarish intensity, would remain with the survivors, and to some extent such memories were represented in the battlefield relics that they held dear. These war objects were a safe way to reach back to an authenticated past, and they were proof that a returned man had been to the front to pick up this casing or that shell fragment.[16] For fifty years, Lieutenant Ernest Edwin Davis, a wartime armourer, kept a deskset for pens and writing material, adorned with bullets and with a No. 5 mills grenade as the centrepiece.[17] The inkwell and bomb had a personal, concrete, and symbolic link to a war that had devastated his generation. Yet while few would deny that the war of the trenches was indeed horrible, why did veterans like Davis want to be reminded daily of it? The answer must be that the war experience had been so powerful and affecting that those who survived did not, or could not, forget about it, and for many those strong feelings would deepen with time. These memories were not necessarily always positive, but they were of such a momentous and complex nature that they could not be disregarded or simply characterized as only horrifying or traumatizing.

FEW VETERANS OF THE WESTERN Front could drive the searing experiences of combat from their minds, but these nightmarish memories were balanced by the comforting recollections of the camaraderie they had felt in the trenches. These friendships were something to be cultivated and sustained in the postwar years, too. The prewar differences of class, region, language, and even religion had often been overcome by the soldiers in a remarkable act of coming together in a place of death. There were still biases and prejudices, but some of the prewar divisiveness was remade by veterans into a new and broader Canadian identity. Soldiers had accepted one another in the trenches or behind the lines, and they would do so again as veterans in Canada. One of the great disillusionments of the veterans returning to Canada was that society had not evolved with them, with political rivalries and open partisanship still intact. However, one must be cautious in suggesting that veterans were great harbingers of a new, friendly, and open Canada. They were not, especially as they held forceful prejudices against those who had not served, particularly new non-English Canadians.[18] The Canada that emerged in the trial of war was forever different, with new heroes, symbols, and a history written in service and sacrifice. But it would be many more decades before the country shed its ingrained prejudices and embraced diversity, and some say it is still an unfinished project.

Soldiers' culture was intricately linked to this wartime spirit of comradeship. While some of this unique culture was buried on the Western Front, much of it survived as soldiers carried it to Canada in their "old kit bags," as the popular song "Pack Up Your Troubles" went, urging the men to "smile, smile, smile." The soldiers' phrases, songs, slang, and sayings from the war continued to be a part of the veterans' vernacular, and, in some cases, they even entered the broader English language. In the late 1920s, two British Great War veterans, John Brophy and Eric Partridge, compiled and published a list of English words and songs from the war. By consulting men of different ranks and regions, throughout the British Empire, they gathered hundreds of words and phrases to reconstitute the soldiers' lexicon, little of which had been recorded during the war years. The authors emphasized that the result was not just a "mere dictionary-list, but a record-by-glimpses of the British soldiers' spirit and life in the years 1914–1918."[19] *Songs and Slang of the British Soldier, 1914–1918* (1930) became a linguistic archive that provided another window into the soldiers' culture and its vernacular underpinning.

E.L.M. Burns, a signalling officer in the Great War who was destined to become one of Canada's most illustrious soldiers, observed after the publication of Brophy and Partridge's book that many of words and slang compiled there were rarely used "in the daily talk of the Canadian troops," while other Canadian phrases and "stock words" were missing. The Canadians, he believed, also influenced the British by introducing some North American slang that circulated widely, such as "bone-head, to get away with it, attaboy, joy-ride, dope, and dozens, perhaps hundreds, of other phrases."[20] However, he never went further than highlighting the missing Canadian slang, and it is clear from soldiers' written discourse and songs that they used much of the same Empire-wide soldiers' slang. Perhaps the difference lay in how the Canadians spoke, how their accent changed words, and how they incorporated Canadianisms into their language. With no wartime audio recordings having survived, this is a part of the secret history that has disappeared.

As the veterans died, many of their words, sayings, and slang phrases were buried with them. But not all. Some of these have been incorporated into the English language. Phrases like "lousy" and "crummy," referring to the lice-infected soldiers, are still used, although they are applied more generally to show disapproval or describe shabbiness. Having a "chat" remains part of the English language, although it no longer refers to picking lice from one's clothes. "Souvenir," of French origin, replaced "keepsake," which was a more common English word for objects of remembrance at the turn of the twentieth century, and the "trench coat" became civilian attire in the postwar years. "Shell shock," the term banned by the military authorities during the war for fear of encouraging "malingerers" who would use mental wounds to escape the front, retains to this day a meaning similar to the one it had in the war. "Firing line," "behind the lines," and "over the top" are all still in use, as is the phrase "going back to the trenches" or some variation of it, to denote re-engaging with a difficult task. The term "No Man's Land" had its origins before the war, but in the postwar world it was infused with new meaning by the trench warfare experience.

If the soldiers' slang filtered into the English language, their songs had even greater influence and longevity. The songs were the war's soundtrack. Soldiers sang them with relish and gusto in the firing line, in the rear areas, in training camps, and on ships. It is not surprising that these songs—from the sentimental to the lewd, from pop hits to rollicking limericks and everything in between—remained important cultural icons after the guns fell silent. Captain Harold McGill, the medical officer for the 31st Battalion, wrote about how the songs triggered his memories for decades after he stopped wearing the uniform, noting, "The hearing of a particular popular air of the period will cause me to recall and fix the date and the place of a war episode."[21] From 1914 to 1918, soldiers' songs mattered and they continued to matter for decades after the war.

Many of the songs were not fit for reprinting or even for singing in polite company, and Brophy and Partridge felt compelled to expurgate the obscenities from their printed songs. However, most soldiers refused to accept the tamed-down versions. In reunions after the war, soldiers sang when they met periodically in small groups or at larger annual affairs. It was part of their shared culture—during both the war and the veteran years—and in these safe environments, there was little that was tame. Legion Halls began to be erected across the country in the late 1920s as sanctuaries for the veterans. Much like the soldiers' wartime dugouts or the *estaminets* behind the lines, the halls were sites to gather together and share—and in this case relive and rejuvenate—wartime culture. Veterans traded freely on their shared stories and rehashed old jokes. Returned veteran Ben Wagner explained that those at home "tried to understand, but you gradually got to the point where you only talked about the war with [other veterans]."[22] Though the scars of war could not be faded by a ditty, the songs were a way for veterans to stay connected with one another, to engage with the past, and to relive wartime camaraderie.[23] As one British veteran testified, "the songs we sang in the Army are bits of history. In them is embalmed that comic fatalism that carried us through four years of hell."[24]

THE CAMARADERIE AMONG MATES, THE relief behind the lines, the gallows humour, the importance of souvenirs, trench art, theatre, and songs that the soldiers created during the war mattered to them long after they put away their uniforms. The wartime stage productions with their uplifting songs were so popular that they continued to be embraced by veterans upon their return to Canada. The postwar Dumbells, gathered together by Mert Plunkett and consisting of performers from many of the best wartime entertainment groups, toured North America to great fanfare. They drew upon their wartime repertoire, honed during hundreds of concerts behind the Western Front, and over the next decade the Dumbells played close to a thousand shows and were seen by an estimated one million Canadians.[25] Sales of sheet music and gramophone albums were brisk and allowed for the further dissemination the troupe's popular songs "Everybody Slips a Little" and "The Dumbell Rag."[26] The content of the shows revealed aspects of the soldiers' secret culture to a wider audience. "Marjorie" remained wildly popular, as Ross Hamilton suggestively sang to the audience about love and longing. Anything anti-American brought an enormous laugh. The Dumbells showcased Canadian wartime culture, and along with Canadiana like the Group of Seven and CBC radio programs, they signalled the emergence of a renewed Canadian cultural nationalism.

1920s Dumbells' song sheet music for the wartime popular song "Oh! It's a Lovely War." The Dumbells played across Canada for over a decade after the war.

The Dumbells had a good run, but their popularity had begun to fade by the late 1920s. The show had grown stale, the performers were fighting over money, and perhaps many veterans no longer felt the need to cheer or jeer. In another attempt to capture lightning in a bottle, a new Dumbells show with female actors was created in 1928 but was met with disapproval, with veterans complaining that the wartime show had been corrupted. The Great Depression ultimately ended the Dumbells' popularity, even though there were reunions over the years, including the final one in 1975 at Toronto's

Lambert Lodge, where four surviving members treated an audience to the old songs, pitter-patter, and jokes. Two years later, the Charlottetown Festival mounted a tribute in the form of *The Legend of the Dumbells*, which was performed again in 2002.

Veterans also mounted their own plays. R.C. Sherriff's *Journey's End* was popular in Canada, as it was throughout the British Empire, and veterans' organizations staged it across the country. While it has come down through history as an antiwar play, Sherriff wrote it as a celebration of comradeship and an opportunity to reveal the spirit of the officers and men who endured the strain of war. One veteran from Peace River, Alberta, part of a local production, admitted that he and his fellow actors "liked the idea of donning our Khaki again and portraying on the stage what we had all once done in grim reality." The play had revived and reinforced the wartime "memories and comradeship of the trenches."[27]

Another postwar play, set in a cheerful *estaminet*, featured soldiers describing their setting as "A little moment of happiness snatched from death and disaster."[28] Theatre critic Hector Charlesworth, in reviewing the veterans-produced play *P.B.I.*, admitted to not understanding the in-jokes that drew laughter from the audience of veterans.[29] There were other war-inspired plays written and dramatized across the country, by groups ranging from professional theatre troupes to collectives of community actors staging local productions. Dr. Norman Craig, a wartime flyer and postwar doctor who had lost most of his boyhood friends during the war, authored and funded the play *You're Lucky If You're Killed* as a fundraising rebuttal to the town leaders of Fergus, Ontario—a group of "unreasoning pacifists," in his words—who refused to allocate funds for a local war memorial.[30] The play was staged in June 1933 and presented the story of a fighter pilot and his inner struggle over leading and losing his comrades in the relentless air battles. The wartime songs played a key part in driving the story and shaping the mood, and many of the cast members were veterans. The proceeds from the play were funnelled into erecting a local memorial in 1935, which bore the names of forty-six Great War service personnel killed in the conflict.

Canadian-made war films were less popular in the Dominion, although this was in part because the market was inundated with American productions that strangled the domestic film industry in the 1920s. Canadians chaffed at some of the American war films, as they invariably claimed that the Yanks had won the war single-handedly, but they also spent money to see them. It took until 1935 for the Canadian official film *Lest We Forget* to be produced, although its appeal was limited because it was a documentary rather than a feature film.[31]

A large crowd lining up for the 1928 film Carry On Sergeant. *One of the banners reads, "Canada's First Mammoth Motion Picture." The crowds did not last for long, and the film was a flop in Canada and around the world.*

The Empire-wide success of Bairnsfather's Old Bill continued into the postwar years in live-action formats. Bairnsfather's cartoons and witty lines had helped soldiers make sense of the war, and Old Bill and his anti-heroic mates were also put on stage, with *The Better 'Ole* playing to packed crowds for over a year at the Oxford Theatre in London. A film of the same name was also wildly popular. Merchandise—from shaving mugs to mascots and spin-off publications—kept Old Bill in the public imagination long after the last round was fired. Emboldened by the movie's success, Bairnsfather turned his hand to another major production. Surprisingly, it was filmed in Cobourg, Ontario. Plagued by delays and cost overruns, *Carry On Sergeant* was a major flop when it was released in 1928. The silent film arrived just as talkies were making their way into theatres, but the film also failed to capture the spirit of the trenches and it never found its audience.[32] Bairnsfather died in 1959, having lost his relevance as a cultural touchstone, although his legacy lives on in the cartoons that touched a generation. Equally important, his military anti-hero, Old Bill, would be the progenitor of sad-sack comic-strip figures like the American Bill Mauldin's Willy and Joe and Canadian William "Bing" Coughlin's Herbie. A host of other anti-heroic military figures, in film and television productions like *Hogan's Heroes* and *M*A*S*H*, would follow.

THE FAILURE OF BAIRNSFATHER'S FILM and the Dumbells' loss of steam occurred a decade after the Great War ended. At the same time, the war's meaning was shifting. The just war of the 1920s, symbolized in local monuments and homages to the dead, had been profoundly reframed by the end of the decade. A vigorous peace movement arose in Canada, as in many other countries, which questioned the use of war to achieve national goals, and also led some to question the very act of remembrance. Indeed, one did not have to be a pacifist to wonder if the war of the trenches, with its millions of dead, really had been a necessary war of noble crusaders against the evil Hun. The phrase "The War to End All Wars" was invoked as robustly as "Lest We Forget," and both expressions spoke to the appalling bloodshed. But the first of these suggested that the Great War had been so terrible that no right-minded, God-fearing nation or peoples would ever again engage is such carnage. That perspective marked a significant shift from just ten years earlier, when the dominant idea had been that the war was fought in support of civilization and that any and all burdens had been shouldered in the pursuit of a just war.

Nearly a decade after the armistice, a high-profile court case also led to Canadians' questioning the necessity of the war's unimaginable losses. In March 1919, Sam Hughes, the former minister of militia and defence, had stood in the House of Commons and accused former Canadian Corps commander Lieutenant-General Arthur Currie of incompetence and possessing a vainglorious desire to win acclaim. The general had been unable to respond effectively to the accusations because he was out of the country at the time, but in 1927 a small-town newspaper in Port Hope, Ontario, repeated the charges against Currie, describing him as a callous butcher who had needlessly sacrificed soldiers' lives. The accusations were untrue, but they shook the country. Currie, the principal of McGill University at the time, sued for libel, hoping to finally bury the ghosts of the past.[33] The war was refought in a Cobourg courtroom, as Currie's battlefield decisions were attacked, his motives interrogated, his character assassinated, and the cost of the war questioned. Currie barely survived the onslaught, and even though he won the case, some Canadians remained unconvinced that his leadership had not led to waste and unnecessary loss of life. The trial was such a strain that Currie suffered a stroke in its aftermath and he never fully regained his health, dying in 1933 at the age of fifty-seven. The sanctified idea that the war was fought for justice and the sacrifice had been worthwhile was increasingly shaken.

The worldwide success of German *frontsoldaten* Erich Remarque's *All Quiet on the Western Front* signalled a greater change in how the war was reimagined. Published in 1929, the novel sold millions of copies globally as Remarque revealed the dirt and drudgery of trench warfare, its futility and its folly, at least as viewed from a muddy trench plagued by mud, rats, and shells. The soldiers in Remarque's narrative were reduced to victims, caught in the industrial mincing machine of modern warfare. "Now it is all suffering," despairs the protagonist, Paul Baumer, "It is all so hopeless and never-ending."[34] The film of the same name, released the next year, further spread the message of the war's futility, and a rush of war books like it were published in almost every country around the world.

There were Canadian novels in this vein, the most infamous being Charles Yale Harrison's *Generals Die in Bed*, but these types of antiwar or disillusionment novels, as the genre came to be called, did not find much purchase in Canada.[35] Harrison's novel was attacked by veterans as denigrating the soldiers' experience, downplaying the key role of camaraderie, and adopting a limited view of the conflict that corrupted the war's memory. Many veterans—or at least those with a venue to share their voice in print—refused to accept that the war had been a pointless waste. Nonetheless, Harrison's novel sold well and has had a long life as a key Canadian literary work.

To cope with their experiences and make sense of their memories of the war, some veterans turned to writing the war from their minds, much as they had in their letters and diaries while serving overseas. This was exorcism by pen. Others ached to capture the war in print before it faded from memory. Some veterans wrote against the influential idea of disillusionment presented in *All Quiet on the Western Front*, while others tried to emulate Remarque's vivid writing and unvarnished presentation of the war in the trenches. All survivors knew they had lived through a historic event. For most ex-soldiers, it took time to come to grips with their experiences. Robert Kentner, who served with the 46th Battalion and went into the fish and seafood business, used his wartime journals and diaries to pen his memoirs during the 1920s while living in Winnipeg. He observed, "The experiences I have had are stamped indelibly upon my memory and nothing can possibly erase them. I can remember what happened the first night I spent in the Line as clearly as I can what I was doing two hours ago. It is the Gravest Chapter in the Book of My Life, the most important and most valuable."[36] Kentner's trials on the Western Front were a "dreadful ordeal," although one that he was "thankful" not to have missed, and he believed that his war experience had shaped him more than any other event in his life. Most veterans would have echoed such sentiments, and their memories of the war were complex and even contradictory, as they wished to forget but also to remember.

Charles Cameron, a lieutenant in the 16th Battalion who served at the front for much of the war and was wounded on the Somme, began compiling his memoirs in 1922. He noted, "During the postwar period there has been a plethora of books, sketches and plays portraying war in its grim and lighter phases, but we have yet to find an effort typifying the wonderful spirt and camaraderie of the Sons of Canada when at war."[37] Cameron's was a common sentiment. Many veterans sought to reclaim some of the comradeship forged during the war, even if only in their own unpublished writings. While the combatant memoirs could be biting and even riven with vitriol, they tended not to line up on one side or another in the war of reputations that was playing out between senior British generals and politicians after the war, especially in Britain.[38] In Canada there was less vitriol and neither Byng nor Currie wrote extensively about their war experiences, and Prime Minister Sir Robert Borden's two-volume work took out the sharpened pen to plunge in many backs, but not those of the soldiers. As for the junior officers and rank and file, most did not know and could not comment on the wider war effort or the strategic decisions that had affected their lives; their observations were limited to their own personal battles. And so most of these memoirs, along with a lesser number of works of poetry and fiction, were attempts to come to grips with the war's effects on individuals rather than assessments of why the war occurred, why it lasted so long, and how it was fought.[39]

Many of the memoirs written in the 1930s, after Remarque's crucial novel, also reflected the suffering that the Great Depression inflicted on so many in Canada and around the world. Capitalism seemed on the verge of collapse as jobs were lost and lives destroyed. The war had been awful in many ways, but it was the economic depression that ended so many dreams. When that was compounded by the rise of dictators like Germany's Hitler and Italy's Mussolini, a new sense of disillusionment was forged. The war seemed to have achieved little except to push Western democracies to the greatest economic crisis in their history and give rise to murderous fascist thugs. There was a stronger collective turn away from the war during this dark decade when so much was lost or taken away. Still, tens of thousands of veterans banded together, found solace in one another, and chose to remember the war as encompassing both sorrow and cheerfulness, a time when they "did their bit," even if they did not want to do it again. Contradictions abound here, and they are important to untangle. At the very least, not all soldiers considered their war experience a disaster. Almost all found value in having served King and country. Canadian wartime gunner Ernest Black wrote his memoirs to leave something for his children and grandchildren. While his war story revealed terrible loss and ghastly deaths, it was also infused with humour and cheerful absurdity. Throughout Black's war, his comrades had seen him through the difficult periods, and those remained his strongest memories of the conflict. Though some traumatic experiences can never be refashioned, there is a natural human tendency to minimize the bad over time, as memory fades. As Black noted, writing nearly fifty years after the armistice, "It seems odd that my memories of a thing so horrible and inhuman as World War I should almost all be pleasant."[40]

Black and others who engaged in the writing process may have found it odd to be reflecting warmly on the war, but most veterans did not write their memoirs. Some were not literarily inclined, and others wished to forget the war. Almost all survivors from the war generation had firm ideas about masculinity and how a man should conduct himself: they stifled the hurt and pain and carried on in silence. Few felt inclined to share their stories with others who had not been there. Whereas once soldiers had talked openly and freely to one another to endure the strain, now, without comrades to share a hole in the ground, they could rarely find the words. When in the company of others who had not served, many took solace in the bottle and in silence. And so the war was obscured and buried deep, often revealed only in short bursts over the course of a lifetime, even as wives and children yearned to know what had happened over there.

CULTURE AND CAMARADERIE HAD BOUND together the soldiers of the trenches, and they turned to one another again in the postwar years. The Great War Veterans Association was established in April 1917, and it grew to tens of thousands of members. Initially formed by wounded veterans returning home, it was an organization devoted to prosecuting the war to the fullest, no matter the cost, including enacting conscription and restricting the rights of some new Canadians, especially those from enemy countries in the war.[41] In deliberate opposition to the hierarchical structure of the army overseas, the returned veterans made their organization egalitarian, with length of service trumping rank, and they even went so far as to call one another "Comrade." During and after the war, there were many ex-soldiers' associations, including special groups for those who were blinded or who suffered from tuberculosis.[42] The Canadian Corps and the CEF disbanded in 1919, but the soldiers found each other in the postwar years. In 1925, after failing to convince successive federal governments to give a $2,000 bonus to every veteran, most of the fragmented associations joined together to form The Canadian Legion of the British Empire Services League. It became the largest and most important voice of veterans, and in 1960 was renamed The Royal Canadian Legion.[43] Through the Legion, members fought for more generous pensions and medical care for veterans and their

A group of Canadian veterans who were part of the Amputations Club of Vancouver, British Columbia. Veterans banded together in the postwar years to take strength from solidarity and camaraderie.

dependants. They also banded together to keep the memory of comradeship alive.

In addition to the Legion, which only had about a third of all veterans sign up for membership before 1939, the unit associations were also important in bringing veterans together. These local groups, most of which were created shortly after the soldiers returned to Canada, were often more enticing for veterans who wished to be reunited with their chums and not lumped together in some monolithic pan-Canadian organization. "The battalion and battery reunion is the one solace left for the dead days of the past," remarked one veteran in *The Legionary* in 1932. "It is there only that one can reopen the door which leads into that room crowded with pictures, which, for the ex-service man, time can never erase."[44] The reunions, held in newly built Legion Halls across the country or, depending on the wealth of a unit, in an armoury or a dedicated regimental building, usually had several hundred attendees. Daily get-togethers were smaller affairs, as men went to visit old comrades, drink, and relive memories after the working day was done. There were also a few formal events each year, usually on the anniversary of a battle or the unit's formation, and those attracted larger crowds. Elaborate meals, toasts, and traditions, along with boisterous songs and storytelling, reinforced the wartime camaraderie. The dark humour of the trenches was frequently on display. One reunion dinner for members of the 15th Battery, Canadian Field Artillery, offered a menu consisting of "Bucket of Blood, Shell-hole Special, and Fish-guts, followed by Ypres Fish-tail, Vimy Mud, or Passchendaele Slime."[45]

As part of the veterans' experience, some men and women, former soldiers and nurses, banded together to return to the battlefields. The expensive trips were out of reach for many veterans, while others had no interest in returning to the slaughter fields. But over the years, Canadians walked the Western Front, armed with Michelin maps and history books. Some brought their wartime letters and diaries to locate old sites, and sometimes a mother and father clutched a son's wartime souvenir as they stood over his grave in Europe, finally having a chance to say goodbye. Belgian and French farms, destroyed on the firing line, had been rebuilt as bed-and-breakfasts that sold "authentic" souvenirs and trench art to the travellers.

Closer to home, in early August 1934 some 75,000 Canadian veterans converged on Toronto for a reunion. One pamphlet observed that the power of memories awakened as "once more we travel down a road that is twenty years away and share again its friendships, romance, laughter and tragedy. . . . We welcome our companions . . . the men of the Canadian Corps . . . who bring back with them that greatest of all heritage . . . comradeship."[46] Parts of the city were cordoned off to create a "village" that was situated "behind the lines," a space that allowed for old soldiers to drink at *estaminets*, sing their songs, and ramble along the streets arm in arm with their comrades from the trenches.[47]

A railway car that carried Canadians to Toronto for the 1934 CEF reunion that drew over 75,000 veterans. The car was covered with soldiers' slang, song lyrics, and sayings written by veterans using chalk to invoke memories of the wartime years. These included Bairnsfather's caption "If you knows of a better 'ole, go to it" and the lyrics "If the sergeant steals your rum, never mind."

A more sombre and reverential reunion, but one also infused with nostalgia and camaraderie, took place when 6,200 veterans and their family members travelled to Vimy Ridge from Canada for King Edward VIII's unveiling of the monument in July 1936. It was the single largest movement of Canadians in peacetime up to that point in history.[48] While many were disappointed to find the battlefields overgrown, the cemeteries filled with their old comrades remained, beautifully manicured by the Imperial War Graves Commission. The soldiers' wartime graffiti also survived in places, especially in underground dugouts and tunnels under Vimy. The engraved scribblings and carvings of soldiers, some done out of boredom, others through a desire to leave their mark, are mute testimony to the men who served on those fronts. Much of this graffiti remains to this day as memorials etched into the landscape of former sites of battle, long after bodies have been reduced to dust.

THE EDITOR OF *The Canadian Machine Gunner* noted towards the end of the war that "when the Hun is finally beaten to his knees and war is over, it is our hope that the *Canadian Machine Gunner* will go on, and that Jack on his ranch in far-off British Columbia will be able, through the medium of its pages, to keep in touch with Bill, who is managing a fishery on the shores of the Gaspé Bay."[49] But the reality was that, with the disbandment of almost all of the CEF regiments and units, all of the trench newspapers were shuttered in 1919 except for *The Listening Post*, the most famous of the Canadian papers, which carried on into the postwar years, publishing episodically up to at least 1925. However, in 1929, after a ten-year hiatus, the 49th Battalion Association began to republish its regimental newspaper, *The Forty-Niner*. It had regular columns like "Where Is My Wandering Boy Tonight?" which tracked Forty-Niners around the world.[50] Drawing upon the language and structure of the wartime paper, the postwar publication also contained cartoons, jokes, poetry, and narratives. To forge a collective identity, the editors republished history pieces and soldiers' memories so that veterans could relive the past or learn for the first time what had occurred in a battle, anchoring their own personal experience to the wider regimental story. The unit's historian observed that the paper "recalled days both grave and gay when 'Billy's Boys' in the words of the old song 'saw the whole show through.'"[51] The bonds of wartime kinship were continually reinforced and strengthened for the men of the 49th through annual dinners, Remembrance Day ceremonies, and the paper, and other units carried out the same commemorative events.

"Year by year the old songs rang out, the hoary jests crackled anew, the back-chat and cross-talk brought about a throw-back in time; the myths and legends of the war were bedecked with fresh frills and furbelows," recounted the 44th Battalion's regimental history for decades after the armistice.[52] Refusing to let memories fade, many units sought to write a chronicle of their wartime experiences, although it was no easy task as trained historians were in short supply in Canada in the 1920s.[53] Official war diaries, kept daily by each unit during the conflict, were an important element of these written histories, along with accompanying appendices and reports, but these were augmented by call-outs to veterans to contribute their memories, letters, and diary entries. The official historian in Ottawa, Colonel A.F. Duguid, who was tasked with writing a history of the entire Canadian Expeditionary Force in eight volumes (and who produced only one in 1938), assisted the regimental historians with records and guidance. He also cautioned them not to be critical of senior commanders. Most of the histories were not of the muckraking sort, but they do provide insight into battle and regimental conditions. They also served as a memorial for the survivors and next of kin.[54] The regimental history of the 42nd Battalion, Royal Highlanders of Canada, was published in 1931. "This book will awaken memories," wrote Major G.G.D. Kilpatrick, the battalion's former chaplain, "it will carry [the men] back to the old days till they feel again on their faces the wind of France, and hear once more the sullen voices of the guns." The history of thousands of men who passed through the unit was offered in the name of the "immortal dead," their families, and the survivors, with its author, Lieutenant-Colonel C. Beresford Topp, noting, "It is not that any sane man can glorify war as such. Those who knew its stark horrors, its abysmal follies, its appalling waste will pray that their sons may never be called to pass through its flames; and yet is there a man of the 42nd who does not recall the years of his service with a sense of pride that he shared in the story that here has been written?"[55] Nostalgia and camaraderie ran as strong themes through these histories, even as the tragedy of the war was freely acknowledged.[56] Few veterans sought to glorify war, but none allowed their service to be forgotten or cast aside as a useless endeavour.

"The ghosts of dear, dead faces dimly rise to the surface," wrote Robert England, as he reflected back on his wartime friends, observing the powerful bleeding of the past into the present. England had spent the interwar years fighting for veterans' rights and he had witnessed many comrades succumb to illness or wounds sustained in the war.[57] Even more withering was time's war against the veterans, which steadily reduced attendee numbers at reunions and regimental associations after the Second World War. About 200 members of the 20th Battalion attended its annual reunion in Toronto in 1953. *The Globe and Mail* reported there were "toasts amid strains of 'Tipperary' and 'Pack Up your Troubles.' Old jokes were tried and new ones tested. . . . But members paused long enough in their reminiscing to salute the fallen and credit those who had kept the diminishing battalion together."[58] In 1958, a journalist described the "thinning ranks" of the veterans, with most of their comrades, to use the wartime slang, having already "gone west." The report added, "The reunions are becoming less frequent, more sparsely attended, and even the bounciest ex-soldiers admit the meetings are beginning to lose their punch."[59]

The 1st Canadian Siege Battery held a reunion on August 9, 1966, when twenty-two veterans gathered in Richmond, Quebec. A written summation of the meeting said, "There were inquires for the other lads, addresses exchanged, family histories compared, memories revived of their narrow escapes and battles, as well as the jokes and funny incidents which occurred in such a vital and intense period of their younger days." The sergeant-major, eighty-three-year-old Joe Jussup, talked of the good and bitter memories, "including the fifty continuous hours of fighting and winning at Passchendaele. He said the memory still bothers me here (touching his heart) 'but not up here' (touching his head): 'We had to do it.'" Some men brought their personal diaries and photographs, sharing them as memory objects, while others were content with "swapping yarns."[60] The war was worth remembering, and the veterans' nostalgia deepened over time, increasingly at odds with how the wider society imagined the war through films, books, novels, and plays. Over the decades, there was a widening chasm between those who served and those who had not, with increasing disagreement over the war's relevance and meaning.

FROM 1929 ONWARDS, THE MEMORY of the war was transformed from a just crusade and a war to liberate an oppressed peoples to a war of brutality and banality. Few understood why it had been fought, and fewer still believed it had been worthwhile. In Britain, over the years, it seemed that the victory had been washed away in a tide of disillusionment, while Germany had seethed in defeat, ripe for a fascist demagogue like Hitler to lead it into greater ruin, along with much of the world. In the face of these titanic world events and the unending horror of war, the importance of the soldiers' culture further receded from social memory. Trench culture had forged camaraderie, allowing soldiers to "stick it" together and laugh at almost anything the war could throw at them. And yet, over time, who could laugh at a

A wartime cartoon, "His Steel Helmet in War and Peace," illustrating a helmet's important role in protecting a soldier on the battlefield, its purpose back in Canada as a useable souvenir, and then, after decades, its function as a relic in a museum. The helmet, as artifact, helps the old veteran to tell the stories of his war years to younger generations, but the cartoon leaves an unanswered question: who will tell the stories once all the veterans are gone?

war that had spawned the rise of dictators and economic ruin? In the 1930s, the Great War was recast by many participants, politicians, and commentators as a pointless, even hopeless cause. The Second World War—with its unambiguous need to stop the Nazis and its ultimate justification as a necessary war by the revelation of the Holocaust—further pushed the memory of the Great War to the periphery.[61] Canadians understood why they had had to fight the war against Hitler, but over time they found it more difficult to make sense of the war against the Kaiser.

Canada emerged unexpectedly in 1945 as a wealthy middle power that had punched above its weight during the Second World War. It would go on to engage more intensely with international bodies and play a part in easing crises far from home. In the aftermath of the war, Canada joined the United Nations and banded together with Western countries to found NATO, a military alliance formed to stave off communism. It fought in the Korean War and embraced a "North Americanism" based on trade, security, and culture. Despite the fact that more than a million veterans from the world wars remained alive in Canada in the 1950s, Canadians adopted the role of "peacekeeper," a designation that grew out of Canada's successful diplomatic negotiations to broker a compromise in the 1956 Suez Crisis. Many of the veterans, scarred by war, freely promoted the country's contribution to peace among or within nations, knowing better than most the horrors of combat. But more than a few were angry that, with the increased emphasis on Canada's role in peacekeeping, the two world wars were pushed to the periphery, losing their importance as touchstones of change in Canadian history and largely being left for veterans to ruminate over in the Legion Halls except on November 11, Remembrance Day.

A new generation of British writers and historians returned to the Great War in the late 1950s, with interest peaking in 1964, the fiftieth anniversary of its start. The histories, novels, plays, and films of this period almost universally emphasized the futility of the war. Many were influenced by contemporary politics, broader societal trends, and a rejection of old certainties. The Great War was depicted as the ultimate hoax, with incompetent and bloodthirsty politicians and generals orchestrating one battlefield massacre after another. The Somme and Passchendaele battles seemed to reveal the bankrupt strategy of the callous generals, although few commentators knew what to make of 1918, the year the Allied forces—with France, Britain, and the latter's dominions in the lead, backed by the growing American armies—smashed the German forces along the Western Front. In totality, however, the war was regarded as a wasting defeat for all combatants, with the cost far outweighing the gains and the end not justifying the means. Few contemplated or cared that German militarism had been defeated or that the French and Belgian oppressed peoples had been liberated. Those reasons for going to war had been displaced by a focus on the crushing battlefield losses. Reinforcing and sometimes leading the way in this reframing of the war's meaning, the eloquent antiwar poetry of Siegfried Sassoon and Wilfred Owen became even more relevant, at least for English-language readers. These former soldiers' verse captured the plight of the seemingly helpless young men who had been manipulated by their elders to fight and then left to rot in the trenches. The emphasis on camaraderie and the many ways that soldiers coped was superseded by the image of the soldiers as victims, fools tricked by propaganda to throw away their lives in blind service to King and country.[62] The wartime soldiers' calls to one another to grin and bear it had been reduced to a long, silent scream from the mouths of broken men whose lives were ended too young or who were haunted by the ghosts of those they outlived.

In a few cases, the soldiers' culture was resurrected, and, as it had been during the war, was used to skewer those in command. But by the 1960s it was all bite and bile with none of the humour-based jousting between leaders and led—that careful and frequently recalculated negotiation of power—that had been common during the war. Joan Littlewood's 1963 play, *Oh! What a Lovely War*, later made into a 1969 film of the same name, presented the soldiers' haunting melodies and songs in a manner intended to eviscerate the generals and lampoon their senseless strategies. And a generation later, the television sitcom *Blackadder Goes Forth* (1986) followed an anti-heroic captain constantly using malingering tricks to try to escape his ultimate destiny of "going over the top." Both productions drew upon the soldiers' dark humour, not to explain how soldiers survived but to reveal the monstrosity of the war effort. Not to be outdone, the mad destabilizers known as *Monty Python* also found the war ripe for satire, with sketches that emphasized the absurdity and futility of soldiers under fire doing anything to avoid going over the top in battle.[63] By the late twentieth century, the just war had long been buried and would remain there, as the millions of Great War veterans from around the world succumbed to age and time, their secret history disappearing with them or being quietly revealed in obscure memoirs.

IN *BLACKADDER GOES FORTH*, THE loud-mouthed, egotistical flying ace Lord Flashheart moans, "I'm sick of this damn war—the blood, the noise, the endless poetry."[64] It's a lovely line and the blood and endless poetry have continued to echo since the 1930s, with the war framed through the lens of futility and gutting loss. Academics towards the end of the twentieth century—especially in France, Britain, and Australia—tried to offer other perspectives. They reconstructed the thinking of the time, and the political and economic factors that had led to the war. They studied how soldiers and civilians were able to withstand the strain. But the scholarship made few inroads into broader societal debates and did little to change the dominant discourse that insisted the war had been unmitigated, senseless butchery. In Canada, the message was a little different: the country's heavy sacrifice was twinned with the redeeming message of how the war had propelled Canada to full nationhood. In this reading of history, Vimy became the primary symbol for Canada's war effort, a legend in which the battle and the monument stood for the emergence of a new country through the trial of combat and the sacrifice of its people.[65] While the Vimy legend did not resonate with all Canadians, the battle took on new symbolic meaning over time, reflecting the changing nature of society. It was a malleable idea grounded in a costly victory. However, soldiers' culture was difficult to locate in the nation-building narrative, and few could conceive of an army of anti-heroes hurling the Germans back from the ridge. They were not anti-heroes, of course, but they embraced these characteristics that were so prevalent in the soldiers' culture to cope and endure before and after the battle. And yet such nuances had long been forgotten and, instead, the solidifying narratives reflected gritty courage, Canadian initiative, and perseverance in the face of a strong enemy and incompetent British allies.

The soldier-as-victim narrative prevails in novels, plays, and films, which depict the war almost exclusively as a tragedy. The classic Canadian novel about the war, Timothy Findley's *The Wars* (1977), thrusts its main character into the madhouse of battle, where he is savaged by his companions, brutalized by combat, and eventually driven to murder as he tries to free a trainload of horses. There is no redemption; there is no camaraderie to see him through; he is broken by the war. Findley's novel has been influential in Canadian literature and is often featured on school curricula. Over time, it became more difficult for Canadians to understand the war as anything other than a forlorn battle in the mud and blood of the trenches. The strategic or societal reasons for why the world went to war in 1914—alliance systems, fear, revenge, diplomatic failure, social Darwinistic ideas of race degeneration, hubris, and the list goes on—no longer made much sense. And none of it reads like the moving poetry and evocative literature that continue to guide us in our quest to know the past. And so the war is usually reduced to the personal—rendered as a terrible conflagration disconnected from the larger contextualized political, cultural, or social currents that had led to the war. It is not wrong to let the eyewitnesses to history be our guides to the past, but when the war is viewed through the lens of personal experience, there can seemingly only be victims. The protagonists of novels and plays are shattered men whose minds and bodies were ripped asunder by the war's awfulness. Shell shock is a powerful trope, used by many novelists and playwrights to frame the war as something akin to a grand act of lunacy. Equally dominant is the image of the damaged survivor of the trenches, who is haunted by his dead comrades and the men he killed.[66] There are no novels or plays of note in which a soldier has a good war, in which the story is told of a bayonet instructor in England who never makes it to the front, of a soldier staffing one of the countless administrative jobs out of reach of shells, or even of a front-line infantryman who emerges unscathed and proud of his service in a time of great turmoil.

This is not to say that the war was a happy romp. The soldiers' experiences at the front were grim beyond belief. Men suffered from dirt and deprivation, and death stalked them daily. And yet, most soldiers did not break down from shell shock or run away from the trenches. They found ways to endure. They stayed in the fight, believing in the cause, aiding their comrades, following their leaders. They were bucked up with rewards, kept in place by discipline, and protected by their culture. Life was hard in every way. But the soldiers were not lurching about seeking release by a bullet. Though some might have claimed to embrace fatalism, even that was a mental shield used to ward off their fear of death and help them to cling stubbornly to life. Soldiers' culture provides evidence that the history of the war need not be reduced to a binary idea of this *or* that but can instead be seen as a more inclusive pairing of this *and* that, and so much more. Even to reclaim the soldiers' culture from obscurity is to broaden the soldiers' story and to provide a new perspective on the constructed meaning and memory of the Great War. An uncovering of the soldiers' hidden society and culture reveals that the combatants were not passive victims but instead active participants in shaping their war experience.

The war novelists, playwrights, poets, and filmmakers have had the greatest impact on how the Great War is understood and remembered. Their works left some veterans who survived late into the twentieth century angry that their wartime experiences had been reduced to images of disempowerment, revulsion, and futility. The deadening disenchantment had seemingly smothered the redeeming impact of camaraderie. Even worse for such survivors was the pity and scorn these works expressed for those who

The Canadian "Brooding Soldier" monument, unveiled in 1923 to mark the Battle of Second Ypres. Carved out of granite, the soldier stands sentry for his fallen comrades. Now that all those who served are gone, how shall we remember this generation of Canadians who served and sacrificed in the Great War?

had fought. New Zealander Charles Edmund Carrington recounted his discomfort over how the war's meaning had moved firmly into the realm of ridicule and contempt: "I never meet an old 'sweat,' as we liked to describe ourselves, who accepts or enjoys the figure in which we are now presented. . . . Just smile and make an old soldier's wry joke when you see yourself on the television screen, agonized and woebegone, trudging from disaster to disaster, knee-deep in moral as well as physical mud, hesitant about your purpose, submissive to a harsh, irrelevant discipline, mistrustful of your commanders. Is it any use to assert that I was not like that, and my dead friends were not like that, and the old cronies that I meet at reunions are not like that?"[67]

There can be no doubt that many veterans looking back on the war carried with them scarring memories of the conflict and the wreckage that accompanied it. Some never came to grips with the grief and guilt of burying young friends, even as they returned to their homes, started families, and grew old. But veterans were able to hold the two seemingly conflicting ideas about the war in their hearts: it was a dreadful slaughter and it was also a titanic event that revealed the best about themselves and their comrades. For many, the redemptive qualities of service and camaraderie were sought after, embraced, and celebrated long after the war in a unique veterans' culture that drew directly from the soldiers' wartime experiences. Decades after the war ended, Governor General Georges Vanier spoke of the honour of having served his country and of having stood beside so many Canadians who also did: "Never have I been so proud of my compatriots than on the battlefield."[68]

THE SOLDIERS OF THE WESTERN Front were a tribe unto themselves. They bore witness to events that we can scarcely comprehend, and they created a culture to protect themselves from the savagery. Their culture was theirs—it was not meant to be shared with or even understood by outsiders. And to further distance themselves from those at home, the soldiers often embraced anti-heroism over heroism. Grim humour edged out the forced optimism of the home front, with its message of "one more push to victory." Soldiers revelled in the bawdy and the vulgar, but they could be equally happy with the maudlin and the spiritual. Their culture was alive with contradictions. This is not surprising if we remember that the trench culture was embraced by some 425,000 men from all parts of Canada, all classes, and almost all religions. This culture was a tool of survival and identity, and it bound together this diverse force. The Canadian soldiers' songs, slang, jokes, and newspapers reinforced the idea of "Canadianness" that was forged in the war. Though intricate connections to the dominant culture of the British Empire remained in postwar Canada, the war changed things forever, perhaps most for recent British immigrants, who found that they were indeed members of a distinct country. Never before had there been anything to bring together Canadians like the cauldron of war, and that terrible conflict forged a new Canadian nationalism.

With John Babcock's death in 2010, Canada lost its last Great War veteran, and all of the world's remaining veterans passed away shortly after that. Though we have letters, postcards, sheet music, souvenirs, artifacts, relics, and all manner of material culture, we have lost that tangible living link to the war. However, most of us who learned about the war in school, or read books and novels depicting it, or watched the plays and films, can conjure up the rumble of shellfire, the clanging of the gas alarms, and the low-ripping sound of machine-gun fire. We can picture the gluey mud, the disgusting rats, and the rotting dead hanging on the barbed wire. That is the dominant narrative of the war and it is not easy to see it any other way. The stand-up comedians, the cross-dressers and ghost story tellers, the Charlie Chaplins and Old Bills, the happy singers and artful dodgers—they have been long buried and are little remembered and even less well understood. And yet they are part of the secret history of the war.

To better understand that conflict a century ago, we need to unravel the soldiers' riddles that they left behind, even though many did not want to share their culture with us, the outsiders. We might start by thinking of those soldiers as not just the black-and-white figures of photographs and film, but as vibrant young men, full of life, colour, jokes, and pranks. They were sons, husbands, uncles, and fathers. They had hopes of surviving the war and of returning, "aprés la guerre," to their old lives, comforting communities, and supportive families. The citizen-soldiers railed against the machine in which they were caught. Some did not make it, devastated in body, mind, and spirit. We have made space for them in our collective memory, but not for the vast majority who survived, or for considerations of how they survived. Canadian soldiers were not simply victims. They had tremendous resiliency and agency. They refused to go under without a fight.

This generation has passed from our world, but their actions and accomplishments, their service and sacrifice, will forever live on in our history. Remember them clothed in battle, armed with deep courage, tough resolve, gallows humour, and camaraderie. While the Great War soldiers are all gone, we can still hear the faint echo of their boisterous songs. *Goodbyeeeeeee, and fuck you.*

ENDNOTES

INTRODUCTION: SOLDIERS' CULTURE

1 Maurice Pope, *Letters from the Front* (Toronto: Pope and Company, 1996) 32.

2 Canadian War Museum (CWM), 19920187-002, Herbert Heckford Burrell diary, 27 December 1916.

3 Canadian Bank of Commerce, *Letters from the Front: being a partial record of the part played by officers of the Bank in the Great European War* (Canada: Canadian Bank of Commerce, 1920) 302.

4 There are thousands upon thousands of books written on culture. The most useful entry is Peter Burke, *What Is Cultural History?* (Cambridge: Polity Press, 2004). My thinking on historicizing culture has been shaped by many books, but I'll single out David Lowenthal, *The Past Is a Foreign Country* (Cambridge: Cambridge University Press, 1985); Michael Kammen, *Mystic Chords of Memory: The Transformation of Tradition in American Culture* (New York: Vintage Books, 1993); John Bodnar, *The "Good War" in American Memory* (Baltimore: The Johns Hopkins University Press, 2010).

5 For soldiers' agency, see G.D. Sheffield, *Leadership in the Trenches* (London: Macmillan, 2000); Craig Leslie Mantle (ed.), *The Unwilling and the Reluctant: Theoretical Perspectives on Disobedience in the Military* (Kingston: CDA Press, 2006); Leonard V. Smith, *Between Mutiny and Obedience: The Case of the French Fifth Infantry Division During World War I* (New Jersey: Princeton University Press, 1994).

6 For work on soldiers' culture, see Stéphane Audoin-Rouzeau, *Men at War 1914–1918: National Sentiment and Trench Journalism in France during the First World War*, trans. Helen McPhail (Providence, RI: Berg, 1992); J.G. Fuller, *Troop Morale and Popular Culture in the British and Dominion Armies, 1914–1918* (Oxford: Clarendon Press, 1990); Samuel Hynes, *The Soldiers' Tale: Bearing Witness to Modern War* (New York: Allen Lane, 1997); John Brophy and Eric Partridge, *Songs and Slang of the British Soldier: 1914–1918* (London: E. Partridge, 1931); Peter Farrugia, "A Small Truce in a Big War: The Historial de la Grande Guerre and the Interplay of History and Memory," *Canadian Military History* 22.2 (Spring 2013) 63–76. For works related to the elite culture, see Paul Fussell, *The Great War and Modern Memory* (New York: Oxford University Press, 1975); Laura Brandon, *Art or Memorial?: The Forgotten History of Canada's War Art* (Calgary: University of Calgary Press, 2006); Modris Eksteins, *Rites of Spring: The Great War and the Birth of the Modern Age* (Toronto: Lester & Orpen Dennys, 1994).

7 Canadian Letters and Images Project (CLIP), Cecil and Louis Duff collection, September 4, 1916.

8 Leslie Frost, *Fighting Men* (Toronto: Clark, Irwin and Company, 1967) 153.

9 Library and Archives Canada (LAC), MG 30 E558, Cecil J. French, French to McAulay, 22 August 1916.

10 CLIP, Memoir by Kenneth Walter Foster, no page numbers.

11 Ralf Sheldon-Williams, *The Canadian Front in France and Flanders* (London: A. and C. Black, 1920) 190.

12 John Harold Becker, *Silhouettes of the Great War* (Ottawa: CEF Books, 2001) 126–8.

13 See Ana Carden-Coybe, *The Politics of Wounds: Military Patients and Medical Power in the First World War* (Oxford: Oxford University Press, 2014); and Jeffrey Reznick, *Healing the Nation: The Culture of Caregiving in Britain during the Great War* (Manchester: Manchester University Press, 2005).

14 CWM, *R.M.R. Growler* 1 (1 January 1916) 1.

15 Richard Holt, *Filling the Ranks: Manpower in the Canadian Expeditionary Force, 1914–1918* (Montreal and Kingston: McGill-Queen's University Press, 2016) 43.

16 On Britishness, see Carl Berger, *The Sense of Power: Studies in the Ideas of Canadian Imperialism* (Toronto: University of Toronto Press, 1970); Chris Champion, *The Strange Demise of British Canada: The Liberals and Canadian Nationalism, 1964–1968* (Montreal and Kingston: McGill-Queen's University Press, 2010); Philip Bucker and Douglas Francis (eds.), *Rediscovering the British World* (Calgary: University of Calgary Press, 2005); Mary Chaktsiris, "Our Boys with the Maple Leaf on Their Shoulders and Straps: Masculinity, the Toronto Press, and the Outbreak of the South African War, 1899," *War and Society* 32.1 (2013) 3–25.

17 Jonathan Vance, "Provincial Patterns of Enlistment in the Canadian Expeditionary Force," *Canadian Military History* 17.2 (Spring 2008) 75–8.

18 On manpower, see J.L. Granatstein and J.M. Hitsman, *Broken Promises: A History of Conscription in Canada* (Toronto: Oxford University Press, 1977); Holt, *Filling the Ranks*; William F. Stewart, *The Embattled General: Sir Richard Turner and the First World War* (Montreal and Kingston: McGill-Queen's University Press, 2015); Jean Martin, "Francophone Enlistment in the Canadian Expeditionary Force, 1914–1918: The Evidence," *Canadian Military History* 25.1 (2016) 1–12; Peter Broznitsky, "For King, Not Tsar: Identifying Ukrainians in the Canadian Expeditionary Force, 1914–1918," *Canadian Military History* 17.3 (2008) 22.

19 Timothy C. Winegard, *For King and Kanata: Canadian Indians and the First World War* (Winnipeg: University of Winnipeg Press, 2012) 6.

20 L. James Dempsey, "Aboriginal Alberta and the First World War," in Adriana A. Davies and Jeff Keshen, *The Frontier of Patriotism Alberta and the First World War* (Calgary: University of Calgary Press, 2016) 61.

21 For the 35,599 figure, see RG 24, v. 1874, Some figures regarding American-born serving with the CEF, 3 November 1928. Of the 35,599 American-born serving in the CEF, 19,966 served overseas and 1,999 were killed in combat and another 139 succumbed to accidents or disease. For a higher figure, see Richard Holt, "British Blood Calls British Blood: The British-Canadian Recruiting Mission of 1917–1918," *Canadian Military History* 22.1 (2013) 27; Holt, *Filling the Ranks*, 86–7. Also see Ronald G. Haycock, "The American Legion in the Canadian Expeditionary Force, 1914–1917: A Study in Failure," *Military Affairs* 43.3 (October 1979) 115–19.

22 Nic Clarke, John Cranfield, and Kris Inwood, "Fighting Fit? Diet, Disease, and Disability in the Canadian Expeditionary Force, 1914–18," *War & Society* 33.2 (May 2014) 80–97.

23 Tim Cook, "From Destruction to Construction: The Khaki University of Canada, 1917–1919," *Journal of Canadian Studies* 37.1 (Spring 2002) 109–43.

24 Tim Cook, "'He was determined to go': Underage Soldiers in the Canadian Expeditionary Force," *Histoire sociale/Social History* 41.81 (May 2008) 41–74.

25 See Nic Clarke, *Unwanted Warriors: The Rejected Volunteers of the Canadian Expeditionary Force* (Vancouver: UBC Press, 2015). At least 189,701 men, aged twenty-one and over, were from "enemy" countries, like Germany, Austria-Hungary, and Turkey. See Chris Sharpe, "Enlistment in the Canadian Expeditionary Force 1914–1918," *Canadian Military History* 24.1 (2015) 26.

26 Jim Woods, *Militia Myths: Ideas of the Canadian Citizen Soldier, 1896–1921* (Vancouver: UBC Press, 2010); and Amy Shaw, "The Boer War, Masculinity, and Citizenship in Canada, 1899–1902," in Patrizia Gentile and Jane Nicholas (eds.), *Contesting Bodies and Nation in Canadian History* (Toronto: University of Toronto Press, 2013) 97–114.

27 Brian MacDowall, "'A Flag that Knows No Colour Line': Indigenous Veteranship in Canada, 1914–1939," (Ph.D. dissertation: York University, 2017) 59.

28 Richard Holt, "British Blood Calls British Blood: The British-Canadian Recruiting Mission of 1917–1918," *Canadian Military History* 22.1 (2013) 33; Robert H. Thompson and Jonathan F. Vance (eds.), *A Passport of First World War Canadians* (Toronto: The World Remembers, 2017) 19.

29 CWM, 2000 0148-001, 58A 1.203.1, letter to Ruth, 1 June 1918.

30 *Canada in Khaki: A Tribute to the Offices and Men Now Serving in the Canadian Expeditionary Force* (London: CWRO, 1917) 1.

31 On religion, Alan Bowker, *A Time Such as There Never Was Before: Canada After the Great War* (Toronto: Dundurn Publishers, 2014); Mark McGowan, *The Imperial Irish: Canada's Irish Catholics Fight the Great War, 1914–1918* (Montreal and Kingston: McGill-Queen's University Press, 2017).

32 LAC, MG 30 E427, Macfie papers, Roy to Muriel, 2 February 1918.

33 Mark David Sheftall, *Altered Memories of the Great War: Divergent Narratives of Britain, Australia, New Zealand and Canada* (London: I.B. Tauris, 2009) 36–42.

34 LAC, A.F. Duguid papers, v. 2, file 6, "The Canadian as a Soldier," (14 July 1920).

35 George Nasmith, *On the Fringe of the Great Fight* (Toronto: McClelland, Goodchild & Stewart, 1917) 80; Harold Peat, *Private Peat* (Indianapolis Bobbs Merrill, 1917) 31; F.W. Bagnall, *Not Mentioned in Dispatches* (North Vancouver: North Shore Press, 1933) 21.

36 Quoted in Tim Cook, "Immortalizing the Canadian Soldier: Lord Beaverbrook and the Canadian War Records Office in the First World War," in Briton C. Busch (ed.), *Canada and the Great War: Wester Front Association Papers* (Montreal and Kingston: McGill-Queen's University Press, 2003) 54.

37 Heather Streets, *Martial Races: The Military, Race and Masculinity in British Imperial Culture, 1857–1914* (Manchester: Manchester University Press, 2004); Doug Owram and R.F. Moyles, *Imperial Dreams and Colonial Realities* (Toronto: University of Toronto Press, 1988).

38 Tim Cook, "Documenting War & Forging Reputations: Sir Max Aitken and the Canadian War Records Office in the First World War," *War in History* 10.3 (2003) 265–5; Jeff Keshen, "The Great War Soldiers as Nation-Builders in Canada and Australia," in Briton Busch (ed.), *Canada and the Great War: Western Front Association Papers* (Montreal and Kingston: McGill-Queen's University Press, 2003) 3–26; Jonathan Vance, *Maple Leaf Empire: Canada, Britain, and Two World Wars* (Oxford: Oxford University Press, 2012) 65.

39 Desmond Morton, *When Your Number's Up: The Canadian Soldier in the First World War* (Toronto: Random House of Canada Ltd., 1993) 278.

40 Y.A. Bennett Bennett (ed.), *Kiss the kids for dad, Don't forget to write: The Wartime Letters of George Timmins, 1916–18* (Vancouver: UBC Press, 2009) 20.

41 See Desmond Morton, *A Peculiar Kind of Politics: Canada's Overseas Ministry in the First World War* (Toronto: University of Toronto Press, 1982).

42 Tim Cook, *The Madman and the Butcher: The Sensational Wars of Sam Hughes and General Arthur Currie* (Toronto: Allen Lane, 2010).

43 CLIP, Jay Batiste Moyer, letter, 17 October 1916.

CHAPTER 1: SURVIVAL CULTURE

1 CLIP, Herbert Irwin, letter, 13 August 1916.

2 J. Clinton Morrison (ed.), *Hell Upon Earth: A Personal Account of Prince Edward Island Soldiers in the Great War, 1914–1918* (Summerside, P.E.I.: J. Clinton Morrison, 1995) 80.

3 Alexander Watson, *Enduring the Great War: Combat, Morale and Collapse in the German and British Armies, 1914–1918* (Cambridge: Cambridge University Press, 2008) 15.

4 R. Lewis, *Over the top with the 25th: Chronicle of Events at Vimy Ridge and Courcellette* (Halifax: H.H. Marshall, 1918) 50.

5 Susan C. McGrath (ed.), *The Long Sadness: World War I Diary of William Hannaford Ball* (self-published, 2014) 14.

6 MHRC, Harold Simpson, *A History of the 2nd Canadian Siege Battery* (self-published, 1966) 69.

7 For a full discussion of wartime deaths, see Tim Cook, *Shock Troops: Canadians Fighting on the Western Front, 1917–1918* (Toronto: Viking, 2008) 613; Tim Cook and William Stewart, "Death in the Canadian Expeditionary Force," *1914–18 International Encyclopedia of the First World War*. http://www.1914-1918-online.net

8 Brian Douglas Tennyson, "'Wild Bill' Livingstone Goes to War: A Diary and Letters, 1916–19," *Journal of the Royal Nova Scotia Historical Society* 12 (2009) 130.

9 See Peter Chasseaud, *Rat's Alley: Trench Names of the Western Front, 1914–1918* (Gloucestershire: Spellmount, 2006); Allyson Booth, *Postcards from the Trenches: Negotiating the Space between Modernism and the First World War* (Toronto: Oxford University Press, 1996) 117; Ross Wilson, *Landscapes of the Western Front: Materiality during the Great War* (New York: Routledge, 2012) 168.

10 Joseph Hayes, *The Eighty-Fifth in France and Flanders* (Halifax: Royal Print and Litho, 1920) 69.

11 Canadian Bank of Commerce, *Letters from the Front*, 149.

12 Tim Cook, *At the Sharp End: Canadians Fighting the Great War* (Toronto: Viking, 2007) 230.

13 Captain R.J. Manion, *A Surgeon in Arms* (Toronto: McClelland, Goodchild & Stewart, 1918) 62.

14 CLIP, George Kempling diary, 26 July 1916.

15 *The Brazier* 4 (18 July 1916) 10.

16 CWM, 20090121-004, Charles Edward Clarke, *One Man's Warfare*, no pagination (n.p.), 30.

17 See, for example, Hugh Kay (eds.), *Battery Action!* (Ottawa: CEF Books, 2002) 99. Also see Annette Becker, "Graffiti et sculptures des soldat," *14/18 Aujourd'hui—Today—Heute* 2 (1999)117–27.

18 CLIP, Cobourg World, William Beattie to Mr. Horne, 5 November 1915.

19 *The Listening Post* 14 (21 April 1916) 83.

20 MHRC, Anita Simpson Hagen (ed.), *World War I Letters from Harold Simpson to His Family in Prince Edward Island* (self-published, 2003) 130.

21 Jay Winter, "Popular Culture in Wartime Britain," in Aviel Roshwald and Richard Stites (eds.), *European Culture in the Great War: The Arts, Entertainment and Propaganda, 1914–1918* (Cambridge: Cambridge University Press, 1999) 333–4; Charles Bishop, *The YMCA in the Great War* (Toronto: T.H. Best, 1921) 64 and 149.

22 L. McLeod Gould, *From B.C. To Baisieux: 102nd Canadian Infantry Battalion* (Victoria: Thos R. Cusack Presses, 1919) 25.

23 Lieutenant-Colonel C. Beresford Topp, *The 42nd Battalion, C.E.F., Royal Highlanders of Canada, in the Great War* (Montreal: Gazette, 1931) 99–100; Ralph Hodder-Williams, *Princess Patricia's Canadian Light Infantry, 1914–1919* (Toronto: Hodder and Stoughton, 1923) 191.

24 Bard Maeland and Paul Otto Brunstad, *Enduring Military Boredom from 1750 to the Present* (Basingstoke, UK: Palgrave Macmillan, 2009).

25 Robert F. Zubkowski, *As Long as Faith and Freedom Last: Stories from the Princess Patricia's Canadian Light Infantry from June1914 to September 1919* (Calgary: Bunker to Bunker, 160).

26 Armine Norris, *Mainly for Mother* (Toronto: Ryerson, 1919) 24.

27 Alexander McKee, *Vimy Ridge* (London: Pan Books, 1968) 47.

28 CWM, 20120055-013, Lieutenant Ralph Jones, 27th Battalion, letter to Brother Harry from "Somewhere in Billets," November 15, 1915.

29 McKee, *Vimy Ridge*, 33.

30 CWM, MHRC, D.G. Scott Calder, "The History of the 28th (Northwest) Battalion," [official report, no date (n.d.)] 2–3.

31 On morale, see Robert Engen, *Strangers in Arms: Combat Motivation in the Canadian Army, 1943–1945* (Montreal and Kingston: McGill-Queen's University Press, 2016); Peter E.

Hodgkinson, "*Glum Heroes": Hardship, Fear and Death—Resilience and Coping in the British Army on the Western Front 1914–1918* (England: Helion & Company Limited, 2016); Alexander Watson, *Enduring the Great War Combat: Morale and Collapse in the German and British Armies, 1914–1918* (Cambridge: Cambridge University Press, 2008); Anthony King (ed.), *Frontline: Combat and Cohesion in the Twenty-First Century* (Oxford: Oxford University Press, 2015).

32 See William Philpott, *War of Attrition: Fighting the First World War* (New York: Overlook Press, 2014).

33 R.J. Manion, *Life Is an Adventure* (Toronto: Ryerson, 1936) 197.

34 CWM, 20060194-001, Albert Hitchcox, 7 August 1917. On the importance of food, see Rachel Duffet, *The Stomach for Fighting: Food and the Soldiers of the First World War* (Manchester: Manchester University Press, 2012).

35 CWM, MHRC, *The Sling* 1 (January 1917) 30.

36 Len Willans, *The Memoirs of a Canadian Soldier: World War I Diary Entries and Letters* (Edmonton: Bobair Media Inc., 2012) 24.

37 CWM, 20120055-013, Lt. Ralph Jones, 27th Battalion, letter to Brother Harry from "Somewhere in Billets" November 15, 1915.

38 Hagen (ed.), *World War I Letters*, 52.

39 Steven E. Sawell (ed.), *Into the Cauldron: Memoirs of Edwards Stanley Sawell, M.C., V.D.* (self-published, 2009) 28.

40 Tim Cook, "'More as a medicine than a beverage': 'Demon Rum' and the Canadian Trench Soldier in the First World War," *Canadian Military History*, 9.1 (Winter 2000) 7–22.

41 Gary Sheffield, *Leadership in the Trenches: Officer–Man Relations, Morale and Discipline in The British Army in the Era of the First World War* (Basingstoke: Palgrave Macmillan, 2000).

42 William Gray, *A Sunny Subaltern: Billy's Letters from Flanders* (Toronto: McClelland, Goodchild & Stewart, 1916) 126.

43 Victor N. Swanston, *Who Said War Is Hell!* (self-published, 1983) 41.

44 See Teresa Iacobelli, *Death or Deliverance: Canadian Courts Martial in the Great War* (Vancouver: UBC Press, 2013).

45 On awards, see Hugh Halliday, *Valour Reconsidered: Inquiries into the Victoria Cross and Other Awards for Extreme Bravery* (Toronto: Robin Brass Studio, 2006); Melvin Charles Smith, *Awarded for Valour: A History of the Victoria Cross and the Evolution of British Heroism* (Basingstoke: Palgrave Macmillan, 2008).

46 There are differing accounts of the number of Victoria Crosses awarded to Canadians during the war, with the number sometimes including or excluding men who had a short residence in Canada before the war, or Canadians who served with Imperial units and did not return to Canada after the war. The sixty-four VCs figure comes from the Directorate of History and Heritage's online exhibition, *Victoria Cross Gallery*.

47 Zubkowski, *As Long as Faith and Freedom Last*, 275.

48 Michael Snape and Edward Madigan (eds.), *The Clergy in Khaki: New Perspectives in British Army Chaplaincy in the First World War* (Burlington, VT: Ashgate, 2013); Richard Schweitzer, *The Cross and the Trenches: Religious Faith and Doubt among British and American Great War Soldiers* (Westport: Praeger, 2003).

49 Arthur Lapointe, *Soldier of Quebec (1916–1919)* (Montreal: Garand, 1931) 38. Also see, Watson, *Enduring the Great War*, 97, 107.

50 CWM, 20110042-002, Robert Miller collection, diary, 3 May 1916.

51 Morton, *When Your Number's Up*, 279.

52 See Duff Crerar, *Padres in No Man's Land: Canadian Chaplains and the Great War* (Montreal and Kingston: McGill-Queen's University Press, 1995).

53 Morrison, *Hell Upon Earth*, 125.

54 Ollie Miller (ed.), *Letters Bridging Time: Tom Johnson's Letters* (self-published, 2007) 25.

55 Morton, *When Your Number's Up*, 293.

56 Deborah Cowley (ed.), *Georges Vanier, Soldier: The Wartime Letters and Diaries, 1915–1919* (Toronto: Dundurn Press, 2000) 116.
57 Manion, *Life Is an Adventure*, 192.
58 Norris, *Mainly for Mother*, 127.
59 On leave, see Sarah Cozzi, *Killing Time: The Experiences of Canadian Expeditionary Force Soldiers on Leave in Britain, 1914–1919* (Master's thesis: University of Ottawa, 2009).
60 Lord Moran, *The Anatomy of Courage* (London: Robinson, 2007) xxii. *Report of the War Office Committee of Enquiry into "Shell Shock"* (Crawley: Imperial War Museum, 2004 [original, 1922]) 30.
61 Patricia Thomas (ed.), *The First World War as I Saw It* (self-published, 2013) 37.
62 Mark Humphries, "War's Long Shadow: Masculinity, Medicine and the Gendered Politics of Trauma, 1914–1939," *Canadian Historical Review* 91.3 (2010) 503–31.
63 Tim Cook, ""Dr. Jekyll and Mr. Hyde: Canadian Medical Officers in the Great War," in Stephen Craig and Dale C. Smith (eds.), *Glimpsing Modernity: Military Medicine in World War I* (Cambridge: Cambridge Scholars Publishing, 2016) 34–59.
64 Norris, *Mainly for Mother*, 125.
65 Mark Humphries, "Wilfully and with Intent: Self-Inflicted Wounds and the Negotiation of Power in the Trenches," *Histoire sociale/Social History* 47.94 (June 2014) 369–97.
66 Christopher Pugsley, *On the Fringe of Hell: New Zealanders and Military Discipline in the First World War* (Auckland: Hodder & Stoughton, 1991).
67 Roger Cooter, "Malingering in Modernity: Psychological Scripts and Adversarial Encounters During the First World War," in Roger Cooter et al. (eds.), *War, Medicine and Modernity* (Stroud: Sutton Publishing, 1998) 130; Joanna Bourke, *Dismembering the Male: Men's Bodies, Britain and the Great War* (London: Reaktion Books, 1999); Tim Cook, *No Place to Run: The Canadian Corps and Gas Warfare in the First World War* (Vancouver: UBC Press,

1999) 157–62; LAC, RG 9, III, v.4105, file 1, DDMS, circular, 2 October 1917.

68 Charles S. Cameron, *War! What of It!* (self-published, 2008) 27.

69 Directorate of History and Heritage, Ottawa, Edwin Pye papers, 74/672/-II-57a, Self-Inflicted Injuries, 11.

70 Percy Leland Kingsley, *The First World War as I Saw It* (self-published, 1972) 51.

CHAPTER 2: DEATH CULTURE

1 Coningsby Dawson, *Khaki Courage: Letters in War-Time* (London: Bodley Head, 1917) 96.

2 See, for example, Janet Oppenheim, *The Other World: Spiritualism and Psychical Research in England, 1850–1914* (Cambridge: Cambridge University Press, 1985); Alex Owen, *The Place of Enchantment: British Occultism and the Culture of the Modern* (Chicago and London: University of Chicago Press, 2004); Pamela Thurschwell, *Literature, Technology and Magical Thinking, 1880–1920* (Cambridge: Cambridge University Press, 2001); Marina Warner, *Phantasmagoria: Spirit Visions, Metaphors, and Media into the Twentieth-First Century* (Oxford: Oxford University Press, 2006); Peter Buse and Andrew Stott, *Ghosts: Deconstruction, Psychoanalysis, History* (New York: St. Martin's Press, 1999).

3 Jay Winter, *Sites of Memory, Sites of Mourning: The Great War in European Cultural History* (Cambridge: Cambridge University Press, 1995) 54.

4 Nicholas Royle, *The Uncanny: An Introduction* (Manchester: Manchester University Press, 2003) 2; also see Sigmund Freud, "The Uncanny," *Art and Literature, Pelican Freud Library*, v. 14, translated by James Strachey (Harmondsworth: Penguin, 1985) 335–76.

5 Tim Cook (ed.), "The Top Ten Books in Canadian Military History," *Canadian Military History* 18.4 (Autumn 2009) 65–74.

6 See Stan McMullin, *Anatomy of a Séance: A History of Spirit Communication in Central Canada* (Montreal and Kingston:

McGill-Queen's University Press, 2004) 58; Winter, *Sites of Memory, Sites of Mourning*, 55; Beth Robertson, *Science of the Séance: Transnational Networks and Gendered Bodies in the Study of Psychic Phenomena, 1918–1940* (Vancouver: UBC Press, 2016).

7 Terry Copp, *The Anatomy of Poverty: The Condition of the Working Class in Montreal, 1897–1929* (Toronto: Oxford University Press, 1974) 25–6, 93–5.

8 Brittany Catherine Dunn, "'Death knows but one rule of arithmetic': Discourses of Death and Grief in the Trenches" (Master's thesis: Wilfrid Laurier University, 2016) 17.

9 Hereward Carrington, *Psychic Phenomena and the War* (New York, 1919) 3, 5–6.

10 On the soldiers' constructed visions of space on the Western Front, see Christopher Schultz, "Violence (Dis)Located: On the Spatial Implications of Violence on the Western Front during the First World War" (Master's thesis: Carleton University, 2010); James Opp and John C. Walsh, *Placing Memory and Remembering Place in Canada* (Vancouver: UBC Press, 2010).

11 CWM, Charles Olson papers, 19801134-011-14, memoir, n.p.

12 CWM, 20060194-001, Albert Hitchcox, 28 October 1917.

13 Jeffrey Booth (ed.), *Opened by Censors* (Aylmer, Ontario: Aylmer Express Ltd., 2008) 186.

14 LAC, MG 30 E42, John McNab papers, diary, 1 November 1917.

15 CWM, John Patrick Teahen papers, 19950023-002, diary entries, vol. 2, pp. 117–18.

16 Coningsby Dawson, *The Glory of the Trenches* (New York: John Lane Company, 1918) 96.

17 Reginald Roy (ed.), *The Journal of Private Fraser: 1914–1918, Canadian Expeditionary Force* (Victoria: Sono Nis Press, 1985) 56.

18 Louis Keene, *"Crumps": The Plain Story of a Canadian Who Went* (Houghton Mifflin Company: New York, 1917) 138.

19 CLIP, Henry Savage, memoir, n.p.

20 George L. Mosse, *Fallen Soldiers: Reshaping the Memory of the World War* (Oxford: Oxford University Press, 1990) 5.

21 James McWilliams and R. James Steel, *The Suicide Battalion* (Edmonton: Hurtig, 1978) 46.

22 CWM, Herbert Heckford Burrell papers, 19920187-002, diary, 31 December 1916.

23 Corporal John Harold Becker, *Silhouettes of War: The Memoir of John Harold Becker, 1915–1919: 75th Canadian Infantry Battalion (Mississauga Horse), Canadian Expeditionary Force* (Ottawa: CEF Books, 2001) 83

24 Norris, *Mainly for Mother*, 38. Also see, Peter E. Hodgkinson, "Human Remains on the Great War Battlefields: Coping with Death in the Trenches" (Master's thesis: University of Birmingham, 2006)

25 Malcolm Brown, *Tommy Goes to War* (Charleston: Tempus Publishing, 2001) 94.

26 Keene, "*Crumps*," 109.

27 LAC, MG 30 D150, Andrew Macphail papers, v.4, folder 4, 5 April 1916.

28 Ross Wilson, "The Burial of the Dead: the British Army on the Western Front, 1914–18," *War & Society* 31.1 (March 2012) 22–41.

29 Bennett (ed.), *Kiss the kids for dad*, 64.

30 On the soldiers' inner life, see Michael Roper, *The Secret Battle: Emotional Survival in the Great War* (Manchester: Manchester University Press, 2009); Carol Acton, *Grief in Wartime: Private Pain, Public Discourse* (New York: Palgrave Macmillan, 2007); Santanu Das, *Touch and Intimacy in First World War Literature* (Cambridge: Cambridge University Press, 2005).

31 Hugh R. Kay, George Magee and F A. MacLennan, *Battery Action! The Story of the 43rd (Howitzer) Battery, Canadian Field Artillery, 1916–1919* (Ottawa: CEF Books, 2002 [original, Toronto: Warwick Bros. & Rutter, 1921]) 118–9.

32 Peter Buse and Andrew Stott, *Ghosts: Deconstruction, Psychoanalysis, History* (Basingstoke: Macmillan, 1999)13.

33 Nasmith, *On the Fringe of the Great Fight*, 178.

34 Lapointe, *Soldier of Quebec*, 37.
35 James Hayward, *Myths & Legends of the First World War* (Oxford: Oxford University Press, 2005), 143.
36 For a useful guide to monster stories, see Carolyn Podruchny, "Werewolves and Windigos: Narratives of Cannibal Monster in French-Canadian Voyageur Oral Tradition," *Ethnohistory* 51. 4 (Fall 2004) 677–700.
37 Hayward, *Myths & Legends*, 144; Fussell, *The Great War and Modern Memory*, 123.
38 David James Corrigall, *The 20th Battalion: The History of the Twentieth Canadian Battalion (Central Ontario Regiment) Canadian Expeditionary Force, in the Great War, 1914–1918* (Toronto: Stone & Cox, 1935) 136.
39 CLIP, Kenneth Walter Foster, Memoirs, n.d.
40 Brian Tennyson (ed.), *Merry Hell: The Story of the 25th Battalion (Nova Scotia Regiment), Canadian Expeditionary Force 1914–1919* (Toronto: University of Toronto Press, 2012) 127.
41 John Lynch, *Princess Patricia's Canadian Light Infantry, 1917–1919* (New York: Exposition Press, 1976) 73.
42 Mary Habeck, "Technology in the First World War: The View from Below," in Jay Winter et al. (eds.), *The Great War and the Twentieth Century* (Yale University Press, 2000) 105–6.
43 CWM, Harry Coombs, 58A 1.197.1, letter to brother, 25 July 1915.
44 Desmond Morton, "A Canadian Soldier in the Great War: The Experiences of Frank Maheux," *Canadian Military History* 1.1–2 (1992) 82.
45 Wilfred Kerr, *Shrieks and Crashes: The Memoir of Wilfred B. Kerr, Canadian Field Artillery, 1917* (Toronto: Hunter Rose, 1929) 144.
46 CWM, 20120162-001, Elgin Eby papers, letter 23 August 1916.
47 LAC, R8258, Gregory Clark papers, file 2-3, undated memoir.
48 Vanessa Ann Chambers, "Fighting Chance: War, Popular Belief and British Society, 1900–1951" (Ph.D. dissertation: University of London, 2007) 37. Also see Fussell, *The Great War and Modern Memory*, 124.

49 Steve Roud, *The Penguin Guide to the Superstitions of Britain and Ireland* (London: Penguin, 2003) 484.
50 Cowley (ed.), *Georges Vanier: Soldier*, 174.
51 Chambers, "Fighting Chance War," 35.
52 Adrian Hayes, *Pegahmagabow: Legendary Warrior, Forgotten Hero* (Huntsville: Fox Meadow Creations, 2003) 29.
53 Eric Story, "'The Awakening Has Come': Canadian First Nations in the Great War Era, 1914–1932," *Canadian Military History* 24.2 (2015) 13; John Steckley and Brian Cummins, "Pegahmagabow of Parry Island From Jennesse Informant to Individual," *Canadian Journal of Native Studies*, 25.1 (2005) 40.
54 CLIP, Herbert Durand, letter, 12 July 1915.
55 CLIP, George Adkins, letter to mother, June 5, 1916.
56 CLIP, *Cobourg World*, letter, Wilfred Throop, 15 November 1915.
57 Sandra Gwyn, *Tapestry of War: A Private View of Canadians in the Great War* (Toronto: HarperCollins, 1992) 154–5.
58 Herbert McBride, *A Rifleman Went to War* (Marines: North Carolina: Small Arms Technical Publishing Company, 1935) 390.
59 See a brief discussion in Watson, *Enduring the Great War*, 97–100; Das, *Touch and Intimacy in First World War Literature*, 83. On the Second World War, see S.P. Mackenzie, *Flying against Fate: Superstitions and Allied Aircrews in World War II* (Kansas: University Press of Kansas, 2017).
60 Jeffrey Williams, *Byng of Vimy* (Toronto: University of Toronto Press, 1992) 132.
61 Charles Edmonds, *A Subaltern's War: Being a Memoir of the Great War from the Point of View of a Romantic Young Man* (London, 1929) 161–2.
62 Stanley Rutledge, *Pen Pictures from the Trenches* (Toronto: HarperCollins, 1992) 55–6.
63 Swanston, *Who Said War Is Hell!*, 30.
64 G.W.L. Nicholson, *The Gunners of Canada: The History of the Royal Regiment of Canadian Artillery* (Toronto: McClelland & Stewart, 1967) 309.

65 J.P. Pollock (ed.), *Letters from Angus, 1915–1916* (self-published, 2005) 98.
66 CLIP, Amos Mayse, 13 August 1917.
67 Morrison, *Hell upon Earth*, 234.
68 CWM, MHRC, Harold Simpson, *The Story of the Second Canadian Siege Battery* (self-published, 1966) 76.
69 LAC, MG 30 E430, William Green, untitled memoir, 16.
70 Majorie Barron Norris (ed.), *Medicine and Duty: The World War I Memoir of Captain Harold W. McGill, Medical Officer, 31st Battalion C.E.F.* (Calgary, Alberta: University of Calgary Press, 2007) 263.
71 CLIP, Charles Henry Savage, memoir, n.p.
72 Cameron, *War! What of It!*, 44.
73 Glenn R Iriam (ed.), *In the Trenches, 1914–1918* (self-published, 2008) 134.
74 George A. Maxwell, *Swan Song of a Rustic Moralist* (New York: Exposition Press, 1975) 106–12.
75 Hereward Carrington, *Psychic Phenomena and the War*, 158–9. On mothers experiencing dream visions, nightmares, and haunting their sons, or their sons' deaths in action, see Michael Roper, *The Secret Battle: Emotional Survival in the Great War* (Manchester: Manchester University Press, 2009) 228–32.
76 CLIP, Wallace Reid to mother, 1 October 1916.
77 LAC, MG 30 E150, Andrew Macphail, v. 4, folder 6, 15 March 1917.
78 Iriam, *In the Trenches*, 136.
79 I have been influenced by Leonard V. Smith, *The Embattled Self: French Soldiers' Testimony of the Great War* (Ithaca: Cornell University Press, 2007); Jessica Meyer, *Men of War: Masculinity and the First World War in Britain* (New York: Palgrave Macmillan, 2009); Roper, *The Secret Battle*.
80 CWM, H.H. Coombs papers, 20020112-002, letter to F. Coombs, 28 August 1918.

CHAPTER 3: VOICING CULTURE: SLANG AND SWEARING

1 *The Listening Post* 27 (10 August 1917) 10.

2 See John Edwards, *Language, Society and Identity* (Toronto: Oxford University Press, 1985); Carol Eastman, *Aspects of Language and Culture* (San Francisco: Chandler and Sharp, 1975); Gordon L. Rottman, *FUBAR: Soldier Slang of World War II* (London: Osprey Publishing, 2007) 10. I have also been influenced by Ged Martin, "Sir John Eh? Macdonald: Recovering A Voice from History," *British Journal of Canadian Studies* XVII (2004) 117–124.

3 W.H. Downing, *Digger Dialects: A Collection of Slang Phrases Used by the Australian Soldiers on Active Service* (Sydney: Lothian Publishing, 1919) Introduction.

4 For a discussion of swearing in societies, see Geoffrey Hughes, *An Encyclopedia of Swearing: The Social History of Oaths, Profanity, Foul Language, And Ethnic Slurs in the English-speaking World* (New York: M.E. Sharpe (2006); James O'Connor, *Cuss Control* (New York: Three Rivers Press, 2000); Ashley Montagu, *The Anatomy of Swearing* (Philadelphia: University of Pennsylvania Press, 2001).

5 Canadian Images and Letters Project (CLIP), Bertram Cox, 5 October 1918.

6 For example, for the influence of American soldiers' slang on the British, and British on American, see Paul Dickson, *War Slang: American Fighting Words and Phrases since the Civil War* (Washington: Potomac Books, 2003) 35–6.

7 Gould, *From B.C. To Baisieux*, 107.

8 E.L. Chicanot, "French—a la Guerre," *The Legionary* 2 (August 1930) 16.

9 Will Bird, *Ghosts Have Warm Hands* (Toronto and Vancouver: Clarke, Irwin, and Company, 1968) 47.

10 Ian Ross Robertson, *Sir Andrew Macphail: The Life and Legacy of a Canadian Man of Letters* (Montreal and Kingston: McGill-Queen's University Press, 2008) 182.

11 CLIP, Bertram Cox, letter, 5 October 1918.
12 W.C. Hawker, "Some Characteristics and Traditions of the Royal Newfoundland Regiment,' *The Veteran* 7.1 (April 1928) 48–9.
13 Richard Holmes, *Tommy: The British Soldier on the Western Front 1914–1918* (London: HarperCollins, 2004) 493.
14 CWM, 58A 2 7.7, George Franklin McFarland Major, memoirs, 21–23 May 1918.
15 CWM, 20000138-001, John Henry Flock, personal diary, unpaginated n.p.
16 *Lingo of No Man's Land* is a slight book of Canadian and British slang, written by an American in the CEF who compiled the words to encourage British recruitment in the United States. Lorenzo Smith, *Lingo of No Man's Land* (London: The British Library, 2014 [original, 1918]).
17 R.B. Fleming (ed.), *The Wartime Letters of Leslie and Cecil Frost, 1915–1919* (Waterloo: Wilfrid Laurier University Press, 2007) 300.
18 Arthur Hunt Chute, *The Real Front* (New York: Harper, 1918)136.
19 Canadian Bank of Commerce, *Letters from the Front*, 139.
20 CWM, 19950008, Samuel Honey papers, Lew to parents, 17 October 1916.
21 CLIP, Bertram Cox, 1 November 1917.
22 A "housewife" was the soldier's sewing kit; a "pull-through" was a weighted rag to pull through a rifle barrel to wipe away gunpowder residue, grit, and dirt.
23 *In and Out* 1 (November 1918) 17.
24 CLIP, Albert Fereday, letter to father, 7 May 1918.
25 Sawell (ed.), *Into the Cauldron*, 110.
26 CWM, Frederick Robinson, 20000148-001, 58A 1.203.1, letter to Ruth, 1 June 1918.
27 "Après La Guerre," *The Iodine Chronicle* 7 (10 May 1916) 2; Rutledge, *Pen Pictures from the Trenches*, 41.
28 Will Bird, *The Communication Trench* (Ottawa: CEF Books, 2000) 50.

29 Tom Spear with Monte Stewart, *Carry On: Reaching Beyond 100* (Calgary: Falcon Press, 1999) 49.

30 On trivialization, see George Mosse, *Fallen Soldiers: Reshaping the Memory of the World Wars* (New York, Oxford University Press, 1990) 133–4.

31 Jean-Yves Le Naour, "Laughter and Tears in the Great War: The Need for Laughter/The Guilt of Humour," *European Studies* 31 (2001) 268.

32 D.E. Macintyre, *Canada at Vimy* (Toronto: P. Martin Associates, 1967) 30.

33 See Humphries, "War's Long Shadow," 503–31.

34 Derek Grout (ed.), *Thunder in the Skies: A Canadian Gunner in the Great War* (Toronto: Dundurn Publishers, 2015) 184.

35 J. George Adami, *The War Story of the CAMC* (Toronto: Canadian War Records Office, 1918) 101–2.

36 Roy (ed.), *The Journal of Private Fraser,* 36–7.

37 Stephen Beames, untitled memoirs, [memoir in author's possession], 31; Canadian Bank of Commerce, *Letters from the Front*, 95.

38 For a brief discussion, see C.L. Berry, "Place Names in Flanders," *The Legionary* 13.10 (May 1938) 6.

39 Dawson, *Khaki Courage*, 56.

40 Alfred Savage, "My Brother Henri," *The Legionary* (June 1956) 36.

41 For literature on French Canada, see Mélanie Morin-Pelletier, "French Canada and the War," *1914–18 International Encyclopedia of the First World War.* http://www.1914-1918-online.net

42 Theodore Dugas, "Un Acadien à la Première Guerre Mondiale," *La Revue d'histoire de la Societé historique Nicolas-Denys* XX.3 (September–December 1992) 32, 40, 42, 50.

43 Remi Tougas, *Stanislas Tougas: Un des plus grands coeurs du 22e Bataillon* (Septentrion, 2005) 97–8.

44 E.L. Chicanot, "French—a la Guerre," *The Legionary* V.2 (August 1930) 16.

45 L. James Dempsey, "Aboriginal Alberta and the First World War," in Adriana A. Davies and Jeff Keshen (eds.), *The Frontier of*

Patriotism Alberta and the First World War (Calgary: University of Calgary Press, 2016) 55.

46 O.C.S. Wallace (ed.), *From Montreal to Vimy Ridge and Beyond: the correspondence of Lieut. Clifford Almon Wells, B.A. of the 8th Battalion, Canadians, B.E.F. November 1915—April 1917* (Toronto: McClelland, Goodchild & Stewart, 1917) 188.

47 Peter Broznitsky, "For King, Not Tsar: Identifying Ukrainians in the Canadian Expeditionary Force, 1914–1918," *Canadian Military History* 17.3 (Summer 2008) 29.

48 Frederick Noyes, *Stretcher-Bearers . . . At the Double!: History of the Fifth Canadian Field Ambulance which Served Overseas during the Great War of 1914–1918* (Toronto: Hunter-Rose, 1937) 128.

49 *The Listening Post* 27 (10 August 1917) 10.

50 LAC, MG 31 G6, ELM Burns papers, v. 9, file Articles, papers—U, Untitled Document on soldiers' slang in the First World War, n.d.

51 LAC, R 8258, Gregory Clark papers, v. 1, diary 1916, 28 April 1916.

52 Brophy and Partridge (eds.), *Songs and Slang of the British Soldier*, 16.

53 David Jay Bercuson, *True Patriot: The Life of Brooke Claxton, 1898–1960* (Toronto: University of Toronto Press, 1993) 40.

54 George A. Maxwell, *Swan Song of a Rustic Moralist* (New York: Exposition Press, 1975) 52.

55 Geoffrey Hughes, *Swearing: A Social History of Foul Language, Oaths and Profanity in English* (London: Blackwell, 1991) 5.

56 LAC, MG 31 G6, ELM Burns papers, v. 9, file Articles, papers—U, Untitled Document on soldiers' slang in the First World War, n.d.

57 CLIP, Charles Savage, memoir, n.p.

58 Daniel Dancocks, *Sir Arthur Currie: A Biography* (Methuen: Toronto, 1985) 18.

59 Ian McCulloch, "'The 'Fighting Seventh': The Evolution and Devolution of Tactical Command and Control in a Canadian Infantry Brigade of the Great War" (Master's thesis: Royal Military College of Canada, 1997) 55.

60 LAC, MG 31 G6, ELM Burns papers, v. 9, file Articles, papers—U, Untitled Document on soldiers' slang in the First World War, n.d.

61 Ollie Miller (ed.), *Letters Bridging Time: Tom Johnson's Letters* (Surrey: Digi-Print Graphics, 2007) 22.

62 *The Listening Post* 20 (10 December 1916) 133.

63 Harold Baldwin, *Holding the Line* (Toronto: G.J. McLeod, 1918) vii–viii.

64 LAC, MG 31 G6, ELM Burns papers, v. 9, file Articles, papers—U, Untitled Document on soldiers' slang in the First World War, n.d.

65 Daniel Dancocks, *Gallant Canadians: The Story of the Tenth Canadian Infantry Battalion, 1914–1919* (Calgary: Calgary Highlanders Regimental Funds Foundation, 1990) 83. Also see Morton, *When Your Number's Up*, 248.

66 Jeff Keshen, "Voices of War: The Press and the Personal," in Adriana A. Davies and Jeff Keshen (eds.), *The Frontier of Patriotism Alberta and the First World War* (Calgary: University of Calgary Press, 2016) 291–2.

67 Richard Holmes, *Firing Line* (London: Pimlico, 1994) 46. I have been influenced here by Peter Layman, "The Fraternal Bond as a Joking Relationship," in Michael S. Kimmel and Michael A. Messner (eds.), *Men's Lives* (New York: Macmillan Publishing Company, 1992) 143–154 and Craig Heron, "The Boys and Their Booze: Masculinities and Public Drinking in Working-Class Hamilton, 1890–1946," *The Canadian Historical Review* 86.3 (September 2005) 411–52.

68 Tim Cook, "'He was determined to go': Underage Soldiers in the Canadian Expeditionary Force," *Histoire sociale/Social History* 41.81 (May 2008) 41–74

69 John W. Lynch, *Princess Patricia's Canadian Light Infantry, 1917–1919* (Hicksville, N.Y: Exposition Press, 1976) 59.

70 Stephen J. Nichol, *Ordinary Heroes: Eastern Ontario's 21st Battalion CEF in The Great War* (self-published, 2008) 10.

71 LAC, MG 30 E220, E.W. Russell papers, memoir, "A Private Soldier's View of the Great War, 1914–1918," 16.

72 CWM, 20000030-009, Thomas Earl Walker papers, Walker to Vie, 8 August 1915.
73 William G. Ogilvie, *Umty-Iddy-Umty: The Story of a Canadian Signaller in the First World War* (Erin, ON: The Boston Mills Press, 1982) 10.
74 Victor Wheeler, *The 50th Battalion in No Man's Land*, (Calgary: Alberta Historical Resources Foundation, 1980) 97.
75 George Anderson Wells, *The Fighting Bishop* (Toronto: Cardwell House, 1971) 202–4.
76 See Hagen (ed.), *World War I Letters*, 71; Hayes, *The Eighty-Fifth in France and Flanders*, 226.
77 Norris, *Mainly for Mother*, 114.

CHAPTER 4: THE WAR'S SOUNDTRACK

1 Heather Robertson, *A Terrible Beauty: The Art of Canada at War* (Toronto: J. Lorimer: Robert McLaughlin Gallery, 1977) 74.
2 On war songs, see Glenn Watkins, *Proof through the Night: Music and the Great War* (University of California Press, 2003); Regina M. Sweeney, *Singing Our Way to Victory: French Cultural Politics and Music during the Great War* (Middletown: Wesleyan University Press, 2001); John Mullen, *The Show Must Go On! Popular Song in Britain in the First World War* (Farnham: Ashgate, 2015); John Brophy and Eric Partridge (eds.), *Song and Slang of the British Soldier: 1914–1918* (London: E. Partridge, 1930); Roy Palmer, *What a Lovely War: British Soldiers' Songs from the Boer War to the Present Day* (London: Michael Joseph, 1990); Les Cleveland, *Dark Laughter: War in Song and Popular Culture* (Westport: Praeger, 1994); John J Niles, et al., *The Songs My Mother Never Taught Me* (New York: Gold Label Books, 1929); Max Arthur, *When This Bloody War Is Over: Soldiers Songs of the First World War* (London: Piatkus, 2001).
3 See Sara Karn, "Songs of War: Anglo-Canadian Popular Songs on the Home Front, 1914–1918" (Major Research Paper: Wilfrid Laurier University, 2017). I have also been influenced by Catherine

Hall and Sonya Rose (eds.), *At Home with the Empire: Metropolitan Culture and the Imperial World* (Cambridge: Cambridge University Press, 2006); David Russell, *Popular Music in England, 1840–1914* (Manchester: Manchester University Press, 1987).

4 Karn, "Songs of War," 23–6, 40.

5 CWM, MHRC, Young Men's Christian Associations of Canada, *Songs for Soldiers* (1914).

6 CWM, MHRC, W.R. Smith, *New War Songs* (1914).

7 Tony Ashworth, *Trench Warfare, 1914–1918: The Live and Let Live System* (London: Palgrave Macmillan, 1980) 48.

8 CWM, 20060227-001, William Davidson collection, letter, 11 May 1917.

9 CWM, 58A 163.14, Waring Cosbie, letter, 23 February 1916.

10 Will Bird, *Ghosts Have Warm Hands* (Ottawa: CEF Books, 1997) 50.

11 On gramophones, see Jay Winter, "Popular Culture in Wartime Britain," in Aviel Roshwald and Richard Stites (eds.), *European Culture in the Great War: The Arts, Entertainment and Propaganda, 1914–1918* (Cambridge University Press, 1999) 333; Edward Moogk, *Roll Back the Years: History of Canadian Recorded Sound and its Legacy* (Ottawa: National Library of Canada, 1975) 59–67; Bishop, *The YMCA in the Great War*, 64 and 149.

12 LAC, MG 30 E8, J.J. Creelman papers, diary, 15 November 1915.

13 CWM, 19790640-003, Andrew Howard Miller, My dearest Ruth, 9 September 1917.

14 CLIP, Amos William Mayse, letter, 26 February 1917.

15 CLIP, Alfred Andrews, diary, 6 August 1915.

16 Richard Graeme, "The Happy Warriors," *The Legionary* (Christmas Number 1934) 34.

17 On the nature of changing folk songs, see Edith Fowke (ed.), *The Penguin Book of Canadian Folk Songs* (London: Penguin Books, 1973) introduction; I. Sheldon Posen, *For Singing and Dancing and All Sorts of Fun* (Toronto: Deneau Publishers, 1988).

18 Brophy and Partridge, *Songs and Slang of the British Soldier*, 4.
19 CWM, 19730066-001, Chester E. Routley papers, The Eighteenth Battalion, 13.
20 George L. Mosse, *Fallen Soldiers: Reshaping the Memory of the World Wars* (New York and Oxford, 1990) 126-7.
21 On this personalization, see Richard Holmes, *Tommy: The British Soldier on the Western Front, 1914–1918* (London: HarperCollins, 2004) 500.
22 CWM, *On Service* 1.5 (July 1916) 8. Also see Amy Shaw, *Crisis of Conscience: Conscientious Objection in Canada during the First World War* (Vancouver: UBC Press, 2009).
23 R.A.L., *Letters of a Canadian Stretcher Bearer*, ed. Anna Chapin Ray (Boston: Little, Brown, and Company, 1918) 101.
24 Brophy and Partridge, *Songs and Slang of the British Soldier*, 11.
25 See Heron, "The Boys and Their Booze," 411–52.
26 Melbert B. Cary, Jr., "Mademoiselle from Armentières," *The Journal of American Folklore* 47.186 (October–December 1934) 369–76.
27 Ernest Black, *I Want One Volunteer* (Toronto: Ryerson Press, 1965) 78.
28 Robertson, *A Terrible Beauty*, 28
29 Sheldon-Williams, *The Canadian Front in France and Flanders*, 119.
30 Arthur, *When This Bloody War Is Over*, 89.
31 Tennyson, "'Wild Bill' Livingstone Goes to War," 130.
32 E.S. Russenholt, *Six Thousand Canadian Men Being the History of the 44th Battalion Canadian Infantry, 1914–1919* (Winnipeg 44th Battalion Association, 1932) 173.
33 Wheeler, *The 50th Battalion in No Man's Land*, 47.
34 Richard Schweitzer, *The Cross and the Trenches: Religious Faith and Doubt among British and American Great War Soldier* (London: Praeger, 2003) 21.
35 CLIP, Harold Simpson, 22 August 1916.
36 Brophy and Partridge, *Songs and Slang of the British Soldier*, 231.
37 Palmer, *What a Lovely War*, 1.

38 On this song being uniquely Canadian, see Brophy and Partridge, *Soldiers' Song and Slang*, 246; CWM, *The Listening Post* 2 (30 August 1915) n.p. It was sung by Lieutenant Ralph Jones, who sent it to his brother, Harry. See CWM, 20120055-013, Ralph Jones, 15 October 1915.
39 Canadian Bank of Commerce, *Letters from the Front*, 59.
40 CWM, *The Brazier* 6 (15 November 1916) 2.
41 John Mullen, "War Memory in British Soldier Songs of the First World War," Stephanie A.H. Belanger and Renee Dickason (eds.), *War Memories: Commemoration, Recollections, and Writings on War* (Montreal and Kingston: McGill-Queen's University Press, 2017) 258.
42 Richard Graeme, "The Happy Warriors," *The Legionary*, Christmas Number (1934) 41.
43 Brett Clifton, "The Experiences of Lethbridge Men Overseas, 1914–1918," in Adriana A. Davies and Jeff Keshen (eds.), *The Frontier of Patriotism Alberta and the First World War* (Calgary: University of Calgary Press, 2016) 81–2.
44 Cited in Emma Hanna, "'When Words Are Not Enough': The Aural Landscape of Britain's Modern Memory of 1914–18," in Angela K. Smith and Krista Cowman (eds.), *Landscapes and Voices in the Great War* (London: Routledge, 2017) 42.
45 Norris, *Mainly for Mother*, 58–9.
46 Rémi Tougas, *Stanislas Tougas (1896–1917)*, 97, 107–9.
47 Cowley (ed.), *Georges Vanier*, 62.
48 Cowley (ed.), *Georges Vanier*, 97; Lapointe, *Soldier of Quebec* , 80.
49 CLIP, Andrew John Napier, 26 September 1915.
50 Roy Ito, *We Went to War: The Story of the Japanese Canadians Who Served during the First and Second World Wars* (Stittsville: Canada's Wings, 1984) 46.
51 Regina M. Sweeney, *Singing Our Way to Victory: French Cultural Politics and Music during the Great War* (Middletown: Wesleyan University Press, 2001) 18.
52 On the importance of humour, see Jean-Yves Le Naour, "Laughter and Tears in the Great War. The Need for Laughter/the Guilt of

Humour," *Journal of European Studies* 31 (2001) 265–75; Tim Cook, "'I will meet the world with a smile and a joke': Canadian Soldiers' Humour in the Great War," *Canadian Military History* 22.2 (Spring 2013) 48–62; Edward Madigan, "'Sticking to a Hateful Task': Resilience, Humour, and British Understandings of Combatant Courage, 1914–1918," *War in History* 20 (2013) 76–98.

53 Canadian Bank of Commerce, *Letters from the Front*, 196.

54 Nicholson, *The Gunners of Canada*, 306.

55 Mike Mountain Horse, *My People, the Bloods* (Calgary: Glenbow-Alberta Institute, 1979) 30. Also see Eric Story, "'The Awakening Has Come': Canadian First Nations in the Great War Era, 1914–1932," *Canadian Military History* 24.2 (2015) 12.

56 Brophy and Partridge, *Songs and Slang of the British Soldier*, 239.

57 CWM, *The Forty-Niner* 1.3, 4.

58 Percy Climo, *Let Us Remember: Lively Letters from World War One* (Colborne: P.L. Climo, 1990) 230.

CHAPTER 5: TRENCH STORIES

1 Rutledge, *Pen Pictures from the Trenches*, 59–60.

2 For an exploration of rumours by psychologists, sociologists, and historians, see Gordon W. Allport and Leo Postman, *The Psychology of Rumour* (New York: Henry Holt, 1947); Joseph Robert White, "'Even in Auschwitz . . . Humanity Could Prevail': British POWs and Jewish Concentration-Camp Inmates at IG Auschwitz, 1943–1945," *Holocaust and Genocide Studies* 15.2 (2001): 266–95; Tamotsu Shibutani, *Improvised News: A Sociological Study of Rumour* (Indianapolis: The Bobbs-Merrill Company, 1966); Patricia Turner, *I Heard it Through the Grapevine: Rumour in African-American Culture* (Berkeley: University of California Press,1993). On the role of rumours in Canada during the Second World War, see Jeff Keshen, *Saints, Sinners and Soldiers: Canada's Second World War* (Vancouver: UBC Press, 2004); J.A. Irving, "The Psychological Analysis of

Wartime Rumour Patterns in Canada," *Bulletin of the Canadian Psychological Association* 3 (1943): 40–4.

3 James Pedley, *Only This: A War Retrospect, 1917–1918* (Ottawa: Graphic Publishers, 1927) 60–1.

4 Lieutenant-Colonel C. Beresford Topp, *The 42nd Battalion, C.E.F., Royal Highlanders of Canada, in the Great War* (Montreal: Gazette, 1931) 98.

5 *The Iodine Chronicle* 14 (22 December 1917) 1.

6 Brophy and Partridge, *Songs and Slang of the British Soldier*, 135; R.B. Fleming (ed.), *The Wartime Letters of Leslie and Cecil Frost, 1915–1919* (Waterloo: Wilfrid Laurier Press, 2007), 126.

7 Bennett (ed.), *Kiss the Kids for Dad*, 35.

8 Cited in Robertson, *A Terrible Beauty*, 67.

9 CLIP, T.C. Lapp, 20 September 1918.

10 *The Listening Post* 29 (1 December 1917) 31.

11 Cowley (ed.), *Georges Vanier*, 105.

12 *The Listening Post* 29 (1 December 1917), 31.

13 Captain W.W. Murray, *The History of the 2nd Canadian Battalion in the Great War* (Ottawa, 1947), 255.

14 CLIP, Bill Hutchinson, letter, 31 December 1916.

15 Gordon Pimm (ed.), *Leo's War: From Gaspé to Vimy* (Ottawa: Historical Committee, 2nd Canadian Battalion, 2007), 97.

16 Karl Weatherbe, *From the Rideau to the Rhine and Back* (Toronto: Hunter-Rose, 1928), 58.

17 *The Listening Post* 24 (20 April 1917) 158–9.

18 See, for example, C. Beresford Topp, *The 42nd Battalion, C.E.F., Royal Highlanders of Canada* (Montreal, 1931), 295.

19 LAC, MG 30 E16, W.H. Hewgill papers, diary, 8 September 1916.

20 Directorate of History and Heritage, Leslie Arthur Catchpole papers, memoir, 81–2.

21 John Horne and Alan Kramer, *German Atrocities, 1914: A History of Denial* (New Haven, 2001), 89–90.

22 David Clarke, "Rumours of Angels: A Legend of the First World War," *Folklore* 113.2 (2002) 151–75.

23 Arthur Machen, *The Bowmen and Other Legends of the War* (London: Simpkin, Marshall, Hamilton, Kent & Co, 1915).
24 Rutledge, *Pen Pictures from the Trenches*, 56.
25 Randal Marlin, *Propaganda and the Ethics of Persuasion* (Peterborough: Broadview Press, 2002) 71–4.
26 CWM, 58A 1 122.2, Herbert Clemens papers, letter, 10 May 1917.
27 Pedley, *Only This*, 298–9.
28 See David Clarke, *The Angel of Mons: Phantom Stories and Ghostly Guardians* (West Sussex: Wiley, 2004).
29 "Canadian was Crucified, Was Clamped to Tree," *Toronto Star*, 11 May 1915, 1; Morton, "A Canadian Soldier in the Great War," 81.
30 On the investigation, see Desmond Morton, *Silent Battle: Canadian Prisoners of War in Germany, 1914–1919* (Toronto: Lester Publishing Limited, 1992).
31 Quotes from LAC, RG 24, v. 817, HQ 54-21-8-48-1. Also see LAC, Sir Arthur Currie papers, MG 30 E100, v. 27, file 7, Currie to Reid, 20 April 1925.
32 Gould, *From B.C. to Baisieux*, 21.
33 Gould, *From B.C. to Baisieux*, 21.
34 CWM, 20000013-008, George Ormsby papers, G to Maggie, 8 May 1915.
35 Robert Graves, *Goodbye to All That* (London, 1960, original in 1929) 154.
36 Morton, *Silent Battle*, 2.
37 Audrey and Paul Grescoe (eds), *The Book of War Letters* (Toronto: McClelland & Stewart, 2003) 112–13.
38 See Tim Cook, "The Politics of Surrender: Canadian Soldiers and the Killing of Prisoners in the Great War," *Journal of Military History* 703 (July 2006) 637–65.
39 Grescoe and Grescoe, *The Book of War Letters*, 112–3. Also see Peat, *Private Peat*, 162.
40 N.M. Christie (ed.), *Letters of Agar Adamson, 1914 to 1919, Lieutenant Colonel, Princess Patricia's Canadian Light Infantry* (Ottawa: CEF Books, 1997) 170.

41 On the morality of gas, see Marion Girard, *A Strange and Formidable Weapon: British Responses to World War I Poison Gas* (Lincoln: University of Nebraska Press, 2008).

42 LAC, RG 9, v. 3982, Folder 3, File 7, "Report on the Periodical Outbursts of Reports Announcing Extraordinary Discoveries Made by the Enemy."

43 G.R. Stevens, *A City Goes to War: History of the Loyal Edmonton Regiment* (Brampton: Charters Publishing, 1964), 53.

44 On censorship, see Jeff Keshen, *Propaganda and Censorship during Canada's Great War* (Edmonton: University of Alberta Press, 1996).

45 On language as a form of resistance, see Chad Bryant, "The Language of Resistance? Czech Jokes and Joke-Telling under Nazi Occupation, 1943–45," *Journal of Contemporary History* 41.1 (2006) 133–51.

46 LAC, Records of the Canadian Broadcasting Corporation, transcripts to Flanders Fields radio program, RG 41, John MacKenzie, 72nd Battalion, tape 1/ page 9.

47 *The Iodine Chronicle* 14 (22 Dec 1917) 11.

48 Morton, *When Your Number's Up*, 245.

49 On demobilization issues, see Desmond Morton and Glenn Wright *Winning the Second Battle: Canadian Veterans and the Return to Civilian Life, 1915–1930* (Toronto: University of Toronto Press, 1987).

50 On Canada's role in the Hundred Days, see Tim Cook, *Shock Troops: Canadians Fighting the Great War, 1917–1918*, vol. 2 (Toronto: Penguin, 2008); J.L. Granatstein, *The Greatest Victory: Canada's One Hundred Days, 1918* (Don Mills: Oxford University Press, 2014).

51 LAC, MG 30 E300, Victor Odlum papers, v. 3, file Currie, Odlum to Edward Kemp, 11 February 1919; also see University of McGill Archives, Hugh Urquhart papers, 4027, box 1, file 12, Alexander Ross to Urquhart, n.d. [1934].

52 On the attack on Currie's reputation, see Tim Cook, "The Butcher and the Madman: Sir Arthur Currie, Sir Sam Hughes and the War

of Reputations," *Canadian Historical Review* 85.4 (December 2004) 693–719.

CHAPTER 6: FROM "SOMEWHERE IN FRANCE"

1 O.C.S. Wallace (ed.), *From Montreal to Vimy Ridge and Beyond: The Correspondence of Lieut. Clifford Almon Wells, B.A., of 8th Battalion Canadians, B.E.F., November, 1915–April, 1917* (Toronto: McClelland, 1917) 223.
2 CWM, Harry Austin McCleave, 20020189-001, 58A 1 185.18, diary, first page.
3 Roy (ed.), *Journal of Private Fraser*, 18.
4 James Robert Johnston (ed.), *Riding into War: The Memoir of a Horse Transport Driver, 1916–1919* (New Brunswick: Goose Lane, 2004) 188.
5 CLIP, William John McLellan, letter to home, 7 May 1917.
6 CWM, 20050023-003, Carman H. Thornton, Call No. 58A 1 218.26, beginning of diary.
7 CWM, 20030153-001, John Wesley McClung, diary, 8 April 1917.
8 Bruce Tascona, *Little Black Devils* (Winnipeg: Frye Publications for Royal Winnipeg Rifles, 1983) 77.
9 Climo (ed.), *Let Us Remember*, 287.
10 Michael Roper, "Maternal Relations: Moral Manliness and Emotional Survival in Letters Home during the First World War," in Stefan Dudink (et al.) *Masculinities in Politics and War: Gendering Modern History* (Manchester: Manchester University Press, 2004) 297; Report of the Ministry, *Overseas Military Force of Canada, 1918* (London: Printed by authority of the Ministry, Overseas Military Forces of Canada, 1919) 88.
11 There is a rich historiography upon which to draw: Martin Lyons, "French Soldiers and their Correspondence: Towards a History of Writing Practices in the First World War," *French History* 17.1; Yuval Noah Hararl, *The Ultimate Experience: Battlefield Revelations and the Making of Modern War Culture* (New York: Palgrave, 2008); L.V. Smith, *The Embattled Self: French Soldiers'*

Testimony of the Great War (Ithaca: Cornell University Press, 2007); Samuel Hynes, *A War Imagined: The First World War and English Culture* (London: Bodley Head, 1990); Michael Roper, *The Secret Battle: Emotional Survival in the First World War* (Manchester: Manchester University Press, 2009); Martha Hanna, *Your Death Would Be Mine: Paul and Marie Pireaud in the Great War* (Cambridge: Harvard University Press, 2006); Maarten Gerritsen, "Corps Identity: The Letters, Diaries and Memoirs of Canada's Great War Soldiers" (Ph.D. dissertation: Memorial University of Newfoundland, 2008); Mélanie Morin-Pelletier, "'The Anxious Waiting Ones at Home': Deux familles canadiennes plongées dans le tourment de la Grande Guerre," *Histoire sociale/Social History* 47.94 (2014) 353–68.

12 LAC, MG 30 E400, Claude Vivian Williams letters, to father, 6 November 1916.

13 See Tim Cook "'My Whole Heart and Soul is in this War': The Letters and War Service of Sergeant G.L. Ormsby," *Canadian Military History* 15.1 (Winter 2006) 51–63.

14 McKee, *Vimy Ridge*, 36

15 CLIP, Charles Willoughby, letter, 30 March 1918.

16 Herb Ross (ed.), *Letters Home: Maritimers and The Great War, 1914–1918* (Halifax: Nimbus, 2014) 99.

17 See Keshen, *Propaganda and Censorship*, 153–59; Meyer, *Men of War*, 16–25.

18 CLIP, Andrew Wilson, letter, 14 November 1917.

19 Norris, *Mainly for Mother*, 116.

20 CLIP, John Sudbury, 13 July 1916.

21 See CWM, 51 A 1.35.3, "Leakage of Military Information," 24 July 1916.

22 LAC, MG 30 E 241, D.E. Macintyre papers, 24 September 1916.

23 CWM, Alfred E. Baggs, letter, 13 March 1916.

24 CWM, Garnet Dobbs, 58A 1, 217.1, 19 June 1918.

25 CLIP, Moyer, Jay Batiste, Letter, December 22, 1916.

26 *The Listening Post* 30 (1 April 1918) 15.

27 Grout (ed.), *Thunder in the Skies*, 227.

28 CWM, Samuel Honey, 19950008-014, 58A 1 112.10, 5 November 1916.

29 LAC, MG 30 E241, D.E. Macintyre papers, diary, 21 December 1915.

30 On the touristic impulse, see James Curran, "'Bonjoor Paree!' The First AIF in Paris, 1916–1918," *Journal of Australian Studies* 23.60 (1999) 18–26.

31 Mosse, *Fallen Soldiers*, 128.

32 CWM, 19750073-005.

33 "A Page of Poetry," *The Brazier* 2 (March 25, 1916) 2.

34 Robert Giddings, *The War Poets* (New York: Orion Books, 1988) 8; Ian F.W. Beckett, *The Great War, 1914–18* (New York: Longman, 2001) 428–9.

35 CLIP, Robert Hale letter, 22 February 1915.

36 Holbrook Jackson (ed.), *Contingent ditties and other soldier songs of the Great War by Frank S. Brown, Sergeant, P.P.C.L.I.* (The Pats) (London: S. Low, Marston, 1915).

37 *Contingent Ditties*, 15.

38 *The Dead Horse Corner Gazette* 1 (December 1915) 39. Also see *The Iodine Chronicle* 5 (20 January 1916) 1.

39 Swanston, *Who Said War Is Hell!*, 23.

40 CLIP, John Sudbury, Poem, 7 May 1916.

41 "Killed even though pardoned," *The Iodine Chronicle* 3 (20 November 1915) 3.

42 Iacobelli, *Death or Deliverance*.

43 *The Iodine Chronicle* 3 (20 November 1915) 4.

44 CWM, 19801134-011-14, memoirs, 35-7.

45 CWM, 20000138-001, John Henry Flock, n.p.

46 Manion, *Life Is an Adventure*, 185.

47 Alexander McClintock, *Best o' Luck: How a Fighting Kentuckian Won the Thanks of Britain's King* (Ottawa: CEF Books, 2000 [original, New York: George H. Doran company, 1917]) 1.

48 Peat, *Private Peat*; Mervin C. Simmons, *Three Times Out*—Told by Private Simmons (Toronto: T. Allen, 1918); Keene, "*Crumps.*"

49 See Brian Douglas Tennyson, *The Canadian Experience of the Great War: A Guide to Memoirs* (Lanham: The Scarecrow Press, 2013) xvii.

50 Norris, *Mainly for Mother*, 109.

51 For other examples, see William Boyd, *With a field ambulance at Ypres: being letters written March 7–August 15, 1915* (Toronto: Musson, 1916); Leslie Buswell, *Ambulance No. 10: personal letters from the front* (Toronto: T. Allen, 1916); Noël Chassé, *Avant la poussée finale* (Quebec: Imprimerie "L'Événement," 1918); R.A.L., *Letters of a Canadian Stretcher Bearer*.

52 CLIP, Frank Cousins, letter, 14 April 1918.

53 CWM, 20060227-001, William Davidson collection, letter, 16 September 1917.

CHAPTER 7: TRENCH NEWSPAPERS

1 CWM, *The Listening Post* 29 (1 December 1917) 17. For other articles, see CWM, *The Splint Record* 3 (10 May 1916) 1; CWM, *The Listening Post* 30 (1 April 1918) 9–10.

2 Mary Vipond, *The Mass Media in Canada*, 4th Edition (Toronto: Lorimer, 2011) 25, 70.

3 RG 25, v. 227, file M-56-97, J.L. Reeves to Beaverbrook, 31 August 1917; James Fox, *British Art and the First World War, 1914–1924* (Cambridge: Cambridge University Press, 2015) 85.

4 Nicholas Hiley, "You Can't Believe a Word You Read: Newspaper-Reading in the British Expeditionary Force, 1914–1918," *Media History* 2.1–2 (1994) 99.

5 Allen Douglas, *War, Memory, and the Politics of Humor: The* Canard Enchaîné *and World War I* (Berkeley: University of California Press, 2002) 8.

6 CWM, 20040015-005, Lawrence Rogers, letter, 8 July 1916.

7 LAC, MG 30 E 241, D.E. Macintyre papers, 17 December 1915.

8 Peat, *Private Peat*, 79.

9 CLIP, Wilbert Gilroy, 10 March 1916.

10 Rutledge, *Pen Pictures from the Trenches*, 107.

11 LAC, RG 9, v. 4746, 176/7, CWRO - The Canadian Daily Record, 31 May 1918.

12 LAC, RG 25, v. 227, file M-56-97, Sir Richard Turner to Perley, 5 March 1917.

13 On the papers, see Fuller, *Troop Morale and Popular Culture in the British and Dominion Armies*; Stephane Audoin-Rouzeau, *Men at War 1914–1918: National Sentiment and Trench Journalism in France During the First World War* (Providence: Oxford Berg, 1992); Graham Patrick Seal, *The Soldiers' Press: Trench Journals in the First World War* (Basingstoke: Palgrave Macmillan, 2013); Robert Nelson, *German Soldier Newspapers of the First World War* (Cambridge: Cambridge University Press, 2011); Robert Nelson, "Soldier newspapers. A useful source in the social and cultural history of the First World War and beyond," *War in History* 17.2 (2010) 167–91; S.P. Mackenzie, "Vox Populi: British Army Newspapers in the Second World War," *Journal of Contemporary History*, 24.4 (1989) 665–81; Alex Souchen, "The Culture of Morale: Battalion Newspapers in the 3rd Canadian Infantry Division, June–August 1944," *Journal of Military History* 77 (April 2013) 523–56.

14 For the most recent edition, see C. Westthorp (ed.), *The Wipers Times: The Famous First World War Trench Newspaper* (London: Conway, 2013).

15 Some of the Canadian journals include: *Action Front!* (53rd Battalion); *Another Garland from the Front* (5th Battalion); *The Brazier* (16th Battalion); *The Canadian Machine Gunner*; *The Dead Horse Corner Gazette* (4th Battalion); *The Forty-Niner* (49th Battalion); *In & Out, N.Y.D.* and *The Sling* (Canadian Army Medical Corps); *The Iodine Chronicle* (No. 1 Canadian Field Ambulance); *The Listening Post* (7th Battalion); *The Message from Mars (*4th Canadian Division); *R.M.R. Growler* (14th Battalion); *The Silent 60th* (60th Battalion); *Tank Tatler (*1st Canadian Tank Battalion); *The Twentieth Gazette* (20th Battalion); *Trench Echo* (27th Battalion); *La Vie Canadienne* (Canadian Section, General

Headquarters); *Vic's Patrol* (24th Battalion); *The Western Scot* (67th Battalion); *The Strafer* (67th Battery); *Action Front!* (53rd Battery); *The O.Pip* (58th Battery); *The Kilt* (72nd Battalion).

16 R.C. Fetherstonhaugh, *The Royal Montreal Regiment: 14th Battalion, CEF, 1914–1925* (Montreal: The Royal Montreal Regiment, 1927) 14.

17 LAC, RG 24, v. 1740, DHS 4-4 pts 1, 4-6, Can War Records - publications, 1919–39, Cruikshank to G.S., 10 March 1920.

18 H.M. Urquhart, *The History of the 16th Battalion* (Toronto: Macmillan Company of Canada, 1932) 25. Also see Colonel W.W. Murray, *The History of the 2nd Canadian Battalion in the Great War* (Ottawa: Published for The Historical Committee, 2nd Battalion, C.E.F., 1947) 10, for the 2nd Battalion paper, *2nd Battalion Bulletin*.

19 *Dead Horse Corner Gazette* 2 (December 1915) 22.

20 LAC, Currie Papers, MG 30 E100, v. 10, file 29, In Memoriam, George Herbert Rae Gibson, 1881–1932.

21 *The Listening Post* 27 (10 August 1917) 7.

22 *The Listening Post* 8 (25 November 1915) 30.

23 *The Listening Post* 1 (10 August 1915) 1.

24 *The Dead Horse Corner Gazette* 1 (October 1915) 1.

25 *The Silent 60th* 1.2 (June 1916) 5.

26 LAC, RG 9, v. 5080, *Vic's Patrol*, 3 June 1916.

27 CLIP, T.W. Johnson to Lulu, 11 October 1917.

28 *In and Out* 1 (November 1918) 6

29 Climo (ed.), *Let Us Remember*, 278.

30 Graham Seal, "'Written in the trenches'": Trench Newspapers of the First World War," *Journal of the Australian War Memorial* 16 (April 1990) 30.

31 Corrigall, *The History of the Twentieth Canadian Battalion*, 7.

32 *The Iodine Chronicle* 8 (15 June 1916) 3.

33 *The Forty-Niner* 1.1, 7.

34 James A. Wood, *The Sense of Duty: Canadian Ideas of the Citizen Soldier, 1896–1917* (Ph.D. dissertation: Wilfrid Laurier University, 2006) 354, note 12.

35 *The Iodine Chronicle* 3 (20 November 1915) 1.
36 *The Forty-Niner* 1.1, 7.
37 *The Listening Post* 15 (18 May 1916) 86.
38 *The Listening Post* 12 (1915) 66; *The Brazier* 8 (February 1917) 2.
39 Stevens, *A City Goes to War,* 24.
40 *The Listening Post* 20 (10 December 1916) 132.
41 Audoin-Rouzeau, *Men at War 1914–1918*, 20.
42 LAC, RG 9, III, v. 4023, 2/12, censorship, trench magazines, 1st Cdn Division, 19 October 1916 to Editors of Dead Horse Corner Gazette; Listening Post; The Brazier, N.Y.D.
43 *The Forty-Niner* 1.3, 4.
44 *The Forty-Niner* 1.7, 9.
45 *The Dead Horse Corner Gazette* 1 (October 1915) 4.
46 *The Listening Post* 19 (October 1916) 118.
47 *The Listening Post* 17 (7 July 1916) 107.
48 Keshen, *Propaganda and Censorship*, 144.
49 Fuller, *Troop Morale and Popular Culture*, 14.
50 Audoin-Rouzeau, *Men at War 1914–1918*, 65.
51 *The Listening Post* 3 (12 September 1915) 1.
52 See Cook, ""Dr. Jekyll and Mr. Hyde," 34–59.
53 LAC, RG 41, v. 16, 72nd Battalion, Private Archie Selwood, 1/11–12.
54 *The Listening Post* 1 (10 August 1915) n.p.
55 *The Listening Post* (17 June 1916) 97.
56 *The Listening Post* 29 (1 December 1917) 30.
57 Cited in Julian Walker, *Words and the First World War: Language, Memory, Vocabulary* (London: Bloomsbury Academic, 2017) 260.
58 *The Silent 60th* 1.2 (June 1916) 15.
59 On the Ross, see Andrew Iarocci, *Shoestring Soldiers: The First Canadian Division at War, 1914–1915* (Toronto: University of Toronto Press, 2008).
60 *The Dead Horse Corner Gazette* 1 (October 1915) 9.
61 LAC, RG 9, v. 5080, *Trench Echo*, Christmas 1915 edition, 13.
62 *The Listening Post* 16 (17 June 1916) 98.
63 *Dead Horse Corner Gazette* 1 (Oct 1915) 5.

64 The ambulance was stationed at La Clytte, a small village in the Somme region.
65 Noyes, *Stretcher Bearers at the Double*, 97.
66 Noyes, *Stretcher Bearers at the Double*, 78.
67 *The Listening Post* 17 (7 July 1916) 108.
68 *The Brazier* 1 (15 February 1916) 7.
69 *The Listening Post* 27 (10 August 1917) 5.
70 *The Iodine Chronicle* 15 (Easter 1918) 4.
71 George Robb, *British Culture and the First World War* (New York: Palgrave, 2002)183.
72 *The Brazier* (February 10, 1917) 5.
73 *The Forty-Niner* 4 (December 1915) 16.
74 Captain W.W. Murray, "The Trench Magazine," *Canadian Defence Quarterly* 5.3 (April 1928) 329.

CHAPTER 8: DRAWN AND QUARTERED

1 Charles and Cynthia Hou, *Great Canadian Political Cartoons, 1820 to 1914* (Vancouver: Moody's Lookout Press, 1997) Preface.
2 Mark Bryant, "Crusader, White Rabbit or Organ-Grinder's Monkey? Leslie Illingworth and the British Political Cartoon in World War II," *European Studies* 31 (2001) 345. Also see, Zbenek Zeman, *Heckling Hitler: Caricatures of the Third Reich* (London: I.B.Tauris, 1987).
3 Valerie Holman and Debra Kelly, "War in the Twentieth Century: The Functioning of Humour in Cultural Representation," *European Studies* 31 (2001) 251.
4 Marcelle Cinq-Mars (ed.), *L'écho du Front: Journaux de Tranchées, 1915–1919* (Outremont, Quebec: Athéna Éditions, 2008).
5 James P. Daughton, "Sketches of the Poilu's World: Trench Cartoons from the Great War," in Douglas Mackaman and Michael Mays (eds.), *World War I and the Cultures of Modernity* (Jackson: University Press of Mississippi, 2000) 20–34.
6 Tonie and Valmai Holt (ed.), *The Best of Fragments from France*

by Capt. Bruce Bairnfather (London: Phin Publishing, 1978) Introduction, part II.

7 Michael Hammond, *The Big Show: British Cinema Culture in the Great War* (Exeter: University of Exeter Press, 2006) 237–8.

8 See Tonie and Valmai Holt, *In Search of the Better 'Ole: The Life, the Works and the Collectables of Bruce Bairnsfather* (Canada: Fitzhenry & Whiteside, 1985).

9 Grace Morris, *But This Is Our War* (Toronto: University of Toronto Press, 1981) 56.

10 Raymond Massey, *When I Was Young* (Toronto: McClelland & Stewart, 1976) 123–4.

11 H.R.N. Clyne, *Vancouver's 29th: A Chronicle of the 29th in Flanders Fields* (Vancouver: Tobin's Tigers Association, 1964) 7.

12 Mark Warby, "If you knows of a better medal . . . ," *Medal News* (October 2017) 23.

13 Stevens, *A City Goes to War,* 66.

14 CWM, 20120055-013, Ralph Jones, letter, February 22, 1916

15 Maurice Pope, *Letters from the Front, 1914–1919* (Toronto: Pope & Co., 1996) 36.

16 Hugh Kay, *Battery Action!: The Story of the 43rd (Howitzer) Battery, Canadian Field Artillery, 1916–1919* (Ottawa: CEF Books, 2002) 46.

17 Brian Douglas Tennyson, *Percy Willmot: A Cape Bretoner at War* (Sydney: Cape Breton University Press, 2007) 170.

18 CWM, 19950008-014, Samuel Honey papers, letter, 6 September 1916.

19 *Oh, Canada* (London: Simpkin and Marshall, 1917) 16.

20 CWM, *The Brazier* 8 (10 February 1917) front page.

21 For sales, see CWM, *The Listening Post* 19 (October 1916) 118.

22 CWM, *The Iodine Chronicle* 14 (22 December 1917) 9.

23 CWM, *The Listening Post* 29 (1 December 1917) 17.

24 CWM, *The Iodine Chronicle* (22 December 1917).

25 Tim Cook, "Wet Canteens and Worrying Mothers: Soldiers and Temperance Groups in the Great War," *Histoire sociale/Social*

History 35.70 (June 2003) 311–30; Cook, "'More as a medicine than a beverage,'" 7–22.

26 CWM, *The Listening Post* (22 March 1917) 153.

27 CWM, "On Doing Their Bit," *The Listening Post* (1 December 1917) 20; CWM, [looking for lice] *Now and Then* (29 March 1917) 7; CWM, *The Iodine Chronicle* 8 (15 June 1916) 3.

28 RG 9, v. 5078, *The Canadian Sapper* (April 1918) 67.

29 CWM, *The Listening Post* (1 December 1917) 15.

30 CWM, *The Twentieth Gazette* 2.3 (December 1916) 20.

31 CWM, "Memories of Christmas," *The Brazier* 8 (February 1917) 4.

32 CWM, *The Listening Post* (25 November 1915) 36. Also see "To the Slacker," which is about the soldiers evening the score when they return home. *The Dead Horse Corner Gazette* 1 (October 1915) 11.

33 CWM, *The Silent 60th* 1.2 (June 1916) n.p. [4].

34 CWM, "Things that never happen," *The Splint Record* 10 (22 December 1917) 16.

35 CWM, [Billeting], *The Forty-Niner* 1.3, 7.

36 Cook, *Shock Troops*, 214.

37 On gallantry medals, see Surgeon Commander F.J. Blatherwick, *Canadian Orders, Decorations, and Medals* (Toronto: The Unitrade Press, 1994); for a critical look at the awarding of medals, see Hugh Halliday, *Valour Reconsidered: Inquiries into the Victoria Cross and other Awards for Extreme Bravery* (Toronto: Robin Brass Studio, 2006). For the Canadian Victoria Cross recipients, see the Directorate of History and Heritage website, Victoria Cross Gallery. The Department of Veterans Affairs website has a slightly higher number of VC recipients.

38 *The Listening Post* (17 June 1916) 97.

39 LAC, RG 9, v. 5079, *The Listening Post* (10 August 1917) 31.

40 Armine Norris, *Mainly for Mother*, 118.

41 CWM, *The Forty-Niner* 1.1, 22. Also see the similar joke in *The Listening Post* 12 (15 March 1916) 66.

42 CWM, 19920187-001, diaries of Herbert Heckford Burrell.

43 Harold Harvey, *A Soldier's Sketches Under Fire* (Toronto: Thomas Allen, 1916) viii, 117–18.
44 *Maclean's*, November 1916, 29.
45 *Maclean's*, March 1918, 31–2.
46 CLIP, David McLean, Dear Margaret, 10 June 1917.

CHAPTER 9: MATERIAL CULTURE

1 Canadian Bank of Commerce, *Letters from the Front*, 189.
2 For other examples, see CWM Military History Research Centre, *The Twentieth Gazette* 2.3 (December 1916) 23; Thomas Dinesen, *Merry Hell: A Dane with the Canadians* (London: Jarrolds, 1929) 225.
3 Nicholas J. Saunders, *Trench Art: Materialities and Memories of War* (Oxford: Berg Books, 2003) 130.
4 Hugh Clout, *After the Ruins: Restoring the Countryside of Northern France after the Great War* (Exeter: University of Exeter Press, 1996) 46.
5 Roy (ed.), *The Journal of Private Fraser*, 85.
6 Wheeler, *The 50th Battalion in No Man's Land*, 198.
7 Robertson, *A Terrible Beauty*, 49.
8 CWM, *The Brazier* 4 (18 July 1916) 8.
9 CWM, 19650038-014, Captain William E. L. Coleman papers, diary, 23 October 1915.
10 Swanston, *Who Said War Is Hell!*, 30.
11 Urquhart, *History of the 16th Battalion*, 339.
12 CLIP, Kenneth Foster, memoir, "Memoirs of the Great War, 1915–1918," n.p.
13 CWM, MHRC, Harold Simpson, *The Story of the Second Canadian Siege Battery* (self-published, 1966) 21.
14 Will Bird, *Ghosts Have Warm Hands* (Ottawa: CEF Books, 1997) 39.
15 Diary transcripts of Frank Morison, 30 May 1915, in author's possession.
16 See Jane A. Kimball, *Trench Art: An Illustrated History* (Davis: Silverpenny Press, 2004); Alan Kerr and Doug Styles, "Private

Stephen Smith and His Trench Art Belts," in Adriana A. Davies and Jeff Keshen (eds.), *The Frontier of Patriotism Alberta and the First World War* (Calgary University of Calgary Press, 2016) 197–200.

17 CWM, AL 2010126.

18 John Lynch, *Princess Patricia's Canadian Light Infantry, 1917–1919* (New York: Exposition Press, 1976) 94.

19 Harold Peat, *Private Peat* (New York: Grosset and Dunlap, 1917) 10.

20 Clare Whittingham, "Mnemonics for War: Trench Art and the Reconciliation of Public and Private Memory," *Past Imperfect* 14 (2008) 113–14.

21 Lapointe, *Soldier of Quebec*, 67.

22 Théodore Dugas, "Un Acadien à la Première Guerre Mondiale," *La Revue d'histoire de la Societé historique Nicolas-Denys* XX.3 (September–December 1992) 50.

23 *Listening Post* 20 (10 December 1916) 128.

24 LAC, MG 30 E 50, Elmer Jones papers, file 9, Prisoners of War and Captured Documents, n.d.

25 Stevens, *A City Goes to War,* 86.

26 CLIP, George Hedley Kempling, diary, September 18, 1916.

27 On the execution of soldiers, see Niall Ferguson, "Prisoner Taking and Prisoner Killing in the Age of Total War: Towards a Political Economy of Military Defeat," *War in History* 11.2 (2004) 148–92; Tim Cook, "The Politics of Surrender: Canadian Soldiers and the Killing of Prisoners in the Great War," *Journal of Military History* 70.3 (July 2006) 637–65.

28 Canadian Bank of Commerce, *Letters from the Front*, 202.

29 Pedley, *Only This*, 345.

30 Climo (ed.), *Let Us Remember*, 221.

31 LAC, transcripts to interviews, *In Flanders' Fields*, RG 41, III-B-1,72nd Battalion, John MacKenzie, tape 2/ page 5.

32 LAC, RG 24, v. 1820, The Battle of Amiens, by N.A.D. Armstrong, 46.

33 CWM, 19920187-002 Herbert Heckford Burrell, diary, 6 May 1917.
34 See Simon Harrison, "Skull Trophies of the Pacific War: Transgressive Objects of Remembrance," *Journal of the Royal Anthropological Institute* 12.4 (December 2006) 817–36
35 Martin O'Malley "Valor of Vimy Ridge Is Still Vivid," *The Globe and Mail*, 9 April 1977.
36 Climo (ed.), *Let Us Remember*, 221.
37 LAC, MG30 E400, Claude Vivian Williams papers, letter, November 18, 1916. I'd like to thank Danielle Teillet for sharing this research with me.
38 See Maria Tippett, *Art at the Service of War: Canada, Art and the Great War* (Toronto: University of Toronto Press, 1984); Brandon, *Art or Memorial?*
39 Nicholas J. Saunders, *Trench Art: A Brief History and Guide, 1914–1939* (London: Leo Cooper, 2001) 54.
40 CWM, 20050153-001, Garnet Edmund Dobbs to Lottie and Walt, 30 April 1918.
41 Kingsley, *The First World War as I Saw It*, 38.
42 Lucie E. Gagné, *Pounding the Enemy: The Diary of the 13th Battery, C.F.A., 1914–1918*, (Ottawa: CEF Books, 2007) 58–9.
43 CWM 20070132-001; CWM 20070132-002; CWM 20070132-003.
44 Pimm (ed.), *Leo's War,* 92 and 102.
45 Climo (ed.), *Let Us Remember*, 175.
46 Wallace (ed.), *From Montreal to Vimy Ridge and Beyond*, 256.
47 Herbert McBride, *A Rifleman Went to War* (Plantersville, South Carolina: Small Arms Technical Publishing Company, 1935) 44–5.
48 Nicholas J. Saunders, "Culture, Conflict and Materiality: The Social Lives of Great War Objects," in Bernard Finn and Barton C. Hacker (eds.), *Materializing the Military* (Baltimore: Johns Hopkins University Press, 2005) 87.
49 Saunders, *Trench Art*, 54; *The Listening Post* 31 (July 1918) 2.
50 CLIP, William Howard Curtis, letter to sister, 18 June 1915.

CHAPTER 10: SOLDIERS' CULTURE BEHIND THE FIRING LINE

1 Norma Hillyer Shephard (ed.), *Dear Harry: The Firsthand Account of a World War I Infantryman* (Burlington: Brigham Press, 2003) 222.
2 CWM, 19930034-020, B.F. Gossage, diary, 19 September 1915.
3 CLIP, James Balfour, 7 August 1915.
4 Zubkowski, *As Long as Faith and Freedom Last*, 287.
5 LAC, RG9 III-C-3 v. 4036, folder 1; file 10, G.H. Fowke to the Secretary War Office, April 12, 1916.
6 Billy Gray (ed.), *More Letters from Billy* (Toronto: McClelland, Goodchild & Stewart, 1917) 40–1.
7 *Letters from the Front*, 58.
8 On the ongoing training, see Bill Rawling, *Surviving Trench Warfare: Technology and the Canadian Corps, 1914–1918* (Toronto: University of Toronto Press, 1992).
9 MHRC, Anita Hagen (ed.), *World War I Letters from Harold Simpson to his Family in Prince Edward Island* (self-published, 2008) 14.
10 Roy (ed.), *The Journal of Private Fraser*, 37.
11 Lapointe, *Soldier of Quebec*, 42.
12 Cowley (ed.), *Georges Vanier*, 130.
13 LAC, MG 30 E249, v. 1, The Diary of the 20th Battery, CFA, by J.C.K. Mackay, 17.
14 Rutledge, *Pen Pictures from the Trenches*, 38.
15 See K. Craig Gibson, "Sex and Soldiering in France and Flanders: The British Expeditionary Force along the Western Front, 1914–1918', *The International History Review* 23 (September 2001), 535–79; K. Craig Gibson, "'My Chief Source of Worry': An Assistant Provost Marshal's View of Relations between 2nd Canadian Division and Local Inhabitants on the Western Front, 1915–1917," *War in History* 7.4 (October 2000) 413–41; Krista Cowman, "Touring behind the Lines: British Soldiers in French Towns and Cities during the Great War," *Urban History* 41.1 (2014) 105–23.

16 CWM, 19980129-003, Clarence McCann collection, letter, 5 March 1916.
17 Robertson, *A Terrible Beauty*, 77.
18 CWM, 20020161-002, Gertrude Mills papers, n.p.
19 Lutz D. H. Sauerteig, "Sex, Medicine and Morality during the First World War," in Roger Cooter, Mark Harrison and Steve Sturdy (eds.), *War Medicine and Morality* (Stroud: Sutton), 1998; Michelle K. Rhoades "Renegotiating French Masculinity: Medicine and Venereal Disease during the Great War," *French Historical Studies* 29.2 (2006) 293–327.
20 Crerar, *Padres in No Man's Land*, 96; Jay Cassel, *The Secret Plague: Venereal Disease in Canada, 1838–1939* (University of Toronto Press, 1987) 123.
21 CWM, "If Every Man Were Straight," 19760148-060, pp. 5–6, 11–12.
22 The number steadily dropped during the war, but there were still 66,346 recorded cases by the end of the war, about one in eight of the men who went overseas. Cook, *Shock Troops*, 176; Morton, *When Your Number's Up*, 200.
23 Desmond Morton, *Fight or Pay Soldiers' Families in the Great War* (Vancouver: UBC Press, 2004) 47–8.
24 CWM, 19801226-276, Assistant Director of Medical Services of 3rd Canadian Division, 10 February 1918.
25 LAC, RG 9, II-B-1, v. 411, file D-35-1, CAS. 4887/32, Headquarters, Canadians, Crowborough, 28 November 1916. Also see correspondence in RG 9, II-B-1, v. 499, file L-7-1.
26 Swanston, *Who Said War Is Hell!*, 47.
27 Johnston, *Riding into War*, 66.
28 Booth (ed.), *Opened by Censor*, 142.
29 Richard Schweitzer, *The Cross and the Trenches: Religious Faith and Doubt among British and American Great War Soldier* (London: Praeger, 2003) 21.
30 Bishop, *The YMCA in the Great War*, 87
31 Frank Carrel, *Impressions of War* (Quebec: The Telegraph Printing, 1919) 72.

32 Shephard (ed.), *Dear Harry*, 104.
33 Philippe Bieler, *Onward Dear Boys: A Family Memoir of the Great War* (Montreal and Kingston: McGill-Queen's University Press, 2014) 67.
34 On Canadian photography, see Peter Robertson, *Relentless Verity: Canadian Military Photographers since 1885* (Toronto: University of Toronto Press, 1973); also see Jane Carmichael, *First World War Photographers* (London: Routledge, 1989).
35 See the correspondence in RG 9, III-A-1, v. 916, v. 66-3, "cameras"; and RG 9, III, v. 4036, 1/13; Grout (ed.), *Thunder in the Skies*, 206.
36 Andrew C. Rodger, "Amateur Photography by Soldiers of the Canadian Expeditionary Force," *Archivaria* 26 (Summer 1988) 163–8.
37 Swanston, *Who Said War Is Hell!*, 31.
38 CWM, 58A 1 153.1-5, Sergeant George Lewis Ormsby, George to Maggie, 6 August 1915.
39 Cook, "'My Whole Heart and Soul is in This War,'" 57–8.
40 Cook, *At the Sharp End*, 248.
41 Climo (ed.), *Let Us Remember*, 273.
42 On the importance of reading, see Amanda Laugesen, *"Boredom in the Enemy": The Intellectual and Imaginative Lives of Australian Soldiers in the Great War and Beyond* (Surrey: Ashgate, 2012).
43 Norris, *Mainly for Mother*, 73.
44 Wells, *From Montreal to Vimy Ridge*, 218.
45 Tennyson, *Merry Hell*, 83.
46 Donald Macpherson, *A Soldier's Diary: The WWI Diaries of Donald MacPherson* (St. Catharines: Vanwell, 2001) 76.
47 "Memoir of Harold Adams Innis" prepared by Anne Innis Dagg. http://www.cjc-online.ca/index.php/journal/article/view/1472/1591
48 CLIP, Private Ernest Taylor, letter, 30 December 1915.
49 Robb, *British Culture and the First World War*, 107. Also see Michael Hammond, *The Big Show: British Cinema Culture in the Great War* (Exeter: University of Exeter Press, 2006).

50 Andrew Horrall, "Charlie Chaplin and the Canadian Expeditionary Force," in Briton C. Busch (ed.), *Canada and the Great War: Western Front Association Papers* (Montreal and Kingston: McGill-Queen's University Press, 2003) 29.
51 *The Brazier* 1 (15 February 1916) 1.
52 CWM, 20040015-005, Lawrence Rogers, letter, 5 March 1916.
53 CWM, 20110042-002, Robert Miller collection, diary, 13 April 1916.
54 Rutledge, *Pen Pictures from the Trenches*, 104–5.
55 *The Listening Post* 21 (25 January 1917) 138.
56 There was the occasional slight hurled towards Chaplin since he was of military age but not serving. See *The Sling*, October 1917, p. 8.
57 CWM, William Shaw Antliff, 58A 1 182.1, letter, 19 March 1916.
58 Brophy and Partridge, *Songs and Slang of the British Soldier*, 243. For another moustache poem, see *The Brazier* 7 (20 December 1916) 1.
59 *The Iodine Chronicle* 2 (15 November 1915) 2.
60 CLIP, Ernest Taylor, letter, 23 January 1916.
61 Libby Murphy, *The Art of Survival: France and the Great War Picaresque* (New Haven: Yale University Press, 2016) 16, 198–9.
62 Murphy, *The Art of Survival*, 204.
63 CLIP, Bill Hutchinson, 16 April 1919.
64 James Dunbar Campbell, "The Army Isn't All Work: Physical Culture and the Evolution of the British Army 1860–1918" (Ph.D. dissertation: University of Maine, 2003); Riedi Eliza and Tony Mason, "'Leather' and the Fighting Spirit: Sport in the British Army in World War 1," *Canadian Journal of History* XLI (2006) 485–516.
65 *The Dead Horse Corner Gazette*, December 1915.
66 CWM, 20020130-001, W.S. Antliff, 2–3 September 1918. Also see Kim Beattie, *48th Highlanders of Canada, 1891–1928* (published by unit, 1932) 113.
67 Fuller, *Troop Morale and Popular Culture*, 91.
68 LAC, MG 30 E 241, D.E. Macintyre, 11 April 1916.

69 LAC, War Diary, 16th Battalion, June 18, 1916.
70 LAC, War Diary 31st Battalion CEF, June 12, 1917.
71 Andrew Horrall, "'Keep-a-Fighting! Play the Game!' Baseball and the Canadian Forces During the First World War," *Canadian Military History*, 10.2 (Spring 2001) 27–40.
72 B.J. Murdoch, *The Red Vineyard* (Great Britain: University Press Glasgow, 1959), 100.
73 Urquhart, *History of the 16th Battalion*, 221.
74 Fuller, *Troop Morale and Popular Culture*, 88.
75 G.W.L. Nicholson, *Canadian Expeditionary Force, 1914–1919: Official History of the Canadian Army in the First World War*, Introduction by Mark Humphries (Montreal: McGill-Queen's University Press, 2015, original, 1962) 384.
76 Tennyson (ed.), *Merry Hell*, 173.
77 CWM, 19730066-001, The Eighteenth Battalion, 119.
78 Corrigal, *The Twentieth*, 41–2.

CHAPTER 11: SHOCK TROUPES

1 Wheeler, *The 50th Battalion in No Man's Land*, 72 and 89.
2 On the importance of theatre, see Andrew Maunder, "'Funny Men and Charming Girls': Revue and the Theatrical Landscape of 1914–1918," in Angela K. Smith and Krista Cowman (eds.), *Landscapes and Voices in the Great War* (London: Routledge, 2017) 19–40; Gordon Williams, *British Theatre in the Great War* (London: Continuum, 2003).
3 On discipline issues, see Tim Cook, "Wet Canteens and Worrying Mothers."
4 UBC, Jack Stickney papers, box 1, letter to Mom, 17 December 1914.
5 Bishop, *The YMCA in the Great War*, 150.
6 John Ellis, *Eye-Deep in Hell* (London: Croom Helm, 1976) 145.
7 LAC, Sam Hughes papers, v. 4, file 8, Captain Richard Ponton to his Dad, n.d. [ca. May 1915].
8 LAC, MG 30 E 241, D.E. Macintyre, diary, 21 September 1917.
9 Andrew Horrall, "Charlie Chaplin and the Canadian

Expeditionary Force," in Briton C. Busch (ed.), *Canada and the Great War: Western Front Association Papers* (Montreal and Kingston: McGill-Queen's University Press, 2003) 28.

10 See G. Lenton-Young, "Variety Theatre," in A. Saddlemyer (ed.), *Early Stages: Theatre in Ontario, 1800–1914* (Toronto: University of Toronto Press, 1990) 166.

11 J.M. McLaren, "Mirth and Mud: The Chronicles of the First Organized Canadian Concert Party to Tour the Trenches During the Great War," *Maclean's Magazine* (1 January 1929) 14.

12 Noyes, *Stretcher-Bearers at the Double!*, 203.

13 Stephen Beames, untitled memoirs, 27–8. Memoir in author's possession.

14 *The Dead Horse Corner Gazette* 1 (December 1915) 33.

15 LAC, The Virtual Gramophone, Lieutenant Gitz Rice. Also see Richard Holt, "British Blood Calls British Blood: The British–Canadian Recruiting Mission of 1917–1918," *Canadian Military History* 22.1 (2013) 29.

16 Hodder-Williams, *Princess Patricia's Canadian Light Infantry*, 140; Jason Wilson, "Soldiers of Song: the Dumbells and Other Canadian Concert Parties of the First World War" (Master's thesis: University of Guelph, 2003) 27.

17 J.M. McLaren, "Mirth and Mud Part Two: Orphans are Orphans," *Maclean's Magazine* (1 March 1929) 66.

18 Wallace (ed.), *From Montreal to Vimy Ridge and Beyond*, 251–2.

19 *The Brazier* 6 (15 November 1916) 1.

20 McLaren, "Mirth and Mud Part Two," 66.

21 David J. Bercuson, *The Patricias: The Proud History of a Fighting Regiment* (Toronto: Stoddart, 2001) 94.

22 Wilson, "Soldiers of Song," 27.

23 Bercuson, *The Patricias*, 94–5.

24 Christie (ed.), Letters of Agar Adamson, 268.

25 Hodder-Williams, *PPCLI*, 140.

26 Patrick Earle, *Al Plunkett: The Famous Dumbell* (New York: Pageant, 1956) 49–50.

27 Bishop, *The YMCA in the Great War*, 101–2.

28 Earle, *Al Plunkett,* 49-50

29 Earle, *Al Plunkett*, 54.

30 McLaren, "Mirth and Mud Part Two," 66.

31 R.F.L. Sheldon-Williams, *The Canadian Front in France and Flanders* (London: A.C. Black, Ltd, 1920) 189–91.

32 Brophy, *Soldiers' Song and Slang*, 243.

33 B. Jones and B. Howell, *Popular Arts of the First World War* (London: Studio Vista Blue Star House, 1972) 130.

34 Wilson, "Soldiers of Song," 101. The 49th Battalion sang a version. See Stevens, *A City Goes to War*, 35.

35 McLaren, "Mirth and Mud," 14.

36 Wilson, "Soldiers of Song," 38, 82.

37 Interview, Alan Cameron, 7 December 2006.

38 Pimm (ed.), *Leo's War*, 92.

39 Ellis, *Eye-Deep in Hell*, 145.

40 Susan Evans Shaw (ed.), *My Darling Girl: Wartime Letters of James Lloyd Evans, 1914–1918* (self-published, 1999) 96.

41 G. Lenton-Young, "Variety Theatre," in A. Saddlemyer (ed.), *Early Stages: Theatre in Ontario, 1800–1914* (Toronto: University of Toronto Press, 1990) 166.

42 Max Arthur, *When This Bloody War Is Over: Soldiers' Songs of the First World War* (London Piatkus, 2001) xxiii–xxiv.

43 For a discussion, see Alon Rachamimov, "The Disruptive Comforts of Drag: (Trans) Gender Performances among Prisoners of War in Russia, 1914–1920," *The American Historical Review* 111.2 (April 2006). Without journal page numbers, but see paragraph 27.

44 Jason Wilson, "Soldiers of Song," 130–1.

45 LAC, MG 30 E351, Claude Craig, diary, 16 July 1918.

46 Corrigall, *The History of the Twentieth Canadian Battalion*, 302.

47 For a misreading of the cross-dressing experience, see David A. Boxwell, "The Follies of War: Cross-Dressing and Popular Theatre on the British Front Lines, 1914–18," *Modernism/modernity* 9.1 (January 2002) 1–20.

48 Wilson, *Soldiers of Song: The Dumbells and other Canadian Concert Parties of the First World War* (Waterloo: Wilfrid Laurier University Press, 2012) 118.
49 Fuller, *Troop Morale*, 105.
50 Ken Tingley (ed.), *The Path of Duty: The Wartime Letters of Alwyn Bramley-Moore* (Calgary: Alberta Records Publication Board, 1998) 74.
51 Arthur, *When This Bloody War Is Over*, xxiii–xxiv.
52 Bishop, *The YMCA in the Great War*, 154.
53 Norman Miles Guiou, *Transfusion: A Canadian Surgeon's Story in War and in Peace* (Yarmouth: Stoneycroft Pub., 1985) 58–9.
54 J. Alexander (Sandy) Bain, *A War Diary of a Canadian Signaller: My Experiences in the Great War, 1914–1918* (Moncton: J.D. Bain, 1986) 73.
55 CWM, 19950008-014, Samuel Lewis Honey papers, 58A 1 112.10, Sam to parents, 26 August 1917.
56 Frederick Scott, *The Great War as I Saw It* (Ottawa: CEF Books, 2000) 242.
57 Patrick O'Neill, "The Canadian Concert Party in France," *Theatre Research in Canada* 4.2 (Fall 1983) 193.
58 Wilson, "Soldiers of Song," 25.

CHAPTER 12: ENTRENCHED CULTURE

1 CWM, Frederick Robinson, 20000148-001, 58A 1.203.1, letter to Ruth, 1 June 1918.
2 CWM, 19980129-003, Clarence McCann collection, letter 22 April 1916.
3 MHRC, Anita Hagen (ed.), *World War I Letters from Harold Simpson to his Family in Prince Edward Island* (self-published, 2008) 169.
4 CWM, 19930034-020 Maj. B.F. Gossage, Diary, December 24, 1915.
5 Robertson, *A Terrible Beauty*, 100. Also see Modris Eksteins, *Rites of Spring: The Great War and the Birth of the Modern Age* (Toronto: Lester & Orpen Dennys, 1994) 228.

6 On the postwar years, see Bowker, *A Time Such as There Never Was Before.*

7 Natascha Morrison, "Looking Backwards, Looking Forwards: Remembrance Day in Canada, 1919–2008" (Master's thesis: Carleton University, 2010); Teresa Iacobelli, "From Armistice to Remembrance: The Continuing Evolution of Remembrance Day in Canada," in Matthew Hayday and Raymond Blake (eds.), *Celebrating Canada: Holidays, National Days, and the Crafting of Identities* (Toronto: University of Toronto Press, 2016).

8 See Amanda Betts (ed.), *In Flanders Fields: 100 Years: Writing on War, Loss and Remembrance* (Toronto: Knopf Canada, 2015).

9 See Pat Jalland, *Death in War and Peace: A History of Loss and Grief in England, 1914–1970* (Oxford: Oxford University Press, 2010).

10 See McMullin, *Anatomy of a Séance*; Winter, *Sites of Memory, Sites of Mourning*; Robertson, *Science of the Séance*; Alan Wilkinson, "Changing English Attitudes to Death in the Two World Wars," in Peter C. Jupp and Glennys Howarth (eds.), *The Changing Face of Death: Historical Accounts of Death and Disposal* (London: Macmillan Press, 1997).

11 Jay Winter, *Remembering War: The Great War Between Memory and History in the Twentieth Century* (New Haven: Yale University Press, 2006) 109.

12 See, for example, CWM, 19740046-001, Allen Oliver, scrapbook; and R.H.T. (ed.), *Victor Gordon Tupper: A Brother's Tribute* (London: Oxford University Press, 1921).

13 CWM, 58A 163.14, Waring Cosbie, letter, 24 February 1917.

14 Cowley (ed.), *Georges Vanier,* 122.

15 See Susan Stewart, *On Longing: Narratives of the Miniature, the Gigantic, the Souvenir, the Collection* (Baltimore: Johns Hopkins University Press, 1984) 133–6; Nicholas Saunders, *Killing Time: Archaeology and the First World War* (Thrupp, U.K.: Sutton Publishing, 2007) 28; Susan M. Pearce, "Objects as Meaning; or Narrating the Past," in Susan M. Pearce (ed.), *Interpreting Objects and Collections* (London: Routledge, 1994) 20.

16 Jon Forrester, "'Mille e tre': Freud and Collecting," John Elsner and Roger Cardinal (ed.), *The Cultures of Collecting* (Harvard University Press, 1994) 244.

17 Canadian War Museum, 19830078-025.

18 See Brock Millman, *Polarity, Patriotism, and Dissent in Great War Canada, 1914–1919* (Toronto: University of Toronto Press, 2016).

19 Brophy and Partridge, *Songs and Slang of the British Soldier*, v.

20 LAC, MG 31 G6, E.L.M. Burns papers, v. 9, file Articles, papers—U, Untitled Document on soldiers' slang in the First World War, n.d.

21 Norris (ed.), *Medicine and Duty*, 264–5.

22 Daphne Read (ed.), *The Great War and Canadian Society: An Oral History* (New Hogtown Press: Toronto, 1978) 207.

23 On songs and nostalgia, see Frederick S. Barrett et al., "Music-Evoked Nostalgia: Affect, Memory, and Personality," *Emotion* 10.3 (2010) 390–403.

24 Cited in Emma Hanna, "'When Words Are Not Enough,' The Aural Landscape of Britain's Modern Memory of 1914–18," in Angela K. Smith and Krista Cowman (eds.), *Landscapes and Voices in the Great War* (London: Routledge, 2017) 43.

25 Wilson, "Soldiers of Song," 130–1.

26 MHRC, Song Sheet music, 19770069-005 and 19870069-005.

27 Vance, *Death So Noble*, 82.

28 Vance, *Death So Noble*, 80.

29 Vance, *Death So Noble*, 131.

30 J. Marshall Craig (ed.), *You're Lucky If You're Killed* (self-published, 2003) xix.

31 Tim Cook, "Canada's Great War on Film: *Lest We Forget* (1935)," *Canadian Military History* 14.3 (Summer 2005) 5–20.

32 Tonnie and Valmai Holt, *In Search of the Better 'Ole: The Life the Works and the Collectables of Bruce Bairnsfather* (Toronto: Fitzhenry & Whiteside, 1985) Chapter 10.

33 Tim Cook, *The Madman and the Butcher: The Sensational Wars of Sam Hughes and General Arthur Currie* (Toronto: Penguin Canada, 2010).

34 Cited in Andrew Frayn, *Writing Disenchantment: British First World War Prose, 1914–1930* (Manchester University Press, 2014) 205.

35 See Jonathan Vance, "The Soldier as Novelist: Literature, History and the Great War," *Canadian Literature: A Quarterly of Criticism and Review* 179 (Winter 2003) 22–37; Zachary Abram, "Canon Fodder: The Canadian Canon and the Erasure of Great War Narratives," in Kellen Kurschinski (eds.), *The Great War: From Memory to History* (Waterloo: Wilfrid Laurier University, 2015) 17–36.

36 Sergeant R.G. Kentner, *Some Recollections of the Battles of World War I* (self-published, 1995) 1.

37 Cameron, *War! What of It!*, ii.

38 On memoirs, see Brian Bond, *The Unquiet Western Front: Britain's Role in Literature and History* (Cambridge: Cambridge University Press, 2002); Dan Todman, *The Great War: Myth and Memory* (London: Hambledon, 2005).

39 See for example, Signaller Frank P. Dixon, *War-Time Memories in Verse* (no publisher, 1937); Captain George Blackstone Field, *Echoes from Ypres* (self-published, 1953).

40 Black, *I Want One Volunteer*, 2–4.

41 See Brock Millman, *Polarity, Patriotism, and Dissent in Great War Canada, 1914–1919* (Toronto: University of Toronto Press, 2016).

42 See Serge Durflinger, *Veterans with a Vision: Canada's War Blinded in Peace and War* (Vancouver: UBC Press, 2010).

43 On the anger of veterans, see Desmond Morton and Glenn Wright, "The Bonus Campaign, 1919–21: Veterans and the Campaign for Re-establishment," *Canadian Historical Review* 64.2 (1983) 147–67; Niall Barr, *The Lion and the Poppy: British Veterans, Politics and Society, 1921–39* (Greenwood, 2005); William F. Stewart, *The Embattled General: Sir Richard Turner and the First World War* (Montreal and Kingston: McGill-Queen's University Press, 2015) 258–61.

44 "Re-Union Memories," *The Legionary* (September–October, 1932) 5.

45 Vance, *Death So Noble*, 132.

46 MHRC, *Behind the Lines* (1934) n.p. Note: ellipses in quote are originals; nothing has been cut by the author.

47 See Jonathan Vance, "'Today they were alive again': The Canadian Corps reunion of 1934," *Ontario History Magazine* LXXXVII. 4 (December 1995) 327–43.

48 See Eric Brown and Tim Cook, "The 1936 Vimy Pilgrimage," *Canadian Military History* 20.2 (Spring 2011) 37–54; David W. Lloyd, *Battlefield Tourism Pilgrimage and the Commemoration of the Great War in Britain, Australia, and Canada, 1919–1939* (Berg: Oxford, 1998).

49 RG 9, v. 5079, "The Canadian Machine Gunner," 1.4, 1.

50 There is no full run of Canadian trench newspapers, although there are large collections at the Canadian War Museum, the Library and Archives of Canada, the Imperial War Museum, McMaster University, and Cambridge University (U.K.).

51 Stevens, *A City Goes to War*, 164. "Billy's Boys" referred to the first lieutenant-colonel, William Griesbach, who rose to command a brigade.

52 Stevens, *A City Goes to War*, 161.

53 See Tim Cook, *Clio's Warriors: Canadian Historians and the Writing of the World Wars* (Vancouver: UBC Press, 2006).

54 See Tim Cook, "Literary Memorials: The Great War Regimental Histories, 1919–1939," *Journal of the Canadian Historical Association* (2002) 167–90.

55 Lieutenant-Colonel C. Beresford Topp, *The 42nd Battalion, C.E.F., Royal Highlanders of Canada, in the Great War* (Montreal: Gazette, 1931) 312, 316.

56 On nostalgia, see Stephen Garton, "Longing for War: Nostalgia and the Australian Returned Soldiers after the First World War," in T.G. Ashplant, et al. (eds.), *The Politics of War Memory and Commemoration* (London: Routledge, 2000) 222–39; Jonathan Vance, '"Today they were alive again': The Canadian Corps Reunion of 1934," *Ontario History* 87/4 (December 1995) 327–44.

57 Robert England, *Discharged A Commentary on Civil Re-establishment of Veterans in Canada* (Toronto: The Macmillan Company of Canada, 1943) 12.

58 "Famed 20th Battalion Relieves Battles of First World War," *The Globe and Mail*, 13 April 1953.

59 "The Thinning Ranks from the First World War," *The Globe and Mail*, 8 November 1958.

60 Percy Climo, *Let Us Remember: Lively Letters from World War One* (1990) 296.

61 On memory, see Jonathan Vance, "An Open Door to a Better Future: The Memory of Canada's Second World War," in Geoffrey Hayes, Mike Bechthold, and Matt Symes (eds.), *Canada and the Second World War: Essays in Honour of Terry Copp* (Waterloo, ON: Wilfrid Laurier University Press, 2012) 461–77; Tim Cook, *Fight to the Finish: Canadians Fighting the Second World War 1944–1945* (Toronto: Allan Lane, 2015) 431–66.

62 There are many commentaries on the soldier as victim, including by the First World War's most prominent historian, Jay Winter. See Jay Winter, *War Beyond Words* (Cambridge: Cambridge University Press, 2017) 11.

63 Monty Python, "Fighting Each Other" sketch, *The Meaning of Life* (film, The Monty Python Partnerships, 1982).

64 *Blackadder* IV, Episode 4—"Private Plane" (British Broadcasting Corporation, 1989).

65 On Vimy's central place in Canada's symbolic landscape, see Tim Cook, *Vimy: The Battle and the Legend* (Toronto: Allen Lane, 2017).

66 See Sherrill Grace, *Landscapes of War and Memory: The Two World Wars in Canadian Literature and the Arts, 1977–2007* (Edmonton: University of Alberta Press, 2014).

67 Hunt Tooley, *The Western Front: Battle Ground and Home Front in the First World War* (Palgrave, 2003) 221.

68 Crowley (ed.), *George Vanier: Soldier*, 302.

ACKNOWLEDGMENTS

All books have their own history. My history with this research started in 1995. I was in the first year of a master's degree at the Royal Military College of Canada, researching my thesis on gas warfare. To locate gas within the soldiers' discourse, I read hundreds of published and archival letter sets, diaries, and memoirs. In addition to finding references to the three-letter word "gas," I found as many to another, "rum." In 2000, I published an article in the *Canadian Military History* journal on the importance of rum as a combat motivator to the Canadian Great War soldier. That article also touched on the importance of rum within the soldiers' culture, as revealed through songs, cartoons, and poetry. I continued to explore these ideas in many of the ten books I published since then, as well as in numerous talks and articles.

At the Canadian War Museum in 2008, I curated the exhibition "Trench Life—A Survival Guide," which explored other aspects of this hidden soldiers' culture and was attended by over 100,000 visitors. While there were many involved in the project, the interpretative planner for that exhibition, Kathryn Lyons, was especially important in helping me draw out key messages for a wide audience. In the ten years after that, I continued to periodically research, analyze, and write about soldiers' culture, even though I was engaged in multiple other projects, exhibitions, and books.

I am grateful to my friends at Penguin Random House Canada, especially my editor, Diane Turbide, for having faith in this book.

There are many hands that have taken this manuscript through production, publication, marketing, and sales, and the dedicated staff at Penguin work tirelessly on behalf of authors. My friend and agent, Rick Broadhead, has been at my side since 2006, always there to pass on encouragement, share hard truths about the business, and support me at every turn. I am especially lucky to work with Tara Tovell, who provided her usual skilled line and copy editing on our eighth book together. Tara's diligence and cheerfulness are inspiring, especially given that when we work together I am always at the end of a very long research and writing process.

My colleagues at the Canadian War Museum have encouraged me over the years and I learn new things every day from them. The relatively small crew at the museum works very hard, but all are dedicated to the key mission and mandate of sharing the stories and material culture of Canada's military history with all Canadians.

I am also lucky to be a part of a large network of military historians in Canada and around the world. I was able to call upon several experts in the field to read through this specific manuscript to offer advice, caution, and commentary. Together they have assisted me in strengthening ideas and in writing a better book, and I am grateful to Dr. Pat Brennan, Dr. Mark Humphries, Dr. Bill Stewart, and Dr. Roger Sarty. Many other scholars, both in Canada and globally, have offered commentary about my work over the previous two decades, and all of them, too numerous to list here, have informed my thinking towards this project.

I would like to thank Brittany Dunn of Wilfrid Laurier University for completing the book's bibliography. As a research fellow at the Laurier Centre for Military Strategic and Disarmament Studies, I gratefully recognize the support from the centre that does so much to encourage scholarship, especially through the flagship journal *Canadian Military History*. I was further supported by the City of Ottawa—which I have proudly called home for forty-five years—through the Creation and Production Fund for Professional Artists. A Canada Council grant for professional writers is also acknowledged with much gratitude.

Dr. Sharon Cook, my mother, an award-winning educator and an author of more than a dozen books, read over the manuscript and offered keen editorial and historical insight. This took time away from Clifford and her beloved granddaughters, but I am grateful to have benefited from her expertise. Thanks also go to Graham and Ankai; and to Sam, Graham, Redden, and Calla. And a shout-out to Jennifer and the Sens.

I think my dad would have liked this book, and he had heard much about it over the years, always offering his thoughts and especially suggesting that I work in more rock and roll. He died four years ago, but I think of him often. While many have influenced my scholarship over the years, he had the greatest impact on me as a writer and historian.

My girls have grown up with the First World War all around them, or at least when they venture into my office. This book seemed to capture their attention more than most, especially the singing, swearing, and supernatural stories. I offer a big hug to them, Chloe, Paige, and Emma, who keep me entertained every day with their stories and experiences. Sarah and I are lucky to share our lives with our lovely girls. Their creative energies feed my own, and those of Sarah, who is my best friend and love. Sarah and I talk daily about research, current affairs, history, and archives, and she offered much insight into this project. Sarah is the one who keeps the Cook family on the path going forward.

SELECT BIBLIOGRAPHY

Library and Archives Canada, Government Records

RG 9, Records of the Department of Militia and Defence

RG 24, Records of the Department of National Defence

RG 25, Records of the Department of External Affairs

RG 41, Records of the Canadian Broadcasting Corporation

Library and Archives Canada, Private Records

Lord Beaverbrook papers, MG 27 II-G-1

E.L.M. Burns papers, MG 31 G6

Gregory Clark papers, R8258 08E

Robert N. Clements papers, MG 30 E156

Claude Craig papers, MG 30 E351

J.J. Creelman papers, MG 30 E8

Sir Arthur Currie papers, MG 30 E100

Cecil J. French papers, MG 30 E558

William Green papers, MG 30 E430

W.H. Hewgill papers, MG 30 E16

Sam Hughes papers, MG 27 IID23

Elmer Watson Jones papers, MG 30 E50

Donald Roy Macfie papers, MG 30 E427

D.E. Macintyre papers, MG 30 E241

Andrew Macphail papers, MG 30 D150

John Peter McNab papers, MG 30 E42

Andrew McNaughton papers, MG 30 E133

Hubert Morris papers, MG 30 E379

G.W.L. Nicholson papers, MG 31 G19

Victor Odlum papers, MG 30 E300

Talbot Mercer Papineau papers, MG 30 E52
E.W. Russell papers, MG 30 E220
John Smith Stewart papers, MG 30 E249
Claude Vivian Williams papers, MG 30 E400

Library and Archives Canada, War Diaries
Unit war diaries, available online

Canadian War Museum
William Antliff papers, 20080038-003 //58A 1 241.1
Alfred E. Baggs papers, 19900227-001 // 58A 1 92.1
Herbert Heckford Burrell papers, 19920187-002 // 58A 1 92.11-13
Charles Edward Clarke papers, 20090121-004 // 58A 1 82.33
Herbert Gordon Clemens papers, 19980050-005 // 58A 1 122.2-8
Captain William E.L. Coleman papers, 19650038-014 // 58A 1 14.1
H.H. Coombs papers, 20020112-002 // 58A 1 197.6
Waring Gerald Cosbie papers, 20020094-001 // 58A 1 163.14
Private Andrew Coulter papers, 20060105-001 // 58A 1 221.1
Leonard Cuff papers, 20080132-001 // 58A 1 269
Sir Arthur Currie papers, 19801226-286 // 58 B 6-5
Elgin Eby papers, 20120162-001 // 58A 1 175.11
William Davidson papers, 20060227-001
Horace Hubert Forster Dibblee papers, 20050172-004 // 58A 1 239.12
Garnet Edmund Dobbs papers, 20050153-001 // 58A 1 217.1
W.M.L. Draycott papers, 19730295-007 // 58A 1 32.1
John Henry Flock papers, 20000138-001 // 58A 1 200.26
E.C. Forrest papers, 19780056-041 // 58E 9 3.2
Major B.F. Gossage, 19930034-020 // 58A 1 13.8
William Hendrie Hay papers, 20030142-001// 58A 1 186.5
Albert Hitchcox papers, 20060194-001 // 58A 1 235.14
Samuel Lewis Honey papers, 19950008-014 // 58A 1 112.15
John Albert House, 20070073-007
Lieutenant Ralph Jones papers, 20120055-013 // 58A 1 280.5
Joseph Harrison MacFarlane papers, 19800218-014 // 58A 1 160.3

Captain Keith Campbell Macgowan papers, 19990026-016 // 58A 1 154.1
Clarence McCann papers, 19980129-003 // 58A 1 151.2-5
Harry Austin McCleave papers, 20020189-001 // 58A 1 185.18
Lieutenant J.W. McClung papers, 20030153-001 // 58A 1 99.9
Major George Franklin McFarland papers, 20000003-002// 58A 1 27.11
Albert Percy Menzies papers, 20100067-002 // 58A 1 228.22
George Metcalf papers, 1990-0066-015
S.C. Mewburn papers, 20030088-028
Andrew Howard Miller papers, 19790640-003 // 58A 1 35.3
Robert Miller papers, 20110042-002 // 58A 1 263.3
Gertrude Mills papers, 20020161-002 // 58A 1 185.24
Victor John Nixon papers, 19810467-005 // 58A 1 34.16
Allen Oliver papers, 19740046-001 // 58E 3 7.1
Charles Olson papers, 19801134-011-14 // 58A 2 7.6
George Lewis Ormsby papers, 20000013-008 // 58A 1153.6
Frederick Robinson papers, 20000148-001 // 58A 1 203.1
Lawrence Rogers papers, 20040015-005 // 58A 1 207.1-5
E.D. Rowe, 58A 1.67.7
Chester E. Routley papers, 19730066-001 // 58A 2 1.5
Howard Scott papers, 19910028-001 // 58A 1 2.14
Martin John Suter papers, 19750073-005 // 58B 6 5.5
John Patrick Teahan papers, 19950023-002 // 58A 113.2
Carman H. Thornton papers, 20050023-003 // 58A 1 218.26
Richard Turner papers, 19710147-001 // 58A 1 9.1
Thomas Earl Walker papers, 20000030-09 // 58A 1 202.6-7
David Watson papers, 19820623-002 // 58A 1 31.13

Canadian War Museum, Military History Research Centre

Behind the Lines (1934)

Calder, D.G. Scott. "The History of the 28th (Northwest) Battalion." Official report, n.d.

Flanders' Fields transcripts

Hagen, Anita Simpson, ed. *World War I Letters from Harold Simpson to His Family in Prince Edward Island*. Self-published, 2003.

"If Every Man Were Straight," 19760148-060.

Simpson, Harold. *A History of the 2nd Canadian Siege Battery*. Self-published, 1966.

Smith, W.R. *New War Songs*. 1914.

Song Sheet music, 19770069-005, 19870069-005

Young Men's Christian Association of Canada, *Songs for Soldiers*. 1914.

Canadian War Museum, Military History Research Centre, Trench Newspapers

Action Front!; *Another Garland from the Front*; *The Brazier*; *The Canadian Machine Gunner*; *The Canadian Sapper*; *The Dead Horse Corner Gazette*; *The Forty-Niner*; *In and Out*; *The Iodine Chronicle*; *The Kilt*; *La Vie Canadienne*; *The Listening Post*; *The Message from Mars*; *Now and Then*; *N.Y.D.*; *On Service*; *The O.Pip*; *R.M.R. Growler*; *The Silent 60th*; *The Sling*; *The Splint Record*; *The Strafer*; *Tank Tatler*; *Trench Echo*; *The Twentieth Gazette*; *Vic's Patrol*; *The Western Scot*; .

Directorate of History and Heritage Archives

Leslie Arthur Catchpole papers

Edwin Pye papers

McGill University Archives

Hugh Urquhart papers

University of British Columbia Archives

Jack Stickney papers

Published Government Documents

Adami, J. George. *The War Story of the* CAMC. Toronto: Canadian War Records Office, 1918.

Canada in Khaki: A Tribute to the Offices and Men Now Serving in the Canadian Expeditionary Force. London: Canadian War Records Office, 1917.

Report of the Ministry. *Overseas Military Force of Canada, 1918.* London: Printed by authority of the Ministry, Overseas Military Forces of Canada, 1919.

Report of the War Office Committee of Enquiry into "Shell Shock" 1922. Crawley: Imperial War Museum, 2004.

Newspapers and Media

Blackadder IV. Episode 4—"Private Plane." BBC, 1989.

The Globe and Mail; *The Legionary*; *Maclean's*; *Toronto Star*; *The Veteran.*

Monty Python. "Fighting Each Other" sketch. *The Meaning of Life.* Film. The Monty Python Partnerships, 1982.

Websites

1914–1918 online—International Encyclopedia of the First World War: http://www.1914-1918-online.net

Canada's Great War Album: http://greatwaralbum.ca/Great-War-Album/About-the-Great-War/Unrest-on-the-homefront/Francis-Cumming

CEF Study Group: http://cefresearch.ca

Directorate of History and Heritage, Victoria Cross Gallery: http://www.cmp-cpm.forces.gc.ca/dhh-dhp/gal/vcg-gcv/index-eng.asp

Virtual Gramophone: Canadian Historical Sound Recordings: https://www.bac-lac.gc.ca/eng/discover/films-videos-sound-recordings/virtual-gramophone/Pages/virtual-gramophone.aspx

Canadian Images and Letters Project

George Adkins; Alfred Andrews; James Balfour; *Cobourg World*; Frank Cousins; Bertram Cox; William Howard Curtis; Alexander Decoteau; Cecil and Louis Duff; Herbert Durand; Albert Fereday; Kenneth Walter Foster; Wilbert Gilroy; Robert Hale; Herbert Irwin; Bill Hutchinson; T.W. Johnson; George Hedley Kempling; Lakefield College School Collection; Thomas Clark Lapp; MacKinnon family; Amos William Mayse; David McLean; William John McLellan; Jay Batiste Moyer; Andrew John Napier; Wallace

Reid; Charles Henry Savage; Harold Simpson; John Sudbury; Ernest Taylor; Charles Willoughby; Andrew Wilson

Articles

Abram, Zachary. "Canon Fodder: The Canadian Canon and the Erasure of Great War Narratives," in Kellen Kurschinski, et al. (eds.) *The Great War: From Memory to History* (Waterloo: Wilfrid Laurier University Press, 2015) 17–36.

Barrett Frederick S., et al. "Music-Evoked Nostalgia: Affect, Memory, and Personality," *Emotion* 10.3 (2010) 390–403.

Becker, Annette. "Graffiti et sculptures des soldat," *14/18 Aujourd'hui—Today—Heute* 2 (1999) 117–27.

Boxwell, David A. "The Follies of War: Cross-Dressing and Popular Theatre on the British Front Lines, 1914–18," *Modernism/modernity* 9.1 (January 2002) 1–20.

Brown, Eric and Tim Cook. "The 1936 Vimy Pilgrimage," *Canadian Military History* 20.2 (Spring 2011) 37–54.

Broznitsky, Peter. "For King, Not Tsar: Identifying Ukrainians in the Canadian Expeditionary Force, 1914–1918," *Canadian Military History* 17.3 (Summer 2008) 21–30.

Bryant, Chad. "The Language of Resistance? Czech Jokes and Joke-telling under Nazi Occupation, 1943–45," *Journal of Contemporary History* 41.1 (2006) 133–51.

Bryant, Mark. "Crusader, White Rabbit or Organ-Grinder's Monkey? Leslie Illingworth and the British Political Cartoon in World War II," *European Studies* 31.123 (2001) 345–66.

Cary, Jr., Melbert B. "Mademoiselle from Armentières," *The Journal of American Folklore* 47.186 (October–December 1934) 369–76.

Chaktsiris, Mary. "'Our Boys with the Maple Leaf on Their Shoulders and Straps': Masculinity, the Toronto Press, and the Outbreak of the South African War, 1899," *War and Society* 32.1 (2013) 3–25.

Clarke, David. "Rumours of Angels: A Legend of the First World War," *Folklore* 113.2 (2002) 151–75.

Clarke, Nic, John Cranfield, and Kris Inwood. "Fighting Fit? Diet,

Disease, and Disability in the Canadian Expeditionary Force, 1914–18," *War & Society* 33.2 (May 2014) 80–97.

Clifton, Brett. "The Experiences of Lethbridge Men Overseas, 1914–1918," in Adriana A. Davies and Jeff Keshen (eds.) *The Frontier of Patriotism: Alberta and the First World War* (Calgary: University of Calgary Press, 2016) 81–92.

Cook, Tim. "Battles of the Imagined Past: Canada's Great War and Memory," *Canadian Historical Review* 95.3 (2014) 414–23.

Cook, Tim. "The Butcher and the Madman: Sir Arthur Currie, Sir Sam Hughes and the War of Reputations," *Canadian Historical Review* 85.4 (December 2004) 693–719.

Cook, Tim. "Canada's Great War on Film: *Lest We Forget* (1935)," *Canadian Military History* 14.3 (Summer 2005) 5–20.

Cook, Tim. "Documenting War and Forging Reputations: Sir Max Aitken and the Canadian War Records Office in the First World War," *War in History* 10.3 (July 2003) 265–95.

Cook, Tim. "Dr. Jekyll and Mr. Hyde: Canadian Medical Officers in the Great War," in Stephen C. Craig and Dale C. Smith (eds.) *Glimpsing Modernity: Military Medicine in World War I* (Cambridge: Cambridge Scholars Publishing, 2016) 34–59.

Cook, Tim. "From Destruction to Construction: The Khaki University of Canada, 1917–1919," *Journal of Canadian Studies* 37.1 (Spring 2002) 109–43.

Cook, Tim. "'He was determined to go': Underage Soldiers in the Canadian Expeditionary Force," *Histoire sociale/Social History* 41.81 (May 2008) 41–74.

Cook, Tim. "'I will meet the world with a smile and a joke': Canadian Soldiers' Humour in the Great War," *Canadian Military History* 22.2 (Spring 2013) 48–62.

Cook, Tim. "Immortalizing the Canadian Soldier: Lord Beaverbrook and the Canadian War Records Office in the First World War," in Briton C. Busch (ed.) *Canada and the Great War: Western Front Association Papers* (Montreal and Kingston: McGill-Queen's University Press, 2003) 46–65.

Cook, Tim. "Literary Memorials: The Great War Regimental Histories, 1919–1939," *Journal of the Canadian Historical Association* (2002) 167–90.

Cook, Tim. "'More as a medicine than a beverage': 'Demon Rum' and the Canadian Trench Soldier in the First World War," *Canadian Military History*, 9.1 (Winter 2000) 7–22.

Cook, Tim. "The Politics of Surrender: Canadian Soldiers and the Killing of Prisoners in the Great War," *Journal of Military History* 70.3 (July 2006) 637–65.

Cook, Tim, ed. "The Top 10 Most Important Books of Canadian Military History," *Canadian Military History* 18.4 (Autumn 2009) 65–74.

Cook, Tim. "Wet Canteens and Worrying Mothers: Soldiers and Temperance Groups in the Great War," *Histoire sociale/Social History* 35.70 (June 2003) 311–30.

Cook, Tim and William Stewart. "Death in the Canadian Expeditionary Force," *1914–18 International Encyclopedia of the First World War*. http://www.1914-1918-online.net

Cooter, Roger. "Malingering in Modernity: Psychological Scripts and Adversarial Encounters During the First World War," in Roger Cooter, et al. (eds.) *War, Medicine and Modernity* (Stroud, UK: Sutton Publishing, 1998).

Cowman, Krista. "Touring behind the Lines: British Soldiers in French Towns and Cities during the Great War," *Urban History* 41.1 (2014) 105–23.

Curran, James. "'Bonjoor Paree!' The First AIF in Paris, 1916–1918," *Journal of Australian Studies* 23.60 (1999) 18–26.

Dagg, Anne Innis. "Memoir of Harold Adams Innis Covering the years 1894–1922," *Canadian Journal of Communication* 29.2 (2004).

Daughton, James P. "Sketches of the *Poilu*'s World: Trench Cartoons from the Great War," in Douglas Mackaman and Michael Mays (eds.) *World War I and the Cultures of Modernity* (Jackson: University Press of Mississippi, 2000) 35–67.

Dempsey, L. James. "Aboriginal Alberta and the First World War," in Adriana A. Davies and Jeff Keshen (eds.) *The Frontier of Patriotism:*

Alberta and the First World War (Calgary: University of Calgary Press, 2016) 51–70.

Dugas, Théodore. "Un Acadien à la Première Guerre Mondiale," *La Revue d'histoire de la Societe historique Nicolas-Denys* 20.3 (September–December 1992).

Farrugia, Peter. "A Small Truce in a Big War: The Historial de la Grande Guerre and the Interplay of History and Memory," *Canadian Military History* 22.2 (Spring 2013) 63–76.

Ferguson, Niall. "Prisoner Taking and Prisoner Killing in the Age of Total War: Towards a Political Economy of Military Defeat," *War in History* 11.2 (2004) 148–92.

Forrester, John. "'Mille e tre': Freud and Collecting," in John Elsner and Roger Cardinal (eds.) *The Cultures of Collecting* (London: Reaktion Books, 1994) 224–51.

Freud, Sigmund. "The Uncanny," *Art and Literature, Pelican Freud Library*, v. 14. Translated by James Strachey (Harmondsworth, UK: Penguin, 1985) 335–76.

Garton, Stephen. "Longing for War: Nostalgia and the Australian Returned Soldiers after the First World War," in T.G. Ashplant, et al. (eds.) *The Politics of War Memory and Commemoration* (London: Routledge, 2000) 222–39.

Gibson, K. Craig. "'My Chief Source of Worry': An Assistant Provost Marshal's View of Relations between 2nd Canadian Division and Local Inhabitants on the Western Front, 1915–1917," *War in History* 7.4 (October 2000) 413–41.

Gibson, K. Craig. "Sex and Soldiering in France and Flanders: The British Expeditionary Force along the Western Front, 1914–1918," *The International History Review* 23 (September 2001) 535–79.

Habeck, Mary R. "Technology in the First World War: The View from Below," in Jay Winter et al. (eds.) *The Great War and the Twentieth Century* (New Haven: Yale University Press, 2000) 99–131.

Hanna, Emma. "'When Words Are Not Enough': The Aural Landscape of Britain's Modern Memory of 1914–18," in Angela K. Smith and

Krista Cowman (eds.) *Landscapes and Voices in the Great War* (London: Routledge, 2017) 41–57.

Harrison, Simon. "Skull Trophies of the Pacific War: Transgressive Objects of Remembrance," *Journal of the Royal Anthropological Institute* 12.4 (December 2006) 817–36.

Haycock, Ronald G. "The American Legion in the Canadian Expeditionary Force, 1914–1917: A Study in Failure," *Military Affairs* 43.3 (October 1979) 115–19.

Heron, Craig. "The Boys and Their Booze: Masculinities and Public Drinking in Working-Class Hamilton, 1890–1946," *The Canadian Historical Review* 86.3 (September 2005) 411–52.

Hiley, Nicholas. "'You Can't Believe a Word You Read': Newspaper-Reading in the British Expeditionary Force, 1914–1918," *Media History* 2.1–2 (1994) 89–102.

Holman, Valerie and Debra Kelly. "War in the Twentieth Century: The Functioning of Humour in Cultural Representation," *European Studies* 31 (2001) 247–63.

Holt, Richard. "British Blood Calls British Blood: The British-Canadian Recruiting Mission of 1917–1918," *Canadian Military History* 22.1 (2013) 27–37.

Horrall, Andrew. "Charlie Chaplin and the Canadian Expeditionary Force," in Briton C. Busch (ed.) *Canada and the Great War: Western Front Association Papers* (Montreal and Kingston: McGill-Queen's University Press, 2003) 27–45.

Horrall, Andrew. "'Keep-a-Fighting! Play the Game!' Baseball and the Canadian Forces During the First World War," *Canadian Military History* 10.2 (Spring 2001) 27–40.

Humphries, Mark. "Between Commemoration and History: The Historiography of the Canadian Corps and Military Overseas," *Canadian Historical Review* 95.4 (September 2014) 384–97.

Humphries, Mark. "War's Long Shadow: Masculinity, Medicine and the Gendered Politics of Trauma, 1914–1939," *Canadian Historical Review* 91.3 (2010) 503–31.

Humphries, Mark. "Wilfully and with Intent: Self-Inflicted Wounds and the Negotiation of Power in the Trenches," *Histoire sociale/Social History* 47.94 (June 2014) 369–97.

Iacobelli, Teresa. "From Armistice to Remembrance: The Continuing Evolution of Remembrance Day in Canada," in Matthew Hayday and Raymond B. Blake (eds.) *Celebrating Canada: Holidays, National Days, and the Crafting of Identities* (Toronto: University of Toronto Press, 2016) 171–90.

Irving, J.A. "The Psychological Analysis of Wartime Rumour Patterns in Canada," *Bulletin of the Canadian Psychological Association* 3 (1943) 40–4.

Kerr, Alan and Doug Styles. "Private Stephen Smith and His Trench Art Belts," in Adriana A. Davies and Jeff Keshen (eds.) *The Frontier of Patriotism: Alberta and the First World War* (Calgary: University of Calgary Press, 2016) 197–200.

Keshen, Jeff. "The Great War Soldier as Nation Builder in Canada and Australia," in Briton C. Busch (ed.) *Canada and the Great War: Western Front Association Papers* (Montreal and Kingston: McGill-Queen's University Press, 2003) 3–26.

Keshen, Jeff. "Voices of War: The Press and the Personal," in Adriana A. Davies and Jeff Keshen (eds.) *The Frontier of Patriotism: Alberta and the First World War* (Calgary: University of Calgary Press, 2016) 287–96.

Layman, Peter. "The Fraternal Bond as a Joking Relationship," in Michael S. Kimmel and Michael A. Messner (eds.), *Men's Lives* (New York: Macmillan Publishing Company, 1992) 143–54.

Le Naour, Jean-Yves. "Laughter and Tears in the Great War: The Need for Laughter/The Guilt of Humour," *European Studies* 31 (2001) 265–75.

Lenton-Young, G. "Variety Theatre," in A. Saddlemyer (ed.) *Early Stages: Theatre in Ontario, 1800–1914* (Toronto: University of Toronto Press, 1990) 166–213.

Lyons, Martin. "French Soldiers and their Correspondence: Towards a History of Writing Practices in the First World War," *French History* 17.1 (2003) 79–95.

Mackenzie, S.P. "Vox Populi: British Army Newspapers in the Second World War," *Journal of Contemporary History*, 24.4 (1989) 665–81.

Madigan, Edward. "'Sticking to a Hateful Task': Resilience, Humour, and British Understandings of Combatant Courage, 1914–1918," *War in History* 20 (2013) 76–98.

Martin, Ged. "Sir John Eh? Macdonald: Recovering A Voice from History," *British Journal of Canadian Studies* XVII (2004) 117–24.

Martin, Jean. "Francophone Enlistment in the Canadian Expeditionary Force, 1914–1918: The Evidence," *Canadian Military History* 25.1 (2016) 1–12.

Maunder, Andrew. "'Funny Men and Charming Girls': Revue and the Theatrical Landscape of 1914–1918," in Angela K. Smith and Krista Cowman (eds.) *Landscapes and Voices in the Great War* (London: Routledge, 2017) 19–40.

Morin-Pelletier, Mélanie. "'The Anxious Waiting Ones at Home': Deux familles canadiennes plongées dans le tourment de la Grande Guerre," *Histoire sociale/Social History* 47.94 (2014) 353–68.

Morin-Pelletier, Mélanie. "French Canada and the War," *1914–18 International Encyclopedia of the First World War.* http://www.1914-1918-online.net

Morton, Desmond. "A Canadian Soldier in the Great War: The Experiences of Frank Maheux," *Canadian Military History* 1.1–2 (1992) 79–89.

Morton, Desmond and Glenn Wright, "The Bonus Campaign, 1919–21: Veterans and the Campaign for Re-establishment," *Canadian Historical Review* 64.2 (1983) 147–67.

Mullen, John. "War Memory in British Soldier Songs of the First World War," Stéphanie A.H. Bélanger and Renée Dickason (eds.) *War Memories: Commemoration, Recollections, and Writings on War* (Montreal and Kingston: McGill-Queen's University Press, 2017) 257–75.

Murray, Captain W.W. "The Trench Magazine," *Canadian Defence Quarterly* 5.3 (April 1928).

Nelson, Robert. "Soldier Newspapers: A Useful Source in the Social and Cultural History of the First World War and Beyond," *War in History* 17.2 (2010) 167–91.

O'Neill, Patrick B. "The Canadian Concert Party in France," *Theatre Research in Canada* 4.2 (Fall 1983) 192–208.

Pearce, Susan M. "Objects as Meaning; or Narrating the Past," in Susan M. Pearce (ed.) *Interpreting Objects and Collections* (London: Routledge, 1994) 19–29.

Podruchny, Carolyn. "Werewolves and Windigos: Narratives of Cannibal Monster in French-Canadian Voyageur Oral Tradition," *Ethnohistory* 51. 4 (Fall 2004) 677–700.

Rachamimov, Alon. "The Disruptive Comforts of Drag: (Trans) Gender Performances among Prisoners of War in Russia, 1914–1920," *The American Historical Review* 111.2 (April 2006) 362–82.

Riedi, Eliza and Tony Mason. "'Leather' and the Fighting Spirit: Sport in the British Army in World War I," *Canadian Journal of History* 41.3 (2006) 485–516.

Rhoades, Michelle K. "Renegotiating French Masculinity: Medicine and Venereal Disease during the Great War," *French Historical Studies* 29.2 (2006) 293–327.

Rodger, Andrew C. "Amateur Photography by Soldiers of the Canadian Expeditionary Force," *Archivaria* 26 (Summer 1988) 163–8.

Roper, Michael. "Maternal Relations: Moral Manliness and Emotional Survival in Letters Home during the First World War," in Stefan Dudink, et al. (eds.) *Masculinities in Politics and War: Gendering Modern History* (Manchester: Manchester University Press, 2004) 295–316.

Sauerteig, Lutz D.H. "Sex, Medicine and Morality during the First World War," in Roger Cooter, et al. (eds.) *War, Medicine and Modernity* (Stroud, UK: Sutton Publishing, 1998).

Saunders, Nicholas J. "Culture, Conflict and Materiality: The Social Lives of Great War Objects," in Bernard Finn and Barton C. Hacker (eds.) *Materializing the Military* (Baltimore: Johns Hopkins University Press, 2005) 77–94.

Seal, Graham. "'Written in the trenches': Trench Newspapers of the First World War," *Journal of the Australian War Memorial* 16 (April 1990) 30–8.

Sharpe, Chris. "Enlistment in the Canadian Expeditionary Force 1914–1918: A Re-Evaluation," *Canadian Military History* 24.1 (2015) 17–60.

Shaw, Amy. "The Boer War, Masculinity, and Citizenship in Canada, 1899–1902," in Patrizia Gentile and Jane Nicholas (eds.) *Contesting Bodies and Nation in Canadian History* (Toronto: University of Toronto Press, 2013) 97–114.

Souchen, Alex. "The Culture of Morale: Battalion Newspapers in the 3rd Canadian Infantry Division, June–August 1944," *Journal of Military History* 77 (April 2013) 523–56.

Steckley, John and Brian Cummins. "Pegahmagabow of Parry Island: From Jenness Informant to Individual," *Canadian Journal of Native Studies*, 25.1 (2005) 35–50.

Story, Eric. "'The Awakening Has Come': Canadian First Nations in the Great War Era, 1914–1932," *Canadian Military History* 24.2 (2015) 11–35.

Vance, Jonathan. "An Open Door to a Better Future: The Memory of Canada's Second World War," in Geoffrey Hayes, Mike Bechthold, and Matt Symes (eds.) *Canada and the Second World War: Essays in Honour of Terry Copp* (Waterloo: Wilfrid Laurier University Press, 2012) 461–77.

Vance, Jonathan. "Provincial Patterns of Enlistment in the Canadian Expeditionary Force," *Canadian Military History* 17.2 (Spring 2008) 75–8.

Vance, Jonathan. "The Soldier as Novelist: Literature, History and the Great War," *Canadian Literature: A Quarterly of Criticism and Review* 179 (Winter 2003) 22–37.

Vance, Jonathan. "'Today they were alive again': The Canadian Corps Reunion of 1934," *Ontario History Magazine* 87.4 (December 1995) 327–44.

Warby, Mark. "If you know of a better medal . . ." *Medal News* (October 2017) 23–4.

White, Joseph Robert. "'Even in Auschwitz . . . Humanity Could Prevail': British POWs and Jewish Concentration-Camp Inmates at IG Auschwitz, 1943–1945," *Holocaust and Genocide Studies* 15.2 (2001) 266–95.

Whittingham, Clare. "Mnemonics for War: Trench Art and the Reconciliation of Public and Private Memory," *Past Imperfect* 14 (2008) 86–119.

Wilkinson, Alan. "Changing English Attitudes to Death in the Two World Wars," in Peter C. Jupp and Glennys Howarth (eds.) *The Changing Face of Death: Historical Accounts of Death and Disposal* (London: Macmillan Press, 1997) 149–63.

Wilson, Ross. "The Burial of the Dead: the British Army on the Western Front, 1914–18," *War & Society* 31.1 (March 2012) 22–41.

Winter, Jay. "Popular Culture in Wartime Britain," in Aviel Roshwald and Richard Stites (eds.) *European Culture in the Great War: The Arts, Entertainment and Propaganda, 1914–1918* (Cambridge: Cambridge University Press, 1999) 330–48.

Monographs and Books

Acton, Carol. *Grief in Wartime Private Pain, Public Discourse*. New York: Palgrave Macmillan, 2007.

Allport, Gordon W. and Leo Postman. *The Psychology of Rumour*. New York: Henry Holt, 1947.

Arthur, Max. *When This Bloody War Is Over: Soldiers Songs of the First World War*. London: Piatkus, 2001.

Ashworth, Tony. *Trench Warfare, 1914–1918: The Live and Let Live System*. London: Macmillan, 1980.

Audoin-Rouzeau, Stéphane. *Men at War 1914–1918: National Sentiment and Trench Journalism in France during the First World War*. Translated by Helen McPhail. Providence, Rhode Island: Berg, 1992.

Barr, Niall. *The Lion and the Poppy: British Veterans, Politics and Society, 1921–1939*. Westport, Connecticut: Praeger, 2005.

Beattie, Kim. *48th Highlanders of Canada, 1891–1928*. Toronto: 48th Highlanders of Canada, 1932.

SELECT BIBLIOGRAPHY

Beckett, Ian F.W. *The Great War, 1914–18*. New York: Longman, 2001.

Bercuson, David J. *The Patricias: The Proud History of a Fighting Regiment*. Toronto: Stoddart, 2001.

Bercuson, David Jay. *True Patriot: The Life of Brooke Claxton, 1898–1960*. Toronto: University of Toronto Press, 1993.

Berger, Carl. *The Sense of Power: Studies in the Ideas of Canadian Imperialism*. Toronto: University of Toronto Press, 1970.

Betts, Amanda, ed. *In Flanders Fields: 100 Years: Writing on War, Loss and Remembrance*. Toronto: Alfred A. Knopf, 2015.

Bishop, Charles. *The Canadian YMCA in the Great War: The Official Record of the Activities of the Canadian YMCA in Connection with the Great War of 1914–1918*. Toronto: National Council of Young Men's Christian Associations of Canada, 1924.

Blatherwick, Surgeon Commander F.J. *Canadian Orders, Decorations, and Medals*. Toronto: The Unitrade Press, 1994.

Bodnar, John. *The "Good War" in American Memory*. Baltimore: The Johns Hopkins University Press, 2010.

Bond, Brian. *The Unquiet Western Front: Britain's Role in Literature and History*. Cambridge: Cambridge University Press, 2002.

Booth, Allyson. *Postcards from the Trenches: Negotiating the Space between Modernism and the First World War*. Toronto: Oxford University Press, 1996.

Bourke, Joanna. *Dismembering the Male: Men's Bodies, Britain and the Great War*. London: Reaktion Books, 1999.

Bowker, Alan. *A Time Such as There Never Was Before: Canada After the Great War*. Toronto: Dundurn Publishers, 2014.

Brandon, Laura. *Art or Memorial?: The Forgotten History of Canada's War Art*. Calgary: University of Calgary, 2006.

Brophy, John and Eric Partridge, eds. *Songs and Slang of the British Soldier: 1914–1918*. London: E. Partridge, 1931.

Brown, Malcolm. *Tommy Goes to War*. Charleston: Tempus Publishing, 2001.

Buckner, Phillip and R. Douglas Francis, eds. *Rediscovering the British World*. Calgary: University of Calgary Press, 2005.

Burke, Peter. *What Is Cultural History?* Cambridge: Polity Press, 2004.

Buse, Peter and Andrew Stott, eds. *Ghosts: Deconstruction, Psychoanalysis, History*. Basingstoke, UK: Palgrave Macmillan, 1999.

Carden-Coybe, Ana. *The Politics of Wounds: Military Patients and Medical Power in the First World War*. Oxford: Oxford University Press, 2014.

Carmichael, Jane. *First World War Photographers*. London: Routledge, 1989.

Carrington, Hereward. *Psychic Phenomena and the War*. New York: American Universities Publishing Company, 1919.

Cassel, Jay. *The Secret Plague: Venereal Disease in Canada, 1838–1939*. University of Toronto Press, 1987.

Champion, Christian P. *The Strange Demise of British Canada: The Liberals and Canadian Nationalism, 1964–68*. Montreal and Kingston: McGill-Queen's University Press, 2010.

Chasseaud, Peter. *Rat's Alley: Trench Names of the Western Front, 1914–1918*. Gloucestershire: Spellmount, 2006.

Cinq-Mars, Marcelle. *L'écho du Front: Journaux de Tranchées, 1915–1919*. Outremont, Quebec: Athéna Éditions, 2008.

Clarke, David. *The Angel of Mons: Phantom Stories and Ghostly Guardians*. West Sussex: Wiley, 2004.

Clarke, Nic. *Unwanted Warriors: The Rejected Volunteers of the Canadian Expeditionary Force*. Vancouver: University of British Columbia Press, 2015.

Cleveland, Les. *Dark Laughter: War in Song and Popular Culture*. Westport, Connecticut: Praeger, 1994.

Clout, Hugh. *After the Ruins: Restoring the Countryside of Northern France after the Great War*. Exeter: University of Exeter Press, 1996.

Clyne, Henry Randolph Notman. *Vancouver's 29th: A Chronicle of the 29th in Flanders Fields*. Vancouver: Tobin's Tiger Association, 1964.

Cook, Tim. *At the Sharp End: Canadians Fighting the Great War 1914 to 1916, Volume One*. Toronto: Viking Canada, 2007.

Cook, Tim. *Clio's Warriors: Canadian Historians and the Writing of the World Wars*. Vancouver: University of British Columbia Press, 2006.

Cook, Tim. *Fight to the Finish: Canadians Fighting the Second World War 1944–1945*. Toronto: Allen Lane, 2015.

Cook, Tim. *The Madman and the Butcher: The Sensational Wars of Sam Hughes and General Arthur Currie*. Toronto: Allen Lane, 2011.

Cook, Tim. *No Place to Run: The Canadian Corps and Gas Warfare in the First World War*. Vancouver: University of British Columbia Press, 1999.

Cook, Tim. *Shock Troops: Canadians Fighting the Great War 1917–1918, Volume Two*. Toronto: Viking Canada, 2009.

Cook, Tim. *Vimy: The Battle and the Legend*. Toronto: Allen Lane, 2017.

Copp, Terry. *The Anatomy of Poverty: The Condition of the Working Class in Montreal, 1897–1929*. Toronto: Oxford University Press, 1974.

Corrigall, Major D.J. *The History of the Twentieth Canadian Battalion (Central Ontario Regiment) Canadian Expeditionary Force: In the Great War, 1914–1918*. Toronto: Stone and Cox Ltd., 1936.

Crerar, Duff. *Padres in No Man's Land: Canadian Chaplains and the Great War*. Montreal and Kingston: McGill-Queen's University Press, 1995.

Dancocks, Daniel G. *Gallant Canadians: The Story of the Tenth Canadian Infantry Battalion, 1914–1919*. Calgary: Calgary Highlanders Regimental Funds Foundation, 1990.

Dancocks, Daniel G. *Sir Arthur Currie: A Biography*. Toronto: Methuen, 1987.

Das, Santanu. *Touch and Intimacy in First World War Literature*. Cambridge: Cambridge University Press, 2005.

Dickson, Paul. *War Slang: American Fighting Words and Phrases since the Civil War*. Washington: Potomac Books, 2003.

Douglas, Allen. *War, Memory, and the Politics of Humor: The* Canard Enchaîné *and World War I*. Oakland: University of California Press, 2002.

Downing, W.H. *Digger Dialects: A Collection of Slang Phrases Used by the Australian Soldiers on Active Service*. Sydney: Lothian Publishing, 1919.

Duffet, Rachel. *The Stomach for Fighting: Food and the Soldiers of the First World War*. Manchester: Manchester University Press, 2012.

Durflinger, Serge. *Veterans with a Vision: Canada's War Blinded in Peace and War*. Vancouver: University of British Columbia Press, 2010.

Eastman, Carol. *Aspects of Language and Culture*. San Francisco: Chandler and Sharp, 1975.

Edwards, John. *Language, Society and Identity*. Toronto: Oxford University Press, 1985.

Eksteins, Modris. *Rites of Spring: The Great War and the Birth of the Modern Age*. Toronto: Lester & Orpen Dennys, 1994.

Ellis, John. *Eye-Deep in Hell*. London: Croom Helm, 1976.

Engen, Robert. *Strangers in Arms: Combat Motivation in the Canadian Army, 1943–1945*. Montreal and Kingston: McGill-Queen's University Press, 2016.

England, Robert. *Discharged: A Commentary on Civil Re-establishment of Veterans in Canada*. Toronto: The Macmillan Company of Canada, 1943.

Fetherstonhaugh, R.C. *The Royal Montreal Regiment, 14th Battalion, C.E.F., 1914–1925*. Montreal: Gazette Print Co. Limited, 1927.

Fowke, Edith, ed. *The Penguin Book of Canadian Folk Songs*. Harmondsworth, UK: Penguin Books, 1973.

Fox, James. *British Art and the First World War, 1914–1924*. Cambridge: Cambridge University Press, 2015.

Frayn, Andrew. *Writing Disenchantment: British First World War Prose, 1914–1930*. Manchester: Manchester University Press, 2014.

Frost, Leslie. *Fighting Men*. Toronto: Clark, Irwin and Company, 1967.

Fuller, J.G. *Troop Morale and Popular Culture in the British and Dominion Armies, 1914–1918*. Oxford: Clarendon Press, 1990.

Fussell, Paul. *The Great War and Modern Memory*. New York: Oxford University Press, 1975.

Giddings, Robert. *The War Poets*. New York: Orion Books, 1988.

Girard, Marion. *A Strange and Formidable Weapon: British Responses to World War I Poison Gas*. Lincoln: University of Nebraska Press, 2008.

Gould, L.M. *From B.C. to Baisieux: Being the Narrative of the 102nd Battalion*. Victoria: Thos. R. Cusack Presses, 1919.

Grace, Sherrill. *Landscapes of War and Memory: The Two World Wars in Canadian Literature and the Arts, 1977–2007*. Edmonton: University of Alberta Press, 2014.

Granatstein, J.L. *The Greatest Victory: Canada's One Hundred Days, 1918*. Don Mills: Oxford University Press, 2014.

Granatstein, J.L. and J.M. Hitsman. *Broken Promises: A History of Conscription in Canada*. Toronto: Oxford University Press, 1977.

Gwyn, Sandra. *Tapestry of War: A Private View of Canadians in the Great War*. Toronto: HarperCollins, 1992.

Hall, Catherine and Sonya Rose, eds. *At Home with the Empire: Metropolitan Culture and the Imperial World*. Cambridge: Cambridge University Press, 2006.

Halliday, Hugh. *Valour Reconsidered: Inquiries into the Victoria Cross and Other Awards for Extreme Bravery*. Toronto: Robin Brass Studio, 2006.

Hammond, Michael. *The Big Show: British Cinema Culture in the Great War*. Exeter: University of Exeter Press, 2006.

Hararl, Yuval Noah. *The Ultimate Experience: Battlefield Revelations and the Making of Modern War Culture*. New York: Palgrave, 2008.

Hayes, Adrian. *Pegahmagabow: Legendary Warrior, Forgotten Hero*. Huntsville: Fox Meadow Creations, 2003.

Hayes, Joseph. *The Eighty-Fifth in France and Flanders*. Halifax: Royal Print & Litho Limited, 1920.

Hayward, James. *Myths & Legends of the First World War*. Oxford: Oxford University Press, 2005.

Hodder-Williams, Ralph. *Princess Patricia's Canadian Light Infantry, 1914–1919*. Toronto: Hodder and Stoughton, 1923.

Hodgkinson, Peter E. "*Glum Heroes*": *Hardship, Fear and Death—Resilience and Coping in the British Army on the Western Front 1914–1918*. England: Helion & Company Limited, 2016.

Holmes, Richard. *Firing Line*. London: Pimlico, 1994.

Holmes, Richard. *Tommy: The British Soldier on the Western Front 1914–1918*. London: HarperCollins, 2004.

Holt, Richard. *Filling the Ranks: Manpower in the Canadian Expeditionary Force, 1914–1918*. Montreal and Kingston: McGill-Queen's University Press, 2016.

Holt, Tonie and Valmai, eds. *The Best of Fragments from France by Capt. Bruce Bairnsfather*. London: Phin Publishing, 1978.

Holt, Tonie and Valmai, eds. *In Search of the Better 'Ole: The Life, the Works and the Collectables of Bruce Bairnsfather*. Toronto: Fitzhenry & Whiteside, 1985.

Horne, John and Alan Kramer. *German Atrocities, 1914: A History of Denial*. New Haven: Yale University Press, 2001.

Hou, Charles and Cynthia. *Great Canadian Political Cartoons, 1820 to 1914*. Vancouver: Moody's Lookout Press, 1997.

Hughes, Geoffrey. *An Encyclopedia of Swearing: The Social History of Oaths, Profanity, Foul Language, And Ethnic Slurs in the English-speaking World*. New York: M.E. Sharpe, 2006.

Hughes, Geoffrey. *Swearing: A Social History of Foul Language, Oaths and Profanity in English*. London: Blackwell, 1991.

Hynes, Samuel. *The Soldiers' Tale: Bearing Witness to Modern War*. New York: Allen Lane, 1997.

Hynes, Samuel. *A War Imagined: The First World War and English Culture*. London: Bodley Head, 1990.

Iacobelli, Teresa. *Death or Deliverance: Canadian Courts Martial in the Great War*. Vancouver: University of British Columbia Press, 2013.

Iarocci, Andrew. *Shoestring Soldiers: The First Canadian Division at War, 1914–1915*. Toronto: University of Toronto Press, 2008.

Ito, Roy. *We Went to War: The Story of the Japanese Canadians who Served During the First and Second World Wars*. Stittsville, Ontario: Canada's Wings, 1984.

Jalland, Pat. *Death in War and Peace: A History of Loss and Grief in England, 1914–1970*. Oxford: Oxford University Press, 2010.

Jones, B. and B. Howell. *Popular Arts of the First World War*. London: Studio Vista Blue Star House, 1972.

Kammen, Michael. *Mystic Chords of Memory: The Transformation of Tradition in American Culture*. New York: Vintage Books, 1993.

Keshen, Jeff. *Propaganda and Censorship during Canada's Great War.* Edmonton: University of Alberta Press, 1996.

Keshen, Jeff. *Saints, Sinners and Soldiers: Canada's Second World War.* Vancouver: University of British Columbia Press, 2004.

Kimball, Jane A. *Trench Art: An Illustrated History.* Davis: Silverpenny Press, 2004.

King, Anthony, ed. *Frontline: Combat and Cohesion in the Twenty-First Century.* Oxford: Oxford University Press, 2015.

Laugesen, Amanda. *"Boredom is the Enemy": The Intellectual and Imaginative Lives of Australian Soldiers in the Great War and Beyond.* Surrey: Ashgate, 2012.

Lloyd, David William. *Battlefield Tourism: Pilgrimage and the Commemoration of the Great War in Britain, Australia and Canada, 1919–1939.* Oxford: Berg, 1998.

Lowenthal, David. *The Past Is a Foreign Country.* Cambridge: Cambridge University Press, 1985.

Mackenzie, S.P. *Flying against Fate: Superstitions and Allied Aircrews in World War II.* Kansas: University Press of Kansas, 2017.

Maeland, Bard and Paul Otto Brunstad. *Enduring Military Boredom from 1750 to the Present.* Basingstoke, UK: Palgrave Macmillan, 2009.

Mantle, Craig Leslie, ed. *The Unwilling and the Reluctant: Theoretical Perspectives on Disobedience in the Military.* Kingston: Canadian Defence Agency Press, 2006.

Marlin, Randal. *Propaganda and the Ethics of Persuasion.* Peterborough: Broadview Press, 2002.

McGowan, Mark. *The Imperial Irish: Canada's Irish Catholics Fight the Great War, 1914–1918.* Montreal and Kingston: McGill-Queen's University Press, 2017.

McKee, Alexander. *Vimy Ridge.* London: Pan Books, 1968.

McMullin, Stan. *Anatomy of a Séance: A History of Spirit Communication in Central Canada.* Montreal and Kingston: McGill-Queen's University Press, 2004.

McWilliams, James and R. James Steel. *The Suicide Battalion.* Edmonton: Hurtig, 1978.

Meyer, Jessica. *Men of War: Masculinity and the First World War in Britain*. New York: Palgrave Macmillan, 2009.

Millman, Brock. *Polarity, Patriotism, and Dissent in Great War Canada, 1914–1919*. Toronto: University of Toronto Press, 2016.

Montagu, Ashley. *The Anatomy of Swearing*. Philadelphia: University of Pennsylvania Press, 2001.

Moogk, Edward. *Roll Back the Years: History of Canadian Recorded Sound and Its Legacy*. Ottawa: National Library of Canada, 1975.

Lord Moran, *The Anatomy of Courage*. London: Robinson, 2007.

Morton, Desmond. *Fight or Pay: Soldiers' Families in the Great War*. Vancouver: University of British Columbia, 2004.

Morton, Desmond. *A Peculiar Kind of Politics: Canada's Overseas Ministry in the First World War*. Toronto: University of Toronto Press, 1982.

Morton, Desmond. *Silent Battle: Canadian Prisoners of War in Germany, 1914–1919*. Toronto: Lester Publishing Limited, 1992.

Morton, Desmond. *When Your Number's Up: The Canadian Soldier in the First World War*. Toronto: Random House of Canada Ltd., 1993.

Morton, Desmond and Glenn Wright. *Winning the Second Battle: Canadian Veterans and the Return to Civilian Life, 1915–1930*. Toronto: University of Toronto Press, 1987.

Mosse, George L. *Fallen Soldiers: Reshaping the Memory of the World War*. Oxford: Oxford University Press, 1990.

Mullen, John. *The Show Must Go On! Popular Song in Britain in the First World War*. Farnham: Ashgate, 2015.

Murphy, Libby. *The Art of Survival: France and the Great War Picaresque*. New Haven: Yale University Press, 2016.

Murray, W.W. *The History of the 2nd Canadian Battalion in the Great War*. Ottawa: Mortimer for The Historical Committee, 2nd Battalion, C.E.F., 1947.

Nelson, Robert L. *German Soldier Newspapers of the First World War*. Cambridge: Cambridge University Press, 2011.

Nichol, Stephen J. *Ordinary Heroes: Eastern Ontario's 21st Battalion C.E.F. in the Great War*. Almonte, Ontario: Self-published, 2008.

Nicholson, G.W.L. *Canadian Expeditionary Force, 1914–1919: Official History of the Canadian Army in the First World War*. Introduction by Mark Humphries. 1962. Montreal and Kingston: McGill-Queen's University Press, 2015.

Nicholson, G.W.L. *Gunners of Canada: The History of the Royal Regiment of Canadian Artillery*. Toronto: McClelland & Stewart, 1967.

Niles, John J., et al. *The Songs My Mother Never Taught Me*. New York: Gold Label Books, 1929.

Noyes, Frederick. *Stretcher-Bearers . . . At the Double!: History of the Fifth Canadian Field Ambulance which Served Overseas during the Great War of 1914–1918*. Toronto: Hunter-Rose, 1937.

O'Connor, James. *Cuss Control*. New York: Three Rivers Press, 2000.

Opp, James and John C. Walsh. *Placing Memory and Remembering Place in Canada*. Vancouver: University of British Columbia Press, 2010.

Oppenheim, Janet. *The Other World: Spiritualism and Psychical Research in England, 1850–1914*. Cambridge: Cambridge University Press, 1985.

Owen, Alex. *The Place of Enchantment: British Occultism and the Culture of the Modern*. Chicago and London: University of Chicago Press, 2004.

Owram, Doug and R.F. Moyles. *Imperial Dreams and Colonial Realities*. Toronto: University of Toronto Press, 1988.

Palmer, Roy. *What a Lovely War: British Soldiers' Songs from the Boer War to the Present Day*. London: Michael Joseph, 1990.

Philpott, William. *War of Attrition: Fighting the First World War*. New York: Overlook Press, 2014.

Posen, I. Sheldon. *For Singing and Dancing and All Sorts of Fun*. Toronto: Deneau Publishers, 1988.

Pugsley, Christopher. *On the Fringe of Hell: New Zealanders and Military Discipline in the First World War*. Auckland: Hodder & Stoughton, 1991.

Rawling, Bill. *Surviving Trench Warfare: Technology and the Canadian Corps, 1914–1918*. Toronto: University of Toronto Press, 1992.

Read, Daphne, ed. *The Great War and Canadian Society: An Oral History*. Toronto: New Hogtown Press, 1978.

Reznick, Jeffrey. *Healing the Nation: The Culture of Caregiving in Britain during the Great War*. Manchester: Manchester University Press, 2005.

Robb, George. *British Culture and the First World War*. New York: Palgrave, 2002.

Robertson, Beth. *Science of the Séance: Transnational Networks and Gendered Bodies in the Study of Psychic Phenomena, 1918–1940*. Vancouver: University of British Columbia Press, 2016.

Robertson, Heather. *A Terrible Beauty: The Art of Canada at War*. Toronto: J. Lorimer: Robert McLaughlin Gallery, 1977.

Robertson, Ian Ross. *Sir Andrew Macphail: The Life and Legacy of a Canadian Man of Letters*. Montreal and Kingston: McGill-Queen's University Press, 2008.

Robertson, Peter. *Relentless Verity: Canadian Military Photographers since 1885*. Toronto: University of Toronto Press, 1973.

Roper, Michael. *The Secret Battle: Emotional Survival in the Great War*. Manchester: Manchester University Press, 2009.

Rottman, Gordon L. *FUBAR: Soldier Slang of World War II*. London: Osprey Publishing, 2007.

Roud, Steve. *The Penguin Guide to the Superstitions of Britain and Ireland*. London: Penguin, 2003.

Royle, Nicholas. *The Uncanny: An Introduction*. Manchester: Manchester University Press, 2003.

Russell, David. *Popular Music in England, 1840–1914*. Manchester: Manchester University Press, 1987.

Russenholt, Edgar Stanford. *Six Thousand Canadian Men: Being the history of the 44th Battalion Canadian Infantry, 1914–1919*. Winnipeg: 44th Battalion Association, 1932.

Saunders, Nicholas J. *Killing Time: Archaeology and the First World War*. Stroud, UK: Sutton Publishing, 2007.

Saunders, Nicholas J. *Trench Art: A Brief History and Guide, 1914–1939*. Barnsley, UK: Leo Cooper, 2001.

Saunders, Nicholas J. *Trench Art: Materialities and Memories of War*. Oxford: Berg Books, 2003.

Schweitzer, Richard. *The Cross and the Trenches: Religious Faith and Doubt among British and American Great War Soldiers*. Westport, Connecticut: Praeger, 2003.

Seal, Graham. *The Soldiers' Press: Trench Journals in the First World War*. Basingstoke, UK: Palgrave Macmillan, 2013.

Shaw, Amy. *Crisis of Conscience: Conscientious Objection in Canada during the First World War*. Vancouver: University of British Columbia Press, 2009.

Sheffield, G.D. *Leadership in the Trenches: Officer–Man Relations, Morale and Discipline in the British Army in the Era of the First World War*. Basingstoke, UK: Palgrave Macmillan, 2000.

Sheftall, Mark David. *Altered Memories of the Great War: Divergent Narratives of Britain, Australia, New Zealand and Canada*. London: I.B. Tauris, 2009.

Sheldon-Williams, Ralf. *The Canadian Front in France and Flanders*. London: A. and C. Black, 1920.

Shibutani, Tamotsu. *Improvised News: A Sociological Study of Rumour*. Indianapolis: The Bobbs-Merrill Company, 1966.

Smith, Leonard V. *Between Mutiny and Obedience: The Case of the French Fifth Infantry Division During World War I*. New Jersey: Princeton University Press, 1994.

Smith, Leonard V. *The Embattled Self: French Soldiers' Testimony of the Great War*. Ithaca: Cornell University Press, 2007.

Smith, Lorenzo. *Lingo of No Man's Land*. 1918. London: The British Library, 2014.

Smith, Melvin Charles. *Awarded for Valour: A History of the Victoria Cross and the Evolution of British Heroism*. Basingstoke, UK: Palgrave Macmillan, 2008.

Snape, Michael and Edward Madigan, eds. *The Clergy in Khaki: New Perspectives in British Army Chaplaincy in the First World War*. Burlington, Vermont: Ashgate, 2013.

Stevens, G.R. *A City Goes to War: History of the Loyal Edmonton Regiment (3 PPCLI)*. Brampton: Charters Publishing Co. Ltd., 1964.

Stewart, Susan. *On Longing: Narratives of the Miniature, the Gigantic, the Souvenir, the Collection*. Baltimore: Johns Hopkins University Press, 1984.

Stewart, William F. *The Embattled General: Sir Richard Turner and the First World War*. Montreal and Kingston: McGill-Queen's University Press, 2015.

Streets, Heather. *Martial Races: The Military, Race and Masculinity in British Imperial Culture, 1857–1914*. Manchester: Manchester University Press, 2004.

Sweeney, Regina M. *Singing Our Way to Victory: French Cultural Politics and Music during the Great War*. Middletown: Wesleyan University Press, 2001.

Tascona, Bruce and Eric Wells. *Little Black Devils: A History of the Royal Winnipeg Rifles*. Winnipeg: Frye Publications for Royal Winnipeg Rifles, 1983.

Tennyson, Brian Douglas. *The Canadian Experience of the Great War: A Guide to Memoirs*. Lanham: The Scarecrow Press, 2013.

Thompson, Robert H. and Jonathan F. Vance, eds. *A Passport of First World War Canadians*. Toronto: The World Remembers, 2017.

Thurschwell, Pamela. *Literature, Technology and Magical Thinking, 1880–1920*. Cambridge: Cambridge University Press, 2001.

Tippett, Maria. *Art at the Service of War: Canada, Art, and the Great War*. Toronto: University of Toronto Press, 1984.

Todman, Dan. *The Great War: Myth and Memory*. London: Hambledon, 2005.

Tooley, Hunt. *The Western Front: Battle Ground and Home Front in the First World War*. New York: Palgrave, 2003.

Topp, Lieutenant-Colonel C. Beresford. *The 42nd Battalion, C.E.F., Royal Highlanders of Canada, in the Great War*. Montreal: Gazette Printing Limited, 1931.

Turner, Patricia. *I Heard it Through the Grapevine: Rumour in African-American Culture*. Oakland: University of California Press, 1993.

Urquhart, H.M. *The History of the 16th Battalion*. Toronto: Macmillan Company of Canada, 1932.

Vance, Jonathan. *Death So Noble: Memory, Meaning, and the First World War*. Vancouver: University of British Columbia Press, 1997.

Vance, Jonathan. *Maple Leaf Empire: Canada, Britain, and Two World Wars*. Oxford: Oxford University Press, 2012.

Vipond, Mary. *The Mass Media in Canada*, 4th Edition. Toronto: Lorimer, 2011.

Walker, Julian. *Words and the First World War: Language, Memory, Vocabulary*. London: Bloomsbury Academic, 2017.

Warner, Marina. *Phantasmagoria: Spirit Visions, Metaphors, and Media into the Twentieth-First Century*. Oxford: Oxford University Press, 2006.

Watkins, Glenn. *Proof through the Night: Music and the Great War*. Oakland: University of California Press, 2003.

Watson, Alexander. *Enduring the Great War: Combat, Morale and Collapse in the German and British Armies, 1914–1918*. Cambridge: Cambridge University Press, 2008.

Westhorp, Christopher, ed. *The Wipers Times: The Famous First World War Trench Newspaper*. London: Bloomsbury, 2013.

Williams, Gordon. *British Theatre in the Great War*. London: Continuum, 2003.

Williams, Jeffrey. *Byng of Vimy: General and Governor General*. Toronto: University of Toronto Press, 1992.

Wilson, Jason. *Soldiers of Song: The Dumbells and other Canadian Concert Parties of the First World War*. Waterloo: Wilfrid Laurier University Press, 2012.

Wilson, Ross. *Landscapes of the Western Front: Materiality during the Great War*. New York: Routledge, 2012.

Winegard, Timothy C. *For King and Kanata*: *Canadian Indians and the First World War*. Winnipeg: University of Manitoba Press, 2012.

Winter, Jay. *Remembering War: The Great War Between Memory and History in the Twentieth Century*. New Haven: Yale University Press, 2006.

Winter, Jay. *Sites of Memory, Sites of Mourning: The Great War in European Cultural History*. Cambridge: Cambridge University Press, 1995.

Winter, Jay. *War Beyond Words*. Cambridge: Cambridge University Press, 2017.

Wood, James. *Militia Myths: Ideas of the Canadian Citizen Soldier, 1896–1921*. Vancouver: University of British Columbia Press, 2010.

Zeman, Zbyněk. *Heckling Hitler: Caricatures of the Third Reich*. London: I.B. Tauris, 1987.

Theses and Dissertations

Campbell, James Dunbar. "The Army Isn't All Work: Physical Culture and the Evolution of the British Army 1860–1918." Ph.D. dissertation: University of Maine, 2003.

Chambers, Vanessa Ann. "Fighting Chance: War, Popular Belief and British Society, 1900–1951." Ph.D. dissertation: University of London, 2007.

Cozzi, Sarah. "Killing Time: The Experiences of Canadian Expeditionary Force Soldiers on Leave in Britain, 1914–1919." Master's thesis: University of Ottawa, 2009.

Dunn, Brittany Catherine. "'Death knows but one rule of arithmetic': Discourses of Death and Grief in the Trenches." Master's thesis: Wilfrid Laurier University, 2016.

Gerritsen, Maarten. "Corps Identity: The Letters, Diaries and Memoirs of Canada's Great War Soldiers." Ph.D. dissertation: Memorial University of Newfoundland, 2008.

Hodgkinson, Peter E. "Human Remains on the Great War Battlefields: Coping with Death in the Trenches." Master's thesis: University of Birmingham, 2006.

Karn, Sara. "Songs of War: Anglo-Canadian Popular Songs on the Home Front, 1914–1918." Major research paper: Wilfrid Laurier University, 2017.

MacDowall, Brian. "'A Flag that Knows No Colour Line': Indigenous Veteranship in Canada, 1914–1939." Ph.D. dissertation: York University, 2017.

McCulloch, Ian. "'The 'Fighting Seventh': The Evolution and Devolution of Tactical Command and Control in a Canadian Infantry Brigade of the Great War." Master's thesis: Royal Military College of Canada, 1997.

Morrison, Natascha. "Looking Backwards, Looking Forwards: Remembrance Day in Canada, 1919–2008." Master's thesis: Carleton University, 2010.

Schultz, Christopher. "Violence (Dis)Located: On the Spatial Implications of Violence on the Western Front during the First World War." Master's thesis: Carleton University, 2010.

Wilson, Jason. "Soldiers of Song: the Dumbells and Other Canadian Concert Parties of the First World War." Master's thesis: University of Guelph, 2003.

Wood, James A. "The Sense of Duty: Canadian Ideas of the Citizen Soldier, 1896-1917." Ph.D. dissertation: Wilfrid Laurier University, 2006.

Soldiers' Memoirs

Adamson, Agar and N.M. Christie, eds. *Letters of Agar Adamson, 1914 to 1919, Lieutenant Colonel, Princess Patricia's Canadian Light Infantry*. Ottawa: CEF Books, 1997.

Bain, J. Alexander (Sandy). *A War Diary of a Canadian Signaller: My Experiences in the Great War, 1914–1918*. Moncton: J.D. Bain, 1986.

Bagnall, F.W. *Not Mentioned in Despatches*. Vancouver: North Shore Press, 1933.

Baldwin, Harold. *Holding the Line*. Toronto: G.J. McLeod, 1918.

Becker, John Harold. *Silhouettes of War: The Memoir of John Harold Becker, 1915–1919: 75th Canadian Infantry Battalion (Mississauga Horse), Canadian Expeditionary Force*. Ottawa: CEF Books, 2001.

Bennett, Y.A., ed. *Kiss the kids for dad, Don't forget to write: The Wartime Letters of George Timmins, 1916–18*. Vancouver: University of British Columbia Press, 2009.

Bieler, Philippe. *Onward Dear Boys: A Family Memoir of the Great War*. Montreal and Kingston: McGill-Queen's University Press, 2014.

Bird, Will. *The Communication Trench*. Ottawa: CEF Books, 2000.

Bird, Will. *Ghosts Have Warm Hands*. Ottawa: CEF Books, 1997.

Black, Ernest. *I Want One Volunteer*. Toronto: Ryerson Press, 1965.

Booth, Jeffrey, ed. *Opened By Censor: A Collection of Letters Home from World War I Veterans from Elgin County*. Aylmer, Ontario: Aylmer Express Ltd., 2008.

Boyd, William. *With a field ambulance at Ypres: being letters written March 7–August 15, 1915*. Toronto: Musson, 1916.

Buswell, Leslie. *Ambulance No. 10: personal letters from the front*. Toronto: T. Allen, 1916.

Cameron, Charles S. *War! What of it! His Memoirs While Serving with the 16th Battalion (Canadian Scottish)*. Victoria: A. Craig Cameron, 2008.

Canadian Bank of Commerce. *Letters from the Front: being a partial record of the part played by officers of the Bank in the Great European War, 1914–1919*. Toronto: Canadian Bank of Commerce, 1920.

Carrel, Frank. *Impressions of War*. Quebec: The Telegraph Printing, 1919.

Chassé, Noël. *Avant la poussée finale*. Quebec: Imprimerie "L'Événement," 1918.

Chute, Arthur Hunt. *The Real Front*. New York: Harper, 1918.

Climo, Percy, ed. *Let Us Remember: Lively Letters from World War One*. Colborne: P.L. Climo, 1990.

Cook, Tim. "'My Whole Heart and Soul is in this War': The Letters and War Service of Sergeant G.L. Ormsby," *Canadian Military History* 15.1 (Winter 2006) 51–63.

Cowley, Deborah, ed. *Georges Vanier, Soldier: The Wartime Letters and Diaries, 1915–1919*. Toronto: Dundurn Press, 2000.

Craig, Grace Morris. *But This Is Our War*. Toronto: University of Toronto Press, 1981.

Craig, J. Marshall, ed. *You're Lucky If You're Killed*. New York: iUniverse, Inc., 2003.

Dawson, Coningsby. *The Glory of the Trenches*. New York: John Lane Company, 1918.

SELECT BIBLIOGRAPHY

Dawson, Coningsby. *Khaki Courage: Letters in War-Time*. London: Bodley Head, 1917.

Dinesen, Thomas. *Merry Hell: A Dane with the Canadians*. London: Jarrolds, 1929.

Dixon, Signaller Frank P. *War-Time Memories in Verse*. No publisher, 1937.

Earle, Patrick. *Al Plunkett: The Famous Dumbell*. New York: Pagant, 1956.

Edmonds, Charles. *A Subaltern's War: Being a Memoir of the Great War from the Point of View of a Romantic Young Man*. London: Peter Davies, 1929.

Field, Captain George Blackstone. *Echoes from Ypres*. Self-published, 1953.

Fleming, R.B., ed. *The Wartime Letters of Leslie and Cecil Frost, 1915–1919*. Waterloo: Wilfrid Laurier University Press, 2007.

Fraser, Donald and Reginald H. Roy. *The Journal of Private Fraser, 1914–1918, Canadian Expeditionary Force*. Victoria, British Columbia: Sono Nis Press, 1985.

Gagné, Lucie E. *Pounding the Enemy: The Diary of the 13th Battery, C.F.A., 1914–1918*. Ottawa: CEF Books, 2007.

Graves, Robert. *Goodbye to All That*. 1929. London: Penguin, 1960.

Gray, William. *A Sunny Subaltern: Billy's Letters from Flanders*. Toronto: McClelland, Goodchild & Stewart, 1916.

Grescoe, Paul and Audrey. *The Book of War Letters: 100 Years of Canadian Wartime Correspondence*. Toronto: McClelland & Stewart, 2003.

Grout, Derek, ed. *Thunder in the Skies: A Canadian Gunner in the Great War*. Toronto: Dundurn Publishers, 2015.

Guiou, Norman Miles. *Transfusion: A Canadian Surgeon's Story in War and in Peace*. Yarmouth: Stoneycroft Pub., 1985.

Hanna, Martha. *Your Death Would Be Mine: Paul and Marie Pireaud in the Great War*. Cambridge: Harvard University Press, 2006.

Harvey, Harold. *A Soldier's Sketches Under Fire*. Toronto: Thomas Allen, 1916.

Hebb, Ross, ed. *Letters Home: Maritimers and The Great War, 1914–1918*. Halifax: Nimbus, 2014.

Iriam, Glenn R., ed. *In the Trenches, 1914–1918*. Self-published, 2008.

Jackson, Holbrook, ed. *Contingent ditties and other soldier songs of the Great War by Frank S. Brown, Sergeant, P.P.C.L.I. (The Pats)*. London: S. Low, Marston, 1915.

Johnston, James Robert. *Riding into War: The Memoir of a Horse Transport Driver, 1916–1919*. Fredericton: Goose Lane Editions, 2004.

Kay, Hugh R., George Magee and F.A. MacLennan, eds. *Battery Action! The Story of the 43rd (Howitzer) Battery, Canadian Field Artillery, 1916–1919*. 1921. Ottawa: CEF Books, 2002.

Keene, Louis. *"Crumps": The Plain Story of a Canadian Who Went*. New York: Houghton Mifflin Company, 1917.

Kentner, Robert George. *Some Recollections of the Battles of World War I*. Fredonia, New York: Irene Kentner Lawson, 1995.

Kerr, Wilfred. *Shrieks and Crashes: The Memoir of Wilfred B. Kerr, Canadian Field Artillery, 1917*. Toronto: Hunter Rose, 1929.

Kingsley, Percy Leland and Patricia Thomas, eds. *The First World War as I Saw It*. Self-published, 2013.

Lapointe, Arthur. *Soldier of Quebec (1916–1919)*. Montreal: Garand, 1931.

LeBoutillier, Leo and Gordon Pimm, eds. *Leo's War: From Gaspé to Vimy*. Ottawa: Partnership Publishers, 2007.

Lewis, R. *Over the top with the 25th: Chronicle of Events at Vimy Ridge and Courcellette*. Halifax: H.H. Marshall, 1918.

Lynch, John. *Princess Patricia's Canadian Light Infantry, 1917–1919*. New York: Exposition Press, 1976.

Machen, Arthur. *The Angel of Mons: The Bowmen and Other Legends of the War*. New York: G.P. Putnam's Sons, 1915.

Macintyre, D.E. *Canada at Vimy*. Toronto: P. Martin Associates, 1967.

Macpherson, Donald. *A Soldier's Diary: The WWI Diaries of Donald MacPherson*. St. Catharines: Vanwell, 2001.

Manion, Captain R.J. *A Surgeon in Arms*. Toronto: McClelland, Goodchild & Stewart, 1918.

Manion, R.J. *Life Is an Adventure*. Toronto: Ryerson, 1936.

Massey, Raymond. *When I Was Young*. Toronto: McClelland & Stewart, 1976.

Maxwell, George A. *Swan Song of a Rustic Moralist*. New York: Exposition Press, 1975.

McBride, Herbert W. *A Rifleman Went to War*. Plantersville, South Carolina: Small Arms Technical Publishing Company, 1935.

McClintock, Alexander. *Best o' Luck: How a Fighting Kentuckian Won the Thanks of Britain's King*. 1917. Ottawa: CEF Books, 2000.

McGrath, Susan, ed. *The Long Sadness: World War I Diary of William Hannaford Ball*. Thousand Oaks, California: Seanachie Press, 2014.

Miller, Ollie, ed. *Letters Bridging Time: Tom Johnson's Letters*. Surrey: Self-published, 2007.

More Letters from Billy. Toronto: McClelland, Goodchild & Stewart, 1917.

Morrison, J. Clinton, ed. *Hell Upon Earth: A Personal Account of Prince Edward Island Soldiers in the Great War, 1914–1918*. Summerside, Prince Edward Island: Self-published, 1995.

Mountain Horse, Mike. *My People, the Bloods*. Calgary: Glenbow-Alberta Institute, 1979.

Murdoch, B.J. *The Red Vineyard*. Great Britain: University Press Glasgow, 1959.

Nasmith, George. *On the Fringe of the Great Fight*. Toronto: McClelland, Goodchild & Stewart, 1917.

Norris, Armine. *Mainly for Mother*. Toronto: Ryerson Press, 1919.

Norris, Marjorie Barron, ed. *Medicine and Duty: The World War I Memoir of Captain Harold W. McGill, Medical Officer, 31st Battalion C.E.F.* Calgary: University of Calgary Press, 2007.

Ogilvie, William G. *Umty-Iddy-Umty: The Story of a Canadian Signaller in the First World War*. Erin, Ontario: The Boston Mills Press, 1982.

Oh, Canada! London: Simpkin and Marshall, 1917.

Peat, Harold. *Private Peat*. New York: Grosset and Dunlap Publishers, 1917.

Pedley, James. *Only This: A War Retrospect, 1917–1918*. Ottawa: Graphic Publishers, 1927.

Pollock, J.P., ed. *Letters from Angus, 1915–1916*. Self-published, 2005.

Pope, Maurice. *Letters from the Front, 1914–1919*. Toronto: Pope and Company, 1996.

R.A.L. and Anna Chapin Ray, eds. *Letters of a Canadian Stretcher Bearer*. Boston: Little, Brown, and Company, 1918.

R.H.T., ed. *Victor Gordon Tupper: A Brother's Tribute*. London: Oxford University Press, 1921.

Roy, Reginald, ed. *The Journal of Private Fraser: 1914–1918, Canadian Expeditionary Force*. Victoria: Sono Nis Press, 1985.

Rutledge, Stanley. *Pen Pictures from the Trenches* (Toronto: HarperCollins, 1992)

Sawell, Edward Stanley and Steven E. Sawell, eds. *Into the Cauldron: Experiences of a CEF Infantry Officer During the Great War: Memoirs of Edward Stanley Sawell, M.C., V.D*. Burlington, Ontario: S.E. Sawell, 2009.

Scott, Frederick. *The Great War as I Saw It*. Ottawa: CEF Books, 2000.

Shaw, Susan Evans, ed. *My Darling Girl: Wartime Letters of James Lloyd Evans, 1914–1918*. Hamilton: Self-published, 1999.

Shephard, Norma Hillyer, ed. *Dear Harry: The Firsthand Account of a World War I Infantryman*. Burlington: Brigham Press, 2003.

Simmons, Mervin C. and Nellie L. McClung. *Three Times and Out*. Toronto: Thomas Allen, 1918.

Spear, Tom with Monte Stewart. *Carry On: Reaching Beyond 100*. Calgary: Falcon Press, 1999.

Swanston, Victor N. *Who Said War Is Hell!* Self-published, 1983.

Tennyson, Brian Douglas, ed. *Merry Hell: The Story of the 25th Battalion (Nova Scotia Regiment), Canadian Expeditionary Force 1914–1919*. Toronto: University of Toronto Press, 2012.

Tennyson, Brian Douglas. *Percy Willmot: A Cape Bretoner at War*. Sydney, Nova Scotia: Cape Breton University Press, 2007.

Tennyson, Brian Douglas. "'Wild Bill' Livingstone Goes to War: A Diary and Letters, 1916–19," *Journal of the Royal Nova Scotia Historical Society* 12 (2009) 119–44.

Tingley, Ken, ed. *The Path of Duty: The Wartime Letters of Alwyn Bramley-Moore*. Calgary: Alberta Records Publication Board, 1998.

Tougas, Rémi. *Stanislas Tougas: Un des plus grands coeurs du 22e Bataillon*. Quebec: Septentrion, 2005.

Wallace, O.C.S., ed. *From Montreal to Vimy Ridge and Beyond: the correspondence of Lieut. Clifford Almon Wells, B.A. of the 8th Battalion, Canadians, B.E.F. November 1915–April 1917*. Toronto: McClelland, Goodchild & Stewart, 1917.

Weatherbe, Karl. *From the Rideau to the Rhine and Back*. Toronto: Hunter-Rose, 1928.

Wells, George Anderson. *The Fighting Bishop*. Toronto: Cardwell House, 1971.

Wheeler, Victor W. *The 50th Battalion in No Man's Land*. Ottawa: CEF Books, 2000.

Willans, Len and Gail Booth, eds. *The Memoirs of a Canadian Soldier: World War I Diary Entries and Letters*. Edmonton: Bobair Media Inc., 2012.

Zubkowski, Robert F., ed. *As Long as Faith and Freedom Last: Stories from the Princess Patricia's Canadian Light Infantry from June 1914 to September 1919*. Calgary: Bunker to Bunker Publications, 2003.

INDEX

Note: Italicized numbers refer to illustrations.

INDEX

C

INDEX

F

INDEX

G

H

INDEX

U

V